Photo by S. G. Payne & Son, Aylesbury.

CASSOWARY.

The female Cassowary is larger than her mate, and her colouring is of equal brilliancy.

THE LIVING ANIMALS OF THE WORLD

THE LIVING ANIMALS OF THE WORLD

A POPULAR NATURAL HISTORY

AN INTERESTING DESCRIPTION OF BEASTS, BIRDS, FISHES REPTILES, INSECTS, Etc., WITH AUTHENTIC ANECDOTES

VOL. II.

BIRDS, REPTILES AND AMPHIBIANS, FISHES JOINTED ANIMALS MOLLUSCS, Etc.

By

W. F. KIRBY, F.L.S.

SIR HERBERT MAXWELL, F.R.S.

W. P. PYCRAFT, A.L.S., F.Z.S.

F. G. AFLALO, F.Z.S.

W. SAVILLE-KENT, F.L.S., F.Z.S.

JOHN BICKERDYKE, M.A.

THEODORE WOOD, F.E.S.

GYAN

Published by

Gyan Publishing House
5, Ansari Road
Daryaganj, New Delhi-110002
Phone: 011-47034999, 9811692060
E-mail: books@gyanbooks.com

Distribution Network
gyanbooks.com
India, USA, Canada, UK, Australia, France

ISBN : 978-81-212-6542-3 (PB)
First Published, 1902

2nd Impression 2022

Printed at: Gyan Press, Delhi.

THE LIVING ANIMALS OF THE WORLD
Author: W.F. KIRBY, HERBERT MAXWELL

THE . .

LIVING ANIMALS OF THE WORLD

A POPULAR NATURAL HISTORY

AN INTERESTING DESCRIPTION OF BEASTS, BIRDS, FISHES REPTILES, INSECTS, ETC., WITH AUTHENTIC ANECDOTES

VOL. II.

Photo by W. P. Dando, F.Z.S., Regent's Park

BIRDS, REPTILES AND AMPHIBIANS, FISHES JOINTED ANIMALS MOLLUSCS, ETC.

BY

W. F. KIRBY, F.L.S.
SIR HERBERT MAXWELL, F.R.S.
W. P. PYCRAFT, A.L.S., F.Z.S.
F. G. AFLALO, F.Z.S.
W. SAVILLE-KENT, F.L.S., F.Z.S.
JOHN BICKERDYKE, M.A.
THEODORE WOOD, F.E.S.

VOL. II.

CONTENTS.

COLOURED PLATES.

ILLUSTRATIONS IN THE TEXT.

Illustrations in the Text, Vol. II.

THE

LIVING ANIMALS

OF

THE WORLD.

BOOK II. BIRDS.

BY W. P. PYCRAFT, A.L.S., F.Z.S.

CHAPTER I.

THE OSTRICH AND ITS KINDRED.

Photo by W. P. Dando, F.Z.S.] [*Regent's Park.*

RUFOUS TINAMOU, BRAZIL.

The tail-feathers of these birds are so small as to appear to be wanting.

THE Ostriches are a very ancient group of birds, and, judging from what we know of their anatomy, they must be regarded as representing the most primitive of living birds. With the exception of a single group, to be discussed presently, all have lost the power of flight. In some, in consequence, the wing has become reduced to a mere vestige. It is a rule in Nature, we may remark, that whenever an organ, such as a wing or a leg or a tail, ceases to be useful, it undergoes forthwith a slow process of reduction or degeneration, growing smaller and smaller in each successive generation, till at last it may even disappear altogether. The loss of flight has been accompanied by a degeneration in the quality of the feathers—that is to say, their serviceability as aids to flight has been entirely lost.

The size of the members of this group varies much. The largest of all is the African Ostrich; the smallest, of the flightless forms, the New Zealand Apteryx. The ostrich-like birds which have retained the power of flight are known as Tinamous, and are natives of South America. All these are smaller than the flightless Apteryx.

TINAMOUS.

The TINAMOUS should perhaps be regarded as standing at the head of the Ostrich Tribe, since they have reached a higher degree of development than any other of its members. They have also preserved the power of flight. In their general appearance they bear a singular resemblance to partridges, though a little careful observation will reveal many points wherein they differ therefrom. They are very confiding and unsuspicious birds—some persons call them stupid

Photo by H. Noble, Esq.] [*Henley.*

RHEA AND YOUNG.

Although the wings of the rhea are large, they fit so closely to the body as to be invisible when closed.

on this account—and in the early morning the species inhabiting the Argentine pampas will, observers tell us, come right up to the isolated houses of the settlers, so that the boys knock them down with stones. The delicate quality of the flesh has caused these birds to be highly esteemed as food, and their trustful nature renders them an easy prey, so much so that in some districts they have been almost exterminated. Large numbers are caught by riding round them in a circle and securing them with a noose. Mr. Hudson, who lived many years in the pampas, assures us that the GREAT TINAMOU is one of the sweetest-voiced of the native birds. The song is composed of "five modulated notes, flute-like in character, and very expressive, and is uttered by many individuals answering each other as they sit far apart, concealed in the grass."

The eggs of the tinamous are to be reckoned among the wonders of bird life, being so highly burnished as to look like beautifully glazed porcelain. The colour varies according to the species, ranging from wine-red, blue-green, and brown to black. The young are almost as remarkable as the eggs, being clothed with a peculiar down, of great complexity of structure, and resembling in some respects the nestling down of the true ostrich.

Photo by H. Noble, Esq.] *[Henley.*

RHEA AND YOUNG ONES.

Although frequently bred in this country, the young do not seem to be easily reared.

THE RHEA.

The RHEA is a native of South America. It is frequently referred to as the SOUTH AMERICAN OSTRICH, and also as the NANDU. The resemblance which it bears to the true ostrich is striking, but it may at once be distinguished therefrom by the fact that it has three toes and a feathered head and neck; furthermore, it is smaller in size, and lacks the conspicuous white wing- and tail-plumes. The tail, indeed, as may be seen from the photographs reproduced is wanting. The rhea must be regarded as standing at the head of the flightless members of the Ostrich Tribe. Its wings, though not large enough to raise its heavy body from the ground, are yet of considerable size.

Photo by Scholastic Photo. Co.] *[Parson's Green.*

RHEA LYING DOWN.

The breast of the larger members of the Ostrich Tribe is provided with a large horny plate, on which they support the body when resting.

In Buenos Aires rheas are hunted with dogs. If a breeze is blowing, the birds raise one wing, which acts as a sail. This done, they can acquire a speed which makes it absolutely impossible for either dog or horse to come up with them. The only chance of ultimately capturing them is by wearing them out by ceaseless pursuit. A chase of this kind may last an hour and a half. Needless to say, for sport of this kind both horses and dogs must be the best of their kind and in "good form." The natives and Indians hunt them on horseback with the "bolas." The bolas, or balls, used for this purpose consist of two round stones covered with leather, and united by a thong of about 8 feet long. One of these is held in the hand and the other whirled round the head and suddenly released, when both go whirling madly round till they strike the rhea's legs, around which they instantly twist, and the victim is a fast prisoner.

The rhea is in danger of disappearing altogether as a wild bird, owing to the ruthless slaughter which is made upon it for the sake of its feathers. For some years back, Mr. Harting tells us, "the number of birds killed has averaged 400,000 per annum, and, as a consequence, the species has already disappeared from nearly half the territory of the River Plate." On some estates in Argentina the wild birds are driven in and plucked.

Like most of the Ostrich Tribe, the male alone performs the duties of incubation, hatching

Photo by J. T. Newman] [*Berkhamsted.*

RHEAS IN TRING PARK.

In spite of its large size, the rhea is not a conspicuous bird in a wild state, the grey plumage harmonising perfectly with the surrounding pampas.

some twenty eggs at a time, the produce of several different females. There are three different kinds of rhea, but they do not differ much one from another. The young are curiously striped. The egg is very large, of a cream colour, and deeply pitted.

Darwin, in his "Voyage of the Beagle," tells us that when he was "at Bahia Blanca, in the months of September and October, the eggs, in extraordinary numbers, were found all over the country. They lie either scattered and single, in which case they are never hatched, and are called by the Spaniards huachos; or they are collected together into a shallow excavation which forms the nest. Out of the four nests which I saw, three contained twenty-two eggs each, and the fourth twenty-seven. In one day's hunting on horseback sixty-four eggs were found: forty-four of these were in two nests, and the remaining twenty scattered huachos. The Gauchos unanimously affirm—and there is no reason to doubt their statement—that the male bird alone hatches the eggs, and for some time afterwards accompanies the young. The cock, when on the nest, lies very close: I have myself almost ridden over one. It is asserted that at such times they are occasionally fierce and even dangerous, and that they have been known to attack a man on horseback, trying to kick and leap on him. My informer pointed out to me an old man whom he had seen much terrified by one chasing him. . . . I understand that the male emu in the Zoological Gardens takes charge of the nest: this habit, therefore, is common to the family.

"The Gauchos unanimously affirm that several females lay in one nest. I have been positively told that four or five hen birds have been watched to go, in the middle of the day, one after another, to the same nest. . . . Although this habit at first appears very strange, I think the cause may be explained in a simple manner. The number of eggs in the nest varies from twenty to forty, and even fifty; and according to Azara even seventy or eighty. Now, although it is most probable, from the number of the eggs found in one district being so extraordinarily great in proportion to the parent birds, and likewise from the state of the ovarium of the hen, that she may, in the course of the season, lay a large number, yet the time required must be very long. . . . If the hen was obliged to hatch her own eggs before the last was laid, the first probably would be addled; but if each laid a few eggs at successive periods in different nests, and several hens . . . combined together, then the eggs in one collection would be nearly of the same age. If the number of eggs in one of these nests is, as I believe, not greater on an average than the number laid by one female in the season, then there must be as many nests as females, and each cock bird will have its fair share of the labour of incubation; and that during a period when the females probably could not sit, from not having finished laying. I have before mentioned the great number of huachos, or deserted eggs; and that in one day's hunting twenty were found in this state. It appears odd that so many should be wasted. Does it not arise from the difficulty of several females

Photo by the Duchess of Bedford] [*Woburn Abbey.*

WHITE RHEAS.

These are only varieties of the common form, not a distinct breed.

associating together, and finding a male ready to undertake the office of incubation? It is obvious that there must at first be some degree of association between at least two females, otherwise the eggs would remain scattered over the wide plains, at distances far too great to allow of the male collecting them into one nest: some . . . have believed that the scattered eggs were deposited for the young birds to feed on. This can hardly be the case . . . because huachos, although often found addled and putrid, are generally whole."

Photo by W. Reid] [Wishaw, N.B.

OSTRICH STANDING BESIDE HER EGGS.

In a wild state both cock and hen take part in the preparation of the nest.

The Ostrich.

The Ostrich is the giant amongst living birds, the full-grown male standing some 8 feet high, and weighing about 300 lbs. It is flightless, the wings being smaller, in proportion to the size of the body, than in the rhea. But the energy which in other birds is employed in sustaining flight in the ostrich is expended in running, so that it has reached a high degree of speed—no less, in fact, than twenty-six miles an hour. When at full speed, it is generally believed the ostrich derives no small help from the wings, which are used sail-wise. Nor is this belief by any means a modern one, for all of us must be familiar with Job's observations on this subject: "What time she lifteth up her wings on high, she scorneth the horse and his rider." The wings are never used in running at full speed, but are of much service in turning, "enabling the bird to double abruptly, even when going at top speed." In justice to the older observers, however, it must be remarked that ostriches *do* run with raised wings, but only at the commencement of the run, or in covering a short distance, when the pace may be considerable; but if circumstances demand "full speed ahead," they are held close to the body, where they offer the least resistance to speed.

With the gradual perfection of its running powers, there has followed a gradual change in the form of the leg. This change has taken place by reduction in the number of the toes. Of the original five with which its ancestors began life only two now remain—the third and fourth. The third is of great size, having apparently waxed great at the expense of the other toes, a growth which seems to be still in progress, inasmuch as the fourth toe is undoubtedly dwindling. It is very small, and gives unmistakable signs of growing smaller, since it has now become nailless. When it has quite disappeared, the ostrich, like the horse, will have but a single toe on each foot—the third. The dainty, mincing step of the ostrich is a delight to watch, and, thanks to the Zoological Gardens, this can be done even in smoky London.

The ostrich, like its cousin of South America, the rhea, commonly associates with herds of the larger mammalia. On the South African veldt the companions of the ostrich are the zebra, wildebeest, and hartebeest, just as on the pampas of South America the rheas are found associated with herds of deer and guanaco.

The egg of the ostrich weighs about 3 lbs., and is of delicious flavour. The empty shell, it has been found by experiment, is large enough to hold the contents of eighteen eggs of the common domesticated fowl. It takes about forty minutes to boil an ostrich egg hard. About fifteen eggs represent the clutch. The nest is a mere depression in the sand. The hen sits by day, and her mate by night; but the eggs are *never* left, as is sometimes stated, to the heat of the sun, so as to lessen the duties of the parent. Such a course would infallibly destroy the eggs, for the sun's rays, especially at noon, are very powerful.

The male and female ostrich differ much in coloration. In the former the trunk is clothed in a vestment of richest black, whilst the quills of the wings and tail-feathers are of pure white: they form the much-prized ostrich plumes. The female is much less splendid, being clothed in sober grey. But these colours are not merely ornamental; they render the male by night and the female by day invisible, owing to the perfect harmony they make with their surroundings, thus affording an interesting illustration of protective coloration.

"All ostriches," says Mr. Cronwright Schreiner, "adults as well as chicks, have a strange habit known as 'waltzing.' When chicks are let out from a kraal in the early morning, they will often start away at a great pace. After running for a few hundred yards they will all stop, and, with wings raised, spin round rapidly for some time, often till quite giddy, when a broken leg occasionally occurs. Adult birds, when running in large camps, will often, if the veldt is good, do the same, especially if startled in the fresh of the early morning. A troop of birds waltzing, in full plumage, is a remarkably pretty sight. Vicious cocks 'roll' when challenging to fight, also when wooing the hen. The cock will suddenly bump down on to his 'knees' . . . open his wings, making a straight line across his breast, and then swing them alternately backwards and forwards . . . as if on a pivot, each wing, as it comes forward, being raised, while that going backward is depressed. The neck is lowered until the head is on a level with the back, and the head and neck swing from side to side with the wings, the back of the head striking with a loud click against the ribs, first on the one side and then on the other. The click is produced by the skin of the neck, which then bulges loosely just under the beak and for some distance downwards. While 'rolling,' every feather over the whole body is on end, and the plumes are open, like a large white fan. At such a time the bird sees very imperfectly, if at all; in fact, he seems so preoccupied that, if pursued, one may often approach unnoticed. I have walked up to a 'rolling' cock and seized him by the neck, much to his surprise. Just before rolling, a cock, especially if courting the hen, will often run slowly and daintily on the points of his toes, with neck slightly inflated, upright and rigid, the tail half drooped, and all his body-feathers fluffed up; the wings raised and expanded, the inside edges touching the sides of the neck for nearly the whole of its length, and the plumes showing separately, like an open fan . . . on each side of his head. In no other attitude is the splendid beauty of his plumage displayed to such advantage."

Photo by W. Reid] [*Wishaw, N.B.*

OSTRICHES TEN DAYS OLD.

The down-feathers of young ostriches are quite different from those of other birds, the tips of each being produced into a horny ribbon.

The males are very fierce while guarding their eggs or fighting for mates, and kick with extraordinary violence with their powerful legs. As an example of their fierceness when aroused, Mr. Cronwright Schreiner, who knows much of these birds, relates a story, told him by a

Photo by Mr. Glenday] [*Cape Town.*

AN OSTRICH FAMILY.

The cock bird is an unusually fine specimen, measuring exactly 8 feet from head to foot.

railway-guard, of an old male who charged a goods-train coming at full speed down a steep gradient. The bird, as soon as he caught sight of the train, at once got on the line, "and advanced fearlessly to fight the monster. As the screeching engine approached, he rushed at it from straight in front, hissing angrily, and kicked. He was cut to pieces the next moment."

The Bedouin tribes hunt the ostrich on dromedaries, so also do the natives of Somaliland, and when near enough shoot it with poisoned arrows. In the Sahara, Canon Tristram tells us it is ridden down on horseback, a method of capture which the Sahara sportsman regards as the greatest feat of hunting.

"The Bushmen," says Mr. Harting, "like the Somalis, kill the ostrich with poisoned arrows, or catch it very cleverly in pit-falls or with the lasso, and the Sukurieh and Hadendawah tribes likewise use the lasso, with which the bird, when once fairly caught, is strangled. . . . A favourite plan is to wait for the birds in a place of concealment, as near as

Photo by Schroeder] [*Zurich.*

A GROUP OF COCK OSTRICHES.

Note the conspicuous tail in these birds; it is wanting in other members of the Ostrich Tribe.

possible to the pools to which they come for water, and then, with a gun loaded with swan-shot, to fire at their necks as they stoop to drink, when perhaps half a dozen are laid low at once. . . . Another plan to which the Bushman often resorts is simpler still. Having found an ostrich's nest, he removes all the eggs, and, ensconcing himself in the nest, quietly awaits the return of the bird, which he shoots with a poisoned arrow before it has time to recover from its surprise at finding him there instead of the eggs. . . . In Senaar the Abû-Rôf bring it down by throwing a curved flat stick from 2½ to 3 feet long, not unlike the Australian boomerang, and made of tough acacia-wood or hard zizyphus."

Mr. Arthur Glynn, of Leydenburg, gives a graphic description of an ostrich hunt, his quarry being a troop of twenty birds—"on sighting which," he tells us, "we immediately gave chase, discovering directly afterwards that a single bull wildebeeste was among them. After a stiff gallop," he says, "of half a mile, we got within seventy yards of the troop; so reining in, we both dismounted and fired, bringing down one ostrich and the wildebeeste bull. . . . We quickly mounted and continued the pursuit, the ostriches never running for any distance in a direct course, but always turning and twisting, which made it difficult for us to keep them in sight. . . . We went sailing on, neck and neck, regardless of holes or anything else, only thinking of the grandly plumaged birds in front of us, our horses straining every nerve to overtake them, as only old stagers know how to run when in pursuit of game. We had now approached within fifty yards, and, jumping down, we fired at two cock birds running separately from the troop, bringing them both down. Hastily mounting, we continued on after the retreating troop; but at this juncture my friend's horse trod in a hole, sending his rider over his head, thereby completely putting him out of the run. I now continued the chase by myself. For a mile the ostriches gained on me, as they continued to run in a straight line, thereby not enabling me to cut off any point, but obliging me to keep in their rear all the time. . . . I got off twice, and fired several fruitless shots, and then continued the chase for certainly two miles without dismounting once. . . . I now got within a hundred yards, and jumped down. . . . The first shot I fired brought down a fine cock bird, but the second struck the ground over the others, turning them to the right along a low ridge. They appeared very much exhausted, and ran with their wings spread out. . . . I saw that they were coming direct for me, and waited until they were close. . . . When the ostriches approached within fifteen yards, I selected the best-looking bird, and put a bullet through him. He ran on for about twenty yards and fell dead."

Photo by W. P. Dando, F.Z.S.] [*Regent's Park.*

SCLATER'S CASSOWARY.

This bird is not yet full grown, the horny casque on the top of the head being much larger in the adult.

Cassowaries and Emeus.

With the Cassowaries and Emeus we have come as near as we can get at the present day to the representatives of the ancient type from which the Ostrich Tribe have sprung. But both these forms are to be regarded as having passed the prime of their development, for, like their allies which we have already considered, they have lost the power of flight. Both emeu and cassowary possess, when adult, one character shared by no other living adult bird: they have what may be called double feathers, each feather possessing two shafts of equal length. They appear to follow a custom of their own in the matter of the coloration of their eggs, since these are never white, like those of the rhea or ostrich, but green, with a very rough surface. The young, like those of the rhea, are striped with alternate black and white stripes. The emeu is found only on the continent of Australia; the cassowary occurs both in Australia and on the neighbouring islands of New Guinea, Ceram, and Aru.

The lot of the Cassowary appears to have been cast in pleasant places, making it possible

Photo by D. Le Souëf] [*Melbourne.*

NEST AND EGGS OF EMEU.

The feet of the old bird, which was standing near, can be seen behind the eggs.

to indulge in the luxury of personal decoration—a decoration, moreover, shared equally by the males and females, both sexes having the head and neck most brilliantly coloured. In some species all the hues of the rainbow are vividly reflected. To show these colours, the feathery covering, still worn by their relatives on the distant continents of Africa and America, has been cast off and the skin left bare. To these gorgeous hues they have added yet other features, for the head is surmounted in many species by a huge casque, or helmet; whilst from the neck depend curious fleshy lobes, or wattles, coloured in accordance with the rest of the bare, coloured skin of this region. Then, too, they have effected quite a novel transformation in the quills of the wing, for these project on either side of the body in a series of shining black spines. Nor is this all, for over and above the energy which they have to spare for personal decoration is a very large reserve to be expended in fighting. The males are very pugnacious, and to give point to this pugnacity they wear a very formidable weapon on the inner toe in the shape of a huge nail, which can inflict a really dangerous wound. It is used in kicking, the foot being brought forwards and downwards with incredible speed and great force. When wounded, these powerful birds are very dangerous to approach. "On more than one occasion a wounded bird has caused a naturalist to take to a tree. The sharp nail of the inner toe is a most dangerous weapon, quite equal to the claw of a large kangaroo, and capable of doing quite as much execution."

Although forest-haunting birds—wherein they differ from their allies, which are plain-dwellers—the cassowaries are adepts at swimming. There is a danger that these beautiful and interesting birds will slowly be exterminated by greedy and thoughtless settlers. The Australian cassowary is already decreasing sadly, being persecuted for the sake of its skin, which is used for rugs and doormats.

The Emeu, though a sort of cousin of the cassowary, boasts none of its splendour; on the contrary, it is a dull, dowdy-looking bird. In size, however, it is much larger than the cassowary. The wings, which are exceedingly small, have numerous tiny quill-feathers—not long, hard spines, as in the cassowary. When in captivity, it exhibits great curiosity; furthermore, it is swift to realise symptoms of fear in the faces of any visitor whom it may have under inspection. Occasionally fear turns into flight, and then, thoroughly entering into the joke, the emeu pursues at top speed. Needless to say, hunting of this kind can only be done in fairly large paddocks or parks; but emeus are frequently so kept.

Photo by D. Le Souëf] [*Melbourne.*

YOUNG EMEUS FIVE DAYS OLD.

Young emeus just out of the shell have the legs beautifully spotted, but these spots are rapidly lost.

A very remarkable and quite unique structure in the emeu is a curious bag or pouch, formed by a sort of out-pocketing of the inner lining of the windpipe. Emerging through a long slit caused by the incompleteness of some of the rings near the middle of the windpipe, the

Photo by Scholastic Photo. Co.] [*Parson's Green.*

YOUNG EMEUS.

After a few weeks the black and white stripes become much less conspicuous.

pouch comes to lie between this tube and the skin. Strangely enough, it is found only in the female, and is used by her chiefly during the breeding-season, when she utters a peculiarly loud booming note, which, it is supposed, is caused by the manipulation of the air in the pouch. When moved by any gentle excitement or pleasure, especially on damp evenings or in the dead of night, she also becomes musical, giving forth a note which has been likened to a gong or muffled drum. The male, which is smaller, fleeter of foot, and more docile and inquisitive, is mute, or at most gives forth a suppressed hiss when angry, or a kind of grunt when distressed.

At one time the emeu roamed over the whole of the mainland of Australia; but now, alas! it is almost exterminated, being found only far inland and in steadily diminishing numbers. Swift of foot and of great powers of endurance, the emeu has afforded in the past much "sport" to the hunting-man, who followed the dogs, doubtless making comparisons the while between his two-legged prey and his four-footed friend Reynard. The hunt does not end till the bird is thoroughly exhausted, when it must be seized at once by the neck, in order to prevent it kicking, for the legs are so powerful that a blow from the foot is dangerous.

Incubation is apparently performed by the male, which sits from fifty-four to sixty-four days. Practically no nest is made, only a shallow hollow being scraped in the sand. The eggs, from seven to thirteen in number, are of a dark bottle-green colour, sometimes lighter, and have the surfaces curiously roughened. The male is smaller than the female, a fact which has led to some confusion, the larger female having at one time been regarded as the male. It will be noted that the emeus not only lack the brilliant colour of the cassowaries, but also the helmet, or casque.

Photo by J. T. Newman] [*Berkhamsted.*

EMEU.

The feathers of the neck of the emeu are much longer than in the rhea; hence the neck seems shorter.

The late Mr. Gould's remarks on the edibility of the emeu are interesting. He says: "Its flesh has been compared to coarse beef, which it resembles, according to Mr. Cunningham, both in appearance and taste, and is good and sweet eating; nothing, indeed,

Photo by Robert D. Carson, Esq.] [Philadelphia.

MANTELL'S KIWI, NEW ZEALAND, NORTH ISLAND.

When feeding, the kiwi makes a sniffing sound, distinctly audible at some distance.

can be more delicate than the flesh of the young ones. There is little fit for culinary use upon any part of the emu, except the hind-quarters, which are of such dimensions that the shouldering of the two hind legs homeward for a mile distance once proved to me as tiresome a task as I ever recollect to have encountered in the colony. I may remark that its flesh proved of the greatest service to Dr. Leichardt and his intrepid companions during their overland route from Moreton Bay to Port Essington, in the course of which, but more particularly between the head of the Gulf of Carpentaria and Port Essington, the sight and capture of the emu was almost a daily occurrence; so abundant, in fact, was it, that he states that he saw in the short space of eight miles at least a hundred, in flocks of three, five, ten, and even more at a time. On the continent of Australia the emu was formerly abundant about Botany Bay and Port Jackson Harbour, but is now only to be seen in the plains of the interior, over whose solitudes it roams in great numbers, and where it breeds, depending on the strength and swiftness of its legs to avoid the pursuit of the stockmen and their dogs. Farther and farther back, however, will it be driven, until it be extirpated, unless some law be instituted to check its wanton destruction."

In a wild state emeus take readily to the water, and have on more than one occasion been seen swimming across a wide river. The South American rhea is also known to be a good swimmer.

The COMMON EMEU is restricted to Eastern Australia. The opposite side of this great continent is inhabited by another and very distinct species, known as the SPOTTED EMEU.

THE APTERYX.

To see the APTERYX at home, we should have to travel to far New Zealand, and to hunt with infinite patience when we got there. Apteryx-hunting, it has been found, to be successful, must be done by the help of dogs. Sir Walter Buller has written some very spirited accounts of such hunts. Europeans, indeed, have been singularly successful in this hunting, whereby they have done much to enhance the value of this bird by hastening its fast approaching and inevitable extermination.

The natives call this bird the KIWI, from its call-note, "ki-i-wi." These cries are uttered during the early hours of the night, ceasing after midnight. They appear to have great penetrating power.

Photo by Robert D. Carson, Esq.] [Philadelphia.

OWEN'S KIWI, NEW ZEALAND, SOUTH ISLAND.

This is the smallest of the kiwis.

CHAPTER II.

THE GAME-BIRDS AND RAILS.

IT is not easy in a few words exactly to define a "game-bird." Anatomical details aside, the most characteristic features are the small head and moderately long neck, and a compact body, in which the wings, when folded, are almost entirely concealed. The hind toe is always present, and the claws are adapted for scratching purposes—that is to say, for scratching up the surface of the ground in the search for seeds as food. The wings are hollowed so as to fit close to the body, and the flight, which is noisy and never long-sustained, is nevertheless often exceedingly rapid. The young are hatched covered with down, and able to run in a few hours after birth.

Photo by C. Reid] [*Wishaw, N.B.*

RED GROUSE.

This is one of the species in which the toes are feathered.

GROUSE AND PTARMIGAN.

The birds of this group are distinguished by the feathery covering which clothes the feet. In some grouse, however, the toes are bare. This causes them to resemble the Pheasant group, from which they may be distinguished by the fact that the toes are fringed with horny processes forming a sort of comb.

Photo by W. F. Piggott] [Leighton Buzzard.

PTARMIGAN.

In winter these birds don a snow-white livery.

The RED GROUSE is the only game-bird which is not found outside the British Islands. It is the bird which perhaps heads the list in the estimation of British sportsmen, who travel north in hundreds every year for the pleasure of the sport it affords. It is furthermore remarkable for the wonderful variety of the seasonal plumages. Both sexes change their dress twice during the year—the female in spring and summer, and the male in autumn and winter. Its Continental relative, the RYPER, has no less than three changes—spring, summer, and winter. For the last season a white dress is adopted, to correspond with its snowy surroundings. The winters in the British Islands are neither long enough nor severe enough to render such change necessary with the red grouse, which is sufficiently protected by its ordinary dress.

Photo by W. F. Piggott] [Leighton Buzzard.

CAPERCALLIE.

This was once a common British bird. The present breed was introduced some years ago, the native birds having been exterminated.

The largest and perhaps the most interesting of all the European game-birds are the CAPERCALLIES, or CAPERCAILZIES. The British species is also known as the COCK-OF-THE-WOOD. He is a handsome black bird, nearly as big as a turkey, weighing from 9 to 17 lbs.

Photo by W. F. Piggott] [Leighton Buzzard.

COMMON PARTRIDGE.

This is the commoner and more esteemed of the two species of British partridges.

In the spring the capercallie, like the blackcock, indulges in a remarkable "love-song," or "play," as it is called. With outstretched neck, tail expanded like a fan, drooping wings, and ruffled feathers, he commences his call, "peller, peller, peller," increasing in rapidity every moment, till he works himself up into a perfect frenzy. At this time he is perfectly unconscious of all around him, and poachers, knowing this, sometimes take advantage to creep up and shoot him. On hearing the cock, the hens assemble from all parts of the forest. The male then descends from the tree to the ground, when "he and his female friends join company" and march away. The capercallie is jealous of trespassers on his domain, and instances are on record where people have been attacked when so infringing.

Like the capercallie, the BLACKCOCK must be sought in the woods, whence he sallies forth to the moors and stubble-fields to feed. The GREY-HEN, as the female of this species is called, lays from six to ten eggs, of a buff colour, spotted with rich brown: both in number and colour they resemble those of the capercallie.

The naturalist Brehm gives a delightful account of the love-making of this bird. During the spring, he says, "the bird utters almost continuously the strangest noises. He holds his tail up and spreads it out like a fan, he lifts up his head and neck with all the feathers erect, and stretches his wings from the body. Then he takes a few jumps in different directions, sometimes in a circle, and presses the under part of his beak so hard against the ground that the chin-feathers are rubbed off. During these movements he beats his wings and turns round and round. The more ardent he grows, the more lively he becomes, until at last the bird appears like a frantic creature. At such times the blackcocks are so absorbed that they become almost blind and deaf, but less so than the capercallie."

North America is very rich in large forms of grouse; and one of the most interesting of these is the PRAIRIE-HEN, remarkable for the possession of a pair of curious bags of a bright orange colour on each side of the neck, which can be inflated with air at will.

"Early in the morning," writes Captain Bendire of the prairie-hen, "you may see them assemble in parties, from a dozen to fifty together, on some dry knolls . . . and their goings-on would make you laugh. The air-sacs are their ornaments, which they display . . . before the gentler sex by blowing them up till they look like two ripe oranges . . . projecting their long, black ears right forward, ruffling up all the feathers of the body till they stand out straight, and dropping their wings on the ground like a turkey-cock. . . . Then it is that the proud cock, in order to complete his triumph, will rush forward at his best speed . . . through the midst of the love-sick damsels, pouring out as he goes a booming noise . . .

Photo by Dr. R. W. Shufeldt] [*Washington.*

TEXAN BOB-WHITE (ABOUT HALF NATURAL SIZE).

This bird takes its name from its note—"Ah-Bob-White."

Photo by C. Reid] [*Wishaw, N.B.*

GOLDEN PHEASANT.

This bird is often kept in aviaries, on account of its magnificent livery.

which may be heard for at least two miles in the still morning air. Every few minutes this display is repeated . . . but they seem careful not to run against each other, for they have not yet got to the fighting-point. After a little while the lady birds begin to show an interest in the proceedings, by moving about quickly a few yards at a time, and then standing still a short time. When these actions are continued by a large number of birds at a time, it presents a funny sight, and you can easily think they are moving to the measure of music."

Photo by W. P. Dando, F.Z.S., Regent's Park.

GOLDEN PHEASANT.

This bird is moulting. In full dress the cape seen in the upper figure is golden with blue-black bars.

The prairie-hens of America possess great economic value, as great, indeed, as the red grouse of the British Islands, enormous numbers of prairie-hens being exported to Europe every year, whilst still greater numbers are consumed by the American people themselves. It is said that American grouse will sometimes eat the shoots of a plant called *kalmia*, which renders the flesh poisonous.

The SAGE-GROUSE is a rather large bird, attaining a weight of 8 lbs., found in the Western United States; it is, indeed, the largest of the American grouse. Its courting habits resemble those of the prairie-hens. From the book containing the above lively description we cull the following:—

"Early one morning in the first week in March, 1877, I had the long-wished-for opportunity to observe the actions of a single cock while paying court to several females near him. . . . His large, pale yellow air-sacs were fully inflated,

Photo by W. P. Dando F.Z.S.] *[Regent's Park.*

SILVER PHEASANT.

A silver pheasant is embroidered as a badge on mandarins' dresses.

Photo by C. Reid] *[Wishaw, N.B.*

ENGLISH PHEASANTS.

These birds are of the ring-necked variety.

Photo by Scholastic Photo. Co.] *[Parson's Green.*

REEVES'S PHEASANT.

This is a native of North and West China, and has been introduced into Britain.

Photo by Scholastic Photo. Co.] *[Parson's Green.*

GOLDEN PHEASANT.

The female is soberly clad, and has no crest or cape.

Photo by W. P. Dando, F.Z.S.] *[Regent's Park.*

AMHERST'S PHEASANT.

This bird is moulting: in full dress the cape is white and the crest blood-red.

Photo by W. P. Dando, F.Z.S.] *[Regent's Park.*

PEACOCK-PHEASANT.

These pheasants take their name from the eye-like spots on the wings.

and not only extended forward but apparently upward as well, rising at least an inch above his head, which consequently was scarcely noticeable, giving the bird an exceedingly peculiar appearance. He looked decidedly top-heavy and ready to topple over on the slightest provocation." He then proceeds to describe the further preparations designed for conquest. The tail is spread fan-wise, and animated with a peculiar quivering motion, whilst the wings are trailed upon the ground. When the correct position has been assumed, he advances with stately, hesitating steps towards his mate, uttering, as he moves, "low, grunting, guttural sounds" resembling those of a purring cat, but louder. This, apparently, is the prescribed method of courting; of many suitors, he is selected who performs best.

The RUFFED GROUSE, like the prairie-hen, has the neck, in the male, ornamented with a frill of long feathers. Like many other birds, the female, when danger, in the shape of prowling beasts, threatens her eggs or young, simulates lameness. So soon as the enemy approaches near enough to be dangerous, up she gets with a great noise of wings, and then flutters along the ground as though wounded. The would-be captor is thus led far from the jealously guarded treasures, and when a safe distance has been covered an end is speedily put to this will-o'-the-wisp chase by the bird suddenly taking wing.

Photo by Scholastic Photo. Co.] [*Parson's Green.*

TEMMINCK'S TRAGOPAN.

Tragopans are remarkable for a fleshy horn above each eye, not noticeable save when the bird is excited.

PARTRIDGES, QUAILS, AND PHEASANTS.

The birds which come under this head are so many in number they may be reckoned by the hundred, and include several forms of exquisite beauty. The legs of many are armed with formidable spurs, with which the males, who are exceedingly pugnacious, fight furiously with their rivals for the possession of some coveted female.

Of the more conspicuous forms we may mention the RED-LEGGED and COMMON PARTRIDGES. In England the former is known more generally as the FRENCH PARTRIDGE—why, it is hard to say. It is a native of South-eastern Europe, whence it was introduced towards the end of the eighteenth century. It is a handsome bird, but not in high favour with sportsmen, since it prefers to escape by running rather than by flight.

Photo by W. P. Dando, F.Z.S.] [*Regent's Park.*

CHINESE TRAGOPAN.

The scarlet plumage of some of the Tragopans is most gorgeous.

Photo by W. P. Dando, F.Z.S.] [Regent's Park.

HIMALAYAN MONAL.

In some parts of India this bird has been exterminated, owing to the demands of the plume-market.

The COMMON PARTRIDGE is the more abundant of the two species. Though more sober in coloration, it is still a beautiful bird. The "horse-shoe" mark, borne on the breast, so characteristic of this bird, is *not* confined to the males, as is generally believed. "Yielding," says Professor Newton, "perhaps in economic importance to the red grouse, what may be called the social influence of the partridge is greater than that excited by any other wild bird."

This bird displays great courage and affection in defence of its eggs or young. A story illustrating this is told of a gentleman near Spilsby, in Lincolnshire, who, "whilst superintending his ploughmen, saw a partridge glide off her nest, so near the foot of one of his plough-horses that he thought the eggs must be crushed; this, however, was not the case. . . . He saw the old bird return to her nest the instant he left the spot. It was evident that the next round of the plough must bury the eggs and nest in the furrow. His surprise was great when, returning with the plough, he came to the spot and saw the nest indeed, but the eggs and bird were gone. An idea struck him that she had removed her eggs; and he found her, before he left the field, sitting under the hedge upon twenty-one eggs. . . . The round of ploughing had occupied about twenty minutes, in which time she, probably aided by the cock bird, had removed the twenty-one eggs to a distance of about forty yards."

The RED-LEGGED PARTRIDGES, their allies the FRANCOLINS, and the GREY PARTRIDGES are all ground-birds; the TREE-PARTRIDGES, as the name implies, are not, or at least less completely so—hence their mention here. They are natives of the Indo-Chinese countries, and the islands of Java, Borneo, and Formosa.

The QUAIL is a little-known British bird, very like a small partridge in appearance. Enormous numbers, Professor Newton tells us, "are netted on the Continent, especially in the spring migration. The captives are exposed in the poulterers' shops, confined in long, cloth-covered cages, with a feeding-trough in front." The bulk "of these are males, which are the first to arrive, and advantage is taken of this circumstance by the bird-catchers, who decoy hundreds into their nets by imitating the call-note of the female. It has been stated that in the small island of Capri, in the Bay of Naples, 160,000 have been netted in a single season, and even larger numbers are on record." An idea of the vast numbers which travel together in

Photo by W. P. Dando, F.Z.S.] [Regent's Park.

HIMALAYAN MONAL.

The female of the monal is quite soberly clad.

Photo by C. Reid] [Wishaw, N.B.

RED COCHINS.

The wings in the typical Cochins are so short as to be useless.

migration may be gathered from Canon Tristram's statement that in Algeria, in April, he found the ground covered with quails for an extent of many acres at daybreak, where on the preceding afternoon not one was to be seen. These are the birds which were so eagerly seized by the Israelites as a welcome change in the diet which had become so monotonous in the days of their early wanderings. The story, so vividly told in the Book of Exodus, is, of course, familiar to all.

The quail lays from nine to fifteen eggs in a feeble apology for a nest. It is said that the curious metallic note "clic-lic-lic" gave origin to the Spanish castanet, for these birds are much esteemed in Spain, being kept in cages for the pleasure their notes afford.

There are five or six other species of quail closely related to the above. The British bird enjoys an enormous range, being found almost everywhere in Europe, Asia, and Africa. The so-called AMERICAN QUAILS—some forty species in number—are generally regarded as belonging to a distinct group.

That ornament to all rural scenery, the PHEASANT, is said to have been introduced from the banks of the river Phasis, in Colchis, Transcaucasia, by the Romans—at least, the original form of pheasant was. Late during the eighteenth century a Japanese and a Chinese form were introduced, and these have freely interbred with the original form, so that pure-bred specimens of any of the three are rare.

The speed of a pheasant on the wing in full flight has been estimated at thirty-eight miles an hour. Occasionally pheasants will take to the water, and are said to swim well.

The number of pheasants reared by hand at the present day is prodigious. In 1883, Professor Newton tells us, 134,000 pheasants' eggs were sold from one estate in Norfolk, while 9,700 fully grown birds were killed upon it. In olden times pheasants were taken in snares or nets, by hawking, and by the cross-bow; but on the introduction of guns these methods were superseded.

Photo by C. Reid] [Wishaw, N.B.

BROWN LEGHORN COCK.

This breed has been derived by crossing White Leghorns with Game-fowl.

Yet another form of pheasant has been introduced into Britain of late years. This is REEVES'S PHEASANT, a truly magnificent bird, with a tail fully 5 feet long in adult males. These birds also interbreed with the more common forms, but not freely.

Beautiful as these pheasants undoubtedly are, they are eclipsed by many of their relatives. Among the most noteworthy of these we may notice the magnificent TRAGOPANS. Rich in coloration of the feathers, these birds have added an additional feature in brilliantly coloured areas of bare skin on the head and neck, which are furthermore rendered conspicuous by being

Photo by C. Reid] [*Wishaw, N.B.*

SILVER-SPANGLED HAMBURGS.

This bird apparently originated in England.

Photo by C. Reid] [*Wishaw, N.B.*

DARK BRAMAS.

The Brama is an Asiatic breed.

developed with "horns" and wattles. These "horns" can be erected at will, a process which causes them at the same time to be greatly increased in size. The bird, with a proud consciousness of his beauty, displays his charms to the full when wooing. Mr. Bartlett tells us that, "after walking about rather excitedly, he places himself in front of the female, with the body slightly crouching upon the legs, and the tail bent downwards; the head is then violently jerked downwards, and the horns and wattle become conspicuous. The wings have a flapping motion, and the bright red patch on them is fully displayed. The whole of the neck appears to be larger than usual during this action, so do the horns, which, moreover, vibrate with every motion. This scene is concluded by the bird suddenly drawing himself up to his full height, with his wings expanded and quivering, the horns erect, and the wattles fully displayed."

Equally splendid, some think more so, are the four species of pheasant known as MONALS or IMPEYAN PHEASANTS. The plumage in this case looks like burnished metal rather than feathers

Photo by C. Reid] [*Wishaw, N.B.*

SILVER WYANDOTTE HEN WITH PHEASANT CHICKS.

This is an American breed, derived by crossing with the Brama.

The head is adorned with a crest either of long or beautifully curled feathers. Monals are found in the same haunts as the tragopans—the highest forest regions of the Himalaya.

But the most gorgeous of all the Pheasant Tribe are perhaps the GOLDEN PHEASANTS. The crimson body and exquisitely beautiful collar of gold barred with black constitute a perfectly royal livery. Since, however, these are amongst the commonest occupants of the aviary, we need not describe them further here. They are natives of China and Tibet.

JUNGLE-FOWL AND THEIR DOMESTICATED DESCENDANTS.

These birds, of which there are four distinct species, are close allies of the domesticated fowls: the descent of these latter, indeed, is traced from the red jungle-fowl of the Himalaya and Central India. The characteristic features of the group are the naked head, bearing the familiar wattles and fleshy comb, and the formidable spurs on the legs.

The varieties of the domesticated jungle-fowl are numerous. The pugnacity of the

Photo by C. Reid] [Wishaw, N.B.

PEACOCK.

Note the perfectly symmetrical distribution of the "eyes" in the "train."

members known as the GAME-BREED is well known, and in the days of cock-fighting large sums of money changed hands over the fierce battles waged by rival game-cocks pitted one against the other—the game-cock, it should be remarked, being the little-modified descendant of the red jungle-cock.

The modern game-cock is purely a show-bird, breeders having changed the type by selecting characters which would render the bird quite unable to hold its own if matched in battle with one of the original breed.

Very different from the wild ancestor is the huge, much-feathered COCHIN. This was introduced into England, not from Cochin-China, as is popularly supposed, but from Shanghai, some fifty years ago. At that time this bird enjoyed the reputation of being wonderfully prolific. This is, alas! no longer a feature of the breed. The show-pen is apparently responsible for this, attention having been paid rather to external appearance than to useful qualities.

The PLYMOUTH ROCK and DORKING are both well-known breeds. The former is of American origin, made by crossing Cochins with a native breed—the Dominique.

The BLACK SPANISH, MINORCAS, LEGHORNS, ANDALUSIANS, etc., constitute what are known as the Mediterranean breeds. They are noted for their great prolificacy. This has been gained by carefully breeding from the most productive birds, but with the result that the instinct to sit has been lost entirely. This is a matter of no consequence, however, as when chicks are required there are plenty of "broody" hens of other breeds which can be made to undertake the duties of foster-mother.

Photo by L. Medland, F.Z.S.] [North Finchley.

BACK VIEW OF PEACOCK.

Note the true tail, like a stout fan, supporting the train.

The HAMBURGS are of two kinds—the SPANGLED, which is of English, and the PENCILLED, of Continental origin.

A very old breed is the POLISH. It figures often in the pictures of the old Dutch masters. One of its chief characteristics is the huge crest of feathers rising from the crown of the head. The development of this crest has had a very extraordinary effect upon the conformation of the bones of the skull, entirely altering the shape of the brain-case.

Photo by Scholastic Photo. Co.] [Parson's Green.

BLACK-CHESTED CRESTED GUINEA-FOWL.

At Durban these birds are often hawked by Kaffir hunters, the flesh being very delicate and much esteemed.

Perhaps the most artificial of all breeds of fowl are the SEBRIGHT BANTAMS. These are diminutive birds, the result of a cross between the Polish with "laced" feathers and a bantam. The feathers of this cross are beautifully "laced"—that is, they are white, edged with black. Another interesting diminutive breed is the JAPANESE BANTAM. The cock carries its tail, which is long, remarkably high, giving a very quaint effect. This breed is further interesting, since it furnishes us with an instance of the breeder's power of localising colour by selection. The tail is black and the body white. Yet another interesting Japanese fowl is the remarkable long-tailed breed in which the tail-coverts grow continuously, attaining a length of from 9 feet to, it is said, 18 feet. The birds are kept for show purposes. The greater part of their lives is passed tethered on high perches. Once a day they are taken down for exercise, when the long feathers are carefully rolled up and securely fastened out of harm's way.

Photo by W. P. Dando, F.Z.S.] [Regent's Park.

BLACK-CHESTED CRESTED GUINEA-FOWL.

This is a black bird, with light blue spots.

THE ARGUS-PHEASANT AND PEACOCK AND THEIR ALLIES.

The ARGUS-PHEASANT most certainly demands notice, on account of the extraordinary development of the wing-quills, which are nearly a yard long, and the wondrous beauty of the pattern thereon. This pattern takes the form of a number of eyes, so shaded as to give the appearance, when fully displayed, of a number of balls lying in a socket. These enormous quills are borne only by the male, and used, like the ornamental feathers of its allies, in captivating the female. When fully displayed, the two wings are spread out to form one huge fan, producing an effect which words cannot adequately describe. The argus-pheasants are found in the forests of Siam, the Malay Peninsula, and Sumatra, and are excessively wary birds.

The PEACOCK is too well known to need a very long description. But a word as to the so-called "tail." This magnificent wealth of plumes does not represent the tail, as is popularly supposed, but is made up of the feathers of the lower part of the back and the upper tail-coverts. These gradually increase in length from before-backwards, culminating in the long and exquisite feathers which form the circumference of the huge, outspread shield. This shield is properly called the "train"; the true tail lies behind it and acts as a support. When the bird is about to display, the "train" feathers are slowly and gently raised till the well-known fan-shaped glory of green and gold and blue is exposed to the fullest possible extent.

Photo by the Duchess of Bedford.

NEST OF BRUSH-TURKEY AT WOBURN ABBEY.

This is made by several birds, of decaying vegetable matter, in which the eggs are laid and left to hatch.

"Watch the bird trying to do his best to persuade his chosen what a handsome fellow he is. He first places himself more or less in front of her, but at some little distance off; and then, watching his opportunity, walks rapidly backwards, going faster and faster and faster, till, arrived within a foot, he suddenly, like a flash, turns round and displays to the full his truly gorgeous vestments. This turning movement is accompanied by a violent shaking of the train, the quills of which rattle like the pattering of rain upon leaves. Often this movement is followed by a loud scream.

"When the train is fully erect, it will be noticed that it lies so far forward that the bird's head and neck appear as if rising from its base. In a side view the whole body, from the front of the wings backwards, appears to lie behind the train."

This bird is a native of India, where it is held in great reverence by the Hindus, and

Photo by C. Reid] [*Wishaw, N.B.*

TURKEY COCK AND HEN.

The curious "tassel" depending from the breast is found in no other bird.

Photo by Kerry & Co.] *[Sydney.*

WALLACE'S PAINTED MEGAPODE.

This bird buries its eggs in the sand, burrowing for each a slanting hole from 3 to 4 feet deep.

in the Hindu States it is not allowed to be killed under any circumstances. There are two, some say three, distinct species of peacock, but they all closely resemble one another.

Brief mention will serve for the GUINEA-FOWLS and TURKEYS, since they are well known to us all. GUINEA-FOWLS are African birds. The farm-yard form, popularly known as "Come-backs," from their peculiar cry "come-back, come-back, come-back," is a descendant of the common helmeted form, of which type there are eight distinct species. Besides these are four crested species; one very beautiful species known as the VULTURE-LIKE GUINEA-FOWL; and one, the rarest of all, known as the BLACK GUINEA-FOWL. Even in the British Museum, writes Mr. Ogilvie Grant, "there are only two examples of it, and neither of these are perfect specimens." It was discovered by M. Du Chaillu. "One day," he says, "I went out hunting by myself, and, to my great joy, shot another new bird, a black wild-fowl, one of the most singular birds I have seen in Africa. . . . The head, where it is bare, is in the female of a pink hue, and in the male of a bright scarlet. . . . Wild they are, and most difficult to approach, and rare, even in the forests where they are at home." They do not travel in huge flocks, like other guinea-fowls, but a male and two females at most.

The familiar form of the TURKEY scarcely needs description; but most people are probably puzzled by its name. Why Turkey? The bird is a native of America, so it certainly cannot have anything to do with its place of origin. Professor Newton has it that it is on account of its call-note, "to be syllabled 'turk, turk, turk,' whereby it may almost be said to have named itself."

The domesticated turkey is descended from the MEXICAN TURKEY, and was probably introduced into Europe during the sixteenth century. This, according to Captain Bendire, is a mountain-living species, and still abundant in the wilder portions of Western Texas and New Mexico. It appears to attain greater bulk than its domesticated descendant, Captain Bendire having recorded a specimen shot by himself which weighed 28 lbs. after having been drawn, and heavier birds are said to occur occasionally.

The Mexicans say that the coyotes catch turkeys by running in circles under the tree in which they are roosting, till the birds get dizzy with watching them, and fall down into the open mouths below!

There are three distinct kinds of turkey—the MEXICAN, AMERICAN, and HONDURAS TURKEY. The last is a very fine bird, with a bright blue head and neck, instead of red. The top of the head is adorned with numerous scarlet, berry-like warts, looking like holly-berries.

The BOB-WHITES, which belong to the group of tooth-billed game-birds known as American Partridges and Quails, demand a brief reference here. The species represented in the illustration on page 399 is common in the lowlands of Texas. It is a very unsuspicious bird, and in consequence falls an easy prey to foxes, hariers, and rattlesnakes, the last-named being the worst enemies, as many as five of these unfortunate birds having been taken at one time from the stomach of one of these monsters, and on another occasion a female and half a dozen of her eggs were similarly discovered.

The MEGAPODES and BRUSH-TURKEYS, though dull and uninteresting-looking birds, are, on account of the facts connected with the propagation of their species, quite remarkable. They do not brood over their eggs, as do other birds, but instead bury them, either in sand in the neighbourhood of warm springs or in heaps of decaying vegetable matter. In the latter case the material is often collected by several birds working together. Mounds of 8 feet high and 60 feet in circumference have been found, the work of the NICOBAR MEGAPODE. Such have been many years in use, material being added each season. Into this mass the female digs down and deposits an egg every second day, covering it up as soon as laid. There it remains till hatched, when the young, probably aided by its mother, forces its way up to the surface, and emerges, *not* a downy nestling as one would expect, but clothed with feathers differing but slightly in texture from those worn in the adult state. Owing to the precocious development, young megapodes are able to fly within an hour after birth.

Photo by Scholastic Photo. Co.] *[Parson's Green.*

RAZOR-BILLED CURASSOW.

So called from the sharp ridge along the top of the beak.

There are many different kinds of megapodes occurring in Australia, Samoa, and the Nicobar and Philippine Islands.

The CURASSOWS and GUANS are very handsome birds, but probably quite unknown to most of our readers, yet they may always be seen in Zoological Gardens. They are closely related to the megapodes, which we have just been discussing; but their nesting habits are quite different. They lay their eggs in nests, either on the ground or in trees, and brood over them like other birds. Many have brilliantly coloured bare skin on the head and handsome crests. They are natives of Central and South America, where they are often kept by the settlers, as they tame easily. It is said that one of the guans, when crossed with the domesticated fowl, becomes intensely pugnacious, and superior to the game-cock for fighting purposes.

Photo by Scholastic Photo. Co.] *[Parson's Green.*

CRESTED CURASSOW.

So called from its crest of curled feathers.

BUSTARD-QUAIL AND PLAIN-WANDERERS.

These are small and quail-like in appearance, though they are probably only distant relatives of the Game-birds. But they are, nevertheless, remarkable birds. A great authority, Mr. A. O. Hume, writing of the INDIAN BUSTARD-QUAIL, says of them: "The most remarkable point in the life-history of these bustard-quails is the extraordinary fashion in which, amongst them, the position of the sexes is reversed. The females are the larger and handsomer birds. The females only call, the females only fight—natives say that they fight for the males, and probably this is true. The males . . . only . . . sit upon the eggs, the females meanwhile larking about, calling, and fighting, without any care for their obedient mates; and, lastly, the males tend . . . the young brood."

The group has a wide geographical range, occurring in Europe, Africa, Madagascar, South Asia, the Indian Archipelago, and Australia.

The Hoatzin.

This bird is one of the puzzles of the ornithologist. Its pedigree is still a mystery, but it is generally believed to have some relation to the Game-birds. Its whole life is passed in trees overhanging water, and its flight restricted to short journeys from tree to tree. In South America, its home, it is known by a variety of names, one of which means Stinking-pheasant. This is in allusion to the peculiar odour of its flesh, which smells, according to some, like musk, and to others like raw hides. Another remarkable feature of this bird is the fact that it has turned its crop into a sort of gizzard, whilst the true gizzard, having been relieved of its functions, has diminished to the size of a hazel-nut. The unusual purpose to which the crop has been put has brought about considerable modification in the form of the breast-bone, which is quite different to that of any other bird.

Photo by J. W. McLellan] *[Highbury.*

HOATZIN.

This is a native of the Amazons Valley, and lives entirely in the trees.

The young of these birds are quite as remarkable as the parents, for almost as soon as they are hatched they crawl out of the nest, along the boughs of the tree in which it rests, to meet the parents coming with food. In these crawling excursions they are aided by the wings, which for a time serve as fore feet. The thumb and first finger are armed with strong claws, with which a firm hold is gained on the bark of the tree. To render these claws effective so long as they are necessary, the quill-feathers of the tip of the wing have their development checked till the others have grown long enough to serve the purposes of flight.

The Rails.

The Rails are all water-loving birds, dwelling in swamps or on the borders of lakes and streams. Although all swim easily, none have webbed feet. The flight is weak; several species, indeed, have lost this power altogether. The body is much compressed, enabling them to pass readily through the narrow interspaces of dense aquatic foliage. The Rails appear to be related on the one hand to the Game-birds, and on the other to the Cranes. In size they vary from a bird as large as a fowl to one as small as a lark.

One of the commonest of the Rails is the Corn-crake, more commonly, perhaps, known as the Land-rail. Its curious grating cry is one of the commonest sounds which the summer brings with it, and one possessing a charm of its own. But rarely seen, it builds its nest in hay-fields, and, when the grass is being cut, sits so closely on its treasures that it is sometimes beheaded by the swinging scythe. In the autumn it falls not infrequently to the sportsmen when partridge-shooting. The corn-crake leaves in the winter for the more congenial climate of Africa, a feat that seems wonderful when its feeble powers of flight are considered. Its near relative the Water-rail is rather a handsome bird, but of shy and retiring habits.

The Weka-rail, a native of New Zealand, is one of the flightless forms to which we have referred. It is about as large as a pheasant, but lacks its splendour, being soberly clad in brown and black. Unlike its relative, it breeds in a burrow, which it digs for itself by the aid of its bill. The name "weka" was given it by the Maoris.

Photo by Scholastic Photo. Co.] [*Parson's Green.*

WEKA-RAIL.

The wings, though fairly large, are useless for flight.

The COMMON WATER-HEN, or MOOR-HEN, is one of the most familiar birds of the London parks. Although frequent enough to be seen upon streams and broads, it is, nevertheless, shy and wary; but in the sanctuary of the public parks all reserve is thrown off. The water-hen, like its allies, is an expert swimmer, in spite of the fact that the toes are not webbed; on the contrary, they are very long and slender. When alarmed, these birds will often submerge the body till only the beak projects above water.

All the members of this group are easily recognised by the bare patch of skin extending from the beak on to the top of the head. In the COOTS this is white; in the WATER-HENS and GALLINULES it is red. The coots and water-hens are clad in sober colours, grey or black; but the gallinules are gorgeously clad in purple, shaded with dark green, olive-brown, and black. MANTELL'S GALLINULE of New Zealand is probably now extinct, the last bird having been killed in 1898.

Photo by W. F. Piggott] [*Leighton Buzzard.*

WATER-RAIL.

This is a common British bird, seldom seen, on account of its retiring habits.

THE FIN-FEET.

These are little-known birds, found in Africa, South America, South-east Asia, and Sumatra. They are closely related to the coots, but differ therefrom in many important particulars. Like the coots, they are river-haunting birds, and have broad flaps of skin fringing the toes, which serve the purpose of a web; but they have much longer necks and tails than the coots and water-hens. Not much is known about them.

CHAPTER III.

PIGEONS AND SAND-GROUSE.

PIGEONS, as a rule, are birds of wonderful powers of flight. The young, which never exceed two in number, are hatched perfectly blind and helpless, and but sparsely clothed. They are nourished by a peculiar milky secretion of the parents' crop known as "pigeons' milk." The operation of feeding is performed by the parent thrusting its beak into the mouth of its offspring and ejecting therein the secretion just referred to. The nest is a very simple structure, being composed of twigs, generally placed in a tree, but sometimes in a cave or hole in a bank. The eggs, which never exceed two in number, are pure white.

Perhaps the most beautiful species occur among the large group known as FRUIT-PIGEONS. Many of these are invested in raiment of vivid green and yellow, forming a little coterie by themselves—the GREEN PIGEONS. Others, on account of their brilliancy, have been designated PAINTED PIGEONS, of which, perhaps, the most beautiful of all is EUGÈNE'S PIGEON. Try to imagine it! The head is pure white, the upper part of the breast a purple-red surrounded by a dull purple band: the under parts are greyish green, shading into white; the flanks green; whilst the upper parts are also green, but of a rich bronze tint. Another group from the Fiji Islands includes a magnificent species, the male of which is clothed in a glorious orange, save the head and throat, which are olive-yellow. His mate is scarcely less beautiful, her plumage being rich green. Another member of the group—the WHITE NUTMEG-PIGEON—is clad in creamy white, with black quills, and a black tip to the tail. It is a native of Borneo. The fruit-pigeons, it should be mentioned, include some of the largest of living pigeons.

Photo by J. T. Newman] [*Berkhamsted.*

A PAIR OF YOUNG PIGEONS IN NEST.

The hair-like down of the young pigeon is quite different to any other nestling down.

Whilst many of the Pigeon Tribe seem to have succeeded in dyeing their feathers with all the hues of the rainbow, others have secured equal glory by a covering which at first sight would rather appear to be of burnished metal than of feathers. The most striking instance of this is found in the magnificent NICOBAR PIGEONS. There are two species of these birds, which occur not only in the Nicobar Islands, from which they take their name, but also in the Malay Archipelago and the Solomon and Pelew Islands. The general tone of the one species is black, but the upper parts are superbly glossed with bronze and copper reflections. The other, from the Pelew Islands, is indigo-blue in general tone. In one of the Nicobar Islands these birds occur in thousands. Furthermore, these two pigeons stand alone, in that the neck-feathers are greatly elongated, forming "hackles" like those of the common fowl.

The largest of living pigeons are the GOURAS, or CROWNED PIGEONS. There are six species,

Photo by L. Medland, F.Z.S.] *[North Finchley.*

SOUTHERN FRUIT-PIGEON.

The flesh of the fruit-pigeon surpasses that of all other birds in delicacy.

Photo by L. Medland, F.Z.S.] *[North Finchley.*

NICOBAR IMPERIAL FRUIT-PIGEONS.

These birds lay but a single egg, which is large.

Photo by W. P. Dando, F.Z.S.] *[Regent's Park.*

NEW GUINEA CROWNED PIGEON.

This is the largest of living pigeons.

Photo by W. P. Dando, F.Z.S.] *[Regent's Park.*

WONGA-WONGA PIGEON.

This bird is found in the brush country of Eastern Australia

all of which are confined to Australasia. They are characterised by a huge and very beautiful fan-shaped crest of feathers which springs from the crown of the head.

At the other extreme stand the NAMAQUA and SCALY DOVES. The former is regarded by Professor Newton as one of the most graceful in form of all the Pigeon Tribe: the latter are scarcely, if at all, larger than the sparrows.

The power of flight of some forms is, however, extremely limited; they bid fair in course of time to become flightless, like the dodo and the solitaire. The most interesting of these is the GREY-NAPED GROUND-PIGEON. Pigeons for the most part display a marked preference for a life among the trees rather than on the ground; but there are some which are essentially ground-dwellers. The species in which this changed habit is most deeply rooted, and probably of longest standing, exhibit one very interesting point of difference from their neighbours of the woods. This difference consists in the very considerably longer legs which mark the ground-haunting bird. The GREY-NAPED GROUND-PIGEON of South-east New Guinea forms an excellent example, inasmuch as the legs are much longer than in any other pigeon. These birds (for there are three species in all) resemble the Megapodes in habit, and frequent hills or dense thickets. They lay one egg, which is deposited at the foot of a tree.

Among domesticated breeds is the ENGLISH POUTER, a bird characterised by its enormous gullet, which can be distended with air whenever the owner wills. The carriage of the body is vertical, not, as in pigeons generally, horizontal. The CARRIER is a breed illustrating the result of long-sustained selection to increase, amongst other characters, the development of the bare skin surrounding the eye and beak of all pigeons, wild or tame. In the SHORT-FACED TUMBLER we have a breed wherein those birds with the shortest beaks have been steadily bred from. To-day so little beak is left that some individuals are hatched which, when grown up, are unable to feed themselves. An example of a radical change in the feathers is the INDIAN FRILL-BACK. In this case the feathers all over the body are reversed, or turned forwards, giving the bird a quite extraordinary appearance. In the JACOBIN we have a breed—and we could cite others—wherein the feathers of the neck are much elongated, and turn upwards and forwards over the head to form a hood.

Photo by L. Medland, F.Z.S.] [*North Finchley.*

MALE BLACK-BELLIED SAND-GROUSE.

Young sand-grouse run directly they are hatched, thus differing from young pigeons.

In general appearance SAND-GROUSE are small, very short-legged birds, with small heads and pointed wings and tail. Their general tone of coloration may be described as sand-coloured, and this has been adopted to render them in harmony with the barren sand-wastes in which they dwell. But some may be described as quite highly coloured, being banded and splashed with chestnut, black, pearly grey, white, and yellow, according to the species.

PALLAS'S SAND-GROUSE is a native of the Kirghiz Steppes, extending through Central Asia to Mongolia and Northern China, and northwards to Lake Baikal, and southwards to Turkestan. Here they may be met with in enormous numbers. In North China large numbers are often caught after a snow-storm. The snow is cleared away, and a small green bean is scattered about. Young sand-grouse differ remarkably in one particular from young pigeons, inasmuch as the former are hatched covered with a thick down, and are able to run about soon after leaving the egg, whilst the pigeon comes into the world very helpless and much in need of clothing. Three eggs are laid by the sand-grouse, and these are double-spotted; whilst the pigeon lays but two, which are white. The eggs of the sand-grouse are laid in a depression in the ground, without any nest.

Photo by Ottomar Anschütz, Berlin.

CROWNED CRANE.

The feathers of the Crest of this bird look not unlike stiff hairs.

CHAPTER IV.

AUKS, GULLS, AND PLOVERS.

THE AUK TRIBE.

THE GUILLEMOT is found all around Britain, and breeds wherever the sea is fringed by cliffs affording ledges for the reception of the eggs. It breeds in colonies often numbering many thousands, and lays but one egg, which is large and pear-shaped. Since the guillemot builds no nest, but lays its egg on the bare rock, this peculiar shape is advantageous, since it revolves on itself, when disturbed, instead of rolling off the ledge into the sea. At the same time thousands of eggs fall into the sea every year owing to the bird's leaving the egg, whilst incubating, in too great a hurry. At Lundy Island one of the sources of amusement for the gaping tourist was that of firing a shot to frighten the birds, with the result that, at each shot, showers of eggs were knocked off the ledges on to the rocks below. The colour of the egg varies infinitely, no two being quite alike. This, it has been suggested, is useful, as the mother is thereby enabled to identify her own egg, even when surrounded by hundreds of others. The young are covered with long down, and when big enough, but still unable to fly, are taken down by the mother to the sea, being carried, some say, on her back: others say the chick is seized by the wing and carried down.

By permission of the Hon. Walter Rothschild, Tring.

WHITE TERN.

There are two species of white tern, almost restricted to the Southern Hemisphere.

The RAZOR-BILL is nearly, if not quite, as common on the coasts of Britain as the guillemot, from which it may be readily distinguished by its beak, which is much compressed from side to side—hence its name of Razor-bill—and deeply grooved. In habits it very closely resembles the guillemot, but in one respect at least it is a more interesting bird, inasmuch as it is related to and closely resembles the now extinct GREAT AUK, the giant of the tribe. The smallest British representative, it should be mentioned, is the LITTLE AUK, a species more nearly allied to the guillemot. It is only a winter visitant to Britain, breeding in huge colonies on the inhospitable shores of Greenland and Iceland.

So quaint a bird as the PUFFIN most certainly finds a place here. One of its most characteristic features is its enormous bill, which is rendered more conspicuous on account of its bright colour. It is bluish at the base, yellow at the tip, and striped with orange. A very remarkable feature of this bill is the fact that it is larger in summer than winter, portions of the sheath being shed in autumn.

Enormous numbers of puffins breed in Ireland; myriads breed on Lundy Island. The Farne Islands, the cliffs of Flamborough, and Scotland are also tenanted by thousands. Puffins breed in holes, which they dig for themselves when occasion requires, but when rabbit-burrows are to be had they prefer these, dispossessing the owners without the slightest compunction. Might, with the puffin, is right, as well as with many other animals.

Young puffins, like young auks and guillemots, are hatched covered with long down. The parents feed them on fish, which they deposit at the mouth of the burrow twenty at a time, and give them to the young bird one by one. When the female is sitting, her mate feeds her in a similar way.

Puffins lay only a single egg, which differs from that of its relatives the Auks and Guillemots in being white. The white colour enables the sitting-bird to see it in the dark burrow.

THE GULL TRIBE.

To get at the real inwardness of the Gull Tribe, so to speak, we must examine their anatomy very closely; then we shall be convinced that they are modified Plovers, and have nothing to do with the Petrels, to which they bear an undoubted resemblance.

TERNS.

Terns are gulls in miniature, on which account it is probable that many a visitor to the seashore passes them unwittingly. But let him watch next time for what look like flocks of tiny, long-winged, and unusually active gulls, now hovering gracefully in the air, and now suddenly plunging headlong like an arrow to the sea, with a force and dash that will surprise him, now that attention is drawn to them. These are terns. From their vivacity and forked tails, they have been aptly named Sea-swallows.

Photo by G. Watmough Webster & Son] [Chester.

TERNS ON A SHINGLE BANK.

Terns lay their eggs among the shingle; from their coloration, these are difficult to detect among the surrounding stones.

There are several species of tern. Like the Gulls, they have a distinctive dress for summer and winter, but the sexes are both dressed alike. The general livery, as with the Gulls, is pearly grey above and pure white below—in summer, in some species, relieved by a black head. One species, the ROSEATE TERN, has the breast suffused with a most exquisite rose-pink, which fades rapidly after death, however. Young terns, in their first plumage, differ conspicuously from their parents, having much brown intermixed with grey.

Terns lay about three eggs, which are deposited among the shingle on the beach; and so closely do the eggs, and later on the young, resemble the surrounding stones that it is almost impossible to find them. As a rule terns breed in colonies, often numbering many thousand birds.

There are exceptions to the rule just laid down as to nest-building. One species of the NODDY TERNS, for example, builds a nest of turf and dry grass, placed in bushes or in low trees. It seems to return to the same nest year after year, adding on each return new materials, till they form masses nearly 2 feet in height. Occasionally it appears to make a mud-nest, placed in the fork of a tree; whilst the superb little WHITE NODDY often deposits

its egg on the leaf of a cocoanut-palm—truly a wonderful site, and still more wonderful when we reflect that it is chosen by one of the Gull Tribe.

About six species of tern commonly occur in the British Islands, and some five or six other species occasionally visit them.

Skimmers.

The Skimmers are tern-like birds, with a very wide geographical distribution, occurring in India, Africa, and North and South America, and remarkable for the very extraordinary form of the beak. The upper jaw is much shorter than the lower, and both are compressed to the thinness of a knife-blade. This beak is associated with, and is probably an adaptation to, an equally remarkable method of feeding, which has been admirably described by Darwin, who watched them feeding in a lake near Maldonado. "They kept their bills," he says, "wide open, and the lower mandible half buried in the water. Thus skimming the surface, they ploughed it in their course; . . . and it formed a most curious spectacle to behold a flock, each bird leaving its narrow wake on the mirror-like surface. In their flight . . . they dexterously manage with their projecting lower mandible to plough up small fish, which are secured by the upper and shorter half of their scissor-like bills."

Photo by Scholastic Photo. Co.] *[Parson's Green.*

HERRING-GULL.

So called from its habit of following the shoals of herrings.

The Gulls.

Gulls are larger and heavier birds than terns, with longer legs, and shorter, thicker beaks. Furthermore, with one exception, the tail is never forked. Like the terns, gulls generally breed in colonies, and these are often of large size. Young gulls, when newly hatched, are quite active. Later, when their feathers have grown, they are found to wear a dress quite different from that of the parents. Sometimes the adult plumage is gained at the end of the first year of existence, sometimes not until after the third year. Gulls feed on everything that comes in their way, from fish caught swimming at the surface of the sea to worms picked up at the plough-tail.

Photo by Scholastic Photo. Co.] *[Parson's Green.*

YOUNG HERRING-GULLS IN THE GREY PHASE OF PLUMAGE.

In their dull grey plumage the young of all gulls are very unlike the adults.

One of the commonest and best known of all the gulls is perhaps the species known as the Black-headed Gull, which has become so common in the heart of busy London, where hundreds may be seen, during the winter months, flying up and down the river, or wheeling about over the lakes in the parks. The black-headed gull receives its popular name on account of the fact that, like some terns and some other gulls, in the spring, the feathers of the head suddenly acquire a sooty-black colour: all trace of this is lost in the winter, save for two patches, one behind each ear.

Photo by W. F. Piggott] *[Leighton Buzzard.*

STONE-CURLEW, OR THICK-KNEE.

The plumage so closely resembles the sandy soil on which the bird lives that concealment is easily effected by crouching close to the ground.

The eggs of this bird are collected in thousands each spring, and sold in London and other markets as plovers' eggs. As many as 20,000 have been taken in a season from the extensive gullery at Scoulton Mere, in Norfolk. Three or four eggs are laid in a nest of rushes, which is always placed on the ground in marshy and often inaccessible spots.

The largest of the Gull Tribe is the GREAT BLACK-BACKED GULL, which is, furthermore, a common British bird; indeed, it is frequently seen flying, together with the last-mentioned species, on the Thames, doing its best to get a full share of the tit-bits thrown by interested spectators from the various London bridges. Unlike the black-headed gull, it has no seasonal change of plumage, but is clad all the year round in the purest white, set off by a mantle of bluish black. The young of this bird has a quite distinct plumage of greyish brown, and hence has been described as a distinct species—the GREY GULL. This dress is gradually changed for the adult plumage, but the process takes about three years.

Photo by W. F. Piggott] *[Leighton Buzzard.*

CURLEW.

So called on account of its note.

The KITTIWAKE is another of the common British gulls, breeding in thousands in favourable localities on the coasts. Its eggs are deposited on the narrowest and most inaccessible ledges of precipitous cliffs. This species sometimes falls a victim to the fashion of wearing feathers. "At Clovelly," writes Mr. Howard Saunders, "there was a regular staff for preparing plumes; and fishing-smacks, with extra boats and crews, used to commence their work of destruction at Lundy Island by daybreak on the 1st of August. . . . In many cases the wings were torn off the wounded birds before they were dead, the mangled victims being tossed back into the water." And he has seen, he continues, "hundreds of young birds dead or dying of starvation in the nests, through the want of their parents' care. . . . It is well within the mark to say that at least 9,000 of these inoffensive birds were destroyed during the fortnight."

Of the SKUA-GULLS there are several species. Their coloration differs from that of the gulls just described in being confined to shades of brown. One of their most remarkable traits is that of piracy. They await their cousins the Gulls coming shoreward from the sea with newly swallowed fish, and then, giving chase, compel the gull, in order to lighten itself and escape, to disgorge its hard-won meal. So swift of flight is the skua that the ejected morsel is caught before it reaches the water.

THE PLOVER TRIBE.

BIRDS of very various size, shape, and coloration are included in this group—that is to say, birds which vary much superficially, but, it must be understood, all undoubtedly closely related. In England they are to be met with almost everywhere. The seashore, the lonely moorland, the desolate marshes, the river's brink, or the woods—all these shelter some one or other of the Plover Tribe. Like the Gulls, many adopt a distinctive dress for the courting-season, which, however, is sometimes worn by the males only, and not by both sexes alike, as in the Gulls. One of the most striking and familiar instances of this change is seen in the GREY PLOVER. In winter the plumage of the upper-parts of this bird is dusky grey, that of the under-parts pure white; but in the spring the former is exchanged for a beautifully variegated mantle of black and white, and the latter becomes uniformly jet-black, save the under tail-coverts, which remain white.

Photo by C. N. Mavroyeni] [*Smyrna.*

WOODCOCK.

The female is larger than the male.

Photo by A. H. P. Cruickshank] [*Wellington.*

OYSTER-CATCHER ON ITS NEST.

Three eggs are laid in a slight hollow in the ground. The oyster-catcher is one of the most wary of the Plover Tribe, and very difficult to approach.

In the DUNLIN, again, we have a similar change, the upper-parts being in winter grey, the under-parts white: in the spring the former become black, with an admixture of rust-colour, and the latter black in so far as the breast is concerned, but the abdomen remains white.

In many of that section of the Plover Tribe distinguished as "Wading-birds," the changes which take place in the spring in the plumage of the upper-parts resemble those already instanced, but the under-parts turn to a rich chestnut instead of black. This occurs in the forms known as the GODWITS, KNOTS, and SANDERLINGS, for example.

In all the instances so far quoted, both male and female are coloured alike, but, as already hinted, occasionally the change of plumage affects the male only. This is the case with the

Photo by W. P. Dando, F.Z.S.] [*Regent's Park.*

DENHAM'S BUSTARD.

This species, when "showing off," fills the gullet with air, having no special air-sac like the great bustard.

RUFF. The importance of this exception is still further increased by the fact that the change in coloration is accompanied by the development of a large frill around the neck, surmounted by two large tufts called "ears," and fleshy, brightly coloured warts around the beak. The coloured picture of the male in its spring dress, which will be found on another page, gives an admirable idea of the typical ruff, but it must necessarily fail to give any indication of one very remarkable fact concerning this frill and the two "ears," and for this reason—no two individuals ever have these peculiar feathers of the same coloration and pattern. The range of colour is certainly not great—the changes being rung, so to speak, on black, white, chestnut, bay, and ash-colour. Diversification is gained by contrasting the "ears" with the frill, and adding bars or streaks to the light coloration, and purple, green, and violet reflections to the dark. These ornaments are donned in a surprisingly short space of time, and are discarded as quickly, for they are scarcely completed by the month of May, and are thrown off again at the end of June. During the time that this resplendent livery is worn the males engage in mimic battles—which may occasionally develop into real ones—arranged apparently for the edification of the females, which, it seems, select as partners, at least for that season, those which please or excite most. This power of pleasing must certainly be considerable, for the ruff is a polygamous species.

Photo by W. F. Piggott] [*Leighton Buzzard.*

GREAT BUSTARDS.

The cock on the right is "showing off."

Formerly the ruff was a common bird in England, but the drainage of the fens and persecution have practically brought about its extermination.

At least two groups of plovers have succeeded in reversing the usual order of things in the matter of sexual plumage. These are the PHALAROPES — which are British birds—and the PAINTED SNIPE, in both of which the female is more brightly coloured and somewhat larger in size than the male. As is the case where this reversal occurs, the duties of incubation fall mainly or entirely upon the smaller and duller male. It is interesting to note, furthermore, that only in the phalaropes is there a seasonal change of plumage: in the painted snipe the same livery is worn all the year round.

Many of the plovers have no seasonal change of plumage, but both male and female wear all the year round, some a more or less markedly bright-coloured livery, as the DOTTEREL and TURNSTONES, others a more sober vestment, as the CURLEWS and SNIPE, for example.

The SNIPE and WOODCOCK may be cited as especially instructive forms in this connection, showing, in regard to the beak, for instance, undoubted proof of this structural modification, the result of adaptation to the peculiar method of seeking their food. This beak constitutes an organ of touch of great sensitiveness, and is used as a probe, to thrust down into the soft soil in the search for hidden worms.

Of the three species of snipe which occur in Britain, probably the one known as the COMMON

Photo by Billington] [*Queensland.*

INDIAN BUSTARDS.

Bustards have very short toes, like many other birds which walk much on sandy soil.

SNIPE is most familiar; but it will, perhaps, be new to some to learn that this bird ranks as a musical performer, on account of a very extraordinary "bleating" or "drumming" noise which it gives forth, especially during the spring of the year—the season of courtship. We cannot describe this noise better, perhaps, than as an unusually high-pitched "hum," produced, it is generally held, by wind driven between the outer tail-feathers by the rapid vibration of the wings as the bird descends, or rather pitches, at a fearful pace, earthwards. These feathers have the shafts peculiarly thickened; and it is interesting to note that the characteristic sound may be artificially produced if they be fastened to a stick and rapidly whirled through the air.

The snipe and woodcock are not the only members of the Plover Tribe whose beaks have undergone marked structural modifications; indeed, many instances could be cited, but two or three must suffice. In the AVOCET the beak turns upwards like an awl, and the bird is in consequence known in some places as the COBBLER'S-AWL DUCK. In one particular, however, the beak differs from an awl, tapering as it does to an exceedingly fine point. When the

Photo by W. P. Dando] [*Regent's Park.*

STANLEY CRANE.

This is a South African species.

bird feeds, it walks along in shallow water with the curved tip of the beak resting on the surface and the head moving swiftly from side to side, the jaws meanwhile being opened and closed with exceeding rapidity, and seizing instantly upon such small crustacea and other organisms as come in their way.

Although all the Plovers might be described as long-legged birds, the STILTS are quite exceptionally so, and afford evidence of modification in another direction. Relatively to the size of the body, the stilts have the longest legs of all living birds. They seek their prey by wading in shallow water, like the Avocets, to which they are closely related. One species—the BLACK-WINGED STILT—occasionally appears in Britain.

Some other members of the Plover Tribe—the JACANA of Brazil, and the WATER-PHEASANT of India, Ceylon, and China, for example—have enormously long toes, as well as claws of great length.

These birds are furthermore remarkable for the possession of formidable weapons of offence, borne on the wrist-joint of the wing, in the shape of long, sharp, and powerful spurs. Similar weapons are carried by certain plovers—the EGYPTIAN SPUR-WINGED PLOVER, for instance.

CHAPTER V.

BUSTARDS AND CRANES.

THE Plover Tribe, Bustards, Cranes, and Rails form a large group of diverse but probably closely related forms.

Of the Bustards, the most interesting and important species is the GREAT BUSTARD. About a hundred years ago this magnificent bird might have been seen any day in such favoured localities as the Yorkshire and Lincolnshire wolds, the Norfolk and Suffolk "brecks," the heaths of Newmarket, or the downs of Berkshire and Wiltshire. It owes its extermination to several causes, foremost among which must be reckoned the reclaiming of waste land and improved methods of agriculture. "The bulk of its body," says Professor Newton, "renders it a conspicuous and stately object; and when on the wing, to which it readily takes, its flight is not inferior in majesty to that of the eagle." The expanse of the outstretched wings of a great bustard is 8 feet, or even more; and the weight of the male may even exceed 35 lbs. The female is smaller.

Photo by Ottomar Anschütz] [*Berlin.*

COMMON CRANE.

This handsome bird used to breed in Britain till the end of the sixteenth century.

Photo by Scholastic Photo. Co., Parson's Green.

MANCHURIAN CRANE.

The piebald plumage of this species is distinctive.

To see the great bustard in a wild state to-day, one would have to travel to Spain. And if one could make a pilgrimage for this purpose during the birds' courting-season, some very wonderful antics on the part of the male would be witnessed. These antics make up what is really a very elaborate love-display. In this performance the bird inflates his neck with wind, draws his head closely down on to the back, throws up his tail, so as to make the most of the pure white feathers underneath, and sticks up certain of the quill-feathers of the wing in a manner that only a great bustard can. Certain long feathers projecting from each side of the head now stand out like the quills of the porcupine, forming a sort of *cheval-de-frise* on either side of the head, and complete the picture, which, in our eyes, savours of the ludicrous. The inflation of the neck is brought about by filling a specially developed wind-bag between the gullet and the skin with air through a small hole under the tongue. For many years it was believed this bag was used as a sort of water-bottle, to enable the bird to live amid the arid wastes which were its chosen haunts. We now know what its real use is. Visitors to the Natural History Museum in London will find, beautifully mounted, a male bustard "in the act of showing off," as it is called, and hard by a dissection of the head and neck, showing this wonderful wind-bag.

Photo by Scholastic Photo. Co.] [Parson's Green.

COMMON CRANE.

The note of the crane is sonorous and trumpet-like

Photo by Scholastic Photo. Co., Parson's Green.

WATTLED CRANE.

So called from the pendent lappets of the throat. It is a South African species.

CRANES.

One of the most beautiful of this group of peculiarly handsome birds was once numbered among British birds; now, alas! like the bustard, it is one of the rarest visitors. Till the end of the sixteenth century the COMMON CRANE reared its young in the fen-lands. In Saxon times we read of a request being made by King Ethelbert to Boniface, Bishop of Mayence, begging him to send over two falcons suitable for flying at the cranes in Kent. In one case, at a feast given by Archbishop Neville in the reign of Edward IV., as many as

204 cranes figured in the menu. Later, it is interesting to note, they seem to have fallen somewhat into disfavour, since we read of a Dr. Muffet, of Wiltshire, somewhere about 1570, declaring cranes to be "distinctly unfit for sound men's tables. . . . Yet being young, killed with a goshawk, and hanged two or three days by the heels, eaten with hot gelentine, and drowned in sack, it is permitted unto indifferent stomachs."

The nest is placed on the ground, and contains from two to three eggs. The young are covered with down, and, like plovers and bustards, run as soon as hatched.

The cranes, like many other birds, notably some of the Plover Tribe, occasionally indulge in spirited outbursts of dancing. Mr. Nelson, writing of the birds of Alaska, tells how one day he was watching two cranes enjoying themselves in this manner. The male suddenly "wheeled his back towards the female and made a low bow, his head nearly touching the ground, and ending by a quick leap into the air. Another pirouette brought him facing his charmer, whom he greeted with a still deeper bow, his wings meanwhile hanging loosely by his side. She replied by an answering bow and hop, and then each tried to outdo the other in a series of spasmodic hops and starts, mixed with a set of comically grave and ceremonious bows."

Photo by Scholastic Photo. Co.] *[Parson's Green.*

SERIEMA.

A South American bird, at one time supposed to be related to the birds of prey.

Cranes vary much in general appearance. Some species have much of the skin round the head bare and brilliantly coloured, such as the Sarus Crane of India and the Crowned Crane.

The White and Whooping Cranes are birds of wondrous beauty. The first-named species has been not inaptly called the "lily of birds." The whole plumage, with the exception of the black quills, is white. The legs are red, as is also the face. Dr. Coues, an American ornithologist of great repute, relates how he once mistook one of these birds—the Whooping-crane—for an antelope. He and a companion saw what they "took to be an antelope standing quietly feeding, with his broad white stern toward us, and only about 500 yards off. We attempted for at least fifteen minutes to 'flag' the creature up to us, waving a handkerchief on a ramrod. . . . This proving unavailing, my friend proceeded to stalk the game, and crawled on his belly for about half the distance before

Photo by L. Medland, F.Z.S.] *[North Finchley.*

WHITE-BACKED TRUMPETERS.

The trumpeters are very aberrant members of the Crane Tribe.

Photo by W. F. Piggott] *[Leighton Buzzard.*

GREAT CRESTED GREBE.

Young grebes in down are beautifully striped.

the 'antelope' unfolded his broad black-tipped wings and flapped off, revealed at length as a whooping (white) crane."

Another very remarkable species is the CROWNED CRANE. This is an African species, and takes its name from the tuft of curiously modified feathers on the top of the head. The coloured plate gives a good idea of its general appearance.

THE SERIEMA.

This is a very hawklike-looking bird; indeed, by some ornithologists it has been regarded as closely allied to the Hawks and Eagles, and more especially to the Secretary-bird (page 467). Really, however, it is a very ancient kind of crane.

The TRUMPETERS, the COURLANS, the KAGU, and the SUN-BITTERN are other ornithological puzzles. Concerning the precise affinities of these birds much is yet to be learnt; they are, however, undoubtedly related to the Cranes. The last mentioned is a small bird, with wonderfully beautiful wings, which it displays with great effect to its mate during the courting-season.

CHAPTER VI.

GREBES AND DIVERS, PENGUINS, AND TUBE-NOSED BIRDS.

THE GREBES AND DIVERS.

THE Grebes and Divers are representatives of an exceedingly ancient type, and are in many ways besides very interesting. Both are common British birds. The greater part of their lives is spent upon the water, and to suit this aquatic existence their bodies are specially modified. One of the principal features of this modification is seen in the position of the legs. These, by a shortening of the thigh-bones in the grebes, leave the body so far back that when the bird walks the body is held vertically. With the divers walking has become an impossibility, and they can only move on land on their bellies, pushing themselves along with the feet. Both grebes and divers

Photo by W. F. Piggott] *[Leighton Buzzard.*

BLACK-THROATED DIVERS.

These very handsome birds breed in Scotland.

Photo by G. W. Wilson & Co., Ltd.] *[Aberdeen.*

ROCK-HOPPER PENGUIN.

The name Rock-hopper is given in allusion to the habit of hopping over boulders of rock.

are expert swimmers, and dive with the greatest ease, remaining long under water. The grebes haunt ponds, lakes, and broads; the divers prefer the open sea. Both feed on fish.

Grebes.

Of the numerous species of grebe, the most familiar are the Great Crested Grebe and the little Dabchick. The former has suffered grievous persecution for the sake of its beautiful breast-feathers, which Fashion decreed should be worn by the gentler sex in the form of muffs or hats. Thus a price was set upon the head of this beautiful and harmless bird, and its ranks were speedily thinned. Some species wear during the nesting-season beautiful chestnut or golden "ears," "horns," or "frills" on the head and neck. The Eared Grebe is especially magnificent at this time.

Divers.

These, as already remarked, are sea-loving birds, but they breed inland on the shores of lakes. There are not many species of divers, but, like the grebes, they assume a special dress during the nesting-season, more beautiful than the winter dress.

THE PENGUINS.

Photo by W. P. Dando, F.Z.S.] *[Regent's Park.*

BLACK-FOOTED PENGUIN.

This bird, also known as the Cape or Jackass-penguin, breeds in burrows or under ledges of rock.

The Penguins may justly be called wonderful birds, and they are undoubtedly of very ancient descent. For countless generations the sea has been their home and refuge, and, in consequence, flight has been abandoned, in exchange for increased swimming-powers, which have been gained by transforming the wing into a paddle. This transformation has resulted in flattening the wing-bones—and so increasing the surface of the hand and arm whilst reducing its thickness—and the suppression of the quill-feathers. The result is a blade-like paddle closely resembling the paddle of the whale, the turtle, or the extinct fish-lizards. With this organ they cleave their way through the water, often far below the surface, in pursuit of food, just as of old their ancestors did through the air. In other diving-birds the wings are kept closely pressed to the side of the body when under water, whilst the locomotion is effected by the feet. The penguin's legs, in consequence of diminished use, have shortened considerably. But besides the wings and legs, the feathery covering has also undergone a certain amount of change. This has been effected by increasing the size of the shaft of the feather and diminishing the vane; as a result, on the front part of the wings these feathers look more like scales than feathers.

Professor Moseley has vividly described the appearance of a flock of penguins at sea. He writes from Tristan d'Acunha: "As we approached the shore, I was astonished at seeing a shoal of what looked like extremely active, very small porpoises or dolphins. . . . They showed black above and white beneath, and came along in a shoal of fifty or more . . . towards the shore at a rapid pace, by a series of successive leaps out of the water and leaps into it again. . . . Splash, splash, went this marvellous shoal of animals, till they went splash through the surf on to the black, stony beach, and then struggled and jumped up amongst the boulders and revealed themselves as wet and dripping penguins."

Like their relatives in other parts of the world, penguins breed in huge communities known as "rookeries," a rookery being peopled by tens of thousands. Their nests, made of small stones, are placed among the tall grass and reached by beaten pathways, exceedingly difficult to walk through. Professor Moseley thus describes a "rookery": "At first you try to avoid the nests, but soon find that impossible; then, maddened almost by the pain [for they bite furiously at the legs], stench, and noise, you have recourse to brutality. Thump, thump, goes your stick, and at each blow down goes a bird. Thud, thud, you hear from the men behind you as they kick the birds right and left off the nests; and so you go for a bit—thump, smash, whack, thud, 'caa, caa, urr, urr,' and the path behind you is strewn with the dead and dying and bleeding. Of course, it is horribly cruel thus to kill whole families of innocent birds, but it is absolutely necessary. One must cross the rookeries in order to explore the island at all, and collect the plants, or survey the coasts from the heights."

Penguins feed principally on crustacea, molluscs ("shell-fish"), and small fish, varied with a little vegetable matter. Although the legs are very short, penguins yet walk with ease, and can, on occasion, run with considerable speed. It would appear, however, as if the largest of the tribe, the EMPEROR-PENGUIN, had become somewhat too bulky to run; for when speed is necessary it lies down upon the snow and propels itself with its feet, travelling, it is said, in this manner with incredible speed.

Penguins, though confined to the Southern Hemisphere, enjoy a wide range and every variety of climate. They are found on the Antarctic ice, on the shores of South Africa, South America, Australia, New Zealand, and inhabit many islands of the southern seas,

Photo by Percy Ashenden] [*Cape Town.*

BLACK-FOOTED PENGUINS BATHING.

The name Jackass is bestowed because the noise made by these birds closely resembles the bray of a donkey.

notably the Falklands, Kerguelen, and Tristan d'Acunha. In size penguins vary greatly. The largest is the EMPEROR-PENGUIN of the Antarctic seas; scarcely smaller is the KING-PENGUIN of Kerguelen Island. The emperor-penguin stands some 3½ feet high, and may weigh as much as 78 lbs. The GENTLE PENGUIN, or "Johnny" of the sailors, is next in size, being but little smaller than the king-penguin; this species inhabits Kerguelen Island and the Falklands. The CRESTED PENGUINS, or ROCK-HOPPERS, of which there are several species, are much smaller; they occur in the Falkland Islands, New Zealand, and the Antarctic. The South African form is known as the BLACK-FOOTED PENGUIN. Its nearest allies are HUMBOLDT'S PENGUIN of Western South America, and the JACKASS-PENGUIN of the Falklands. The smallest of all is the little BLUE PENGUIN of South Australia and New Zealand, standing only 17 inches high.

Photo by W. P. Dando, F.Z.S.] *[Regent's Park.*

KING-PENGUIN.

This is one of the largest of the Penguins.

THE TUBE-NOSED BIRDS.

UNTIL recently these birds were believed to be closely related to the Gulls, but it is now generally agreed that they are really distant relatives of the Divers and Penguins. The association with the Gulls was pardonable, for they certainly bear a superficial resemblance to them. The birds now under discussion may be readily distinguished from the Gulls by the fact that the nostrils open into a tube on the top of the beak, or a pair of tubes, one on either side—hence the name of the group. Like the Gulls, they are sea-birds and web-footed. Their young are downy and for a time helpless. One egg is laid, which is white, and in some cases spotted with red at the large end. As a rule no nest is made, but the egg laid on the bare ground, in a hole or burrow or in crevices of rocks. The Albatrosses build a nest of earth, tufts of grass, and moss, the whole structure raising the sitting-bird well above the ground. The Giant and Fulmar Petrels also build nests. The albatross is said by Professor Moseley to hold the egg in a pouch while sitting, as in the case of the king-penguin. The nature of this pouch has never been described.

Although occurring in the seas of all parts of the world, the Southern Hemisphere must be regarded as their headquarters, since here the greatest number of species are found. All are carnivorous, and—with the exception of one small group, the Diving-petrels of the Strait of Magellan—are birds of powerful flight. A large number of species belong to this group, but an enumeration of all would be wearisome. A few of the more striking have, therefore, been selected for description.

THE ALBATROSSES.

It was an albatross which brought such woe upon the ancient mariner whose pitiful story is so feelingly told by Coleridge. But the tables are occasionally turned, for men falling overboard in southern seas are liable to be attacked by these powerful giants. The albatross is mostly renowned for its majestic flight. Mr. Froude has given us a wonderful description of this flight, which is quoted with approval by Professor Newton. It runs as follows: "The albatross wheels in circles round and round, and for ever round the ship—now far behind, now sweeping past in a long, rapid curve, like a perfect skater on an untouched field of ice. There is no effort; watch as closely as you will, you rarely or never see a stroke of the mighty pinion. The flight is generally near the water, often close to it. You lose sight of the bird as he disappears in the hollow between the waves, and catch him again as he rises over the crest; but how he rises and whence comes the propelling force is to the eye inexplicable: he alters merely the angle at which the wings are inclined; usually they are parallel to the water and horizontal; but when he turns to ascend or makes a change in his direction, the wings then point at an angle, one to the sky, the other to the water."

Professor Hutton, speaking with similar enthusiasm of the wonderful flight, gives us, however, another side to the picture. "Suddenly," he says, "he sees something floating on the water, and prepares to alight; but how changed he now is from the noble bird but a moment before, all grace and symmetry! He raises his wings, his head goes back, and his back goes in; down drop two enormous webbed feet, straddled out to their full extent; and with a hoarse croak, between the cry of a raven and that of a sheep, he falls 'souse' into the water. Here he is at home again, breasting the waves like a cork. Presently he stretches out his neck, and with great exertion of his wings runs along the top of the water for seventy or eighty yards, until, at last, having got sufficient impetus, he tucks up his legs, and is once more fairly launched in the air."

For the wonderful photographs of the albatross at home we are indebted to the Hon. Walter

By permission of the Hon. Walter Rothschild] [*Tring.*

NESTING ALBATROSSES ON LAYSAN ISLAND.

This colony was of enormous size, and included thousands of birds.

Rothschild. They are from his book on the avifauna of Laysan Island, in the North Pacific. Unfortunately for the albatrosses and other birds, traders have been attracted to Laysan for the sake of the guano deposits. The birds were strictly protected during the occupation of Mr. Preece, but when he left they had no friend to shield them, and their eggs were taken in cart-loads, as the accompanying photograph shows.

When an albatross makes love, Professor Moseley tells us, he stands "by the female on the nest, raises his wings, spreads his tail and elevates it, throws up his head with the bill in the air, or stretches it straight out forwards as far as he can, and then utters a curious cry. . . . Whilst uttering the cry the bird sways his neck up and down. The female responds with a similar note, and they bring the tips of their bills lovingly together. This sort of thing goes on for half an hour or so at a time."

Photo by D. Le Souëf] [*Melbourne.*

WHITE-CAPPED ALBATROSS ON EGG.

Professor Moseley describes the egg of the albatross as being held in a sort of pouch.

There are several different kinds of albatross. The largest measures over 11 feet across the outstretched wings. They are inhabitants of the southern seas.

After the Albatrosses, the largest bird of the group is the GIANT PETREL. The sailors call it "Break-bones," "Nelly," or "Stinker." In habits it differs much from its aristocratic relative the albatross, haunting the coasts in search of dead seals and whales, and the bodies of other birds. Professor Moseley aptly likens it to the vulture: "It soars all day along the coast on the look-out for food. No sooner is an animal killed than numbers appear as if by magic, and the birds are evidently well acquainted with the usual proceedings of sealers, who kill the sea-elephant, take off the skin and blubber, and leave the carcase. The birds gorge themselves with food, just like the vultures, and are then unable to fly. I came across half a dozen at Christmas Harbour in this condition. We landed just opposite them; they began to run to get out of the way. The men chased them; they ran off, spreading their wings, but unable to rise. Some struggled

By permission of the Hon. Walter Rothschild] [*Tring.*

CARTING ALBATROSS EGGS ON THE ISLAND OF LAYSAN.

At one time these birds were protected; as this photograph testifies, this is no longer the case.

into the water and swam away, but two went running on, gradually disgorging their food, in the utmost hurry, until they were able to rise, when they made off to sea."

The FULMAR PETREL is a British bird. On St. Kilda, Professor Newton tells us, from 18,000 to 20,000 young are killed in one week in August, the only time when, by the custom of the community, they are allowed to be taken. These, after the oil is extracted, serve the islanders for winter food.

The STORM-PETREL is a small bird which breeds abundantly in St. Kilda and the Orkneys, and so fearless that it will allow itself to be taken from the nest by hand. Immediately this is done, the bird vomits a quantity of pure oil from its mouth. The wild-fowlers make use of this habit, capturing the bird, collecting the oil, and setting the prisoner free again. A story is related of a storm-petrel which was kept in a cage for three weeks. It was fed by smearing its breast with oil, which the bird swallowed by drawing the feathers separately through its beak. These birds are popularly supposed to be seen only before stormy weather, and therefore are not welcomed by sailors, who call them "Devil's Birds" and "Witches." This bird seems to commend itself to some palates; thus the late Mr. Seebohm says: "Cooked on toast, like snipe, we found them delicious eating, very rich, but not at all fishy."

We cannot refrain from a brief mention of the remarkable little DIVING-PETREL—remarkable because of its unlikeness to all the other Petrels and its strong resemblance to the Auks. But its tubular nostrils and certain anatomical characters proclaim its true affinities. "This is a petrel," says Professor Moseley, "that has given up the active aerial habits of its allies, and has taken to diving, and has become specially modified by natural selection to suit it for this changed habit, though still a petrel in essential structure." On two occasions Professor Moseley met with them in the Strait of Magellan, and describes the water as being covered with these birds in flocks extending over acres, which were made black with them.

CHAPTER VII.

STORKS, HERONS, AND PELICAN TRIBE.

THE Storks, Herons, and Pelican Tribe form a group of closely allied but externally very unlike birds, distantly related to the Petrels on the one hand, and the Cranes and Hawk Tribe on the other.

THE STORKS.

Photo by L. Medland, F.Z.S.] *[North Finchley.*

FULMAR PETREL.

Like the vulture, this bird will so gorge itself with food as to be unable, for a time, to fly.

There are few birds which have figured more prominently in the realms of fairy-tale and fable than the WHITE STORK. To-day it is almost universally held in affectionate regard, and in Holland, Denmark, and Germany is afforded the strictest protection, every effort being made, in localities where it is plentiful, to induce it to build its nest upon the house-roof. Sometimes, to effect this, its fondness for a stage of some sort being known, a cart-wheel is set up, and this generally proves successful, the grateful bird erecting thereon its nest. Once occupied, it may be held by several generations of tenants; and year by year additions are made to the nest, so that the original shallow structure at last attains a height of several feet. The material used in its construction consists of sticks and other substances. He considers himself a fortunate man indeed who can boast a stork's nest on his house.

To show how widespread is the regard in which this bird is held, we may mention that in Morocco, according to Colonel Irby, "almost every Moorish hovel has its stork's nest on the top, a pile of sticks lined with grass and palmetto-fibre," and he goes on to relate that in "Morocco and Fez, and some other large towns in the Moorish Empire, there is a regular storks' hospital, and that, should one be in any way injured or fall from the nest, it is sent to this institution, or rather enclosure, which is kept up by subscriptions from wealthy Moors, who regard the stork as a sacred bird."

Though the nest appears to be generally placed upon buildings, it is, when these fail, built in trees, and the selection of such sites must be regarded as representing the original practice of the species.

The stork is one of the very few birds which appear to be quite dumb. It supplies the want of a voice by a very remarkable clapping noise made by the long, horny beak. But even this noise is rarely made, and appears to be prompted by unusual excitement. "During the breeding-season," Mr. Howard Saunders tells us, "storks keep up a clappering with their bills, and this sound may frequently be heard proceeding from a number of birds circling in the air at such a height as to be almost invisible."

The affection displayed by storks for their young is proverbial. They feed them by thrusting their beaks down into the gaping little mouths, and injecting the half-digested remains of their last meal, which may represent reptile, frog, or fish, varied by a small mammal, young bird, worms, or insects.

The white stork is a really beautiful bird. Except the quill- and some of the smaller wing-feathers, which are black, the plumage is snow-white, whilst the bill and the legs are bright red. Like the swallow, it performs extensive migrations, travelling in flocks, numbering many thousands, at an immense height.

By permission of the Hon. Walter Rothschild, Tring.

WHALE-HEADED STORK.

A rare species, remarkable for the huge size of the beak.

Scarcely less beautiful is the BLACK STORK, and, like its white-plumaged ally, it is also an occasional visitant to Britain. It is a handsome bird, having the plumage of the upper-parts black, richly glossed with purple, copper, and green; the under-parts pure white; and the legs and beak red. But it is far less sociable, and consequently less known, than the white stork, shunning the haunts of men, and seeking seclusion for its nest in the lofty trees of large forests.

The largest members of the Stork Tribe are the ADJUTANT-STORKS and JABIRUS. The adjutants are also, to our eyes at least, singularly ugly birds. In spite of this very natural disadvantage, they have won a very high place in the regard of the people among whom they dwell, on account of the fact that, both in Africa and India, they perform, with the vultures, the work of scavengers. Yet there is something of quaintness about these birds, if they are watched from a distance too great to reveal the character which imparts the ugliness to which we have referred, and their actions not seldom border on the grotesque. The name Adjutant has been bestowed upon them on

Photo by Ottomar Anschütz] [*Berlin.*

WHITE STORKS.

The right-hand figure shows the bird making the curious clappering with its beak.

Photo by Ottomar Anschütz] [*Berlin.*

WHITE STORK.

A parent bird returning with a frog for its young.

account of the peculiar gait, which bears a fanciful resemblance to the measured pacing of an officer on parade. Like all the Storks, they have large bodies and very long legs, but they have outstripped all their relatives in the enormous size of the beak. The features which have earned this unenviable reputation for ugliness are the peculiarly unkempt and unwashed appearance of the head and neck. These are but scantily clothed in very shabby, brown-looking down-feathers; and the neck is made still more, we might almost say, repulsive by the presence of a large bare pouch, which can be distended with air to an enormous size at will. The Arabs, on account of this pouch, call the species resident with them "The Father of the Leather Bottle." Some, however, say that the correct translation of the native name would be "The Father of the Beak." But it is not only on account of their scavenging propensities that the adjutants are esteemed, for it is from the under tail-coverts of these birds that the much-prized "marabou" or "comercolly" feathers are obtained—at least the finest kinds; for some appear to be furnished by that chief of scavengers, the vulture. More precious still "is the celebrated stone called Zahir mora, or poison-killer, of great virtue and repute as an antidote to all kinds of poison," to be procured only by splitting open the head of the bird before death. Needless to say, the existence of this stone lives only in popular superstition, though how many poor birds have fallen victims thereto is not pleasant to contemplate.

Photo by W. P. Dando, F.Z.S., Regent's Park.

ADJUTANT-STORK.

The curious wind-bag is well shown.

Photo by W. P. Dando, F.Z.S., Regent's Park.

ADJUTANT-STORK.

This shows the bird in a rather unusual attitude.

Photo by Scholastic Photo. Co., Parson's Green.

JABIRU STORK.

This bird stands between 4 and 5 feet high.

Adjutants choose almost inaccessible pinnacles of rock on

which to build their nests, though they sometimes nest in trees. From two to four white eggs are laid, from which, if all goes well, as many young, covered with fluffly white down, are hatched.

The JABIRUS are distant relatives of, and scarcely inferior in size to, the Adjutants. There are three species, one occurring in the Indian Peninsula, New Guinea, and Australia, one in Africa, and one in South America. It is to this last species that the name Jabiru correctly applies. Furthermore, there can be no doubt that it is one of the handsomest of its tribe. The whole plumage is pure white, and the upper-parts are made additionally resplendent by an indescribable satin-like gloss. The beautiful whiteness of its plumage is enhanced by the fact that the head and neck, bill and feet, are jet-black. Some would give the palm of beauty to the AFRICAN SADDLE-BILLED STORK. Black and white, as in the American form, are the contrasting "colours"; but the plumage of the body, instead of being pure white, is plentifully enriched with black, with beautiful purple reflections.

Photo by D. Le Souëf] [*Melbourne.*

FLAMINGOES.

In flight the long neck and legs are fully extended, giving the bird a very remarkable appearance.

More or less nearly allied to the Storks are several species familiar enough to the professional ornithologist, but not very well known generally. One of the rarest and most interesting of these is the WHALE-HEADED or SHOE-BILLED STORK of the Nile, remarkable for its enormous boat-shaped bill. More common but equally interesting are the beautiful FLAMINGOES. Apart from the brilliancy of their colour, the most noticeable feature of these birds is the curious beak, which is bent downwards at a sharp angle, and provided on its inside with horny plates resembling those of the Ducks and Swans. The tongue of this bird, unlike that of the Stork Tribe generally, is thick and fleshy, and also resembles that of the duck.

The flamingo is the only member of the Stork Tribe which builds a mud-nest. Its foundation laid often in as much as 15 inches of water, and rising above the surface from 6 to 8 inches, with a diameter at the top of 15 inches, it forms a pile of no mean size. Strangely enough, though these birds are never so happy as when wading "knee" deep in water, yet after the construction of the nest the incubation of the eggs is delayed so long

Photo by Charles Knight] *[Aldershot.*

FLAMINGOES.

On account of the swan-like neck and "strainers" along the edges of the beak, these birds have been regarded as long-legged members of the Duck Tribe, but they seem more nearly related to the Storks.

that before they are hatched the water has disappeared, leaving a burning plain of sun-baked mud. On the top of this nest the parent sits with its long neck neatly curled away among the back-feathers, with its long legs doubled up, and projecting behind her for some distance beyond the tail. Until quite recently it was believed that the bird incubated its eggs by sitting *astride* the nest, the length of the legs forbidding any other position: this has now been proved beyond cavil to be an entirely erroneous opinion.

The eggs, two in number, are peculiar in that they are encased in a thick outer chalky coat, which on removal reveals a greenish-blue shell.

The characteristic crooked beak of the adult is not at all apparent in the young bird, and only appears as it approaches maturity.

The huge flocks in which these birds consort are graphically described by Mr. Abel Chapman as follows: "In herds of 300 to 400, several of which are often in sight at once, they stand feeding in the open water, all their heads under, greedily tearing up the grasses and water-plants from the bottom. On approaching them, which can only be done by extreme caution, their silence is first broken by the sentries, who commence walking away with low croaks; then hundreds of necks rise at once to full extent, every bird gaggling its loudest, as they walk obliquely away, looking back over their shoulders, as though to take stock of the extent of the danger. Pushing a few yards forward, up they all rise, and a more beautiful sight cannot be imagined than the simultaneous spreading of the crimson wings, flashing against the sky like a gleam of rosy light. In many respects these birds bear a strong resemblance to geese. Like them, flamingoes feed by day; and great quantities

Photo by W. P. Dando, F.Z.S.] *[Regent's Park.*

EUROPEAN FLAMINGOES.

These birds breed in the South of France and Spain.

of grass, etc., are always floating about the muddy water when a herd has been feeding. Their cry is almost indistinguishable from the gaggling of geese, and they fly in the same catenarian formations."

The SPOONBILLS and IBISES also belong to the Stork Tribe. The former are remarkable chiefly for the strange spoon-shaped bill: one species, a few hundred years ago, nested in England. This remarkable beak is associated with a peculiar method of feeding, well described by the late Mr. Wolley. During the operation, he says, "the beak was passed sideways through the water, and kept open till something palatable came within its grasp; but the action by which the bird effected this was most singular; for instead of turning only its head and neck, it turned its whole body from left to right and from right to left, like the balance-wheel of a watch; its neck stretched out and its beak immersed perpendicularly to about half its depth: this semicircular action was kept up with great vigour and at a tolerably quick march."

A graphic description by Mr. Alfred Crowley of a visit to the breeding-haunts of the

Photo by W. P. Dando, F.Z.S.] *[Regent's Park.*

SPOONBILL.

So called on account of its spoon-shaped bill.

Photo by W. P. Dando, F.Z.S.] *[Regent's Park.*

SACRED IBIS.

Sacred to the ancient Egyptians, it is known to the Abyssinians to-day as "Father John."

spoonbill, about fifteen miles from Amsterdam, in 1884, is well worth reproducing here: "Taking a small boat in tow, we were punted across the open water, over which were flying numbers of sand-martins, swifts, common and black terns, and black-headed gulls, the reeds being full of coots, moorhens, sedge- and reed-warblers, etc., and in the distance we saw, rising above the reeds occasionally, a small spoonbill or purple heron. On nearing a large mass of reeds, one of the boatmen struck the side of the punt with the pole, when up rose some fifty spoonbills and eight or ten purple herons; and as we came closer to the reeds there were soon hovering over our heads, within easy shot, some 200 of the former, and fifty or sixty of the latter. Strange to say, not a note or sound escaped from the spoonbills, and only a few croaks from the herons. On reaching the reeds, we moored our punt, and two of the men, wading in the mud, took us in the small boat about fifty yards through the reeds, where we found ourselves surrounded by spoonbills' nests. They were placed on the mud among the reeds, built about 1 foot or 18 inches high and 2 feet in diameter at the bottom, tapering to 1 foot at the top, where there was a slight depression, in which lay four eggs, or in most cases four young birds, many ready to leave the nest, and several ran off as we

Photo by J. T. Newman] [*Berkhamsted.*

YOUNG HERONS FOURTEEN DAYS OLD IN NEST.

Photographed in the top of a pine-tree 60 feet from the ground, in Lord Clarendon's Park.

approached. In the nests with young there was a great difference in age and size, one being about a day or so old, and the oldest nearly ready to leave the nest—some two or three weeks old—so that evidently the birds lay their four eggs at considerable intervals, and begin to sit on depositing the first. After wandering about, a matter of difficulty on account of the mud, we found a clutch of only three eggs, and one of four, which I managed to blow. We also obtained two clutches of eggs of the purple heron, but some of the latter had young."

The IBISES, though much alike in form, are strangely diverse in colour. One species was sacred to the ancient Egyptians. The reverence and affection they showed to this bird, above all others, is probably largely due to its migrating habits, which obtained in that far past just as they do to-day. The naturalist Brehm says on this subject: "When the Nile, after being at its lowest ebb, rose again, and the water assumed a red tinge, then the ibis appeared in the land of the Pharaohs as a sure guarantee that the stream—the giver and preserver of life, which the people in their profound reverence raised to the rank of a god—would once again empty the well-spring of plenty over the thirsty land. The servant and messenger of an all-bounteous Deity commanded of a necessity a reverence of a poetic and distinguished character, by reason of its importance: he too must be a god."

Another species, the GLOSSY IBIS, occurs sometimes in Britain. Perhaps the most beautiful of all is the SCARLET IBIS of America, numbers of which can be seen in the Zoological Gardens of London. On account of the curved, sickle-shaped bill the Ibises were at one time believed to be related to the Curlews: this, however, is now known to be quite incorrect.

It was at one time believed that "the ibis [was] adopted as a part of the arms of the town of Liverpool. This bird is termed a *Liver*, from which that flourishing town derived its name, and is now standing on the spot where the *Pool* was, on the verge of which the *Liver* was killed." The arms of the town of Liverpool, however, as Mr. Howard Saunders points out, are "comparatively modern, and seem to have no reference to the ibis. The bird which was adopted in the arms of the [extinct] Earls of Liverpool was described in a former edition of 'Burke's Peerage' as a cormorant, holding in the beak a branch of seaweed. In the Plantagenet seal of Liverpool, which is believed to be of the time of King John, the bird has the appearance of a dove, bearing in its bill a sprig of olive, apparently intended to refer to the advantages that commerce would derive from peace."

The glossy ibis has been found breeding in colonies of thousands in Slavonia. The nests are large structures formed of sticks and a few weeds, never far from the water, and many even, in the colony referred to, were so near the surface that they appeared to be floating. The eggs, three or four in number, are of a beautiful greenish blue. The young, while still unable to fly, climb actively among the branches of the trees in which the nest is placed, clinging so firmly with the feet as to be removed with difficulty.

By permission of Professor Bumpus] [*New York.*

GREAT BLUE HERON.

This bird ranges from the Arctic regions to the West Indies and South America

Photo by W. P. Dando, F.Z.S.] *[Regent's Park.*

COMMON NIGHT-HERON.

This bird occasionally visits the British Islands.

THE HERONS AND BITTERNS.

In the first mentioned of these two groups the COMMON HERON is the best known in the British Islands. Indeed, there must be few who have not encountered it in a wild state at some time or another. In suitable spots it may occasionally be met with standing mid-leg in water on the look-out for eels and other fish and frogs, a diet varied by an occasional young bird or small mammal. Sometimes this prey is hunted, so to speak, the bird walking along with a slow, measured step, striking with lightning rapidity and wonderful precision the moment its victim is sighted, whilst at others it stands motionless, as when fishing, striking the instant the unsuspecting eel or flounder comes within range.

From the earliest times until the reign of William IV. the heron was specially protected by law, being held in high regard both as an object of sport and a desirable addition to the dinner-table. So late as James I.'s time an Act was passed making it illegal to shoot with any gun within 600 paces of a heronry. The favourite way of taking the heron was by hawking, a sport which has furnished material in abundance both for poet and painter.

Herons breed in more or less extensive colonies, the nests—somewhat bulky structures, made of sticks and lined with twigs—being placed in the tops of high trees. From four to six is the normal number of eggs, and these are of a beautiful sea-green colour. The young are thinly clad in long, hairy-looking down, and for some considerable time are quite helpless.

Similar in appearance to the common heron is the American GREAT BLUE HERON, though it is by no means the largest of the herons, as its name might seem to imply. This distinction belongs to the GOLIATH HERON. A native of Africa, it is remarkable not only for its size, but for an extraordinary development of long, loose feathers hanging down from the lower part of the breast, and bearing a strange resemblance to an apron, concealing the upper part of the legs.

Passing over many species, we pause to descant on the EGRETS. These are numbered

Photo by Scholastic Photo. Co.] *[Parson's Green.*

YOUNG COMMON HERONS.

These birds have not yet acquired their full plumage.

amongst the most unfortunate of birds, and this because of the gracefulness and beauty of certain parts of the plumage worn during the breeding-season, which are coveted alike by Eastern magnates and Western women. The feathers in question are those known as "egrets," or, more commonly, "ospreys"; and their collection, as Professor Newton points out, causes some of "the most abominable cruelty practised in the animal world." The wearing of these feathers can no longer be excused; for Sir William Flower in England, and Professor W. E. D. Scott in America, have given the greatest publicity to the horrible barbarities and sickening scenes which are perpetrated by the men sent to gather in this harvest. The egrets, however, are not the only victims, as a glance at the milliners' windows will show, the distorted and mangled bodies of almost every known species of the smaller

Photo by Dr. R. W. Shufeldt] *[Washington.*

GREEN HERON.

This is a North American bird of skulking and nocturnal habits.

birds being therein displayed! Many of those who wear these "ornaments" offend unwittingly; it is certain that if they realised the suffering and waste of life that this method of decoration entails they would eschew any but ostrich feathers for ever.

The CATTLE-EGRET, better known as the BUFF-BACKED HERON, breeds in the southern portion of the Spanish Peninsula, where from March to autumn it is very common in the marshes of Andalusia, thousands congregating there, herding with the cattle, from the backs of which they may be often seen picking off the ticks; hence the Spaniards give them a name meaning "cattle-cleaners."

The NIGHT-HERONS are comparatively small birds, and derive their name from their habit of turning night into day, waking up only as the shades of evening fall to hunt for food; only during the breeding-season is this habit broken through, when they are obliged to hunt for food for their young during the daytime. They breed in colonies, in bushes or low trees in the neighbourhood of swamps. In some places they are protected—as, for instance, round the Great Honam Temple at Canton, where these birds are held sacred.

Colonel Swinhoe, says Mr. Howard Saunders, describes the nests "as placed thickly in some venerable banyans, the granite slabs that form the pavement beneath the trees being bedaubed with the droppings of old and young, while from the nests arose the chattering cry of the callow broods, for which the parent birds were catering the whole day long, becoming more active at sunset. As darkness set in, the noise and hubbub from the trees rose to a fearful pitch."

In Hungary large numbers of herons and egrets breed together in the marshes, egrets and night-herons breeding together with the common and purple herons. Landbeck, an enthusiastic ornithologist, writes of such heronries: "The clamour in these breeding-places is so tremendous and singular in its character as almost to defy description; it must be heard before a person can form any idea of what it is like. At a distance these hideous noises blend with a confused roar, so as in some way to resemble the hubbub caused by a party of drunken Hungarian peasants; and it is only on a nearer approach the separate notes of the two species, the common and the night-heron, can be distinguished—namely, 'craik' and 'quâck,' to which the notes of the young, 'zek-zek-zek,' . . . in different keys, serve as an accompaniment. When close to, the noise is tremendous and the stench unbearable. This, together with the sight of dozens of young herons in every stage of putrefaction and teeming with maggots, is perfectly sickening, though the contemplation of life and movement in this immense heronry is a matter of interest to the true ornithologist. . . . The tops of the highest trees are usually occupied by the nests of the common heron; a little lower down is the habitation of the shy and beautiful GREAT EGRET, while in the forks of the lowest branches the night-heron takes up her abode. All these species build in one and the same tree, the nests numbering not infrequently as many as fifteen in a single tree, and yet peace invariably reigns amongst all these varieties. High over the trees appears the common heron, laden with booty, announcing his arrival with a hoarse 'craaich,' when, changing his note to a goose-like 'da-da-da-da,' he either jerks the provender down the throats of the ever-hungry youngsters or throws it up before them, when the fish are greedily swallowed, amid a desperate accompaniment of 'gohé-é-é-é, gohé-é-é-é,' a sound much resembling the frantic cry of a calf which is being lifted into a farmer's market-cart. The conduct of the more cautious egret is very different. Circling far above the nest, she first satisfies herself that no foe is hidden below before she alights among her family, which are much quieter and less hasty than their cousins. The night-herons, on the contrary, approach their nests from all sides, high and low, their crops filled with frogs, fish, and insects. A deep 'quâk' or 'gowek' announces the arrival of the old bird already from some distance, to which the young answer, while feeding, with a note resembling 'queht, queht,' or 'quehaoâheh, quehoehah. As soon as the parents have taken their departure the youngsters recommence their concert, and from every nest uninterrupted cries of 'tzik, tzik, tzik, tzek-tzek, tzek,' and 'gétt, gétt-gett,' are

Photo by W. P. Dando, F.Z.S.] *[Regent's Park.*

BUFF-BACKED HERON.

This bird habitually picks insects from the backs of cattle.

the order of the day. This amusement is varied by the nestlings climbing out among the branches till they reach the top of the tree, whence they can have a good look-out, and can see the old birds returning home from a long distance, though they are in many cases often mistaken in their identity."

A common North American bird is the so-called GREEN HERON, known by many local aliases, such as "Fly-up-the-Creek," "Chalk-line," and "Chuckle-head." Seen at short range, its plumage is lustrous and beautiful, but this disappears as soon as the bird takes wing. The nest is of very loose construction; and a story is told of one which was such a shaky concern that every time the old birds jarred it a stick fell off, and the structure grew smaller and smaller, until the day when the young were ready to fly there were but three sticks left; finally these parted, and the little herons found themselves perching on the branch that once held the nest!

THE BITTERNS.

These are birds of a remarkable type of coloration, adapted to aid their skulking habits. The coloration partakes so completely of the nature of the undergrowth among which they dwell, that, aided by certain peculiar habits described below, they succeed in harmonising so perfectly with their surroundings as to render themselves invisible to their enemies.

The best-known species is the COMMON BITTERN, though this epithet is no longer applicable, for at the present time it is but an occasional visitant to Britain. Once it was plentiful enough, as the frequent references both in prose and poetry bear witness. These references have been inspired mainly by its very peculiar note, made apparently only during the breeding-season. This sound is variously described as "booming," "bellowing," and "bumping," and many are the theories which have been invented to account for its origin. Thomson, in "The Seasons," says that it is made whilst the beak is thrust into the mud:—

Photo by Scholastic Photo. Co.] *[Parson's Green.*

INDIAN CATTLE-EGRET.

This is a species of buff-backed heron, and earns its name from its habit of hovering round cattle for the sake of picking off the ticks by which they are infested.

> The bittern knows his time, with bill ingulf'd
> To shake the sounding marsh.

Chaucer, that it is caused whilst it is immersed under water; and Dryden represents it as made by thrusting the bill into a reed. Mr. J. E. Harting is one of the few who have actually watched the bird during the production of the sound, and from him we gather that it is made by expelling the air from the throat whilst the head is held vertically upwards.

The protective coloration and the peculiar habits associated therewith have only recently been recognised. These birds, when threatened, do not take flight, but immediately bring the body and the long neck and pointed head into one vertical line, and remain absolutely motionless so long as the cause of alarm persists. The peculiar coloration of the body harmonises so perfectly with the surrounding undergrowth, that, as just remarked, detection is well-nigh impossible. Although the pattern and tone of the coloration vary in the various species of bittern—which occur all over the world—this principle of protection obtains in all.

The drainage of the fens is answerable for the extinction of the bittern in England.

We would draw special attention to the great length of the feathers on the neck, which, when the bird is excited, are extended on either side to form an enormous feather shield. This is admirably shown in the photograph below, which represents a bittern preparing to strike. It is a curious fact that, when extended, the hind part of the neck is protected only by a thin coat of down. When the excitement has passed, the elongated feathers fall again, and, curling round the unprotected area, give the bird the appearance of having a perfectly normally clothed neck.

A wounded bittern will strike at either man or dog, and is extremely dangerous, owing to the sharpness of its dagger-like bill. If a dog advances on one not entirely disabled, the bird immediately turns itself upon its back, and fights with beak and claws, after the fashion of a wounded hawk or owl. Owing to the way in which the neck can be tucked up, by throwing it into a series of curves, and then suddenly extended, great danger attends the approach of the unwary.

The bittern is by no means particular in its choice of food, small mammals, birds, lizards, frogs, fishes, and beetles being alike palatable. The writer remembers taking from the gullet and stomach of one of these birds no less than four water-voles, three of which had apparently been killed only just before it was shot, for the process of digestion had hardly begun.

On migration these birds appear to travel in flocks of considerable size, since Captain Kelham reports having seen as many as fifty together high up in the air, when between Alexandria and Cairo. Curiously enough, they flew like "a gaggle" of geese—in the form of a V; but every now and then he noticed they, for some reason or other, got into great confusion.

At one time the flesh of the bittern was much esteemed as food for the table, being likened in taste and colour to the leveret, with some of the flavour of wild-fowl. Sir Thomas Browne, who flourished during the middle of the seventeenth century, says that young bitterns were considered better eating than young herons.

In the fourteenth century it bred in considerable numbers in the fens of Cambridgeshire, and was so highly esteemed as a bird for the table that the taking of its eggs was forbidden. At a court-baron of the Bishop of Ely, according to Mr. J. E. Harting, held at Littleport in the eleventh year of the reign of Edward II., several people were fined for taking the eggs of the bittern and carrying them out of the fen, to the great destruction of the birds. Decreasing steadily in numbers, the bittern continued to breed in Britain till the middle of the nineteenth century, one of the last nests being taken in Norfolk in 1868.

Photo by J. L. Bonhote, Esq.

COMMON BITTERN.

Preparing to attack (side view).

Photo by Henry King, Sydney.

AUSTRALIAN COCKATOO.

The sulphur-coloured crest of this bird is arranged in the form of a horse-shoe.

Photo by Ottomar Anschutz, Berlin.

MACAW.

Next to the brilliancy of its colouration, the most striking feature about this bird is its huge beak.

Photo by W. Saville-Kent, F.Z.S.

MALE RUFF IN FULL BREEDING PLUMAGE.

This wonderful plumage is worn only for a few weeks in the year.

Photo by Henry King, Sydney.

LAUGHING JACKASS.

This bird is a species of Kingfisher, and has acquired its name on account of its most extraordinary cry.

Photo by W. P. Dando, F.Z.S.] *[Regent's Park.*

EGYPTIAN PELICAN.

In the Pelicans the two sexes are coloured alike.

Photo by the Duchess of Bedford] [*Woburn Abbey.*

CRESTED PELICAN.

This bird derives its name from the curiously curled feathers on the top of the head and nape of the neck.

THE PELICAN TRIBE.

The members of the Pelican Tribe may be readily distinguished from other living birds by the fact that all their toes are united in a common fold of skin or web. In the Ducks and other web-footed birds only the front toes are so united.

The Pelican Tribe embraces several apparently dissimilar forms, whose only claim to be grouped together, judged from a superficial point of view, lies in the fact that they possess the peculiar type of foot above mentioned. With the general appearance of the Pelican itself probably every one is familiar, but we had better mention here that the other representatives of the group with which we have now to deal are the Cormorants and Gannets, common on the British coasts, and the less-known Darters, Frigate-birds, and Tropic-birds; these, as we know from their anatomy, are all closely allied forms, and with the Pelicans make up a somewhat isolated group whose nearest allies appear to be the members of the Stork Tribe.

The PELICAN figures largely in ecclesiastical heraldry as the type of maternal tenderness. Tradition has it that the bird, in admonishing its young, occasionally did so with such violence as to slay them. Remorse immediately following, the distracted parent drew blood from its own breast, and therewith sprinkled the victims of its wrath, which thereupon became restored to life again. The exhaustion following on this loss of blood was so great that the young had perforce to leave the nest to procure food for themselves and the sinking parent. If any, through lack of filial affection, refused to aid in this good work, the mother, on recovering strength, drove them from her presence, but the faithful children she permitted to follow her wherever she went.

One of the most remarkable features of the pelican is the pouch which hangs suspended from the under side of the beak. This is capable of great distension, and is used, when fishing, as a sort of bag-net, of which the upper jaw serves as the lid. The young are fed by the female, which, pressing her well-filled pouch against her breast, opens her mouth and allows them to take their fill therefrom.

Pelicans display great sagacity when fishing, a flock often combining to form a horse-shoe, and, driving the fish into a mass, take their fill. This method, of course, is only possible when fishing in the estuaries of rivers or lakes, where the fish can be "rounded up," so to speak. Clumsy as the pelican looks, it is yet capable of wonderful powers of flight; indeed, it shares the honour with the vultures, storks, and adjutants as an expert in the peculiar form of flight known as "soaring."

A North American species of pelican is remarkable in that during the breeding-season the beak is ornamented with a peculiar horny excrescence, which is shed as soon as that period is over.

Pelicans are natives of the tropical and temperate regions of the Old and New Worlds, and live in flocks often numbering many thousands. The nest is placed on the ground, and therein are deposited two white eggs. The young are helpless for some time after hatching.

In all some six-and-thirty species of CORMORANTS are known to science, of which two are commonly to be met with round the British coasts, one of which also travels inland to establish itself on such lakes and rivers as may afford it support.

Photo by D. Le Souef] [*Melbourne.*

YOUNG AUSTRALIAN PELICAN.

Pelicans, like gannets and cormorants, are hatched perfectly naked and quite blind.

In various parts of the world cormorants are taken when young and trained to catch fish: sometimes for sport, or—as in China—to furnish a livelihood for their owners. At one time the Master of the Cormorants was one of the officers in the Royal Household of England, the post having been created in 1611 by James I. The method of hunting is as follows:—After fastening a ring around the neck, the bird is cast off into the water, and, diving immediately, makes its way beneath the surface with incredible speed, and, seizing one fish after another, rises in a short space of time with its mouth full and throat distended by the fish, which it has been unable to swallow by reason of the restraining ring. With these captures it dutifully returns to its keeper, who deftly removes the fish, and either returns the bird to the water, or, giving it a share of the spoil, restores it to its perch.

Cormorants nest either in trees or on the ground; they lay from four to six eggs, and the young feed themselves by thrusting their heads far down the parents' throats and helping themselves to the half-digested fish which they find there.

The cormorant has a certain sinister appearance equalled by no other bird, so that its introduction in Milton's "Paradise Lost" (Book IV., 194) seems particularly appropriate. Satan, it will be remembered, is likened to a cormorant:—

Photo by W. Saville-Kent, F.Z.S.] [*Milford-on-Sea.*

YOUNG PELICANS.

Young pelicans never develop long down-feathers, like gannets and frigate-birds.

> So clomb this first grand Thief into God's
> fold
> . . . .
> Thence up he flew, and in the Tree of Life,
> The middle tree and highest there that grew,
> Sat like a cormorant.

The curious bottle-green plumage, green eyes, long hooked beak, and head surmounted by a crest of the smaller sea-loving representative of the two British species were doubtless familiar enough to Milton before blindness overtook him.

Some of our readers may have made the acquaintance of the cormorant's nearest ally, the DARTER, or SNAKE-NECK, in the Fish-house at the

Zoological Gardens of London. For the sake of those who have not, we may say that the darter may be described as a long-necked cormorant, with somewhat lighter plumage. The head is small and flat, and armed with a pointed, dagger-like bill, whose edges are finely toothed, with needle-like points projecting backwards. The neck is very long and slender; hence its name of Snake-neck. Furthermore, it is remarkable for a very strange "kink," formed by a peculiar arrangement of the neck-bones—an arrangement intimately associated with its peculiar method of capturing its prey, which, as with the cormorant, is pursued under water. How dexterously this is done may be seen any day in the Fish-house at the Zoological Gardens, where, as we have already mentioned, these birds are kept. At feeding-time they are turned loose into a large tank into which a number of small fish have been placed. The birds dive as soon as they reach the water, and with surprising speed chase their prey till within short range. Then, by a sudden bayonet-like lunge, made possible by the peculiar "kink" in the neck, a victim is transfixed, brought to the surface, released from the bill by a series of sudden jerks, tossed into the air, and dexterously caught and swallowed.

Photo by Scholastic Photo. Co.) *[Parson's Green.*

CORMORANT.

In the spring a slight crest is developed, and a white patch appears on the thigh.

The darter is found in Africa, India, the Malay region, Australia, and South America, frequenting the banks of rivers, lakes, and swamps, sometimes singly, sometimes in pairs or in immense flocks.

Very different from either of the foregoing species, both in build and coloration, is the GANNET. In its habits it is also different. The adult bird is about the size of a goose, white in colour, and armed with a powerful pointed bill. The young have a quite distinct plumage, being deep brown, speckled with white, this livery being worn for nearly three years.

The greater part of a gannet's lifetime seems to be spent upon the wing, a fact which implies a very different method of feeding from that followed by the cormorant and darter; and this is actually the case. Preying upon shoals of herring, mackerel, sprats, or pilchards, the birds, flying singly or in flocks, as soon as the fish are discovered, rise, soar in circles to such a height as experience shows best calculated to carry them by a downward motion to the required depth, and then, partially closing the wings, plunge upon their prey, and rarely without success, the time which elapses between the plunge and the immersion being about fifteen seconds. A flock of gannets feeding is a really wonderful sight, and can be witnessed in many places around the British coasts, for the gannet is one of the very common British birds. The pilchard-fishermen off the Cornish coast learn when the shoals are at hand, and the direction in which they are travelling, by the actions of these birds. A very cruel experiment is sometimes practised upon the gannet, based upon its well-known method of fishing. A herring is tied to a beam and set adrift, and the bird, not noticing the trap, plunges with its usual velocity upon the

By permission of the Hon. Walter Rothschild] *[Tring.*

FRIGATE-BIRDS AT HOME.

The feathers of frigate-birds are used for head-dresses in the Pacific Islands.

Photo by Scholastic Photo. Co.] *[Parson's Green.*

YOUNG GANNETS, FIRST YEAR.

The plumage at this stage is very dark brown, each feather being tipped with white.

fish, with the result that it is killed instantly by the shock of the contact.

Gannets breed in colonies of thousands on the islands off the east and west coasts of Scotland. They lay but a single egg, in a nest composed of seaweed deposited in inaccessible crags of precipitous cliffs. The young are at first naked; later they become clothed with long white down. "At one time," says Mr. Howard Saunders, "young gannets were much esteemed as food, from 1,500 to 2,000 being taken in a season during the month of August. They are hooked up, killed, and flung into the sea, where a boat is waiting to pick up the bodies. These are plucked, cleaned, and half roasted, after which they are sold at from eightpence to a shilling each. . . . The fat is boiled down into oil, and the feathers, after being well baked, are used for stuffing beds, about a hundred birds producing a stone of feathers."

Photo by Scholastic Photo. Co.] *[Parson's Green.*

GANNET, SECOND YEAR.

The white plumage of the neck is just beginning to appear.

Gannets present one or two structural peculiarities of sufficient interest to mention here. In most birds, it will be remembered, the nostrils open on each side of the beak; but in the gannet no trace of true nostrils remains; and the same may almost be said of the cormorant and darter. In gannets, however, a slight indication of their sometime existence remains, though the nostril itself no longer serves as an air-passage; and these birds are compelled to breathe through the mouth. Again, the tongue, like the nostrils, has also been reduced to a mere vestige. Stranger still is the fact that immediately under the skin there lies an extensive system of air-cells of large size, which can be inflated or emptied at will. Many of these cells dip down between the muscles of the body, so that the whole organism is pervaded with air-cells, all of which are in connection with the lungs.

Photo by Scholastic Photo. Co.] *[Parson's Green.*

GANNET, FULL PLUMAGE.

The fully adult plumage is not attained till the bird is three years old.

The FRIGATE- and TROPIC-BIRDS, which now remain to be described, are probably much less familiar to our readers than the foregoing species.

Photo by Valentine & Sons, Ltd.] *[Dundee.*

GANNETS ON THE BASS ROCK.

The Bass Rock is the only breeding-station of the gannet on the eastern coast of the British Islands.

FRIGATE-BIRDS are remarkable in more ways than one. To begin with, their general appearance may be described as that of a small, long-winged, fork-tailed albatross, mounted upon particularly diminutive legs, so short as to do little more than raise the body off the ground. Their flight is wonderfully graceful, and capable of being sustained for considerable periods; for, like the gannets, they pass most of their time on the wing. They feed upon surface-fish, which they capture from the surface of the water without alighting, or upon fish which they take from the gannets of the neighbourhood.

Frigate-birds build their nests in trees, on low bushes, or on the ground, and sometimes upon ledges of precipitous cliffs. The nest is a loose structure composed of sticks, and its construction is accompanied by much pilfering from one another. Only a single egg is laid.

About the beginning of January the male acquires a very remarkable pouch of brilliant scarlet skin, which hangs beneath the beak. Frigate-birds are found all over the world within the tropics.

The TROPIC-BIRDS, or BOATSWAIN-BIRDS, as they are sometimes called, are more like gulls or the heavier species of terns in general appearance, and in no way resemble superficially the forms with which they are associated, save in the fact that all the toes are enclosed in the same web. A study of their anatomy, however, leaves little doubt that these birds are really members of the Pelican Tribe.

Either pure white, relieved with black, or of a beautiful apricot-yellow, with similar black markings, with a powerful bill and long tapering tail, the tropic-bird is one of the most beautiful of sea-birds. There are altogether about six species of tropic-birds, distributed over the Pacific and Indian Oceans. They nest in hollows of cliffs or holes in trees, and lay a single egg, which bears some resemblance to that of a kestrel.

CHAPTER VIII.

SCREAMERS, DUCKS, GEESE, AND SWANS.

FAMILIAR as are most of our readers with all save the first mentioned of these birds, yet few probably suspect how great a wealth of forms this group displays. All are more or less aquatic in their habits, of heavy build, with long necks and small heads, short legs, and short wings and tails. The young are hatched covered with a peculiar kind of down, which more nearly resembles that of the Ostrich Tribe than the down of other birds, and they run about or accompany their parents to the water either immediately or a few hours after hatching. Several species have become domesticated, and in some cases have given rise to peculiar breeds, whilst many are much in demand for the purpose of enlivening ornamental waters.

Photo by W. P. Dando, F.Z.S.] *[Regent's Park.*

CRESTED SCREAMER, OR CHAKA.

The Crested and Horned Screamers are the only members of the family without webbed feet.

The least-known members of the group are the very remarkable and extremely interesting SCREAMERS of South America, of which there are three species. These are large birds, presenting some resemblances to the Game-birds on the one hand and the Geese on the

Photo by J. T. Newman, [*Berkhamsted.*

AYLESBURY DUCK.

This is one of the most esteemed of all domesticated breeds.

other. Not only the beak, but the skull, in certain characters, recalls that of the Game-birds. The body may be described as goose-like, but in the longer legs and enormous toes, which are not connected by a web, these birds recall the Megapodes, or Mound-builders (page 411).

The screamers are generally regarded as primitive members of the group with which they are now associated; but in many respects they are quite peculiar. Not the least interesting of their habits is the great predilection they observe for soaring in the air at immense altitudes, uttering the while the curious cry to which they owe their name. Several birds often do this at once. Yet stranger is the fact that they not seldom gather together in vast flocks to sing in concert. Mr. Hudson, for instance, states that the species known as the CRESTED SCREAMER on one occasion surprised him by "an awful and overpowering burst of 'melody,'" which saluted him from half a million of voices at an out-of-the-way spot in the pampas one evening at nine o'clock; and, again, once at noon he heard flock after flock take up their song round the entire circuit of a certain lake, each flock waiting its turn to sing, and only stopping when the duty had been performed.

Like the gannet, these birds are richly supplied with air-cells between the body and the skin, and between many of the muscles; so highly are these cells developed, that it is said a crackling sound is emitted when pressure is applied to the skin.

The wings of these birds are armed each with a pair of powerful and sharp spurs, recalling those of certain of the Plover Tribe (page 421), though in the latter only one spur is present on each wing.

The division of the remainder of this group into Ducks, Geese, and Swans is generally recognised, but no hard-and-fast line can yet be drawn between the several sections. We must regard them as representing adaptations to peculiar modes of life, which appear to be most marked in the duck-like forms. These may be divided into FRESH-WATER DUCKS, SALT-WATER DUCKS, SPINY-TAILED DUCKS, and MERGANSERS.

Of the FRESH-WATER DUCKS, the most familiar is the WILD-DUCK, or MALLARD. This is a resident British bird, and also the parent of the domesticated stock, which frequently closely resembles the wild form. In this species, as with the majority of the fresh-water ducks,

Photo by J. W. McLellan] [*Highbury.*

POCHARD.

This is one of the diving-ducks.

Photo by W. F. Piggott] [*Leighton Buzzard.*

EIDER-DUCK.

It is the down of this bird which is so much in demand for quilts.

the males wear a distinctive livery; but the males for a few weeks during the summer assume more or less completely the livery of the female, a process aptly described as going into "eclipse." The assumption of the female dress at this season is necessary, since it harmonises completely with the surrounding foliage, and so effectually conceals the bird at a time when it is peculiarly helpless; for, as with all birds, the quills or flight-feathers are cast off by the process known as moulting once a year, but instead of being replaced in pairs, and the flight remaining unaffected, they are shed all at once, so that escape from enemies must be sought by concealment.

Usually among birds the male has the more powerful voice, but with the mallard and its allies the reverse is the case, the female giving forth the loud familiar "quack, quack," whilst the note of the male sounds like a feeble attempt to answer its mate, but smothered by a cold in the head. This peculiar and characteristic subdued voice is associated with a remarkable bulb-shaped bony enlargement at the bottom of the windpipe, just where it branches off to the right and left lungs, the female being without this swelling.

The nest is composed of grass, and lined with down plucked by the female from her own breast, with the sole object, it is generally believed, of keeping the eggs warm; but it is possible that the down is removed as much for the sake of bringing the warm surface of the body in closer contact with the eggs. The site chosen for the nest is exceedingly varied; usually the nest is placed on the ground and near the water, but sometimes in a hedgerow or in a wood, and occasionally in trees, and instances are on record where the deserted nests of hawks and crows have been appropriated. At such times the young seem to be brought to the ground by the parent, which carries them down in her bill. It is some time before the wings of the young birds are big enough to carry them; indeed, they are quite full grown in so far as the body is concerned. At this stage they are known as "flappers." Advantage was at one time taken of their helplessness in the "sport" known as "flapper-shooting." On other occasions numbers of people assembled and "beat" a vast tract of country, driving these young flappers before them to a given spot where nets were placed, in which as many as 150 dozen have been taken at one time. Fortunately this practice has been abolished by Act of Parliament.

Several very distinct

Photo by W. F. Piggott] [*Leighton Buzzard.*

SHELDRAKE.

The female bird is just entering her nest at the bottom of a long burrow.

domesticated breeds of ducks have been derived from the mallard. The commonest breed differs but little, save in its great size, from the wild parent form, but the most esteemed are those known as the ROUEN and AYLESBURY. The PENGUIN-DUCK is the most aberrant and the ugliest of these breeds, having a peculiarly upright, awkward carriage, and very small wings.

The SALT-WATER DUCKS, or DIVING-DUCKS, are for the most part of a heavier build than the foregoing species, and many are of a sombre coloration. All the species are expert divers, and in consequence have the legs, which are short, placed far backwards, and this causes them to assume a more upright carriage when on land. The curious bony bulb at the base of the windpipe found in the fresh-water species becomes in the salt-water forms greatly enlarged, and its walls incompletely ossified, leaving large spaces to be filled by peculiarly delicate sheets of membrane. The majority of the species in this section frequent the open sea, but some occur inland.

One of the most useful, and at the same time most ornamental, of this section is the EIDER-DUCK, the male in full plumage being a truly magnificent bird: the female, as in the majority of ducks, is clad in sober colours. In Iceland and Norway the eider-duck is strictly protected, a fine being imposed for killing it during the breeding-season, or even for firing a gun near its haunts. This most unusual care is, however, by no means of a disinterested kind, but is extended solely that certain privileged persons may rob the birds of their eggs and the down on which they rest, the latter being the valuable eider-down so much in demand for bed-coverlets and other purposes. "The eggs and down," says Professor Newton, "are taken at intervals of a few days by the owners of the 'eider-fold,' and the birds are thus kept depositing both during the whole season. . . . Every duck is ultimately allowed to hatch an egg or two to keep up the stock." Mr. W. C. Sheppard gives an interesting account of a visit to an eider-colony on an island off the coast of Iceland. "On landing," he says, "the ducks and their nests were everywhere. Great brown ducks sat upon their nests in masses, and at every step started from under our feet. It was with difficulty we avoided treading on some of the nests. On the coast of the opposite shore was a wall built of large stones . . . about 3 feet high and of considerable thickness. At the bottom, on both sides of it, alternate stones had been left out, so as to form a series of square apartments for the ducks to nest in. Almost every apartment was occupied. . . . The house itself was a marvel. The earthen walls that surrounded it, and the window embrasures, were occupied by ducks. On the ground the house was fringed with ducks. On the turf slopes of its roof we could see ducks, and a duck sat on the door-scraper. The grassy banks had been cut into square patches, about 18 inches having been removed, and each hollow had been filled with ducks. A windmill was infested, and so were all the outhouses, mounds, rocks, and crevices. The ducks were everywhere. Many were so tame that we could stroke them on their nests, and the good lady told us that there was scarcely a duck on the island that would not allow her to take its eggs without flight or fear."

Photo by W. Reid] [*Wishaw, N.B.*

PARADISE-DUCKS.

This species is a native of New Zealand, where the photograph was taken. The bird on the right with the white head is the female.

The nest is composed externally of seaweed, and lined with down, which is plucked by the female from her breast as incubation proceeds, till eventually it completely conceals the eggs. Each nest yields about one-sixth of a pound, and is worth, on the spot, from twelve to fifteen shillings a pound.

The POCHARDS, SCAUPS, GOLDEN-EYES, and SCOTERS are relatives of the eider-duck; but since all resemble the latter in their general mode of life, we need not consider them here.

The MERGANSERS and SMEWS, to which reference has been made, differ markedly from all the ducks so far considered in the peculiar formation of the bill, which is relatively long and narrow, with its edges armed with sharp, tooth-like processes projecting backwards towards the back of the mouth. These processes are really only horny spines, and have no relation to

Photo by the Duchess of Bedford] [*Woburn Abbey.*

CAPE BARREN GOOSE.

This bird is a native of South-east Australia and Tasmania, and remarkable for its short beak.

teeth, although they are used, as teeth would be, for holding slippery prey, such as fish, which form the greater part of the diet of these birds.

So far, in all the ducks which we have considered, the male differs conspicuously from the female in plumage; but in the forms we are now about to describe both sexes are coloured alike.

The first is the COMMON SHELDRAKE, which seems to lie somewhere on the borderland between the Ducks and the Geese. It is a very beautiful bird, conspicuously marked with broad bands of orange-chestnut, white, and black. The beak being coral-red in colour, and further ornamented by a peculiar fleshy knob at its base, serves to set off the glossy bottle-green colour of the head and neck. As appears to be invariably the case where both sexes are coloured alike, the female builds her nest in a hole, generally a rabbit-burrow, whilst the young have a distinct livery, duller in tone than that of the parent. The female sheldrake breeds in Britain, and may be frequently seen at sea flying in small parties, which have been likened to a flock of butterflies.

Photo by W. Saville-Kent, F.Z.S.] *[Milford-on-Sea.*

AUSTRALIAN PYGMY GOOSE.

The pygmy geese are expert divers.

The GEESE include birds of somewhat conspicuous coloration, besides a considerable number of more subdued aspect. The sexes are distinguished by different names, the female being known as the Goose, the male as the Gander, whilst the young is the Gosling. As we have already mentioned, there is no hard-and-fast line to be drawn between the three sections of this group. The Ducks are connected by the Sheldrakes with the Geese, through the Spur-winged Goose, the Egyptian and Orinoco Geese, and certain other species which cannot be alluded to on this occasion.

The SPUR-WINGED GEESE, of which there are two species, are African birds, and derive their name from the long spur seated on the wing.

A still more remarkable form is the HALF-WEBBED GOOSE, so called from the fact that its feet are only partially webbed. It has a black-and-white plumage, a hooked beak, and a large warty prominence on the front of the head. It spends most of its time perched on the branches of the Australian tea-trees, and rarely enters the water. The windpipe is peculiar, being coiled in several folds between the skin and the breast-muscles.

From these peculiar forms we pass to the true geese. The largest living species is the CHINESE or GUINEA-GOOSE of Eastern Siberia, regarded as the stock from which the domesticated geese of Eastern countries have been derived.

European domesticated geese have been derived from the GREY or GREY-LAG GOOSE, a species at one time exceedingly common in England, breeding in considerable numbers in the fen districts, where the young were frequently taken and reared with the large flock of domesticated geese commonly kept at that time for the sake of their feathers. The grey-lag goose, however, has long ceased to breed in England, though a few still nest in Scotland. The most important breeds derived from the grey-lag are the TOULOUSE and EMDEN. Other British species are the BEAN-GOOSE, PINK-FOOTED and WHITE-FRONTED GEESE, and the "BLACK" BRENT and BARNACLE-GEESE, in all of which the sexes are precisely similar in coloration and subdued in tone.

In the New World some very beautiful white geese are found, which are still more interesting in that the females have a different coloration. These are the KELP- and UPLAND-GEESE of Patagonia and the Falklands. The female of the kelp-goose is brownish black above and black barred with white below, whilst the female of the upland-goose is rufous and black in colour. The latter may be seen in London parks.

Lastly, we have a few species known from their small size as PYGMY GEESE of Australia, India, and Africa. Perhaps the best known is the Indian species, called the COTTON-TEAL.

Photo by W. P. Dando, F.Z.S.] *[Regent's Park.*

BLACK-NECKED SWAN.

The fleshy knob at the base of the bill is of a bright red colour.

Photo by the Duchess of Bedford] [*Woburn Abbey.*

TRUMPETER- AND WHOOPER-SWANS.

The trumpeter is the bird in the foreground: the whooper is remarkable for its musical note, resembling the word "whoop" quickly repeated.

They are tiny birds, resembling small ducks rather than geese, and dive admirably, a feat which the larger species do not perform.

The SWANS are linked with the Geese through a very beautiful South American species, known as the COSCOROBA SWAN. It is the smallest of all the swans, pure white in colour, save the tips of the greater wing-quills, which are black, and the coral-red bill and feet.

Of all the swans, probably the best known is the MUTE SWAN, the semi-domesticated descendants of which are so common on ornamental waters. For hundreds of years the latter were jealously guarded, none but the larger freeholders being allowed to keep them, and then not without a licence from the Crown; with this licence was coupled an obligation to mark each swan with a particular mark, cut with a knife or other instrument through the skin of the beak, whereby ownership might be established.

It would seem that these swans and their descendants were not derived from the native wild stock, but were introduced into England, it is said, from Cyprus by Richard I. At the present day large "swanneries" have almost ceased to exist. Perhaps the largest is that of the Earl of Ilchester, at Abbotsbury, near Weymouth. In 1878 between 1,300 and 1,400 swans were to be seen there at one time, but latterly the number has been reduced to about half.

Although swans do not perhaps stand so high in the general esteem as table delicacies as with our forefathers, there are yet many who appreciate the flesh of this bird; but the St. Helen's Swan-pit at Norwich is the only place in England where they are systematically fattened for the table. Here from 70 to 200 cygnets—as the young swans are called—caught in the neighbouring rivers, are placed early in August, and fed upon cut grass and barley till Christmas, when they are fit for table, weighing, when "dressed," about 15 lbs., and fetching, if purchased alive at the pit, about two guineas each. The pit is constructed of brickwork, and is about 74 feet long, 32 feet wide, and 6 feet deep—the water, admitted from the river, being about 2 feet deep. The food is placed in floating troughs. The birds, "when so disposed," says Mr. Southwell, "leave the water by walking up a sloping stage, and thus obtain access to a railed-in enclosure, where they may rest and preen themselves."

The beautiful swan-like carriage, so familiar in the floating bird, seems to belong only to the mute swan, the other species of white swans carrying the neck more or less straight, and keeping the wings closely folded to the body.

No greater anomally could at one time have been imagined than a BLACK SWAN. For centuries it was considered to be an impossibility. We owe the discovery of such a bird to the Dutch navigator Willem de Vlaming, who, more than 200 years ago, captured the first specimen at the mouth of what is now known, in consequence, as the Swan River. A year after their capture accounts reached England through the burgomaster of Amsterdam, and these were published by the Royal Society in 1698. The bird is now fairly common on ornamental waters, where its sooty-black plumage, set off by pure white quill-feathers and coral-red bill, contrasts strongly with the typical snow-white mute swan, generally kept with it.

Equally interesting is the handsome BLACK-NECKED SWAN of South America. In this species the plumage is pure white, save that of the neck, which is black. The distribution of this species is practically the same as that of the Coscoroba swan. Breeding freely in confinement, it has become a fairly common bird on ornamental waters. It shares with the mute swan the reputation of gracefulness when afloat, swimming with the neck curved and wings raised.

Photo by W. Reid] *[Wishaw, N.B.*

AUSTRALIAN BLACK SWANS AND CYGNETS.

The cygnets are light-coloured, like those of the white swans

CHAPTER IX.

BIRDS OF PREY AND OWLS.

BIRDS OF PREY.

AT one time the boundaries of this group were much larger than now, for within them were included at least one form which has since proved to belong to the Crane Tribe: we allude to the Seriema (page 428), and also to the Owls. This classification was based on the very remarkable superficial resemblance to the typical birds of prey which those forms bear. Modern ornithologists regard as birds of prey only the forms known as the New World Vultures, the Secretary-bird, and the Falcons, Eagles, Vultures, Buzzards, and the numerous smaller forms commonly classed as "Hawks."

Photo by Scholastic Photo. Co.] *[Parson's Green.*

CONDOR.

The habit of standing with the wings expanded is a very common one with these birds.

THE NEW WORLD VULTURES.

These may be distinguished from their distant relatives of the Old World by the fact that the nostrils are not divided from one another by a partition, and by their much weaker feet. The head and neck in all, as in the true vultures, is more or less bare, and, furthermore, is often very brilliantly coloured, in which last particular these birds differ from the typical vultures.

One of the most important members of the group is the CONDOR, one of the largest of flying birds, and when on the wing the most majestic. "When the condors," says Darwin, "are wheeling in a flock round and round any spot, their flight is beautiful. Except when rising off the ground, I do not recollect ever having seen one of these birds flap its wings. Near Lima I watched several for nearly half an hour, without once taking

Photo by W. P. Dando, F.Z.S.] *[Regent's Park.*

CONDOR.

The bare skin of the head and neck is of a dark purple colour, the ruff encircling the neck being of pure white down-feathers.

off my eyes; they moved in large curves, sweeping in circles, descending and ascending, without giving a single flap." One which he shot measured, from tip to tip of the fully expanded wings, 8½ feet.

The condor, like its smaller relatives, hunts by sight, and not, as was at one time believed, by smell, feeding on the dead bodies of guanacos which have died a natural death or been killed by pumas, and upon other dead animals. In the neighbourhood where sheep and goats are kept, they are much dreaded, as they will attack the young kids and lambs. The flock-owners on this account wage constant war against them, capturing them by enclosing a carcase within a narrow space, and when the condors are gorged galloping up on horseback and killing them, for when this bird has not space to run it cannot rise from the ground. Sometimes the trees on which they roost are marked, and when night falls a man climbs the tree and captures them with a noose, for they are very heavy sleepers.

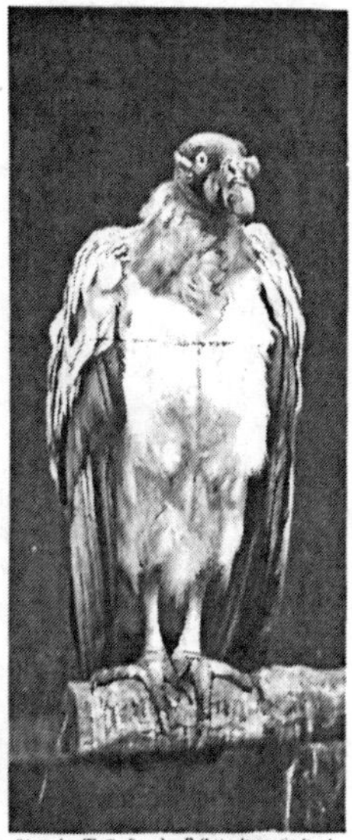

Photo by W. P. Dando, F.Z.S., Regent's Park.

KING-VULTURE.

The fleshy crest on the beak is developed in the females as well as in the males.

The condor ranges from the Andes of Ecuador, Peru, and Chili southwards to the Rio Negro on the east coast of Patagonia. It lays two large white eggs on a shelf of bare rock projecting from precipitous cliffs, and the young are said to be unable to fly till after they are a year old. As will be seen in the photographs, the head of the male is crowned by a bare, fleshy caruncle, which, like the surrounding bare skin, is of a dull reddish colour: lower down the neck is a frill of pure white down, which forms a conspicuous contrast with the glossy black plumage of the rest of the body and wings.

The KING-VULTURE is a much smaller bird, but the bare parts of the head are much more brilliantly, even gaudily coloured, the combinations being orange, purple, and crimson. The plumage is creamy white and black. It is a comparatively rare bird, and but little is known concerning its breeding habits. The female is much more soberly clad than her mate. The king-vulture has a more northerly range than the condor, extending from Brazil to Mexico, Texas, and Florida.

Photo by W. P. Dando, F.Z.S.] [*Regent's Park.*

BLACK VULTURES.

When disturbed, these birds eject foul-smelling matter.

The commonest of the New World vultures is the TURKEY-BUZZARD, which is found over the whole of temperate and tropical America. Of the four species commonly known as Turkey-buzzards, three are exclusively South American—the fourth

Photo by Robert D. Carson, Esq.] *[Philadelphia.*

CALIFORNIAN VULTURE.

The bare parts of the head are of a brick-red colour.

ranges as far north as New York and British Columbia, and in the Southern and Middle United States is very common, perambulating the streets or perching on the house-tops.

Other species are the small BLACK VULTURE, a dull, uninteresting-looking bird, and the CALIFORNIAN VULTURE. This latter is a large species, and in the expanse of wing may even exceed the condor. At one time its extermination seemed certain, owing to its falling a victim to the poisoned meat laid out by the stock-keepers for carnivorous mammals, but in the more barren and inaccessible regions it appears to be on the increase.

THE SECRETARY-BIRD.

The second of the three main divisions into which the Birds of Prey are divided is reserved for the SECRETARY-BIRD. This bird derives its name from the crest of long feathers which bear a fanciful resemblance to the quill-pens a clerk is supposed to stick above his ear. It differs from all the other members of the Hawk Tribe in the exceedingly long legs, which in the young are said to be so fragile as to fracture if the bird is suddenly alarmed. It feeds chiefly on insects and reptiles, especially snakes, for which last it seems to have a special liking. It attacks even the most venomous species, striking at them with its powerful wings and pounding them with its feet, jumping upon them with great force, till rendered helpless, when they are at once swallowed head-foremost. On account of its great value as a snake-eater it has been accorded special protection, though unfortunately there is a tendency on the part of English settlers to relax this, on account of the fact that it will occasionally eat animals coming within the scope of "game." Valuable as the latter may be, there yet seems no justification for such a course.

The secretary-bird, which is a South African species, though extending northwards as far as Abyssinia, builds a huge nest of sticks in low bushes, under which will often be found numerous nests of the Cape sparrow, apparently the only available site on the veldt, where bushes are scarce. Here the sparrows are efficiently protected from the icy winds which so frequently sweep across this region, and apparently suffer no fear of personal violence from the fierce owners of the domicile above them. When sitting, the female secretary is fed by her mate. The young do not appear to leave the nest for five or six months. They are frequently taken from the nest and brought up as household pets, becoming not only very tame, but exceedingly useful.

THE EAGLE AND FALCON TRIBE.

From the perplexing wealth of species displayed among the forms herein bracketed together, we can only select a few examples, which embrace, however, all the more important and interesting forms.

Beginning with the more lowly, we start with those members of small or medium size known as KITES, and as an example of the group take the species known in the British Islands as the KITE or GLEAD. In former days this bird was extremely common in England, being found in numbers not only in the rural districts, but in London itself, where, as old records of the fifteenth century show, it occurred in such numbers near London Bridge as to excite the wonder of foreigners visiting the city. These birds found an abundance of food in the garbage of the streets, and also of the Thames itself—"an observation," remarks Mr. Finn, "which throws a lurid light upon the city sanitation."

In the days of falconry the kite was royal game, not, however, by legal enactment, but by reason of the fact that none but specially trained falcons could secure a prey with such wonderful powers of flight. Consequently the price of a falcon which had attained this degree of skill was beyond the purse of any but a king.

Save on the wing, the kite is not a handsome bird, its general colour being of a pale reddish brown; but those who have had the good fortune to watch its flight are one and all impressed. Cowper admirably expresses the general admiration in the lines:—

> Kites that swim sublime
> In still repeated circles, screaming loud.

The kites may be distinguished from other members of the tribe by their forked tails. Somewhat of a scavenger, as we have already hinted, the kite feeds also upon such small game as moles, frogs, young birds, rabbits, snakes, and fish. Its partiality for young birds caused it to be much dreaded in the farmyard in the days when it was common; and when, with the introduction of modern and improved firearms, game-preserving became more strenuously prosecuted, its doom was sealed, for a ceaseless war was waged against it, which ended only with its extermination.

Nearly allied to the Kites, the HONEY-BUZZARDS next claim attention. The name Honey-buzzard is a misnomer, for honey forms no part of the bird's food. This species exhibits, however, a quite remarkable partiality for the immature stages of wasps and bees, the nests of which it tears in pieces with its feet, so as to lay bare the coveted morsels, devouring them on the spot, perfectly regardless of the stings of the infuriated insects, which seem unable to penetrate its feathers. When its favourite food is not to be had, it will feed upon corn, earth-worms, beetles, slugs, small birds' eggs, and moles—a diet sufficiently

Photo by Scholastic Photo. Co.] *[Parson's Green.*

SECRETARY-BIRD.

In full plumage the tail of this bird is much longer.

strange for a bird of prey. Honey-buzzards appear to be exemplary parents, for they are said to construct a bower of leafy boughs above the nest to screen the young from the sun, the boughs being replaced as they wither by fresh ones.

The honey-buzzard occurs but rarely in England, and nowhere appears to be a very common bird, though it is said to be more frequently met with in Arabia and Egypt than elsewhere. On migration, however, it appears in unusually large numbers, the late Lord Lilford recording an occasion when he observed many hundreds crossing the Straits of Gibraltar from Spain to Africa. These were apparently on their autumnal migration to warmer winter quarters.

The dash, energy, and courage which we are wont to associate with the Hawk Tribe have certainly not been manifest in the members of the order which we have examined so far; but these attributes will be evident enough in the majority of the species with which we are now about to deal. One of the most interesting of these fiercer forms is the OSPREY, or FISHING-HAWK. As its name implies, it feeds largely upon fish, which it captures with great dexterity, seizing them either with its feet from the surface of the water, or by plunging entirely beneath the surface, when it disappears amid a shower of spray, to emerge a moment later with a fish writhing in its talons. To ensure a firm grip of its slippery prey, the soles of its feet are armed with rough tubercles, whilst the foot is furthermore remarkable in that the outer toe can be turned backwards, so as to lie parallel with the hind toe—an arrangement rare in birds of the Hawk Tribe, but characteristic of the Owls and some other birds. At times, it would seem, the osprey seizes a fish too large to be raised from the water, when, owing to the firm hold which the claws have taken, the bird is unable to release itself, and is speedily dragged beneath the surface and drowned. Some have suggested that the bird falls a victim, not to inability to free itself, but rather to its obstinacy.

Photo by W. P. Dando, F.Z.S., Regent's Park.

EGYPTIAN KITE.

Feeding on garbage of all kinds, kites are useful birds in hot countries.

The osprey is now rare in Great Britain, though it breeds occasionally in the wilder parts of Scotland. It enjoys an extensive range, however, being found all over the world. In America it appears to be very common. On an island "off the eastern extremity of Long Island, New York," writes Professor Newton, "300 nests were counted. The old birds were rearing their young close together, living as peaceably as so many rooks, and were equally harmless to other birds." Colonies of this kind are rare among birds of prey.

Whilst the fiercer raptorial birds, which hunt and kill their prey, live only upon small or medium-sized animals, a certain section, known as the VULTURES, feed upon the carcases of the largest mammals which they find either in the throes of death or already dead, and even far advanced in decomposition. Gathering to the feast in large crowds, even the largest bodies are soon demolished; and on this account the vultures are to be reckoned amongst the most useful of birds, speedily removing matter which in hot countries would rapidly endanger the health of neighbouring communities.

Many years ago a great controversy was waged over the question of the faculty which guides the vulture in the discovery of its food, since it was a matter of common knowledge that the traveller might sweep the

Photo by W. Saville-Kent, F.Z.S.] [*Milford-on-Sea.*

AUSTRALIAN OSPREY.

This species of osprey is confined to Australia and the Austro-Malay Islands.

horizon in vain for a sign of these birds, yet, should a camel from a caravan fall out and die, or men fall in warfare, within an incredibly short space of time a crowd of vultures would be squabbling over the dead. Some held that the vulture was guided by scent, others by sight, and this latter view is now almost universally accepted. The bird's natural habit of soaring at an immense height enables it to survey not only immense tracts of country, but the actions of its neighbours soaring at the same altitude, though perhaps miles away. So soon as one descries food it betrays the fact by its actions, making off in the direction of the prospective feast; it is then followed immediately by its yet more distant neighbour, and this by a third, and so the first serves as a guide to all the other soaring birds for miles around. This flight has been admirably expressed by Longfellow in "Hiawatha."

We need here mention only one or two of the more important species of vulture, and among these one of the most interesting is the LAMMERGEIR, or BEARDED VULTURE. This species is one of the least vulture-like of the tribe, not only in general appearance, but also in habits, and is to be regarded as near the ancestral stock, whose descendants have become more and more addicted to feeding upon dead bodies.

Photo by Charles Knight] [*Aldershot.*

BEARDED VULTURE.

It is called the Bearded Vulture on account of the tuft of bristles hanging from the chin.

The lammergeir, or bearded vulture, is a bird of large size and majestic flight, differing from all other vultures in that the head and neck are clothed in feathers, whilst the nostrils are covered by long bristles. Beneath the bill hangs a tuft of bristles like those covering the nostrils; hence its name of Bearded Vulture; and this, coupled with a remarkable red rim to the eyes, gives the bird an almost diabolical appearance. It lives partly upon living animals and partly upon carrion, bones apparently being especially relished; these it breaks by dropping them from a height upon the rocks below, probably to get at the marrow. Land-tortoises are treated in a similar manner, and it was possibly this species which caused the death of the poet Æschylus, on whose bare head a tortoise is alleged to have been dropped. It was at one time common in Europe, and is still fairly numerous in West Africa, though rare in the East and South. Many stories are told of its strength and daring, some of which concern the carrying off of young children; but these are probably mythical, modern observers generally agreeing that the bird is by nature far from courageous.

The more typical vultures differ from the lammergeir in having the head and neck more or less bare, and often conspicuously coloured, or covered with a short velvety down. The CINEREOUS, GRIFFON, PONDICHERRY, and EGYPTIAN VULTURES may be cited as examples of these.

The CINEREOUS or BLACK VULTURE is a heavy and repulsive-looking bird, feeding entirely on garbage. On the wing, however, this vulture shares with its relatives the admiration of all who have been privileged to watch it; sailing in graceful circles in the blue sky of the tropics, or hurrying from all quarters of the compass to some ghoulish feast, it forms a spectacle, once seen, never to be forgotten. It is found on both sides of the Mediterranean, and extends eastwards to India and China.

This species, like the GRIFFON-VULTURE, has the head and neck down-covered, thus standing in strong contrast with the PONDICHERRY and SACRED VULTURES of India and Africa, which have bare heads and necks ornamented by loose folds or lappets of skin of a pinkish colour. These vultures hunt in pairs, and are very self-assertive, driving away all other birds from their prey. They build enormous nests of sticks in bushes and trees, thus differing from the vultures previously described, which generally nest on ledges of rock on precipitous cliffs. These nests are made of sticks, lined with straw and leaves. A single egg is laid, which is white with red markings. The largest species rivals the condor in size.

The EGYPTIAN VULTURE, sometimes known as PHARAOH'S HEN, is the smallest of the vultures. The plumage is white; the head, throat, and fore part of the neck are naked and of a lemon-yellow colour; whilst the feet are pink and the eyes crimson. Not only is it a carrion-feeder, but it will also follow the plough, picking up worms and grubs. This species occurs in Europe, breeding in Provence and Savoy, the Madeiras, Cape Verde, the Canaries, North and South Africa, and India. On three occasions it has wandered to Great Britain.

We pass now to the EAGLES, a group the exact limits of which it is impossible to define, since the forms so designated merge insensibly into Buzzards, Hawks, Harriers, and so forth.

Eagles occur all over the world, save only in New Zealand. An eagle, it is interesting to note, is the bird of Jove, the emblem of St. John and Rome, and at the present day of the American Republic. It also plays an emblematic part in Germany, Austria, and Russia.

Of the true eagles, perhaps the best known is the GOLDEN EAGLE, or MOUNTAIN-EAGLE—a British bird, breeding still, though in diminishing numbers, in Scotland. In Ireland it is fast verging on extinction, trap, gun, and poison having wrought its destruction. In times past it bred in the Lake District of England. Abroad it is found over the greater part of Europe, Northern Asia, India and China, and Northern Africa, and America as far south as Mexico. It is a very fierce and powerful bird, attacking such

Photo by Scholastic Photo. Co.] *[Parson's Green.*

GRIFFON-VULTURE.

This bird has once been taken in the British Islands.

Photo by Scholastic Photo. Co.] *[Parson's Green.*

RÜPPELL'S VULTURE.

An African species, closely allied to the griffon.

large animals as antelopes, wolves, and foxes, as well as the more helpless fawns, lambs, hares and rabbits, and ducks, geese, grouse, and so on.

Very different from the free-roving golden eagle and its allies is the South American HARPY-EAGLE. This is a denizen of the forest, of great size and enormous strength, as the powerful bill and feet testify. Whilst other eagles are conspicuous for their powers of flight, the present species is rarely seen on the wing, being strictly a forest-dweller, with short wings and tail, and of a somewhat owl-like plumage, the feathers being very soft. At rest it is one of the most striking of all the eagles. The head is crested, the under parts of the body are white, and the upper dark grey, banded with black. It feeds upon sloths, peccaries, and spider-monkeys.

Photo by Scholastic Photo. Co.] [Parson's Green

ANGOLAN VULTURE.

A common West African bird, living upon fish and carrion.

So recently as 1897 another forest-dwelling species was discovered in the Philippines, and this also preys largely upon monkeys. Its nearest ally is apparently the harpy-eagle, and, like this species, it is a bird of large size and very powerful. It is further remarkable for the enormous size of the beak, which differs from that of all other members of this group in being much compressed from side to side.

Photo by W. P. Dando, F.Z.S.] [Regent's Park.

PONDICHERRY VULTURE.

This Indian species is remarkable for the loose flaps of skin which hang down on each side of the head.

The sea, as well as the mountain and the forest, is also, as it were, presided over by members of this group, which are in consequence called SEA-EAGLES. One species, the WHITE-TAILED EAGLE, OR ERNE, is reckoned among British birds, though it is fast verging on extinction. In former days it bred on the sea-cliffs of Scotland and Ireland, and in the Lake District. The nest, or eyrie, as it is called, is commonly placed on inaccessible cliffs, but sometimes on the ground or in a tree, and, as is usual with the group, is made of sticks, with a lining of finer materials. This eagle feeds principally upon fish, though hares, lambs, and rabbits and carrion are occasionally taken.

The Hawk Tribe, generally speaking, have the wings comparatively short, the legs long and slender, and the edges of the beak with a sinuous outline and unnotched; but it is impossible to sharply define the group. The best-known species are the SPARROW- and GOS-HAWKS. The first named is still a common British bird, but the latter has now become very rare indeed. In both species the male is a much smaller bird than the female, and is also more brightly coloured. The GOS-HAWK was at one time used in falconry; it is a bird of extremely ferocious disposition, and in the days when hawks were used for sporting purposes had to be kept very safely tethered, as, if it gained its liberty, it would at once proceed to kill every other hawk and falcon in the "mews."

Photo by W. P. Dando, F.Z.S.] [Regent's Park.

EGYPTIAN VULTURE.

This is one of the foulest feeders of the Vulture Tribe.

The Falcon Tribe is divisible into two sections—the one containing the American CARRION-HAWKS, and the other the FALCONS.

The CARRION-HAWKS, or CARACARAS, are long-legged birds which spend most of their time on the ground and run well. They are said to hunt, not seldom in packs, after the fashion of wild dogs. One species at least affords an admirable example of mimicry—so rare among birds. This is the CURASSOW-HAWK, so called from its resemblance to the curassow, one of the Game-birds. The resemblance is evidently advantageous, for thereby the hawk is enabled to sit quietly at rest till its prey comes within easy reach, mistaking the hawk for the inoffensive curassow.

Photo by Scholastic Photo. Co.] [Parson's Green.

WEDGE-TAILED EAGLE.

This is an Australian species, feeding chiefly upon carrion.

The FALCONS form an exceedingly interesting group, if only on account of the part which they played in the sports of mediæval England. Birds of large size and forms as small as sparrows are included within the group; all are very powerful on the wing, and all feed on living prey, though, in the case of the diminutive forms, this may consist mainly, if not entirely, of insects. The members of the Falcon Tribe may be distinguished from the majority of the larger hawks by the fact that the eyes are dark hazel-brown instead of yellow, and that the bare, yellow, waxy-looking band of skin at the base of the beak, so characteristic of the Birds of Prey, is not sharply defined, but scantily clothed with fine bristles, passing insensibly into the feathers of the crown of the head.

Some of the best-known members of this section of the group are the PEREGRINE and JER-FALCONS, and the KESTREL, HOBBY, and MERLIN. Only the peregrine and the kestrel, however, can now be called common.

The PEREGRINE is the falcon held so much in esteem by falconers, by whom the female only was called the "falcon," the male, which is smaller, being known as a "tiercel." The female was used for the capture of the larger game, such as herons and rooks; whilst the male was flown only at partridges, and sometimes magpies.

Photo by Dr. R. W. Shufeldt, Washington.

AMERICAN SPARROW-HAWK.

One of the smallest and handsomest of the American hawks.

In a wild state the peregrine falcon is regarded by other birds with the greatest fear and terror. Ducks feeding on the banks of streams or lakes, on perceiving it, immediately take to the water; whilst plovers and lapwings rise to an immense height in the air, and remain there for hours. Mr. Ussher, who has had many opportunities of studying this bird in Ireland, where it is quite common, relates an instance of the tenacity with which it follows its prey, in this case a lapwing. "The falcon," he says, "after several stoops, cleverly avoided by the lapwing, was so near clutching, that the poor bird, quite worn out, dropped into the water, and the falcon, after rising from her stoop, poised a moment on her wings, and then quietly lowering herself with extended legs, lifted the lapwing from the water and bore her off."

The eyrie is generally found half-way up some precipitous cliff: no nest is made, but the eggs are laid on the earth or gravel covering the selected ledge. When eggs are found in a nest, the latter has always been taken from some other bird, even the eagle being occasionally dispossessed. Three or four eggs are laid, which are very beautiful and variable in their coloration. The young are attended by their parents long after they are able to fly.

The JER-FALCONS are birds of large size and great beauty, and at one time were much in request by falconers, probably largely on account of their appearance, for they lack the power and spirit of the peregrine. Grey and black and white and black are distinctive colours of the various species, which are inhabitants of northern regions.

The KESTREL, or WIND-HOVER, is one of the commonest birds of prey, much and most unjustly persecuted by gamekeepers. In its general appearance it closely resembles its much smaller relative, the so-called "SPARROW-HAWK" of America, shown in the photograph on this page by Dr. Shufeldt. The American sparrow-hawk, it should be mentioned, is really a species of kestrel, and, like the British kestrel, belongs to the Falcon group of the Birds of Prey. Like the peregrine falcon, the kestrel does not build a nest, but takes possession of the deserted nests of crows and magpies, or deposits its eggs on the bare earth of a recess in some cliff or quarry which is overhung by a projecting shelf of rock. Occasionally a hole in a tree is chosen, the eggs then resting on the rotten wood at the bottom. That the kestrel is of a more confiding disposition than the majority of its tribe seems to be proved by the fact that it will often deposit its eggs in nesting-boxes, if these are placed in suitable spots. On some

Photo by Scholastic Photo. Co.] *[Parson's Green.*

VOCIFEROUS SEA-EAGLE.

This is an African species.

Photo by Scholastic Photo. Co.] *[Parson's Green.*

IMPERIAL EAGLE.

Occurs in Southern Europe and North-west Africa.

Photo by W. Saville-Kent, F.Z.S.] *[Milford-on-Sea.*

CRESTED EAGLE.

A powerful and savage bird from South America.

Photo by Scholastic Photo. Co.] *[Parson's Green.*

CHILIAN SEA-EAGLE.

This bird feeds on carrion which it finds on the beach.

English estates the harmlessness of this bird is fully recognised, and every encouragement is given it to breed by the erection of these nesting-boxes. By way of illustration we may cite a case where, on an estate in Kent in 1900, five of these boxes were erected 20 or 30 feet from the ground round a single field, all of which were tenanted by kestrels; and though a thousand young pheasants were reared in this field, not a single one of these was missed by the keepers. Besides its human enemies, the kestrel has to contend with crows and rooks, which spare no efforts to seize its eggs whenever the opportunity presents itself. The eggs, it should be mentioned, are of a bright ruddy colour, but, like those of the peregrine falcon, lose much of their freshness of colouring during incubation. Four or five in number, they are laid at intervals of two days or so, incubation commencing with the deposition of the first egg; as a result, the first nestling hatched may be more than a week older than the last.

Photo by W. P. Dando, F.Z.S.] [*Regent's Park.*

ROUGH-LEGGED BUZZARD.

Frequent in the British Islands.

The food of the kestrel appears to consist mainly of mice, but frogs, earthworms, grasshoppers, cockchafers, and other beetles are also taken. Kestrels will also eat dead animals, as is proved by the fact that they are not seldom found dead from eating poisoned rats laid out for magpies. One instance is on record where a kestrel was taken with its claws entangled in the fur of a stoat, which fiercely defended itself. It is an easy matter, for those who will take the trouble, to find out what is the staple diet of the kestrel; for if the nest and its neighbourhood be searched, numerous small rounded pellets of the size of a chestnut will be found, which, when broken up, will prove to be composed of the hard and indigestible parts of what has been swallowed. The majority of such pellets are made up of the fur and bones of mice.

The little AMERICAN "SPARROW-HAWK," which, as we have already pointed out, is really a species of kestrel, appears to be almost exclusively insectivorous during the summer months, preying mainly upon grasshoppers. An American ornithologist, Mr. Henshaw, writing on the subject, remarks that during a scourge of grasshoppers the sparrow-hawks assembled in hundreds; and although on this occasion, owing to the vast myriads in which these insects had collected, the birds could make no visible impression, yet

Photo by W. P. Dando, F.Z.S.] [*Regent's Park.*

MARTIAL HAWK-EAGLE.

The Hawk-eagles show a marked preference for woody districts.

By permission of Percy Leigh Pemberton, Esq.

PEREGRINE FALCON.

A favourite in falconry.

they must have done an immense amount of good. Ornithologists from all parts of the United States unanimously agree that grasshoppers form the staple diet of this hawk, though mice and gophers are also largely eaten, and especially during the winter months, when insect food is scarce.

Of the PYGMY FALCONS there are several species, ranging from the Eastern Himalaya, through Tenasserim and Burma, to the Malay Islands and the Philippines. The smallest is the RED-LEGGED FALCONET of Nepal, Sikhim, and Burma. It feeds largely upon insects, such as dragon-flies, beetles, and butterflies, hawking them with a swallow-like speed. Occasionally the members of this little group are said to hunt down and kill birds larger than themselves.

OWLS.

FEW birds have been more misrepresented in literature than the OWLS. For centuries they have been depicted as birds of ill omen, and accused of all kinds of diabolical practices. Shakespeare, for example, repeatedly makes the owl do duty for some evil sign, or fulfil some dire purpose. Thus in *Macbeth*, Act II., Scene ii.,

> It was the owl that shriek'd, the fatal bellman,
> Which gives the stern'st good-night.

And later on, in Act IV., it is an owl's wing which he makes the witches add to their caldron of noisome things, when brewing their deadly potion. In Spain the scops and tawny owls are believed to be devil's birds, and are accused of drinking the oil from the lamps suspended before the shrines of saints. The gamekeeper nails their bodies up on the barn door as offenders of the worst type, whilst the Malagasy believe owls to be the embodiments of evil spirits.

It is therefore a relief to find this unwarrantable prejudice is not absolutely universal, since amongst some people, at least, the owl has found some favour. The best-known instance of this is the

Photo by Ottomar Anschütz] *[Berlin.*

SPECTACLED OWL.

A South American bird with a somewhat remarkable coloration.

Photo by C. N. Mavrogeni] [*Smyrna.*

EAGLE-OWL.

An occasional visitor to the British Isles.

case of the Greeks, who made the owl the symbol of wisdom, and chose as an emblem, singularly enough, the species known as the Little Owl, a bird which is notorious for its ludicrous behaviour, so much so that it has earned for itself the reputation of being the veritable buffoon of birds. Its grotesque and ridiculous antics are utilised by Continental bird-catchers, who use it as a lure to attract small birds, tethering it for this purpose near nets, snares, or twigs smeared with bird-lime.

Amongst other birds, strangely enough, the owl appears to be as much disliked as the fiercer and more dangerous members of the Hawk Tribe, and in consequence, should one venture abroad during the day or be discovered in its retreat, the alarm is given, and every small bird within call is summoned to take part in a general mobbing.

Although proverbially unpalatable, the Little Owl is said to be eaten in Italy, as are other species in the various countries in which they are found.

Varying considerably in size, the owls, nevertheless, present a very general uniformity in appearance. All are remarkable for the peculiar softness of their plumage, which imparts to the wings the almost unique power of absolutely silent flight, the sound being deadened or muffled, so that the prey can be approached suddenly, and seized before escape is possible. This is very necessary when hunting in twilight hours. The owls are almost the only birds in which the outer toe is reversible, or capable of being turned either forwards or backwards. Futhermore, the members of this group are remarkable for the fact that the eyes look directly forward, instead of outwards, as in other birds, and that the feathers of the face are arranged round each eye in the form of a disk, and thus impart the familiar owl-like visage, seen elsewhere only among certain of the Hawk Tribe known as "Harriers."

Four species of owl are to be found sparsely distributed over Great Britain. We may regard as the typical owl the species known as the TAWNY or WOOD-OWL. It is the largest of the resident owls in England; and would be much more abundant but that it is subjected to a rigorous and foolish persecution, born of long-standing prejudice and ignorance; it stands accused of the heinous offence of eating game, a charge which has never yet been fully proved. The benefits it confers are great, but, unfortunately, unrecognised, for its chief food consists of rats and mice. This is the bird which gives utterance to that weird "hoo-hoo—hoo-hoo-hoo,"

Photo by W. P. Dando, F.Z.S., Regent's Park.

VIRGINIAN EAGLE-OWL.

A common North American species, feeding largely on small mammals.

one of the most charming of the many delightful sounds that break the stillness of the summer nights. It is interesting to note that this species is unknown as a wild bird in Ireland.

Other and fairly common species in England are the LONG- and SHORT-EARED OWLS, both remarkable for the fact that the aperture of the ear, which is of enormous size, is of a different shape on the right and left sides of the head. These owls, furthermore, are characterised by the possession of a pair of feathery tufts, or "horns," springing from the top of the head, which can be erected or depressed at pleasure. These horns are found in many species of owl not necessarily closely related. The species under consideration are of medium size, with large eyes of a most wonderful golden-yellow colour, standing in strong contrast with those of the tawny owl, which are nearly black. Like the tawny owl, these two species, and especially the short-eared, live largely on rats and mice. The last-named bird also devours great numbers of dor-beetles and cockchafers.

Photo by Dr. R. W. Shufeldt] *[Washington.*

AMERICAN LONG-EARED OWL.

This is a young bird which has not yet completely lost its down-feathers.

Amongst the largest of the tribe are the EAGLE- and SNOWY OWLS, both of which are occasionally met with in Great Britain. The eagle-owl may be described as a largely magnified long-eared owl in general appearance, though, as a matter of fact, the two are not very closely related. The snowy owl, as its name implies, is white in colour, the white being relieved by more or less conspicuous black markings. This white livery, assimilating with its snowy surroundings, allows the wearer to approach its prey unperceived on the snow. Whilst the snowy owl is confined to northern regions, the eagle-owl enjoys a wide distribution, and is represented by numerous species, one of which, as we have remarked, occasionally visits Great Britain. The larger species of eagle-owl are the most ferocious members of the order, and prey largely upon hares, rabbits, and the large game-birds; whilst the snowy owl, though selecting similar prey, does incalculable good by devouring those destructive little rodents known as the lemmings.

Photo by W. P. Dando, F.Z.S.] *[Regent's Park.*

TAWNY OWL.

One of the commonest British owls.

Solitary as owls usually are, some, as the AMERICAN BURROWING-OWLS, live in what may be called colonies; and, stranger still, they live in burrows, which they share with the original excavators. Occurring both in North and South America, it is not surprising to find that the creatures with whom the burrowing-owls elect to take up their abode are very varied, belonging for the most part to numerous groups of burrowing mammalia. In the prairies of North

America they appear to quarter themselves upon the prairie-dogs, ground-squirrels, and badgers; and in the pampas of South America upon the Patagonian cavy, the viscacha and armadillos, and occasionally lizards. It seems to be no unusual thing to find, in addition to the bird and mammal tenants of a single burrow, one or more full-grown examples of the much-dreaded rattle-snake—a truly wonderful happy-family, if all accounts are to be believed. But many competent to speak on the matter throw out dark hints which would appear to show that the owl quarters itself on the tenants of a burrow too weak to resist its intrusion upon their domicile, and that occasionally this most masterful bird renders itself still more objectionable by devouring the progeny of its hosts, and sometimes even the hosts themselves.

The species known as PYGMY OWLS and LITTLE OWLS we mention here only on account of their small size, one member of the former group being little bigger than a lark. Thus they stand in strong contrast with the giant snowy and eagle-owls.

Photo by Dr. R. W. Shufeldt] *[Washington.*

SCREECH-OWL.

A common North American bird, feeding on small animals of all kinds.

Photo by Frans Monsen] *[Breda.*

BARN-OWL.

This is a British owl, evincing a preference for church-towers in which to roost and breed.

Finally, we have the WHITE or BARN-OWL, which with its allies forms a group distinguished from all the other owls by certain well-marked structural characters. The barn-owl is also to be found in Great Britain, but is growing, like all the other owls in this area, more and more rare every year, owing to persecution at the hands of gamekeepers. It is a handsome bird, of a pale buff-yellow, mottled with grey above to pure white beneath, and with the characteristic facial disk peculiarly well developed. It breeds in holes in trees, ruins, and church towers, and feeds almost entirely on mice and rats. From the piercing note which it occasionally utters, it is also known as the SCREECH-OWL.

Photo by C. N. Macrogeni, Smyrna.

HOOPOE FLYING.

This photograph displays the crest fully elevated, and likewise shows the beautifully banded colouration of the under surface of the wing, as well as the position of the wings in flight.

CHAPTER X.

NIGHT-JARS, SWIFTS, AND HUMMING-BIRDS.

NIGHT-JARS.

Photo by A. S. Rudland & Sons.

COMMON NIGHT-JAR.

Known also as Fern-owl and Goat-sucker.

IT is probable that the NIGHT-JARS are the nearest allies of the Owls. As pointed out in the last chapter, although the latter have acquired the habits of the Hawk and Eagle Tribe, they are not really connected with that group by descent.

Soberly clad, so as to be in complete harmony with its surroundings, with large eyes, huge mouth, and peculiarly short beak, beset with long bristles, the night-jar may be distinguished at once from all other British birds. By day it hides, squatting close to the ground, or perched on the thick branch of a tree; but when on the latter, it sits along and not across the bough, like other birds, the complete harmony between its plumage and the bark rendering it as invisible as when on the ground.

Not until the spring has far advanced does this bird leave its winter resort in Africa for Europe, making its presence known by its conspicuous habit of hunting its food (which consists of moths and beetles) after twilight has fallen. Later, its extraordinary churring note is heard—

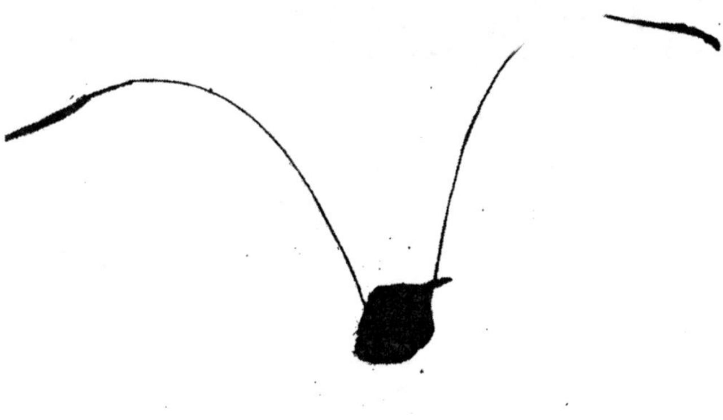

Photo by A. S. Rudland & Sons.

PENNANT-WINGED NIGHT-JAR (FRONT VIEW).

The long and graceful plumes are much-lengthened quill-feathers, and by their resemblance to the waving grass in which the bird nests afford protection.

a note which has been likened to the noise made by a spinning-wheel, and so powerful as to be audible half a mile off. This note is made while on the ground: on the wing, while toying with its mate, another equally peculiar sound is made, which has been likened to the noise made by swinging a whip-thong through the air.

No nest is made by this bird; but the eggs, two in number and beautifully marked, are laid on the bare ground. The young are covered with down, and remain in the nest for some time.

Another very remarkable feature is the fact that the claw of the middle toe has its inner edge curiously serrated, forming a sort of comb, the function of which is unknown. This comb-like claw occurs also in some few other birds—bitterns, for instance.

A very remarkable kind is the PENNANT-WINGED NIGHT-JAR, in which one of the quill-feathers in each wing is produced into a "pennant" of some 17 inches in length. The shaft of the feather is bare for the greater part of its length, and terminates in a feathery blade. It is an Abyssinian species about which not much is known.

Photo by W. Saville-Kent, F.Z.S.] [Milford-on-Sea.

MORE-PORKS.

So called from the note they utter.

Some of the night-jars, as the New World NIGHT-HAWK and the Old World EARED NIGHT-JARS, are particularly owl-like, a resemblance imparted by long "ear-like" tufts of feathers which rise from the back of the head. Others, as the MORE-PORK of the Tasmanian colonist, or the FROG-MOUTH, as it is called in Australia, are remarkable for the huge size of the mouth, bounded, as it appears to be, by huge lips, represented by the short, round-edged beak.

Very nearly related to the night-jars is the OIL-BIRD of South America, which lives in caves in Trinidad, Ecuador, and Peru, where it builds a nest which has been likened in appearance to a huge cheese, and in which are laid from two to four white eggs. Like the night-jars, these birds feed by night, emerging from their gloomy retreats at twilight with much noise and in great numbers. Their food, however, is entirely of a vegetable nature, consisting of oily nuts or fruits.

The young, soon after they are hatched, become perfect masses of fat, and on this account are much in demand by the Indians, who make a special business of killing them and extracting the oil.

SWIFTS.

In general appearance SWIFTS bear a strong superficial resemblance to Swallows; in reality they are related, not to those harbingers of spring, but to the Night-jars on the one hand and the Humming-birds on the other.

The COMMON SWIFT arrives in England during the early part of May, and stays till the end of August, or sometimes till September has half run its course. Black in colour, relieved only by a white throat, it has little in the sense of beauty to recommend it; nevertheless, there are probably few who do not cherish tender feelings towards this bird.

Photo by W. Saville-Kent, F.Z.S.] [*Milford-on-Sea.*

MORE-PORK.

This is one of the most owl-like of the Night-jars.

Photo by J. T. Newman] *[Berkhamsted.*

SWIFT.

A common British bird during the summer months.

The swift has great buoyancy of spirits, as is manifested by the wild, exuberant bursts of screaming to which it gives voice as it rushes in small parties down the lanes or along the less-frequented thoroughfares of towns as morning breaks or evening falls, and occasionally throughout the day. The greater part of its life is spent upon the wing (indeed, it appears to rest only when incubating or sleeping), and of all the smaller birds it is the most graceful in flight, turning and twisting in fairy mazes high in the heavens for hours at a time.

The swift chooses for its nesting-place the eaves of houses and holes in church towers, and occasionally a crevice in the face of a quarry. The nest is formed of bits of straw, dry grass, and a few feathers, glued together by a secretion of the salivary glands into a compact crust; in this the bird deposits from two to four white eggs. The young, which are hatched naked and blind, never develop down-feathers, but soon become more or less imperfectly clothed in a mass of tiny spines, representing the budding feathers; these give the bird somewhat the appearance of a young hedgehog.

In adaptation to its remarkable powers of flight, the wing has undergone considerable modification in form, so that it differs from that of all other birds. On the other hand, the legs, being so little required, have diminished considerably, and are remarkable for their smallness—a fact which hampers the bird considerably, should it happen to alight on level ground, for, owing to the great length of the wings, it can arise only with considerable difficulty.

Nearly allied to the common swift is SALVIN'S SWIFT, remarkable on account of its nest, which has been described by Dr. Sharpe as the most wonderful in the world. About 2 feet long and 6 inches in diameter, it looks rather like the sleeve of an old coat than a nest. It is made entirely of the downy seeds of plants, which, floating through the air after the fashion of such seeds, are caught by the birds when on the wing, and, partly felted and partly glued by the salivary secretion, are woven slowly into the characteristic woolly domicile. The site and manner of fixation of the nest are scarcely less wonderful, for it is suspended from the flat surface of some projecting piece of rock on the face of a cliff, and is thus almost inaccessible; yet, as if to make assurance doubly sure, two entrances are made, one at the bottom, which is really blind, and one at the top, near its foundation, if we may call it so, which leads into the nursery.

Still more swallow-like in general appearance are the diminutive EDIBLE SWIFTS, so called, not on account of the palatability of the birds themselves, but of their nests, which are in great demand by the wealthy Chinese for conversion into birds'-nest soup. It has already been remarked that the salivary glands are unusually active in the swifts, their secretion bearing a very important part in the construction of the nest, and serving as a kind of cement. It is, therefore, not surprising that in some members of the group we find this secretion playing a still more prominent part, forming, at least in one species, the entire material of the nest. "With these nests," writes Dr. Sharpe, "a large trade is done with China from many of the Malayan Islands, over 3,500,000 nests having been known to be exported in a single year from Borneo to the latter country. . . . In Borneo and other places the caves in which the swiftlets build are leased to the collectors for a considerable sum; but it is only the white nests, made of the pure secretion, which are of any real value. The nests of those species which mix into their nests grass or feathers are not appreciated as an article of commerce."

Photo by A. S. Rudland & Sons.

EDIBLE SWIFT.

The nests of this bird are used for soup; five are seen in this photograph.

Colonel Legge gives some extremely interesting particulars concerning the nesting habits of these birds in Ceylon. "It is noteworthy," he writes, "that the partially fledged young—which were procured on this occasion for me, and which I kept for the night—scrambled out on to the exterior of the nest, and slept in an upright position, with the bill pointing straight up. This is evidently the normal mode of roosting resorted to by this species. The interior of this cave, with its numbers of active tenants, presented a singular appearance. The bottom was filled with a vast deposit of liquid guano, reaching, I was informed, to a depth of 30 feet, and composed of droppings, old nests, and dead young fallen from above, the whole mingled into a loathsome mass, with water lodged in the crevices, and causing an awful stench, which would have been intolerable for a moment even, had not the hundreds of frightened little birds, as they screamed and whirred in and out of the gloomy cave with a hum like a storm in a ship's rigging, powerfully excited my interest, and produced a long examination of the colony. This guano-deposit is a source of considerable profit to the estate, the hospitable manager of which informed us that he had manured 100 acres of coffee with it during that season."

HUMMING-BIRDS.

It is generally admitted that HUMMING-BIRDS are nearly related to Swifts, with which, however, they stand in the strongest possible contrast in the matter of plumage—the latter being always inconspicuously coloured, whilst the former are for the most part clad in vestments so gorgeous as to render it extremely difficult to describe them in sober language. Moreover, so great is the wealth of species—some hundreds in number—and so varied are the form and coloration, and so closely do the various types pass one into the other, that their classification is a matter of extreme difficulty.

Photo by W. Saville-Kent, F.Z.S.] [Milford-on-Sea.

RUBY-THROATED HUMMING-BIRDS.

About 500 distinct species of humming-birds are known.

Confined to the American Continent and certain islands adjacent thereto, humming-birds range from Canada to Tierra del Fuego in a horizontal direction, and rise vertically in the mountain-range of Chimborazo to a height of 16,000 feet above the sea-level—"dwelling," as Professor Newton describes it, "in a world of almost constant hail, sleet, and rain, and feeding on the insects which resort to the indigenous flowering plants."

Humming-birds surpass all others in the wondrous beauty of their plumage, which depends not so much on colour as metallic lustre reflecting all the hues of the most precious stones—amethyst, ruby, sapphire, emerald, and topaz gleaming and sparkling from their bodies with a fire and intensity truly marvellous. "In some cases," as Professor Newton aptly describes it, "this radiance beams from the brow, in some it glows from the throat, in others it shines from the tail-coverts, in others it sparkles from the tips of elongated feathers that crest the head or surround the neck as with a frill, while again in others it may appear as a luminous streak across the cheek. . . . The feathers that cover the upper parts of the body very frequently have a metallic lustre of golden green, which in other birds would be thought sufficiently beautiful, but in the [humming-birds] its sheen is overspread by the almost dazzling splendour that radiates from the spots where Nature's lapidary has set her jewels."

Besides this brilliancy of colour and variety in form—variety due to the development of these crests and frills, or to the forking and elongation of the tail-feathers—still further changes are brought about by the modification of the bill, which may be produced into a long straight style, longer than the body of the bird, or turned up like that of the avocet or down like that of the curlew. These changes are adaptations to the bird's methods of feeding, some seeking their food from the long tubular corollas of flowers, and requiring, therefore, very elongated beaks, others from more open and easily accessible flowers, whilst others hunt among leaves, especially the under-surfaces, the quarry consisting mainly of insects attracted by the honey secreted by the flowers, or those living on the leaves. Not only the beak but the tongue also has undergone great modification in this group, its outer sheath curling up on each side into a thin scroll, so as to form a pair of tubes, the exact use of which is unknown. The wings, like those of the swift, have undergone a certain amount of change in the relative proportion of the several regions, and in the form and number of the quill-feathers, whilst the legs have become considerably reduced in size. In some species each leg is surrounded by a little tuft of down, which may be black, brown, or snow-white in colour. In size these birds vary from 8 inches to scarcely more than 3 inches.

"The beautiful nests of humming-birds," writes Professor Newton, "than which the fairies could not have conceived more delicate . . . will be found on examination to be very solidly and tenaciously built, though the materials are generally of the slightest—cotton-wool, or some vegetable down, and spiders' webs. They vary greatly in form and ornamentation—for it would seem that the portions of lichen which frequently bestud them are affixed to their exterior with that object, though probably concealment was the original intention. They are mostly cup-shaped; and the singular fact is on record, that in one instance, as the young grew, the walls were heightened by the parents, until at last the nest was more than twice as big as when the eggs were laid and hatched."

CHAPTER XI.

PARROTS, CUCKOOS, AND PLANTAIN-EATERS.

PARROTS.

"THE art of taming wild animals," writes Mr. Jenks in his "History of Politics," "and making them serve the purposes of man, is one of the greatest discoveries of the world." He holds—and there can be little question as to its reasonableness—"that the domestication of animals converted the savage pack into the patriarchal tribe," and that the earliest domesticated animals were pets. How great a share, then, PARROTS may have had in this civilisation and advancement no man can tell, for it is impossible to say how long these beautiful birds may have been esteemed as pets, or how early they were introduced to the notice of the civilised peoples of past generations. Certain it is, however, that for more than 2,000 years they have been held in the highest esteem.

Modern discovery has added enormously to the list of known parrots, so that to-day more than 500 different species have been described, and these may be divided into NESTORS, LORIES, COCKATOOS, COCKATEELS, MACAWS, and KAKAPOS.

Photo by W. Reid] *[Wishaw, N.B.*

KEA

Also known as the Mountain-nestor.

Photo by D. Le Souef] [*Melbourne.*

NEW ZEALAND KEA.

The kea frequents the slopes of lofty snow-covered mountains.

Of the first named, the best known is the KEA, or MOUNTAIN-NESTOR, of the South Island, New Zealand. Dull in coloration, and not striking in appearance, it has earned an unenviable notoriety, which appears to rest as much upon fable as upon fact. It seems that, since the introduction of sheep into this part of the world by the settlers, this bird has found a diet of flesh more stimulating than one of fruit. Exactly how this came to be is not known. Two explanations have been advanced. The first has it that the birds settled on the skins of the sheep slaughtered for their wool, and picked off pieces of fat therefrom, as well as various tit-bits from the carcases of the same, and thus found out how toothsome—or beaksome—mutton was. From this they went a step further, and did the slaughtering for themselves. Parties of them now go a-hunting, worry a sheep till exhausted, then dig down through the back, and so wound the intestines that death results. Another explanation is that the birds in the original instance mistook the sheep's backs for the huge masses of lichen common to this region, of which the birds are very fond. Not finding it to their taste at the top, they dug deep, and soon came to the flesh, which, like the forbidden fruit, proved more palatable than that which was provided for them by a bountiful Nature. The result is, that they have become a menace to sheep-farmers, and are on this account in danger of extermination. It has, however, been denied recently that the damage inflicted is anything like so serious as was at one time reported, since on one run, where the damage was unusually large, only 1 in 300 sheep was so attacked. This bird has also been said to attack horses.

Very different, in general appearance and in esteem, are the LORIES. Like the Nestors, the tip of the upper jaw, or beak, is smooth, or nearly so; and in this respect these two groups are to be distinguished from all the other parrots; but in the gorgeousness of their plumage they far eclipse their congeners. Absent in New Zealand, they are found elsewhere throughout the Australasian region, inclusive of Polynesia, and are highly esteemed as pets, combining great beauty with a very docile disposition and considerable talking powers.

The birds of this section are also known as BRUSH-TONGUED PARROTS, from the presence of a remarkable "brush" borne on the end of the tongue. This is a special adaptation, enabling the birds to feed upon honey; some, indeed, have this brush particularly well developed, and are almost entirely honey-seekers, whilst others, wherein the brush is less developed, live largely on fruits. Professor Moseley tells us that honey literally poured from the mouths of BLUE MOUNTAIN-LORIES which he shot at Cape York.

Photo by D. Le Souef] [*Melbourne.*

NEW ZEALAND KAKA.

The Maoris keep this bird as a lure.

The COCKATOOS are abundant in the Australian region, but have their headquarters in the Malay Archipelago. Besides the familiar white-crested form so commonly kept in England, the group includes an iron-grey coloured bird with a bright red head, and a huge black species, which represents the giant of the order. It is a funereal-looking bird, the largest specimens inhabiting New Guinea. One of its most striking features is the beak, which is of enormous size. Its tongue differs from that of other parrots in that it is slender and cylindrical in shape, and of a deep red colour, instead of thick, fleshy, and black. It frequents, Mr. Wallace tells us, the lower parts of the forest, feeding upon various fruits and seeds, but displaying a marked partiality for the kernel of the canary-nut, which grows on a lofty forest-tree; "and the manner in which it gets at these seeds," writes Mr. Wallace, "shows a correlation of structure and habits which would point to the canary as its special food. The shell of this nut is so excessively hard that only a heavy hammer will crack it; it is somewhat triangular, and the outside is quite smooth. The manner in which the bird opens these nuts is very curious. Taking one end-ways in its bill, and keeping it firm by a pressure of the tongue, it cuts a transverse notch by a lateral sawing motion of the sharp-edged lower mandible. This done, it takes hold of the nut with its foot, and, biting off a piece of leaf, retains it in the deep notch by the upper mandible, and again seizing the nut, which is prevented from slipping by the elastic tissue of the leaf, fixes the edge of the lower mandible in the notch, and a powerful rip breaks off a piece of the shell. Again taking the nut in its claws, it inserts the very long and sharp point of the bill, and picks out the kernel, which is seized hold of, morsel by morsel, by the extensile tongue."

Of the typical parrots, the best known is the common GREY AFRICAN PARROT, with a red tail, so valued on account of its great talking powers. Other species of this section which should be mentioned here are the PYGMY PARROTS, MACAWS, HAWK-BILLED PARROT, BUDGERIGARS, and OWL-PARROT.

The first named are the smallest of all the tribe, remarkable as well for the splendour of the plumage as their size, which is less than that of the common sparrow.

The LONG-TAILED MACAWS, representing the most showy and gaudily coloured of all the Parrot Tribe, inhabit the tropical forests of South America. Mr. Bates describes a flock of scarlet-and-blue macaws, which he came across one day, as looking like a cluster of flaunting banners among the crown of dark green leaves of a bacaba-palm.

The superb HYACINTHINE MACAW is one of the rarest of the Parrot Tribe, and was found by Bates in the interior of Brazil. As its name implies, it is of a deep hyacinthine colour, relieved by a bare patch of pure white skin round the eyes. It feeds on the nuts of several palms, especially those of the macuja. These nuts, which are so hard as to be difficult to break without a heavy hammer, are crushed to a pulp by the powerful beak of this macaw.

Crests among parrots are common enough, but only one species wears a frill; this is the HAWK-BILLED PARROT of the Amazon Valley. It is closely related to the large and well-known AMAZON PARROTS, and has been aptly described as a most extraordinary bird. Its coloration is striking—green above, with a brown head; the frill or ruff around the neck shows up in strong contrast, being dark red, with blue edges, and barred with blue. The feathers of the breast and abdomen, like the frill, are also red and blue, whilst the under-surfaces of the tail and wings are black. It is only when the bird is excited or angry that the ruff is raised.

Photo by W. Saville-Kent, F.Z.S.] *[Milford-on-Sea.*

BLACK COCKATOO.

Found in pairs in thick forests.

The HANGING-PARROTS are about the same size as the well-known "love-birds," and remarkable for their habit of sleeping suspended head-downwards by one foot from the boughs of trees. They are all brilliantly coloured birds, and have a fairly wide range, extending from India and the Philippines through the Malay region as far east as Duke of York Island.

The Australian BUDGERIGARS, or GRASS-PARRAKEETS, need no description here; but it is interesting to note that nearly allied to them is a small species known as the SWAMP- or LONG-TAILED GROUND-PARRAKEET. As its

Photo by Scholastic Photo. Co.] *[Parson's Green.*

COCKATOO.

Cockatoos in a wild state often congregate in immense flocks.

Photo by Ottomar Anschutz] [Berlin.

LEADBEATER'S COCKATOO.

Has a red crest, banded with yellow and tipped with white.

name implies, it is a ground-dwelling species, and, in accordance with this habit, has considerably longer legs than the tree-haunting species. This lengthening of the leg in arboreal species is seen also among pigeons and many other birds.

The most interesting, perhaps, of all the parrots is the remarkable KAKAPO, or OWL-PARROT, of New Zealand. Like the species just described, it is also a ground-dweller; furthermore, it differs from all other members of the tribe in being flightless, and, like the flightless members of the Ostrich Tribe, has completely lost the deep keel from the breast-bone, which gives support to the muscles which move the wings. It is a large bird, green in colour, mottled with yellow and black, and derives its name of Owl-parrot from the fact that the feathers of the face radiate from the eye outwards to form a kind of disk. When eating grass, it is said to graze, nibbling after the fashion of a rabbit. Occasionally it is said to climb trees, descending with extended wings, so as to break the force of its career. It has been described as a playful and affectionate pet in captivity, displaying also great cleverness and intelligence. Unfortunately it is growing more and more rare, so that its final extermination is only a question of time—the ravages of dogs, cats, and pigs, introduced by the settlers, being mainly the agents of destruction.

Once common all over New Zealand, the range of the owl-parrot is now restricted to the mountainous regions of North Island and the northern half of South Island. During the day it remains concealed in the holes in rocks or under roots of trees, and if disturbed is difficult to rouse. When taken from its retreat, it runs swiftly, and tries to hide, seeking shelter, if possible, under a heap of soft, dry grass. At sunset, however, it becomes very animated, and travels—at least when possible—in companies, making tracks a foot or more wide across the herbage. It feeds greedily upon mosses, ferns, seeds, berries, and, it is said, even lizards, giving vent, when devouring some favourite morsel, to a kind of grunting noise.

Photo by C. Reid] [*Wishaw, N.B.*

MACAW.

The flight of these gorgeously clad birds is very powerful.

The kakapo nests in holes under trees and rocks, laying two or three eggs, which, like those of the Parrots, are white.

The natives take advantage of its feeble powers of flight, hunting it on foot by torchlight, aided by dogs, which, it is said, are not seldom seriously wounded by the powerful bill.

When the breeding-season is over, these birds appear to live in small communities, four or five occupying the same hole. They are apparently gifted with some fore-sight, inasmuch as they lay up a store of food, to be drawn upon during bad weather.

Cuckoos and Plantain-eaters.

The Cuckoo Tribe is somewhat unfortunate in that the numerous members of which it is composed are completely overshadowed by the prominence which has been given to the Common Cuckoo. Few birds, indeed, have managed to secure so much attention, the poet in particular having sung its praises without stint. This enthusiasm undoubtedly is but an echo of the general popular senti-ment, for there are few birds to which we in Britain extend a more hearty welcome, its well-known cry possessing a peculiar charm for lovers of the country. Coming to us in April, and leaving again in July, its stay is of the shortest; but during the greater part of this time its whereabouts may generally be known by the familiar call "cuckoo, cuckoo," though undergoing certain characteristic changes as the months glide by.

Apart from its song, one of the most interesting things concerning the cuckoo is the fact that it goes about in disguise—the disguise of the ass in the lion's skin with a vengeance; for it is clothed in the garb of that terror of the countryside, the sparrow-hawk. Nay, more; it has also most successfully imitated the flight of that bogy; and this to frighten little birds—not, however, for the mere purpose of creating consternation amongst them, but for far more sinister ends.

Somehow or another, in cuckoo society, the rearing of a family is a responsibility which is utterly repudiated. Great pains seem to have been taken to evade this duty, and yet to ensure the continuity of their distinguished house. The oviparous method of reproduction, which obtains in the feathered world, has been turned to good account—in fact, everything depends upon this. It seems to have suggested itself as far more convenient to drop an egg here and there into a neighbour's nursery, and leave the work of bringing it to life to the owners thereof. But to carry out this system of distributing foundlings requires tact,

Photo by Kerry & Co.] [Sydney.

BLUE MOUNTAIN-PARROTS.

A honey-eating species.

Photo by J. Peat Millar] [*Beith.*

YOUNG CUCKOO EJECTING EGG.

The egg is held in position by the head and wings.

cunning, and the mutual co-operation of both the male and his—at least temporary—wife; hence the disguise. The plan of execution very frequently adopted is for the male to hover over the treasure-house of the intended foster-parents hawk-wise. This is sure to call forth an attack from the poor little wretches threatened, which ends in an apparently hasty retreat of the marauder, followed by his fearless assailants. No sooner is the coast clear, however, than the wily female, taking her egg in her beak, slips quietly up to the nest and deposits her burden.

Let us imagine that this home so lately threatened is that of the modest little hedge-sparrow, and take a peep during the absence of the owners, after quiet has established itself once again. Lying side by side with the tiny sky-blue eggs of the hedge-sparrow we should find the relatively large, greyish-green or reddish-grey egg of the cuckoo. What a contrast! If the hedge-sparrows notice this too, they evidently do not mind, for they invariably hatch it with their own.

But some birds are not so accommodating as this, and would ruthlessly destroy or reject any egg surreptitiously introduced into the nest. Consequently more deception has to be practised. The hawk-like garb still serves its purpose to draw off the intended dupes from the nest; but this is not enough, for to deposit an egg of the normal cuckoo type would be worse than useless, since it would meet with instant destruction on the return of the owners of the nest. But the cuckoo, strange to say, has proved equal to the occasion, and meets the difficulty by laying an egg to match those in the nest. The Redstart, Wagtail, Sedge-warbler, Red-backed Shrike, and Meadow-pipit may be cited as instances of—shall we say exclusive?—birds which must be circumvented by "colourable imitations." Perhaps the most wonderful of the cuckoo successes in this direction is the imitation of the redstart's egg, which is blue.

Naturally these facts have given rise to much speculation, but even now we cannot regard the discussion as finally settled. Some ornithologists held that the egg of every individual cuckoo was subject to great variations, and that the place of deposit of each egg was determined only after the bird had ascertained its colour. If this were true, surely we should find blue cuckoos' eggs in hedge-sparrows' as well as redstarts' nests. But we don't! Others have sought to explain the existence of mimicking eggs to the influence of the food peculiar to the foster-parent upon the germ of the young female cuckoo, which, through this channel, became transmitted to all its descendants. To support this hypothesis it was necessary to throw overboard the old individual variability explanation, and to adopt one that is certainly nearer the truth—to wit, that each cuckoo chooses the nest of that species in which itself was reared as a depository, in turn, for its own egg, and only when such is not available will it select some other species, and trust to luck for its adoption. This would certainly account for many anomalies; but as it seems that there are more eggs unlike than like those of the selected foster-parents, it cannot be a perfect explanation.

A third explanation takes that part of the second for granted which assumes that cuckoos select nests of the species which served them as foster-parents, and explains the mimicry, when this occurs, as due to the results of natural selection.

Our interest, however, in the domestic economy of the common cuckoo is not to be allowed to drop with the incubation of the egg. The perfidy of the parents seems to have cast a sombre shadow over the cradle of the offspring, an evil spell destined to bear fruit with terrible suddenness; for the young, before it is many hours old, and while yet blind and naked, perpetrates its first act of wrong-doing by committing murder! There is no case here of wilful or ignorant misrepresentation and slander, such as many of our feathered friends are made to suffer at our hands—no foolish prejudice such as has blasted the reputation of some of our most guiltless and useful of bird-citizens. The witnesses of the crime of which we speak are many and unimpeachable. The facts are as follows:—

The parent cuckoo deposits her egg in the nest of some other bird with those of the owners thereof. All are hatched. In a few hours after the arrival of the young cuckoo the foster-brothers and -sisters invariably disappear, and are not seldom found in the immediate neighbourhood of the nest. That they must have been removed by force is certain; but this force cannot be attributed to the natural parents. The evidence of the first witnesses, therefore, was worthy of all consideration; and since their accounts have been frequently

Photo by Billington] [*Queensland.*

PHEASANT-CUCKOO.

The hind toe terminates in a spur-like claw; hence these cuckoos are known as Lark-heeled Cuckoos.

confirmed by most trustworthy observers, we must now admit the charge proved. One of the best known of these accounts is that of Mrs. Hugh Blackburn. She has given us a vivid picture of this most extraordinary of domestic tragedies. The victims in this instance were meadow-pipits. Finding a pipit's nest with a cuckoo's egg therein, she kept it carefully under observation. At one visit she found the pipits hatched, but not the cuckoo. Forty-eight hours later the cuckoo had not only arrived, but ousted his foster-brothers and -sisters, who were found lying outside the nest, but yet alive. They were replaced beside the cuckoo, which at once reopened hostilities for the purpose of maintaining its absolute possession of the nursery. This it did by burrowing under one of them, which, balanced upon its back, it proceeded to eject by climbing up the nest tail-foremost, till, reaching the brim, it could relieve itself of its burden by heaving it over the edge and down the bank. Pausing a moment, it then felt backwards with its wings to make sure the pipit was really gone, and, having satisfied itself on this point, subsided to the bottom of the nest. Next day, when the nest was visited, the remaining pipit was found outside the nest cold and dead. "But what struck me most," she writes, "was this: the cuckoo was perfectly naked, without a vestige of a feather or even a hint of feathers, its eyes were not yet opened, and its neck seemed too weak to support the weight of its head. The pipits had well-developed quills on the wings and back, and had bright eyes partially opened, yet they seemed quite helpless under the manipulations of the cuckoo, which looked a much less developed creature."

The GREAT SPOTTED CUCKOO of South Europe and North Africa is a species which, though parasitic, does not seem to have sunk to such a depth as the common cuckoo. Its eggs very closely resemble those of certain magpies and crows within its breeding-area, and it is in the nests of these that they are deposited. We may assume that mimicry has been resorted to, and become perfected by the same means as have accomplished this end in the case of the common cuckoo. We notice here, however, two points of difference therefrom. In the first place, from two to four eggs are left in each nest instead of one; and, secondly, the young cuckoos seem to live in perfect amity with their foster-brothers and -sisters—there is no ejection of the rightful heirs.

Photo by J. T. Newman] [*Berkhamsted.*

CUCKOO ONE DAY OLD IN HEDGE-SPARROW'S NEST.

The young bird has its mouth open, ready for all the food the foster-parents can collect.

Having pledged themselves to a course of deception and treachery, there is no telling the lengths to which such conduct may lead. We have already seen that the bird has succeeded in laying what we may call forged eggs, but we come now to an instance where the young has also to be disguised. This is furnished by a species of cuckoo known as the KOEL, inhabiting Palawan, an island in the Philippines. This bird shifts its parental duties upon the shoulders of a species of myna inhabiting the same island. Now, the mynas are black, and their young, as is often the case where both sexes are coloured alike, resemble the parents, and are black likewise. With the cuckoo the case is different. The male and female are conspicuously different in coloration, the former being black, the latter brown. In such cases it is the rule for the young to wear the livery of the female. If this rule were adhered to in the case of the cuckoo, destruction would be more than probable, for the mynas would as likely as not destroy so outrageous a departure from myna custom as a brown youngster. But the koel has proved equal to the occasion, by the simple expedient of attiring the young in the male instead of the female livery. Later on in life the rule for the exchange of plumage is reversed, and the young female doffs the temporary black dress of the male for the brown one of the adult female, instead of *vice versâ*.

Photo by J. T. Newman] [Berkhamsted.

YOUNG CUCKOO.

A young cuckoo remains in the nest till fully fledged.

All cuckoos, however, are not parasitic, the species known as LARK-HEELED CUCKOOS—from the presence of a long, spine-like claw on the hind toe—building a nest and hatching their own eggs. They have a wide range, being found in Africa from Egypt to Cape Colony, Madagascar, India, China, New Guinea, and Australia.

As a rule, the Cuckoos are not conspicuously coloured, but some species are clad in a livery resplendent with metallic colours. These are represented by the Indian and Australian BRONZE CUCKOOS and the African GOLDEN CUCKOOS. One of the most beautiful of all is the African EMERALD CUCKOO, in which the upper-parts are of a vivid emerald-green, whilst the under-parts are bright yellow.

Finally, we must mention the GROUND-CUCKOOS, which are comparatively long-legged, terrestrial forms, with small wings. One of the best known is an inhabitant of the Southern United States, from Texas to New Mexico, Southern Colorado, and California. "It has obtained the name of ROOD-RUNNER," writes Dr. Sharpe, "from the speed with which it flies over the ground, some idea of which may be gained from a statement of Colonel Stevenson, that, when in Southern California, he saw, on two occasions, the ranchmen of that part of the country chase one of these birds on horseback for a distance of a mile or more at full speed, when the cuckoo, though still in advance, would suddenly stop and fly up among the upper limbs of some stunted tree or bush near the roadside, and the rider, having kept the bird in view all the way, would dismount and easily take the exhausted bird from its perch alive."

That the African PLANTAIN-EATERS, or TOURACOS, are related to the Cuckoos there can be no doubt, although they do not bear any very close superficial resemblance to them. Striking in appearance and of beautiful plumage, they owe as much of the interest which now centres on them to the chemist as to the ornithologist. Long ago it was noticed that the rich crimson colour of the wing-quills disappeared after exposure to a heavy rain, having been

Photo by J. T. Newman] [*Berkhamsted.*

YOUNG CUCKOO IN REED-WARBLER'S NEST.

This photograph was taken in August, an unusually late date to find these birds in the nest.

apparently washed out—a supposition justified by the discovery still later that the water in which captive species had been bathing was strongly tinged with colour. A little more than thirty years ago these facts came under the notice of Professor Church, who, as a result of a thorough examination of the mystery, was enabled to announce the discovery of a new animal pigment containing copper, which he called "turacin."

There are twenty-five different species of plantain-eaters, which are divided into two groups—those which have red in the quills and those without. All are forest-dwellers, feeding upon various wild fruits, building a nest of sticks resembling that of a pigeon, and laying therein three white eggs. The majority of the species are crested and brilliantly coloured, but a few are quite soberly clad. The largest of the tribe is nearly 3 feet long, and a brief description of its coloration will serve to convey a notion of the beauty of the more gorgeously clad members. In this species, then, the upper surface of the body is blue, the tail yellow, with a blue base and black bar across the tip, the under surface of the body rufous brown, the bill yellow, with a scarlet tip, and the eye red.

Though the tops of the highest trees seem to be their favourite resort, these birds are found also among the dense tangled masses of creepers near the ground, flitting, when disturbed, in graceful curves, and alighting with crest erected and the tail turned sharply upwards. The powers of flight appear to vary among the different species, some being described as decidedly clumsy on the wing, whilst others, on the contrary, are light and graceful. Shy and very restless, they are very difficult to procure, when wounded running with great speed, and taking shelter in holes in trees. Their flesh is esteemed a great delicacy by the natives. Save during rain or the heat of midday, they appear to be very noisy birds, having a harsh note, varied with cat-like mewings.

CHAPTER XII.

ROLLERS, KINGFISHERS, HORNBILLS, AND HOOPOES.

CROW-LIKE birds of brilliant coloration, the ROLLERS have earned their name from the habit of occasionally rolling or turning over in their flight, after the manner of tumbler-pigeons. One species at least visits Britain occasionally, only to be shot down at once by the insatiable pot-hunter and collector of rare birds. They are birds of wide distribution, occurring over the greater part of the Old World, and, as we have already remarked, of brilliant coloration, blue and green, varied with reddish, being the predominating colours. As with all birds of beautiful plumage, they are subjected to much persecution,

Photo by W. Saville-Kent, F.Z.S.] [Milford-on-Sea.

AUSTRALIAN LAUGHING-KINGFISHER.

The Laughing-kingfisher, or Laughing-jackass, derives its name from its extraordinary note, resembling a demoniacal laugh.

Photo by W. F. Piggott. [*Leighton Buzzard.*

KINGFISHERS AT HOME.

The plumage of this bird is remarkable for the beauty of its iridescent hues.

thousands upon thousands being killed every year in India alone, to supply the demands made by milliners for the decoration of ladies' hats.

Rollers frequent forest country, and travel in pairs or in small companies: some species are entirely insectivorous; others eat also reptiles, frogs, beetles, worms, and grain. Four or five white eggs are laid in a nest made of roots, grass, hair, and feathers, and built in walls, under the eaves of buildings, or in holes of trees or banks.

Equally beautiful as a whole, and far more widely known, are the KINGFISHERS. But just as the common cuckoo has come to overshadow the rest of its tribe, so the COMMON KINGFISHER eclipses all its congeners. For centuries a wealth of fable, held together by a modicum of fact, served to secure for this bird a peculiar interest; whilst to-day, though shorn of much of the importance with which these fables had invested it, this kingfisher is still esteemed one of the most interesting and beautiful of its tribe.

Green and blue are the predominating colours of its upper- and bright chestnut-red of its under-surface; but owing to structural peculiarities of the feathers of the upper-parts, the reflection of the green and blue areas changes with the direction of the light from which the bird is viewed, in the same way that the peacock's train-feathers change according as the light falls upon them.

As is the rule where both sexes are brilliantly coloured, this bird breeds in a hole, which in the present species is generally excavated in the bank of a stream, but sometimes in an old gravel-pit or chalk-pit, a mile or even more from the water. Occasionally the crumbling soil under the roots of an old tree affords sufficient shelter. No nest is made, although what is equivalent to a nest is ultimately formed from the bird's habit of ejecting the indigestible parts of its food on to the floor of the space in which the eggs are laid. In course of time this becomes a cup-shaped structure; but whether, as Professor Newton remarks, by the pleasure of the bird or the moisture of the soil, or both, is unknown. With care the nest may be removed entire, but the slightest jar reduces the whole to the collection of fish-bones and crustacean skeletons of which it was originally composed. There is a tradition, not yet extinct, to the effect that these "nests" are of great pecuniary value, and scarcely a year passes without the authorities at the British Museum being offered such a treasure, at prices varying from a few pounds to a hundred. The nest-chamber is approached by a tunnel sloping upwards, and varying from 8 inches to 3 feet in length, terminating in a chamber some 6 inches in diameter, in which the eggs are laid. These, from six to eight in number, have a pure white, shining shell, tinged with a most exquisite pink colour, which is lost when the eggs are blown.

The young seem to be reared under very unsanitary conditions, for the ejected fish-bones and other hard parts are not reserved entirely for the nest, but gradually distributed along the tunnel approaching it; later, fish brought for the young, but dropped on the way, and the fluid excreta of the parents are added, forming a dripping, fetid mass swarming with maggots. The young, on leaving the nest, are at first tenderly fed and cared for by the parents, but towards the end of the summer seem to be driven away to seek new fishing-grounds for themselves.

Of the many legends that have grown up around this bird, some are well worth repeating. Specially interesting is one related by Professor Newton on the authority of the French naturalist Rolland. This has it that the kingfisher was originally a plain grey bird, and acquired its present bright colours by flying towards the sun on its liberation from Noah's ark, when its upper-surface assumed the hue of the sky above it, and its lower plumage was scorched by the heat of the setting sun to the tint it now bears. Not a few virtues were also attributed to this bird. Its dried body would, it was believed, avert thunder-bolts, or, kept in a wardrobe, preserve from moths the woollen stuffs contained therein, whilst, hung by a thread from the ceiling of a room, it would serve like the more conventional weather-cock to point the direction of the prevailing wind.

Persecuted though it is, the kingfisher is by no means a rare bird in England, and those who will may generally see it by the banks of some slowly flowing stream or lake, or even shallow brook, sometimes even by the seashore. It feeds upon small aquatic insects and crustacea and small fishes, sometimes even, it is said, upon leeches. Perched on some bough overhanging the water, or stump or railing on the bank, it watches patiently, silent and motionless. The moment its prey comes within striking distance it plunges down upon it, disappearing for a moment beneath the surface, to appear the next with its capture in its beak. If this be a fish, it is held crosswise, and borne upwards to the station from which the plunge was made, there to be stunned by a few sharp blows, tossed into the air, dexterously caught, and swallowed head-foremost. At times, however, perhaps when hunger presses, more activity in the capture of food is displayed, the bird hovering suspended over the water, after the custom of the kestrel-hawk.

Although essentially fish-eating birds, a considerable number live far removed from water, obtaining a livelihood by the capture of insects in forest regions, whilst some appear to feed mainly on reptiles. These are known as Wood-kingfishers, to distinguish them from the Water-kingfishers, the typical member of which group has been just described.

Of the WOOD-KINGFISHERS, or KINGHUNTERS, as they are also called, the most beautiful are the RACKET-TAILED KINGFISHERS, so called from the fact that the two middle tail-feathers are produced into two long rods, terminating in a spoon-shaped enlargement. Although represented by no less than twenty distinct species, they have a somewhat limited range, being found only in the Moluccas, New Guinea, and Northern Australia. One of the handsomest of all is the one occurring in Amboina, an island in the Malay Archipelago, where it was discovered by Mr. A. R. Wallace. The

Photo by Scholastic Photo. Co.] *[Parson's Green.*

LAUGHING-KINGFISHERS.

This species has comparatively dull-coloured plumage.

bill, he tells us, is coral-red, the under-surface pure white, the back and wings deep purple, while the shoulders, head, and nape, and some spots on the upper part of the back and wings, are pure azure-blue. The tail is white, narrowly edged with blue. These birds live upon insects and small land-mollusca, which they dart down upon and pick up from the ground just as the fish-eating species pick up a fish.

Photo by C. N. Mavrogeni] [*Smyrna.*

KINGFISHER.

The photograph shows the nature of the favourite haunts of this species.

Of the forest-haunting species, however, the best known is probably the large and, for a kingfisher, dull-coloured LAUGHING-JACKASS, or SETTLER'S CLOCK, of Australia. Its food is of a very mixed character—small mammals, reptiles, insects, and crabs being devoured with equal relish. Since it is not seldom to be seen bearing off a snake in its bill, it may be regarded as a useful bird—supposing, of course, the snake to be of a poisonous variety. A good idea of the bird in its native haunts is given by the late Mr. Wheelwright. "About an hour before sunrise," he writes, "the bushman is awakened by the most discordant sounds, as if a troop of fiends were shouting, whooping, and laughing around him in one wild chorus. This is the morning song of the 'laughing-jackass,' warning his feathered mates that daybreak is at hand. At noon the same wild laugh is heard, and as the sun sinks into the west it again rings through the forest. I shall never forget the first night I slept in the open bush in this country. It was in the Black Forest. I woke about daybreak after a confused sleep, and for some minutes I could not remember where I was, such were the extraordinary sounds that greeted my ears: the fiendish laugh of the jackass, the clear, flute-like notes of the magpie, the hoarse cackle of the wattle-birds . . . and the screaming of thousands of parrots as they dashed through the forest, all giving chorus, formed one of the most extraordinary concerts I have ever heard, and seemed, at the moment, to have been got up for the purpose of welcoming the stranger to this land of wonders on that eventful morning. I have heard it hundreds of times since, but never with the same feelings that I listened to it then. The laughing-jackass is the bushman's clock, and being by no means shy, of a companionable nature, and a constant attendant on the bush-tent and a destroyer of snakes, is regarded, like the robin at home, as a sacred bird in the Australian forests. It is an uncouth-looking bird . . . nearly the size of a crow, of a rich chestnut-brown and dirty white colour, the wings slightly chequered with light blue, after the manner of the British jay. The tail-feathers are long, rather pointed, and barred with brown. . . . It is a common bird in all the forest throughout the year, breeds in the hole of a tree, and the eggs are white."

Whilst the Kingfishers are remarkable for the wondrous beauty of their coloration, the HORNBILLS, their allies, attract our attention rather by the grotesqueness of their shape, due to the enormous size of the bill, and the still more remarkable horny excrescences which surmount it in not a few species, forming what is known as a "casque." Absent in some of the smaller and possibly more primitive forms, its gradual development may be traced, beginning with a series of corrugations along the ridge of the base of the bill, gradually increasing, to form, in the most extreme cases, huge superstructures of quaint shapes, and apparently of great solidity. As a matter of fact, however, these casques are practically hollow, save in the case of the HELMET-HORNBILL of the Malay countries, in which the horny sheath is backed by solid supports of bone, whilst the front of the sheath itself is of great thickness and surprising density, and is used by the natives for carving and making brooches and other ornaments. The use of this powerful hammer—for such it may possibly be—is unknown.

Hornbills are forest-birds, feeding upon fruit and insects, the latter being captured on the wing. With large bill and wings, a long tail, and a relatively small body and short legs, they are rather unwieldy birds, and yet, for many reasons, unusually interesting. Their nesting habits are unique, and quite worth recounting here at some length. Of the many accounts, one of the most interesting, as well as one of the latest, is that of Mr. Charles Hose, of Borneo.

"The nest," he writes, "is always built in the hollow of a large tree—the hollow, be it noted, being always due to disease of the tree or the ravages of termites, not to the personal labours of the birds. The bottom of this cavity is often plugged by a termites' nest and accumulation of decayed wood, and on the upper surface of this is made the nest, a very rough-and-ready structure, composed simply of the feathers of the female. The hollow of the tree communicates with the exterior air by means of a long aperture, which, just before the period of incubation, is closed up almost entirely by the male, simply leaving a long slit open, up and down which the beak of the enclosed female can move. The substance used in thus closing the aperture closely resembles some vegetable resin, and is probably composed of a gastric secretion, combined with the woody fragments of fruit. It should be noticed that this slit is always in close proximity to the nest, so that the female can easily protrude her beak

Photo by W. Reid] *[Wishaw, N.B.*

LAUGHING-JACKASS.

Frequently known as the Settler's Clock.

Photo by Scholastic Photo. Co.] *[Parson's Green.*

CRESTED HORNBILL.

The Hornbills derive their name from the great size of the bill.

for food without moving from her sitting position. During incubation the male bird supplies the female with food in the form of pellets of fruit, seeds, insects, portions of reptiles, etc., the pellets being enclosed each in a skin of rubber-like consistency. While feeding the female, the male clings to the bark of the tree, or sits on a branch if conveniently near, and jerks these pellets into the gaping beak of the hen, two to four pellets forming a meal. During mastication (for it is a mistake to suppose that the hornbills always bolt their food entire) some fragments of the pellets fall to the ground, and seeds which these fragments may contain take root, germinate, and sprout, and the natives can judge approximately of the date of incubation by the age of the seedlings. When these are four-leaved, the eggs have been hatched out for two or three weeks. At this stage, though not always so early, the mother bird leaves the nest, breaking down the gluey substance with her beak to effect an exit; having left the nest, the aperture through which she left is carefully closed up again, leaving the slit as before, and now both male and female devote their energies to feeding the young birds, which in course of time follow the example of their mother and leave their place of imprisonment. It is more than probable that this gluing up first of the mother bird and her eggs and afterwards of the nestlings alone is solely a means of protection against predacious carnivora. . . .

"The nesting-season is during May and June, and it is noteworthy that the birds, if undisturbed, return to the same nesting-place every year. The saplings at the foot of the tree, sprung from seeds dropped in the first year of paring, afford signs to the natives of the number of years during which the tree has been occupied. If during paring or incubation the female or female and young are destroyed, the male takes to himself another mate, and repairs to the same nesting-place; if, however, the male and female are destroyed, the nest is never reoccupied by other pairs. An interesting incident was observed while on Mount Dulit. Espying on a tree the external signs of a hornbill's nest, and a male rhinoceros perched close by, I shot the male, and while waiting for my Dyak collectors to make a ladder up the tree to secure the female, I observed several young male birds fly to the nest and assiduously ply the bereaved widow with food, a fact which seems to indicate a competition in the matrimonial market of the bird-world as severe as that among human beings. It is no easy matter to procure embryos or nestlings of hornbills, for the natives are inordinately fond of both as articles of diet, and, further, are always anxious to secure the tail-feathers of the adults to adorn their war-coats and hats.

"The native method of catching the female during incubation is ingenious, though decidedly brutal. The tree is scaled, the resin-like substance is broken away, and the frightened bird flies from her nest up the hollow trunk of the tree, but is ignominiously brought down by means of a thorny stick (the thorns point downward), which is thrust after and twisted about until a firm grip in her plumage is obtained. The Dyaks, never very faithful observers of nature, believe that the female is shut up by the male, so that after hatching her eggs she may die, the maggots in her putrefying body affording food for the young. One very curious habit of the rhinoceros-hornbill which I have not hitherto seen noted is the rapid jumping up and down on a branch with both feet together. This jumping motion is imitated by the Kyans and Dyaks in their dances, the figure being known to the Kyans as 'wan blingong.'"

Photo by W. P. Dando, F.Z.S.] *[Regent's Park.*

CONCAVE-CASQUED HORNBILL, INDIA.

The noise made by hornbills on the wing is said to resemble that of a steam-engine.

That the HOOPOES, unlike as they may be in general appearance, are nevertheless intimately related to the Hornbills there can be no doubt. Graceful in contour and pleasing in coloration, it is a pity that the species which so frequently visits Britain, and has on more than one occasion nested there, should be so ruthlessly shot down immediately its presence is discovered. Save the wings and tail, the body is of a light cinnamon colour, whilst the head is surmounted by a magnificent crest of black-and-white-tipped feathers, which can be raised or depressed at the pleasure of the bird: the excepted portions of the plumage—the wings and tail—are buff, varied with bands of black and white. Thus it may be truthfully said to be a conspicuously coloured bird; yet this same livery seems also to come under the head of protective coloration, for we are assured that, when danger threatens, the bird throws itself flat upon the ground, spreads out its wings, and at once becomes transformed into what rather resembles a heap of rags than a bird. Escape by flight, however, instead of subterfuge, seems also at times to be resorted to, since, when pursued by a falcon, it will mount rapidly to a great height, and not seldom effect its escape.

Photo by Scholastic Photo. Co.] *[Parson's Green.*

GROUND-HORNBILL.

The legs of the ground-hornbill are much longer than those of its allies.

The domestic habits of the hoopoe are, however, by no means so charming as one would expect to find in so beautiful a bird. "All observers agree," writes Professor Newton, "in stating that it delights to find its food among filth of the most abominable description, and this especially in its winter quarters. But where it breeds, its nest—usually in the hole of a tree or of a wall—is not only partly composed of the foulest materials, but its condition becomes worse as incubation proceeds, for the hen scarcely ever leaves her eggs, being assiduously fed by the cock as she sits

Photo by Scholastic Photo. Co.] [Parson's Green

HOOPOE.

An occasional visitor to the British Isles.

(a feature strongly recalling the custom of the Hornbills), and when the young are hatched their fæces are not removed by their parents, as is the case with most birds, but are discharged in the immediate neighbourhood of the nest, the unsanitary condition of which can readily be imagined. Worms, grubs, and insects generally, form the hoopoes' food, and upon it they get so fat in autumn that they are esteemed a delicate morsel in some of the countries of Southern Europe, and especially by the Christian population of Constantinople."

Beside the EUROPEAN HOOPOE, which also extends into Northern Africa, four other species are known, three of which are African, whilst a fourth ranges from India to Hainan.

Nearly related to the birds we have just described are the WOOD-HOOPOES. They differ from their allies in being crestless, having a more curved bill, and a plumage of metallic purple, with a white patch on the wings and white markings on the tail. Their habits resemble those of their more highly coloured relatives.

CHAPTER XIII.

BEE-EATERS, MOTMOTS, TODIES, COLIES, AND TROGONS.

IN the present chapter we deal with a number of birds of singular beauty and gracefulness. In their coloration green predominates, thus recalling the Rollers, Parrots, Plantain-eaters, and Kingfishers, all of which groups, as we have seen, contain a large proportion of green species.

The BEE-EATERS, like the Kingfishers, Hornbills, and Hoopoes, have a foot of quite peculiar structure, the middle and outer toes being joined together throughout the greater part of their length. They are an Old World group, ranging from the British Islands to Australia, in the American Continent their place being taken by the Motmots and Jacamars, of which we shall speak presently. They are especially plentiful in the African region, somewhat less so in the Indian, the temperate regions of the Old World possessing but few species.

On rare occasions one species visits the British Islands. This is, furthermore, one of the most beautiful of the group. It has the head, neck, upper back, and a broad wing-bar of a ruddy-brown colour; the lower back buff colour; green wings and tail, with black tips to the middle tail-feathers, which are longer than the rest. The forehead is pale green and white; the ear-coverts are black; and the throat bright yellow, divided from the greenish-blue under-parts by a black band. "The name Bee-eater," writes Mr. Evans, "is well deserved, for in Spain [it] is a perfect pest to the bee-keeper, catching the workers as they enter and leave the hives." Like the Kingfishers, the indigestible parts of the food are cast up and deposited around the eggs, though bee-eaters do not appear to form a nest of them, as with the Kingfishers.

From four to six eggs of a beautiful glossy white colour are deposited in holes in banks, or—and this is worthy of special notice—in tunnels bored vertically downwards in level ground for a distance of from 3 to 10 feet. How this is done is a mystery, for the bird's beak and feet look by no means equal to such a task. No nest appears to be made, the eggs being deposited at the extremity of the burrow without further preparation. Two species of the group, however, are said to form an exception, constructing a nest of straw and feathers.

Photo by A. S. Rudland & Sons.

BEE-EATER.

A native of the Malay countries. The long feathers on the throat are bright scarlet.

These two, as well as the members of the genus to which the British bird belongs, apparently breed in colonies.

Unfortunately for the bee-eater, its flesh is palatable, whilst its plumage is in great demand for millinery purposes. Its persecution is of long standing, since more than 300 years ago Belon witnessed a particularly cruel experiment practised by the boys in Crete. Transfixing a beetle with a bent pin, to the head of which a thread was tied, and then holding its other end with their hand, they would let the insect fly. The bee-eater, which catches most of its prey on the wing, would dart upon it, and, swallowing the bait, be caught by the hook.

Not unlike the Bee-eaters in general appearance and coloration, the MOTMOTS are birds of peculiar interest, and this on account of a remarkable habit of one of their tribe—a habit which is perfectly unique, and to which we shall return presently. Belonging, as we have already remarked, to the New World, they range from Southern Mexico to Paraguay, inhabiting dense forests, and being but rarely seen. The plumage is somewhat loose in character—green, blue, cinnamon, and black in colour. The beak has the margins serrated, or saw-like; whilst the feet resemble those of the Kingfishers and Bee-eaters. As with the Bee-eaters, no nest is made. The eggs, three or four in number and creamy white in colour, are deposited in a hole bored by the birds themselves in a tree or bank, both sexes sharing in the work of incubation. Their food consists of insects caught in the air, small reptiles, and fruit.

The remarkable habit to which we have referred is displayed by the species known as the RACKET-TAILED MOTMOT, from the fact that the two middle tail-feathers project beyond the others, and have the greater part of the shaft bare, but terminating in a spoon-shaped expansion. In this there is nothing unusual, for such racket-feathers are common amongst birds. In this particular case, however, the feathers were originally entire, and acquired their characteristic shape artificially, the bird nibbling away the vane on either side of the shaft with its bill until the required shape is obtained. Such an act of conscious decoration on the part of a bird is elsewhere unknown throughout the whole class.

The TODIES are diminutive allies of the Motmots, frequenting hilly districts and woods. They sit with the beak pointed upwards, the head drawn in close to the body, and the plumage puffed out, apparently oblivious of all around them—at least it would seem so, since at such times they may be caught with a butterfly-net. Like their larger allies, they are green in coloration, but have a light red throat, and yellowish-white or pinkish under-parts, with green or pink flank-feathers. They vary in length from 3 to 4½ inches.

Photo by A. S. Rudland & Sons.

RACKET-TAILED MOTMOT.

Note the mutilated tail-feathers.

The COLIES, or MOUSE-BIRDS, of South Africa are small, crested, long-tailed, loose-plumaged birds whose exact relationships are somewhat puzzling. The name Mouse-bird is given on account of the habit of creeping along the boughs of trees with the whole foot applied to the branch. The toes are peculiar in that all turn forwards, and are commonly so retained. About ten species are known, ranging from Abyssinia southwards.

Resplendent without doubt are the majority of the forms which we have been lately considering, but probably the palm for gorgeous coloration should be given to the TROGONS—at least they must be allowed to share the honours with the Humming-birds.

The most splendid of all is the QUEZAL, the male of which has a train of great length, resembling at first sight a tail. But, as in the peacock, this is formed by enormously elongated tail-coverts, concealing the true tail. These tail-coverts differ, however, markedly from those in the peacock in that they are not erectile, but pendent. The head is ornamented with a large, rounded crest; the ground-colour of the upper parts of the plumage is of brilliant metallic green; the under parts from the chest downwards are of a deep blood-red. Certain of the covert-feathers of the wing form elegant drooping plumes, hanging down on either side and giving a wonderfully beautiful effect.

The late Mr. Salvin's account of this bird in its wild state is well worth quoting. Hunting with a native for this bird in the forest, where alone it is to be met with, he writes: "A distant clattering note indicates that the bird is on the wing. He settles—a splendid male—on a bough of a tree, not seventy yards from where we are hidden. Cipriano wants to creep up to within shot, but I keep him back, wishing to risk the chance of losing a specimen rather than miss such an opportunity of seeing the bird in its living state, and of watching its movements. It sits almost motionless on its perch, the body remaining in the same position, the head only moving from side to side. The tail is occasionally jerked open and closed again, and now and then slightly raised, causing the long tail-coverts to vibrate gracefully. I have not seen all. A ripe fruit catches the quezal's eye, and he darts from his perch, hovers for a moment, picks the berry, and returns to his former position. This is done with a degree of elegance that defies description."

CHAPTER XIV.

TOUCANS, HONEY-GUIDES, JACAMARS AND PUFF-BIRDS, BARBETS AND WOODPECKERS.

GAUDY in plumage, and somewhat ungainly in appearance, it must nevertheless be admitted that the TOUCANS form an exceedingly interesting group of birds. On account of their huge and gaily coloured beaks, they have been imagined to be related to the Hornbills; but even judging by this character, the two groups may be readily distinguished; for whereas the typical beak of the hornbill is surmounted by a large casque, the beak of the toucan is never so ornamented. The solid appearance of the beak in the toucan, by the way, is as much a fiction as with the hornbill, since the horny sheath is supported, not on a core of solid bone, but on a frame of delicate bony filigree-work, the spaces being filled by air. The coloration of the plumage (which is somewhat loose in character), as well as of the bare skin round the eye and the beak-sheath, is most brilliant, and displays immense variation amongst the different species.

Shy and restless in their habits, toucans travel generally in small flocks amongst the forest-trees and mangrove-swamps in search of food, which consists mainly of fruits and seeds, varying this diet occasionally with ants and caterpillars. It is to this diet of fruit that the great size of the bill and its peculiar saw-like edges are to be traced—at least this is the opinion of the great traveller-naturalist Bates, who had so many opportunities of watching these birds. "Flowers and fruit," he writes, "on the crowns of the large trees of South American forests grow principally towards the end of slender twigs, which will not bear any considerable weight. All animals, therefore, which feed principally upon fruit, or on insects contained in flowers, must, of course, have some means of reaching the ends of the stalks from a distance. Monkeys obtain their food by stretching forth their long arms, and in some instances their tails, to bring the fruit near to their mouths; humming-birds are endowed with highly perfected organs of flight, with corresponding muscular development, by which they are enabled to sustain themselves on the wing before blossoms whilst rifling them of their contents; [and the long bill of the toucan enables it] to reach and devour fruit whilst remaining seated, and thus to counterbalance the disadvantage which its heavy body and gluttonous appetite would otherwise give it in the competition with allied groups of birds."

Photo by A. S. Rudland & Sons.

TROGON.

Trogons haunt the recesses of the thickest forests.

Toucans appear to be much esteemed as articles of food—at least during the months of June and July, when these birds get very fat, the flesh being exceedingly sweet and tender. They nest in holes of trees at a great height from the ground, and lay white eggs.

One of the most remarkable of the group is the CURL-CRESTED TOUCAN, from the fact that the feathers on the crown of the head are peculiarly modified to form scroll-like, glossy curls, which have been compared to shavings of steel or ebony. Mr. Bates writes: "I had an amusing adventure one day with one of these birds. I had shot one from a rather high tree in a dark glen in the forest, and entered the thicket where the bird had fallen to secure my booty. It was only wounded, and on my attempting to seize it set up a loud scream. In an instant, as if by magic, the shady nook seemed alive with these birds, although there was certainly none visible when I entered the jungle. They descended towards me, hopping from bough to bough, some of them swinging on the loops and cables of woody lianas, and all croaking and fluttering their wings like so many furies. If I had had a long stick in my hand, I could have knocked several of them over. After killing the wounded one, I began to prepare for obtaining more specimens and punishing the viragos for their boldness. But the screaming of their companion having ceased, they remounted the trees, and before I could reload every one of them had disappeared."

With neither charm of colour nor peculiar shape, the small African birds known as HONEY-GUIDES are some of the most remarkable of birds, and this on account of a quite unique habit of inducing other animals, not even excepting man, to hunt for them. Sir John Kirk, writing of its habits in the Zambesi district, says: "The honey-guide is found in forests and often far from water, even during the dry season. On observing a man, it comes fluttering from branch to branch in the neighbouring trees, calling attention. If this be responded to—as the natives do by whistling and starting to their feet—the bird will go in a certain direction, and remain at a little distance, hopping from one tree to another. On being followed, it goes further; and so it will guide the way to a nest of bees. When this is reached, it flies about, but no longer guides; and then some knowledge is required to discover the nest, even when pointed out to within a few trees. I have known this bird, if the man, after taking up the direction for a little, then turns away, come back and offer to point out another nest in a different part. But if it does not know of two nests, it will remain behind. The difficulty is that the bird will point to tame bees in a bark hive as readily as to those in the forest. This is natural, as the bee is the same, the bark hive . . . being simply fastened up in a tree, and left for the bees to come to. . . . The object the bird has in view is clearly the young bees. It will guide to nests having no honey, and seems equally delighted if the comb containing the grubs is torn out, when it is seen pecking at it."

Photo by A. S. Rudland & Sons.

CURL-CRESTED TOUCAN.

So called from the curiously curled feathers on the head, resembling black and glistening shavings.

An old rumour had it that honey-guides occasionally lured men on to spots where lions or other large and dangerous beasts lay hid. No credence whatever is now given to such tales, it being readily understood that the bird's course may by accident pass directly above perils of this kind, without the slightest cognisance of this on the part of the bird.

The honey-guide, however, presses into its service one of the lower mammals—the ratel. The fondness of this animal for bees is well known, and by none better than this little bird, which, by pointing out nests to its more powerful companion, earns as a reward the broken bits which remain after the feast.

Allies of the sombre-coloured Honey-guides are the JACAMARS and PUFF-BIRDS. The former are rather handsome birds, though small, having the upper-parts of a metallic coppery golden green, and more or less rufous below. Ranging from Mexico to South Brazil, they may usually be found on the outskirts of forests, near water, sitting perched on the bare boughs of lofty trees for hours at a time. They feed on moths and other insects, caught on the wing, and brought back and crushed against the bough before swallowing. They lay white eggs in the holes of trees.

The PUFF-BIRDS, though closely allied to the foregoing, are more soberly clad. Black, brown, and rufous in hue, they lack the resplendent metallic markings of the Jacamars. Their geographical range extends from Guatemala and Honduras to Argentina. Though numerous species and genera are known, the nest and eggs appear to have been discovered in the case of one species only: these were found in a hole in a bank, and contained two shining white eggs.

The BARBETS are possibly more closely related to the Honey-guides than the Jacamars and Puff-birds. Brilliantly coloured, and having a plumage exhibiting violent contrasts of red, blue, purple, and yellow, on a green ground, sometimes with crests, bare skin round the eye, and brightly coloured bills, the barbets are, in spite of a somewhat hairy appearance, exceedingly attractive birds.

Forest-dwellers, like their allies, they feed upon fruit, seeds, insects, bark, and buds; but so noiseless are they said to be when feeding that their presence is betrayed only by the falling of berries they have accidentally released.

It is interesting to note that the geographical range of the barbet is much wider than that of its immediate allies, extending through tropical Asia, Africa, and America.

The Woodpecker Tribe constitutes a large group, generally divided into two sections—the WOODPECKERS and the WRYNECKS.

The former are characterised by their large heads and very powerful bills and long and exceedingly stiff tails. The feet are also peculiar, two toes pointing directly forwards and two backwards. Beak, feet, and tail are all specially adapted to the peculiar habits of these birds, which pass their lives upon trees, climbing the trunks, and searching the interstices of the bark for ants, or drilling holes into the unsound portions of the trunk itself for the purpose of extracting the grubs which feed upon decaying wood.

Photo by A. S. Rudland & Sons.

HONEY-GUIDE.

The name is bestowed on account of its remarkable habit of drawing attention to bees' nests.

Photo by A. S. Rudland & Sons.

A FAMILY OF GREATER SPOTTED WOODPECKERS.

This woodpecker is a British species.

That ants and other small insects form the staple diet of the woodpecker is evident from the extraordinary length of the tongue. This is a long, worm-like structure, capable of being protruded many inches from the beak, and covered with a sticky secretion, so that, thrust into colonies of ants, it quickly becomes covered with them, to be withdrawn immediately into the mouth and cleared again for further action.

Woodpeckers are all birds of bright plumage, some particularly so, and have a wide geographical distribution, inhabiting all parts of the world save Madagascar, the Australasian region, and Egypt.

Three species occur in the British Islands, though they are exceedingly rare in Scotland and Ireland. The GREEN WOODPECKER is a particularly handsome bird. Grass-green is the predominating colour of its livery, relieved by a light scarlet cap, a golden patch over the lower part of the back, and chequered bars on the wings and quills.

Photo by W. F. Piggott] [*Leighton Buzzard.*

LESSER SPOTTED WOODPECKERS

One of the members of the group is using its stiff tail feathers as a support.

Scarcely less beautiful, in their way, are the GREATER and LESSER SPOTTED WOODPECKERS. The plumage of these birds has a very rich effect, steely blue-black and white being contrasted with scarlet.

The SPOTTED and BLACK WOODPECKERS are remarkable for a curious drumming sound, so powerful as to be distinctly audible even a mile off. It appears to be caused by hammering vigorously on the bark of some rotten branch, the bird's head moving with amazing rapidity as it beats out this curious tattoo.

Three North American species, known as SAP-SUCKERS, have the curious habit of piercing the boles of trees for the purpose of procuring the sap which flows copiously when the tree is so "tapped." Another species of the same region seems to be possessed of a persistent dread of famine, storing up immense quantities of nuts, which it appears never afterwards to use. These nuts are tightly fixed into holes in the bark of trees, and in such numbers that "a large pine 40 or 50 feet high will present the appearance of being closely studded with brass nails, the heads only being visible."

The WRYNECKS differ from the Woodpeckers mainly in that the tail-feathers are soft instead of spiny. Although sombre, the plumage is yet very beautiful, having a velvety appearance, variegated with pearl-grey, powdered or dusted over a general groundwork of nut-brown, buff, and grey. Bars and fine lines add still more to the general effect, and render description still more difficult. One species is common in England. It is known also as the CUCKOO'S MATE and the SNAKE-BIRD. The former name is given in allusion to the fact that it arrives with the cuckoo, the latter from its strange habit of writhing its head and neck, and also on account of its curious hissing note, made when disturbed on its nest. It has the long, worm-like tongue of the woodpecker, but without a barbed tip.

The habit of writhing the head and neck often serves the wryneck in good stead. Nesting in a hole in a tree, escape is difficult so soon as the discoverer has come to close quarters. The untried egg-collector, for instance, peering down into the nest, and seeing nothing distinctly, but only a moving head, and hearing a hissing sound, imagines the hole to be tenanted by a snake, and beats a hasty retreat, only to catch a glimpse, a moment later, of the bird hurrying out of its perilous hiding-place. Should he, however, discovering the true state of affairs, put down his hand and seize the bird, it will adopt yet other resources. Clinging tightly to its captor's finger, it will ruffle up its feathers, stretch out its neck, and at the same time move it jerkily and stiffly about, and finally, closing its eyes, hang downwards, as if dead. Then, before the puzzled captor has had time to realise what has happened, it loosens its hold and takes instant flight.

The young are easily, though rarely, tamed, and form extremely interesting pets, feeding readily from the hand, and affording endless amusement by their remarkable manner of capturing flies and other insects; but they do not appear to live long in confinement.

The wryneck is one of the few birds which will persistently go on laying eggs, no matter how many times they may be stolen from the nest. A case is on record where as many as forty-two were laid in a single summer by one bird—an exceedingly cruel experiment.

Photo by C. Reid, Wishaw.

WAXBILLS.

Waxbills are relatives of the Weaver birds, and take their name from the waxen appearance of the beak, which is coral red.

Photo by C. Reid, Wishaw.

INDIGO FINCHES.

The Indigo Finch or Indigo Bird is a well known member of a group of American Finches, of which the Nonpareil Finch is another representative.

Photo by Dr. R. W. Shufeldt] [*Washington.*

AMERICAN CROW.

In some parts of the United States this crow, everywhere regarded as a pest, is replaced by the raven.

CHAPTER XV.

THE PERCHING-BIRDS.

SUCH an enormous host are included under this head—nearly 6,000 out of the total of 13,000 known birds—and so great are the difficulties connected with their systematic arrangement, that it has been considered best to begin the present chapter with the highest instead of the lowest types of the group.

The extensive group of Perching-birds is defined mainly from the characters afforded by the structure of the voice-organ, and these are of much too technical a nature to be discussed

Photo by C. Reid] [*Wishaw, N.B.*

JACKDAWS.

It is believed that the Jackdaw is the bird referred to by Shakespeare as the Russet-pated Chough (*Midsummer-Night's Dream*, iii. 2).

here. Suffice it to say that, on account of these characters, the group is further divided into two sections, and each section again divided into two.

THE CROWS, ORIOLES, FINCHES, AND THEIR ALLIES.

At the head of the tribe stands, by general though by no means universal consent, the Crow-Family, of which the recognised chief is the RAVEN, a bird which has for thousands of years commanded a more than passing interest amongst mankind. Renowned as the truant from the Ark, or as the wonderful minister of the prophet Elijah, there are few even of the youngest amongst us who do not know of its striking personality. The poet and the dramatist have both made use of the raven, and it would seem that it has even found a place in the mythology of the Red Indian. The smaller relatives of this celebrated bird, the Rook, the Carrion-crow, and the Jackdaw, and more distantly the Jay and the Magpie, are doubtless as familiar to our readers as the raven.

Although probably unknown to many, the Chough, with its glossy black plumage and brilliant red bill and feet, is a British bird, and lives still in certain parts of England, though fast verging on extinction.

Another very remarkable member of the family is the Huia, and this on account of the fact that the male and female differ markedly in respect of the shape of the bill, this being in the female long and sickle-shaped, and in the male short and cone-shaped. This bird frequents the wooded regions of North Island, New Zealand, living upon grubs found in decaying wood, and on berries. The female procures the grubs by probing the holes which they have made in the sounder wood, the male by breaking away the decayed portions of the tree; but occasionally it happens that, having cleared away as much of the decayed material as possible, the latter is unable to reach his prey, in which case he calls up the female, and yields his find to her, to extricate with her longer bill. So great a difference in the form of the bill in the sexes of the same species is elsewhere unknown among birds.

Photo by Dr. R. W. Shufeldt] [*Washington.*

YOUNG AMERICAN BLUE JAY (NATURAL SIZE).

The blue jay is a most remarkable mimic.

The Crows hold the important position of head of the Class birds, yet they are far outshone in splendour by many of the groups already examined, though, with the exception perhaps of the Humming-birds, these all pale before the Birds of Paradise.

Varying in size from a crow to a thrush, the best known of the latter is the Great Bird of Paradise, which was discovered towards the end of the sixteenth century, if not earlier. On their first discovery it was popularly supposed that these birds lived in the air, turning always to the sun, and never alighting on the earth till they died, for they had neither feet nor wings. Hence the Malay traders called them "God's Birds," the Portuguese "Birds of the Sun," and the Dutch "Paradise-birds." Seventeen or eighteen inches long, these birds have the body, wings, and tail of a rich coffee-brown, which deepens on the breast to a blackish violet or purple-brown. The top of the head and neck are of a delicate straw-yellow, the feathers being short and close-set, resembling velvet. The throat-feathers have a scaly appearance, and are emerald-green in colour. The flank-feathers on either side of the body form a dense mass of long, delicate, waving plumes, sometimes 2 feet in length, of an intense orange colour, and shining with a wonderful gloss. These feathers can be raised and spread out at pleasure, so as to almost conceal the wearer in a fountain-like rain of feathers. This wonderful plumage is worn by the male only, the female being quite plainly dressed. In May, when they are in full dress, the males

Photo by C. Reid] [*Wishaw, N.B.*

A PAIR OF MAGPIES.

When taken young, the magpie is easily tamed, and can be taught to imitate human sounds.

assemble early in the morning to exhibit themselves, forming what are known as "dancing-parties," which take place on the topmost boughs of some giant tree. "From a dozen to twenty birds assemble together," writes Mr. Alfred Russel Wallace, "raise up their wings, stretch out their necks, and elevate their exquisite plumes, keeping them in continual vibration. Betweenwhiles they fly across from branch to branch in great excitement, so that the whole tree is filled with waving plumes in every variety of attitude and motion." The native hunter marks these playing-places, builds a shelter of palm-leaves in a convenient situation among the branches, and ensconces himself under it before daylight, armed with a bow and a number of arrows terminating in a round knob. When the dance is in full swing, he shoots through the roof of his shelter with the blunt arrows, stunning every bird he strikes, which, falling down at once, are immediately picked up by a boy in waiting below. Often a considerable number will be thus secured before the alarm is taken.

Without coloured figures, or very numerous photographs from living birds, which we can hardly hope to get, it would be impossible, except at the risk of being wearisome, to describe all the wonderful combinations of form and colour which the feathers of the birds of paradise display. Breast-shields of metallic sheen, fans and crests in wonderful variety, feathers of a texture like velvet, or gorgeous colours, confuse one in their variety and combination.

Let it suffice to mention only the last discovered species—the KING OF SAXONY'S BIRD OF PARADISE. "Velvety black above," writes Dr. Sharpe, "and yellowish below, there is nothing very striking in the aspect of the bird itself, which is smaller than our song-thrush. But the 'streamers' which it carries! Poised . . . on either side of the head is a long, shaft-like plume, from which depends, on the lower side only, a series of little flags of blue enamel, each quite separate from the one which precedes it, and not of a feathery structure in the least."

Photo by Scholastic Photo. Co.] [Parson's Green.

CORNISH CHOUGH.

Very nearly extinct as a British bird.

Close allies of the Birds of Paradise are the remarkable BOWER-BIRDS of Australia. Conspicuously beautiful in coloration as are some members of this tribe, they are celebrated not so much on this account as for an extraordinary habit of constructing "bowers" or "playing-grounds"—a trait which appears absolutely unique among birds. "These constructions," observes Mr. Gould, "consist in a collection of pieces of stick or grass, formed into a bower; or one of them (that of the SPOTTED BOWER-BIRD) might be called an avenue, being about 3 feet in length, and 7 or 8 inches broad inside; a transverse section giving the figure of a horse-shoe, the round part downwards. They are used by the birds as a playing-house, or 'run,' as it is termed, and are used by the males to attract the females. The 'run' of the SATIN-BIRD is much smaller, being less than 1 foot in length, and, moreover, differs from that just described in being decorated with the highly coloured feathers of the Parrot Tribe. The SPOTTED BOWER-BIRD, on the other hand, collects around its 'run' a quantity of stones, shells, bleached bones, etc.; they are also strewed down the centre within."

Photo by W. Saville-Kent, F.Z.S.] [Milford-on-Sea.

KING BIRD OF PARADISE.

A native of New Guinea; remarkable for the curled tail-feathers.

More wonderful still are the structures reared by the GARDENER-BIRD of New Guinea, presenting, as Professor Newton remarks, "not only a modification of bower-building, but an appreciation of beauty perhaps unparalleled in the animal world. . . . This species . . . builds at the foot of a small tree a kind of hut or cabin . . . some 2 feet in height, roofed with orchid-stems that slope to the ground, regularly radiating from the central support, which is covered with a conical mass of moss, and sheltering a gallery around it. One side of this hut is left open, and in front of it is arranged a bed of verdant moss, bedecked with blossoms and berries of the brightest colours. As these ornaments wither they are removed to a heap behind the hut, and replaced by others that are

Photo by W. Saville-Kent, F.Z.S.] *[Milford-on-Sea.*

QUEENSLAND RIFLE-BIRD.

This unique Australian representative of the Birds of Paradise is about the size of a pigeon. Its plumage is black with a purple sheen; the throat is brilliant metallic emerald-green, like that of a humming-bird.

fresh. The hut is circular and some 3 feet in diameter, and the mossy lawn in front of it nearly twice that expanse. Each hut and garden are, it is believed, though not known, the work of a single pair of birds, or perhaps of the male only; and it may be observed that this species, as its trivial name implies, is wholly inornate in plumage. Not less remarkable is the more recently described 'bower' of the GOLDEN BOWER-BIRD. . . . This structure is said . . . to be piled up almost horizontally around the base of a tree to the height of from 4 to 6 feet, and around it are a number of hut-like fabrics, having the look of a dwarfed native camp." Allied species, though building no bowers, yet clear a space of ground some 8 or 9 feet in diameter, on which to display themselves, and ornament this with little heaps of gaily tinted leaves, replacing them as they fade with fresh specimens.

We pass next to the birds of the Starling Family, of which the BRITISH STARLING is the type. A bird so familiar needs no description here; but we may draw attention to the many interesting phases of plumage this species undergoes.

The first plumage is a uniform greyish brown. Later black feathers, with large white spots at the tips, make their appearance among the brown. These spotted feathers eventually replace the brown, and the bird enters upon a second quite distinct phase—a black, spotted with white. Gradually this gives place to a plumage entirely unspotted, the feathers on the breast being spear-shaped. In the adult dress a wondrous variety of metallic reflections is acquired—green, purple, and violet.

Associating in the autumn and winter in large flocks, starlings move from place to place in search of food. Sometimes the number of birds in these combined flocks rises to an enormous figure. One of the largest of these gatherings recorded in England existed on the property of the late Mr. Miles near Bristol. "This locality is an evergreen plantation . . . covering some acres, to which these birds repair

Photo by W. Saville-Kent, F.Z.S.] *[Milford-on-Sea.*

RED BIRD OF PARADISE.

Found only on the small island of Waigiou, off the north-west coast of New Guinea.

of an evening . . . by millions, from the low grounds about the Severn, where their noise and stench are something altogether unusual. By packing in such myriads upon evergreens, they have stripped them of their leaves, except just at the tops, and have driven the pheasants, for whom the plantation was intended, quite away from the ground. In the daytime, when the birds are not there, the stench is still excessive. Mr. Miles was about to cut the whole plantation down, to get rid of them, two years ago, but I begged him not to do so, on account of the curiosity of the scene, and he has since been well pleased that he abstained."

A similar but still larger congregation has been described; in this, about the year 1845, from 150,000 to 200,000 starlings were computed to rest every night, between the end of October and the end of March, in certain trees in the gardens of the Zoological Society in Dublin. The roof of St. Patrick's Cathedral, in the heart of Dublin, has from time to time been resorted to, as many as 2,000 seeking shelter there. "Possessing very considerable powers of wing," observes Yarrell, "these are turned to account in an extraordinary manner by the birds composing the flock. They wheel, close, open out, rise and descend, as if each were obeying a commander, and all this is done with the utmost marvellous precision while the flock is proceeding at a rapid pace through the air. At times it may extend in a long and nearly straight thread; suddenly an undulation is visible along the line, and in a moment it takes the form of a thin and smoke-like cloud; another moment, and it is a dense and almost perfect globe; then possibly, having preserved this appearance for a perceptibly longer time, it becomes pear-shaped, and in another instant has assumed a spiral figure; an instant after it has spread out like a sheet, and its members are streaming softly along the ground, perhaps to alight, or perhaps once more to mount aloft and circle as before." There are few more magnificent sights in the world than a flock of starlings when performing evolutions of this kind.

Photo by C. Reid] *[Wishaw, N.B.*

YOUNG STARLINGS.

Starlings, if taken when young, are easily tamed and make excellent pets.

Differing much, not only in general appearance, but also in coloration, from the common starling is the Rose-coloured Starling, so called from the beautiful rose-pink colour of the back and breast, set off by the rest of the plumage, which is black, glossed with violet, blue, and green reflections. This handsome bird occasionally visits Britain. Feeding largely upon locusts, these birds are much affected in their movements by the peregrinations of these pests; and this accounts for the sporadic appearance of the rose-coloured starling in huge flocks in places where it is generally seldom seen.

Dull in appearance, ungraceful in flight, and with a harsh, unmusical note, the starling

Photo by J. T. Newman] [*Berkhamsted.*

COMMON STARLING.

Starlings appear to be on the increase in Scotland, whilst larks are said to be on the decrease, owing to the destruction of their eggs by the former.

known as the OX-PECKER would seem at first sight to have little to recommend it; yet it is one of the benefactors of the larger African mammals, clearing them of flies and other insect-pests. Buffaloes, rhinoceroses, elephants, are alike grateful for its services, as it climbs about their huge bodies, picking off the liliputian enemies by which they are beset. But little appears to be known of the breeding-habits of these birds.

In strong contrast to the dull-looking Ox-birds are the beautiful GLOSSY STARLINGS and GRACKLES. The AFRICAN GLOSSY STARLINGS, indeed, represent the most beautiful of all the members of the Starling Tribe. In one of the handsomest and best-known species—the LONG-TAILED GLOSSY STARLING—metallic green and purple-violet are the predominating tones in the plumage, glossed with copper reflections, and relieved by black or darker bars of green and purple. In another species—the GREEN GLOSSY STARLING of Eastern Africa—the shimmer of the plumage is so wonderful that the exact shades of colour are difficult to describe, in that they change completely, according to the light in which the bird is held.

The GRACKLES, or HILL-MYNAS, are Indian birds, with glossy black plumage, relieved by bare flaps of yellow skin projecting backwards from the head immediately behind the eye. These birds make excellent pets, learning both to whistle and talk.

We come now to the beautiful ORIOLES—birds belonging to the temperate and tropical parts of the Old World. The males, as a rule, are clad in a vestment of brilliant yellow and black, but in some species the under-parts are relieved by rich crimson. One species—the GOLDEN ORIOLE—has on several occasions visited the British Islands, and even in one or two instances has nested there. But, as with all brightly plumaged birds in England, no sooner is their presence discovered than they are doomed to fall to the gun of some local collector.

The HANG-NESTS, COW-BIRDS, and RICE-BIRDS are American birds, bearing in many respects a resemblance to the Starlings, chiefly, perhaps, in the form of the beak. Generally black in plumage, in many bright colour is conspicuous.

HANG-NESTS range from North and Central America to Southern Brazil. As a rule they are brilliantly coloured, the livery being bright orange and yellow, set off by black and white. The majority of the numerous species build remarkable nests, looking like long stockings, which they hang from the under side of the bough of a tree; they are composed of coarse grass deftly woven together.

The COW-BIRDS are mostly South American, though the United States possess two or three species. Some, like the Cuckoos, are parasitic, dropping their eggs into the nests of other birds, to be hatched by the owners: the young cow-bird, however, dwells in harmony with his foster-brothers and -sisters, instead of ejecting them from the nest, like the young cuckoo. The name Cow-bird is bestowed upon these birds on account of the persistent way in which they haunt herds of cattle for the sake of the flies which congregate about those animals.

The RICE-BIRDS are represented by some rather showy forms, and others of wonderful powers of song. The typical RICE-BIRD, or BOB-O-LINK, is an especial favourite as a songster. Thoreau writes of this song: "It is as if he [the bird] touched his harp with a wave of liquid melody, and when he lifted it out the notes fell like bubbles from the strings. . . . Away he laun and the meadow is all bespattered with melody." Where rice is extensively cultivated, howe this bird is by no means so enthusiastically welcomed, causing immense destruction to the standing crops—flocks numbering, it has been said, some millions alighting in the fields and leaving too little grain to be worth the trouble of gathering.

We pass now to a group of exceedingly interesting birds, some of which are remarkable on account of the beauty of their plumage, others from their wonderful nesting-habits. The group includes many familiar as cage-birds, such as the LONG-TAILED WIDOW-BIRDS, the RED-BEAKED WAXBILLS, AMADAVATS, JAVA SPARROW, GRASS-FINCHES, MUNIAS, and so on, all of which are embraced under the general title of WEAVER-BIRDS, a name bestowed on account of their peculiar nests.

Photo by Dr. R. W. Shufeldt] [*Washington.*

MEADOW-LARK (NATURAL SIZE).

Known also as the Meadow-starling. This bird, a native of the Eastern United States, has occurred three times in the British Islands, but it is doubtful whether these specimens were wild.

Abundant in Africa, and well represented in South-eastern Asia and Australia, these birds bear a strong family resemblance to the Finches, from which they differ in having ten primary quills in the wings.

One of the most peculiar is the South African LONG-TAILED WHYDAH- or WIDOW-BIRD. Strikingly coloured, this bird is rendered still more attractive by the extremely elongated tail-feathers, which are many times longer than the body, so long, indeed, as to impede its flight, which is so laboured that children commonly amuse themselves by running the bird down. Kaffir children stretch lines coated with bird-lime near the ground across fields of millet and Kaffir corn, and thereby capture many whose tails have become entangled among the threads.

In brilliancy of coloration the Whydah-birds—for there are several species—are pressed hard

...e BISHOP-BIRDS, the handsomest of which is the red species. Sociable in habits, this ...d, throughout the year consorts in immense flocks, which in the summer consist chiefly of males.

Of the more remarkable nest-builders, the most conspicuous are the BAYA SPARROWS, or TODDY-BIRDS, of India and Ceylon, and the SOCIABLE WEAVERS. The former suspend their nests by a solidly wrought rope of fibre from the under side of a branch, the rope expanding into a globular chamber, and then again contracting into a long, narrow, vertical tube, through which the birds make their exit and entrance. The latter—the SOCIABLE WEAVER-BIRD of Africa—builds a still more wonderful structure. As a thing apart it has no existence, a number of birds, varying from 100 to 300, joining their nests together, so as to form a closely interwoven structure, resembling, when finished, a gigantic mushroom. The structure is built among the branches of large trees, so that the tree looks as though it had grown up through a native hut, carrying the roof with it. Cartloads of grass are required to rear this structure, which is nearly solid. Seen from below, it presents a flat surface riddled with holes; these are the entrances to the nests.

Photo by W. F. Piggott] *[Leighton Buzzard.*

HAWFINCH.

A resident in the eastern and midland counties of England.

Closely resembling the typical Finches in general appearance, and often gorgeous in coloration, is the group known as the TANAGERS, of which more than 400 distinct species are known to science. Exclusively American, the majority of the species are found in Central and South America, though a few move northwards into the United States in summer. The most beautiful are the SCARLET, CRIMSON-HEADED, and WHITE-CAPPED TANAGERS. The last-named is generally allowed to be the loveliest of the group. The entire plumage of both sexes is a beautiful cornflower-blue, surmounted by a cap of silvery-white feathers, a crimson spot on the forehead looking like a drop of blood. The identical coloration of the sexes is worth noting, as among the tanagers generally the female is dull-coloured.

Among the Finches there is a considerable variety of coloration, though but little in bodily form; they are all attractive birds, and have the additional advantage that many are British. Distributed over both the northern and temperate regions of the Eastern and Western Hemispheres, they are unknown in Australia. The group, which comprises a very large number of species, may be divided into three sections—GROSBEAKS, TRUE FINCHES, and BUNTINGS.

The GROSBEAKS, as their name implies, are characterised by the great stoutness of the beak, and some, as the EVENING-GROSBEAKS of America, are remarkable for their beauty.

Well-known British members of this section are the HAWFINCHES and GREENFINCHES. Common in many parts of England, though rare in Scotland and Ireland, the HAWFINCH contrives to make itself much disliked by the gardener, owing to its fondness for peas, though it fully compensates for the damage done in this direction by the numbers of noxious insects it destroys. The nest is a very beautiful structure; outside it is composed of twigs intermixed with lichens, inside of dry grasses lined with fine roots and hair. The site chosen

Photo by C. Reid] [*Wishaw, N.B.*

YOUNG CHAFFINCHES.

The chaffinch is one of the commonest of the British finches.

Photo by C. Reid. [*Wishaw, N.B.*

HOUSE-SPARROWS.

The sparrow is to be reckoned among the few really harmful British birds.

Photo by J. T. Newman] *[Berkhamsted.*

BULLFINCH.

Black varieties are occasionally taken in a wild state. Caged specimens fed on hemp-seed frequently turn black.

varies, a favourite place being an old apple- or pear-tree in an orchard; but the woods and fir plantations are not seldom resorted to. The GREENFINCH is an equally common British bird. Of a more confiding disposition than the hawfinch, it makes an excellent cage-bird, becoming with judicious treatment exceedingly tame. It is a useful bird, travelling during the autumn and winter in large flocks, and feeding on the seeds of wild mustard and other weeds. Its nest differs conspicuously from that of the hawfinch, being a somewhat untidy structure, composed of fibrous roots, moss, and wool, lined with finer roots, horsehair, and feathers.

Among the TRUE FINCHES, distinguished from the Grosbeaks by their less powerful bills, are several other well-known British birds. Of these, none are better known than the CHAFFINCH. Gay in appearance and sprightly in habit, this is a general favourite everywhere, and much in demand as a cage-bird. His short though delightful song possesses a peculiar charm, coming as it does with the earliest signs of returning spring. The fascination of this song has never been better expressed than in Browning's lines:—

O to be in England
Now that April's there;
And whoever wakes in England
Sees, some morning, unaware,
That the lowest boughs of the brushwood sheaf
Round the elm-tree bole are in tiny leaf,
While the Chaffinch sings on the orchard bough
In England now!

The nest, which is an exceptionally beautiful structure, takes about a fortnight to build. Closely woven, it appears to consist mainly of wool, into which moss and lichens of various colours are deftly woven. The outside is cunningly decorated with bits of lichen and the inner bark of trees, such as the birch, the whole being secured by a thin veil of spiders' webs. The lichen and bark serve to render the nest inconspicuous by blending it with the general appearance of the bush or small tree in a forked bough of which it is placed. Inside the wool is more closely felted even than on the outside, and this is covered with fine hairs, amongst which a few feathers are intermixed. The work of building seems to be done by the female only, though the male helps by bringing the materials.

Of the GOLDFINCH, LINNETS, and BULLFINCH, by far the most popular and beautiful is the GOLDFINCH, which is, and probably will long remain, one of the most prized of cage-birds. Gifted "with the fatal gift of beauty," this bird is much persecuted by bird-catchers; and indeed, partly owing to the depredations of these men, and partly to improved methods of agriculture, which have diminished its feeding-area, this handsome bird is growing more and more rare every year.

Next to the goldfinch perhaps the LINNET is most sought after as a cage-bird. Large numbers are taken during the autumn, when the birds congregate in large flocks before departure on migration. Those captured in the spring are said to be very impatient of confinement, and only a small percentage seem to survive.

The linnet is one of the most variable of birds in the matter of plumage, and for a long while the opinion was generally held, especially by bird-catchers, that several distinct species—

the RED, BROWN, and GREY LINNETS—existed. It is now known that these are all phases of plumage common to one species. In the male in full summer dress the forehead and centre of the crown are blood-red, whilst the breast is of a glossy rose-red; but these bright colours do not seem to be acquired so universally as is the case with other birds which don a special breeding-dress, nor are they ever developed in captivity. Occasionally what are called LEMON-BREASTED varieties of the linnet occur in which the rose-colour of the breast is replaced by yellow.

The BULLFINCH, though one of the common British birds, is by no means so abundant as the two foregoing species; for whilst the other two travel in small flocks, the bullfinch is a solitary bird. Few birds perhaps have earned a more evil name than the bullfinch, which is accused by the gardener of inflicting enormous damage on the flower-buds of fruit-trees in winter and spring. "On the other hand," writes Mr. Hudson, "he is greatly esteemed as a cage-bird, and the bird-catchers are ever on the watch for it. But the effect in both cases is pretty much the same, since the hatred that slays and the love that makes captive are equally disastrous to the species." That it is diminishing in many districts there can be no doubt, and perhaps its final extermination is only a matter of time. Though by no means a remarkable songster in a wild state, in captivity it is capable of learning to whistle strains and airs of human composition with some skill, good performers fetching high prices.

Photo by J. T. Newman] [*Berkhamsted.*

GREENFINCH.

Commonly known as the Green Linnet.

The SPARROW and the wild CANARY of Madeira—from the latter of which our cage-pets have been derived—are also members of the Finch Tribe, but are too well known to need fuller mention.

Closely allied to the Finches are the BUNTINGS, which are really only slightly modified finches. Several species are British birds, one of the commonest being the CORN-BUNTING, a bird which bears a wonderful resemblance to a skylark, from which, however, it may be distinguished by its large beak and small claw on the hind toe.

The YELLOWAMMER, or YELLOWHAMMER, is another familiar roadside form in England, which scarcely needs description.

The most celebrated of all the buntings is the ORTOLAN, or GREEN-HEADED BUNTING, a bird resembling its congener the yellowhammer, but lacking its bright coloration. It has acquired fame from the delicate flavour of its flesh, and to supply the demand for this delicacy immense numbers are netted annually by the bird-catchers of the Continent. Wintering in North Africa, these birds leave Europe in September in large flocks, and it is during this migration and the return journey in the spring that their ranks are so mercilessly thinned. Common over the greater part of Europe, it is somewhat surprising that the ortolan does not occur more frequently in the British Islands, where it is only an occasional spring and autumn visitor.

The SNOW-BUNTING, or SNOWFLAKE, is a regular winter visitant to the British Islands, some pairs indeed remaining to breed in the Highlands of Scotland every year, whilst its presence serves to enliven some of the dreariest spots of high northern latitudes. The male in breeding-dress is a handsome bird, having the upper-parts black and the under white; its mate is somewhat duller, the black parts being obscured by greyish white, fulvous, and blackish

Photo by W. F. Piggott] [*Leighton Buzzard.*

LINNET.

One of the most popular cage-birds. The so-called Red-brown and Grey Linnets are but phases of plumage of the same species. The bird in the right-hand corner is a greenfinch.

brown, whilst the white parts are less pure in tone. The full dress of the male is rarely seen in the British Islands, save in specimens procured from Scotland; for in winter, when the snow-bunting is chiefly captured, the plumage is altogether more rufous.

Unlike the buntings so far described, the REED-BUNTING is to be found only in marshy places, but in suitable localities it may be found in the British Islands all the year round, being as common a species as the corn-bunting, and therefore not calling for special description here.

The eggs of the buntings are remarkable for the curious scribble-like markings which cover them, and serve readily to distinguish them from those of any other British bird.

CHAPTER XVI.

LARKS, TITMICE, HONEY-EATERS, AND THEIR KINDRED.

CONFINED almost entirely to the Old World, where they are represented by more than one hundred species, many of which have undergone considerable specialisation in the matter of plumage, so as to enable them to live in desert regions, the LARKS constitute a well-marked group, into the characters of which we need not enter here.

The best-known member of the group is the SKYLARK. Common throughout the British Islands, and of sober coloration, no bird is more universally beloved, and this largely on account of the sweetness of its song, which is second only to that of the nightingale. Poets and prose-writers alike have sounded its praises, many in passages that will be remembered as long as our language lasts. The skylark is one of the few birds which sing while on the wing; the peculiar nature of the flight at this time all must have watched, entranced the while by the beauty of the song.

Grahame, in his "Birds of Scotland," happily describes the nest as follows :—

The daisied lea he loves, where tufts of grass
Luxuriant crown the ridge; there, with his mate,
He founds their lowly house, of withered bents,
And coarsest speargrass; next, the inner work
With finer and still finer fibres lays,
Rounding it curious with its speckled breast.

This bird displays great affection for its young, removing them under the fear of impending danger, or if the nest is meddled with. Occasionally, however, the bird sits close, instead of seeking safety by flight.

Brighton enjoys the credit of consuming more larks than any other place in England, except London. It has been estimated that the number of larks annually entering the metropolitan markets alone reaches a total of 400,000—20,000 or 30,000 being often sent together; and the numbers eaten elsewhere in the country must be enormous, quite as large, indeed, as abroad. Most are captured from the hosts which arrive on the east coast of Scotland and England from the Continent on approach of severe weather, the birds making their appearance in thousands, forming a constant and unbroken stream for two or three days in succession.

Close allies of the Larks, the WAGTAILS and PIPITS come next under consideration. The former range over the Old World, but are unknown in Australia and Polynesia. The pipits have a similar range, but one species is found in, and is peculiar to, Australia. Like wagtails, pipits are unknown in Polynesia; only two species occur in America.

The WAGTAILS are generally black and white, grey and white, grey with yellow breasts, or yellowish green with yellow breasts. In the last-mentioned case, as in some specimens of the YELLOW WAGTAIL, the yellow predominates. These birds frequent streams and stagnant waters, like the RED and GREY WAGTAILS; or corn-fields and meadows, as in the case of the YELLOW WAGTAIL. All these are commonly met with in the British Islands.

Photo by C. Reid] [*Wishaw, N.B.*

SKYLARKS.

The numbers of skylarks seem to increase with the spread of agricultural improvement.

The PIPITS are duller-coloured than the Wagtails, have shorter tails, and evince less fondness for the water. The MEADOW-, ROCK-, and TREE-PIPITS are the commonest British species.

Neither Wagtails nor Pipits are much given to perching, but the TREE-CREEPERS spend their lives upon trees, some being specially modified for this mode of life, their tail-feathers being stiff and terminating in sharp points. By pressing its tail closely against the tree-trunk up which it is climbing, the bird obtains a wonderfully reliable support. Beginning at the bottom of a trunk, creepers quickly work their way up in a spiral direction, or sometimes in jerky zigzags, searching every crevice for tiny insects, their eggs and larvæ, and flitting from the higher branches, when these are reached, to the base of another tree.

Creepers are mostly dull-coloured, but the WALL-CREEPER has crimson patches on the wings. This bird, which has occurred in Britain, haunts mountain-cliffs. The TREE-CREEPER, a resident in Britain, builds its nest behind pieces of loose bark, or under tiles, or in crevices of trees, walls, or hollow branches. In this nest are laid from six to nine eggs, pure white, spotted with red, or with a creamy ground-colour, with the spots thicker round the large end.

Intermediate in position between the Creepers and the Titmice are the NUTHATCHES. Chiefly inhabitants of the northern parts of both hemispheres, they extend as far south as Mexico, whilst in the Old World they occur plentifully in the Himalaya. The largest species is found in the mountains of Burma. One species is frequently met with in England, and occasionally in Scotland, but is unknown in Ireland.

Photo by A. S. Rudland & Sons.

YOUNG SKYLARKS.

Several broods are reared by each pair of birds in a season.

The ENGLISH NUTHATCH may serve us as a type of the group. "Its habits," writes Dr. Sharpe, "are a combination of those of the tit and woodpecker. Like the former bird, the nuthatch seeks diligently for its insect-food on the trunks and branches of trees, over which it runs like a woodpecker, with this difference, that its tail is not pressed into the service of climbing a tree, nor does it generally ascend from the bottom to the top, as a woodpecker so often does. On the contrary, a nuthatch will generally be found in the higher branches, and will work its way down from one of the branches towards the trunk, and is just as much at home on the under side of a limb as the upper. Its movements are like those of a mouse rather than of a bird, and it often runs head-downward, or hangs on the under side of a branch and hammers away at the bark with its powerful little bill. The noise produced by one of these birds, when tapping at a tree, is really astonishing for a bird of its size, and, if undisturbed, it can be approached pretty closely. Its general food consists of insects, and in the winter the nuthatches join the wandering parties of tits and creepers which traverse the woods in search of food. . . . In the autumn it feeds on hazel-nuts and beech-mast, breaking them open by constant hammering; and, like the tits, the nuthatches can be tempted to the vicinity of houses in winter, and become quite interesting by their tameness."

The nuthatch nests in hollow trees, plastering up the entrance with mud, and leaving an aperture only just sufficient to enable it to wriggle in and out. A remarkable nest may be seen at the British Natural History Museum. It was built in the side of a haystack, to which the industrious birds had carried as much as 11 lbs. of clay, and had thus made for themselves a solid nest in an apparently unfavourable position.

The TITMICE occur in one form or another all over Europe, Asia, and Africa, and in the New World as far south as Southern Mexico. The family may be divided into TRUE, CRESTED, LONG-TAILED, and PENDULINE TITS and REEDLINGS, all but the penduline tits being represented in England.

Of the true tits, the best known is the BLUE TIT, which is no stranger even in London parks. Travelling in small bands throughout the autumn and winter, they may frequently be met with during a country walk, their presence being made known by a pretty tinkling little note. This method of travelling is obviously advantageous, for the discovery of food at this time is an arduous task, and, if undertaken individually, many would surely starve, as Professor Newton points out: "A single titmouse searching alone might hunt for a whole day without meeting with a sufficiency, whilst, if a dozen are united by the same motive, it is hardly possible for the place in which the food is lodged to escape their detection, and, when discovered, a few call-notes from the lucky finder are enough to assemble the whole company to share the feast. . . . One tree after another is visited by the active little rovers, and its branches examined: if nothing be forthcoming, away goes the explorer to the next that presents itself, merely giving utterance to the usual twitter that serves to keep the whole body together. But if the object of search be found, another chirp is emitted, and the next moment several members of the band are flitting in succession to the tree, and eagerly engaged with the spoil."

Photo by J. T. Newman] *[Berkhamsted.*

NUTHATCH.

Apparently unknown in a wild state in Ireland, and rare in Scotland, in England fairly common.

These little birds display great affection for their old nesting-places. An instance is on record where, so far back as 1785, a pair built their nest in a large earthenware bottle placed in the branches of a tree in a garden at Oxbridge, near Stockton-on-Tees. With two exceptions only, this bottle was tenanted by a pair of these birds every year till 1873. In 1892 Professor Newton, who had this account from Canon Tristram, was informed that the occupancy had ceased for four years.

The LONG-TAILED or BOTTLE-TIT is a British species, deriving its name from the long tail. It is a pretty little bird, black and rose-colour above, with a rose-coloured abdomen, and the head, throat, and breast white. It enjoys the distinction of being one of the smallest British birds, and is found in woods and plantations all over England, though less common in Scotland. These tits have a curious habit of roosting during the winter, six or seven huddling together in a row, with three or four others perched on their backs, and two or three on the top.

The nest, which is placed in a tree or bush, is a model of industry. Oval in shape, and roofed, with a small aperture near the top, it is composed of moss, lichen, and hair, closely felted and lined with an enormous collection of feathers, Macgillivray having counted 2,779 in a single nest.

Other species of titmice occurring in Britain are the GREAT, MARSH-, COAL-, and CRESTED TITS.

Photo by J. T. Newman] [*Berkhamsted.*

MARSH-TIT SEARCHING FOR INSECTS.

The marsh-tit may be distinguished from its ally, the coal-tit, by the absence of white on the nape of the neck.

Whether the REEDLINGS, or BEARDED TITS, as they are generally called, are really true titmice or peculiarly modified buntings is a moot-point. There is but one species, which is British, though found also on the Continent; but it is unfortunately becoming more and more rare every year. The general colour of the upper-parts is cinnamon-rufous, except the head, which is pearly grey: between the bill and the eyes hangs a tuft of long black feathers; hence the name Bearded Tit. The under-parts are white, tinged with yellow and pink, whilst the wings are variegated with white, black, and red. This tit lives in beds of reeds fringing the "broads" of the eastern counties of England, though even there it is now exceedingly rare.

The same uncertainty that obtains with regard to the position of the Reedlings confronts the ornithologist with regard to the affinities of the liliputian GOLD-CRESTS. About six species are known, from the northern and temperate parts of the Old and New Worlds, extending as far south in the latter as Mexico. Two occur in Britain: one, known simply as the GOLD-CREST, or GOLDEN-CRESTED WREN, is fairly common; the other, the FIRE-CREST, or FIRE-CRESTED WREN, is much rarer, but differs very little from its relative in general appearance.

The GOLD-CREST is olive-green above, yellowish grey below, with a conspicuous crest of bright yellow and orange, banded on each side by two black lines. It has the distinction of being the smallest British bird; and it is partly on account of its smallness, and partly owing to its shy, retiring habits, seeking concealment among the foliage, that it is so seldom seen, save by those who know where to look for it; and these may find it all the year round in suitable places.

In the spring this bird may be observed suspended in the air for a considerable time over a bush or flower, singing very melodiously, though few naturalists have ever witnessed this display. Mr. W. H. Hudson, one of these few, writes: "I have observed the male, in the love-season, hovering just above the bush, in the topmost foliage of which its mate was perched and partly hidden from view. It is when engaged in this pretty aerial performance, or love-dance, that the golden-crested wren is seen at his best. The restless, minute, sober-coloured creature, so difficult to see properly at other times, then becomes a conspicuous and exceedingly beautiful object; it hovers on rapidly vibrating wings, the body in an almost vertical position, but the head bent sharply down, the eyes being fixed on the bird beneath, while the wide-open crest shines in the sun like a crown or shield of fiery yellow. When thus hovering, it does not sing, but emits a series of sharp, excited chirping sounds."

The nest is a singularly beautiful structure, made of fine, dry grass, leaves, moss, and spiders' webs, woven closely together, lined with feathers, and suspended like a hammock beneath a branch of yew or fir. In this are laid from six to ten eggs of a pale yellowish white, spotted and blotched with reddish brown.

The numbers of British gold-crests are vastly increased by the arrival on the eastern

Photo by C. Reid] [*Wishaw, N.B.*

GREAT TIT.

Known also as the Ox-eye; it is very pugnacious in captivity, killing birds even as large as itself.

coast of gold-crests from the Continent. "In autumn," writes Mr. Howard Saunders, "immense flocks sometimes arrive on our east coast, extending quite across England and the Irish Channel, and into Ireland. In 1882 the migration wave of this description, commencing on August 6 and lasting for ninety-two days, reached from the Channel to the Færoes; in 1883 the migration lasted eighty-two days; and again in 1884 for a period of eighty-seven days. . . . On such occasions bushes in gardens on the coast are covered with birds as with a swarm of bees; crowds flutter round the lanterns of lighthouses, and the rigging of fishing-smacks in the North Sea is thronged with weary travellers. In April a return migration occurs."

We pass now to the consideration of a few families of birds unknown in Britain, but interesting on account of the fact that they afford us another set of instances of adaptation to attain particular ends, so frequently to be met with in Nature. All the birds in question, though probably not related, have peculiarly modified tongues, apparently specially designed to aid in sucking up honey from flowers.

The first group for consideration are the HONEY-EATERS of New Zealand and Australia. So great is the transformation which the tongue in these birds has undergone, that it forms one of the most elaborate organs of its kind, surpassing even that of the Humming-birds. A description of this organ without the aid of anatomical terms and diagrams would be useless. Suffice it to say it is long, capable of being thrust out of the mouth, and brush-like. It is used to thrust up the tubes of honey-bearing flowers, as well for the sake of the juice as for the insects gathered in such situations to feed on it.

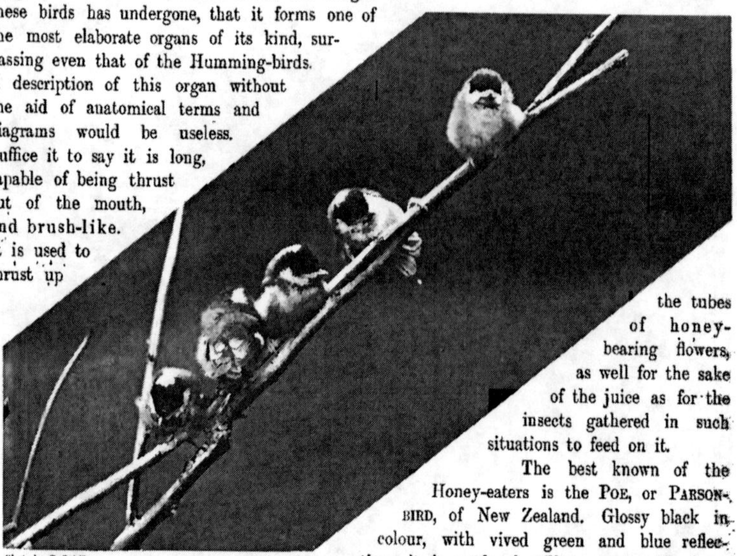

Photo by C. Reid] [Wishaw, N.B.

COAL-TITS.

These birds show the white patch on the nape very distinctly. It is a common British bird, staying with us the whole year round.

The best known of the Honey-eaters is the POE, or PARSON-BIRD, of New Zealand. Glossy black in colour, with vived green and blue reflections, it is rendered still more attractive by a pair of white tufts of feathers hanging from the front upper part of the neck, whilst on the back of the neck in the same region the feathers are of a loose structure, long, and curled forwards. Other honey-eaters are the WHITE-EYES, SUN-BIRDS, and FLOWER-PECKERS.

The WHITE-EYES, so called from a ring of white feathers around the eye, have a wide distribution, being found in Australia, India, Africa, Madagascar, and Japan. Besides honey they are very partial to fruit, particularly figs and grapes, and also capture insects on the wing, after the fashion of fly-catchers.

The SUN-BIRDS correspond in the Old World to the Humming-birds in the New, having, like the latter, a metallic plumage, varied in its hues and wondrous in its beauty; but they are not entirely dependent upon this lustre for their charm, for much of their splendour is gained from the non-metallic portion of the plumage, which is often vividly coloured. The females are dull-coloured, whilst the males lose their beauty in the winter season. These birds are inhabitants of the tropical regions of Africa, India, and Australia, and seem to revel in the burning rays of the noonday sun.

Nearly allied to the Sun-birds are the FLOWER-PECKERS of the Indian and Australian regions. These are all small birds, remarkable as much for the beauty of their nests as for the splendour of their plumage. The nests are purse-like structures, made of white cotton-like material, and suspended from a branch instead of, as usual, resting on it. One of the most beautiful birds of the whole group, which includes numerous species, is the Australian DIAMOND-BIRD. Of a general ashy-grey colour, this species is splashed all over with spots of red, yellow, orange, and black, whilst the tail-coverts are rich dark red.

Photo by W. F. Piggott] *[Leighton Buzzard*

RED-BACKED SHRIKES.

Also called Butcher-birds, from their habit of killing small birds and mammals and hanging them up on thorns.

Photo by W. Reid] *[Wishaw, N.B.*

AUSTRALIAN MAGPIE.

A common South Australian form, known also as the Piping-crow.

CHAPTER XVII.

SHRIKES, THRUSHES AND THEIR ALLIES, SWALLOWS, LYRE-BIRDS, CHATTERERS, BROAD-BILLS, ETC.

THE Shrike Family are an exceedingly interesting group of birds, of world-wide distribution and of great diversity of appearance, varying in size from a bird as small as a titmouse to one as large as a thrush, and presenting a considerable range of coloration, some being very brightly, others dull coloured. From the hooked beak, and the presence of a notch in the tip of the upper jaw, they were considered by the older naturalists to be allies of the Birds of Prey, a decision still further supported by their hawk-like habit of capturing living prey in the shape of small birds and mice; whilst the remarkable custom of impaling their victims, still living, on thorns has earned for them the popular name of BUTCHER-BIRDS. The limits of the family, owing to the diversity of the forms involved, have not as yet been finally determined by naturalists, some having included species which others hold have no place there.

Five species are commonly included in the list of British birds, although only two occur with any frequency: of these, the GREAT GREY SHRIKE visits Great Britain every winter; whilst the smaller RED-BACKED SHRIKE is an annual summer visitor to those islands, breeding, however, only in England, occurring but occasionally in Scotland, and being almost unknown in Ireland, where only one specimen has ever been recorded.

The RED-BACKED SHRIKE, writes Dr. Sharpe, "reminds us of a fly-catcher in the way in which [it] captures its food, for it has undoubtedly favourite perches, on which it sits, and to which it returns after the capture of an insect. It is frequently to be seen on telegraph-wires, where it keeps a sharp look-out in every direction, and a favourite resort is a field of freshly cut grass. It also captures a good many mice and small birds, not pursuing them in the open like birds of prey, but dropping down on them suddenly. In the British Museum is a very good specimen of the larder of a red-backed shrike, taken with the nest of the bird by Lord Walsingham in Norfolk, and showing the way in which the shrike spits insects and birds on thorns; and the species has been known . . . to hang up birds even bigger than itself, such as blackbirds and thrushes, as well as tits of several kinds, robins, and hedge-sparrows, while it will also occasionally seize young partridges and pheasants."

Photo by W. F. Piggott] *[Leighton Buzzard.*

REED-WARBLER.

A common British bird, arriving in April, and leaving again in September.

Though undeniably unmusical, the red-backed shrike is nevertheless able to imitate with considerable success the notes of other small birds, decoying them by this means within striking distance—an accomplishment shared also by other members of the Shrike Family. The present species is attractively clothed in a plumage varied with black, grey, rufous, and chestnut-brown, the last being the predominating hue of the upper-parts; hence the name Red-backed Shrike.

The habits of its congener, the GREAT GREY SHRIKE, are precisely similar. A caged specimen which had become very tame would take food from its captor's hands. When a bird was given it, the skull was invariably broken at once, after which, holding the body in its claws, the shrike would proceed to tear it in pieces after the fashion of a hawk. Sometimes, instead, the carcase would be forced through the bars of the cage—in lieu of thorns—and then pulled in pieces.

Very different in appearance from the members of the Shrike Family are a group of possibly allied forms known as WAX-WINGS. Of pleasing but sober coloration, they are remarkable for certain curious appendages to the inner quill-feathers, of a bright sealing-wax red colour, from which they derive their name: similar wax-like appendages occur also, sometimes, on the tail-feathers.

Breeding in the Arctic Circle, wax-wings occur in both the Old and New Worlds, though some species peculiar to the latter region lack the wax-like appendages characteristic of the majority of the species. These birds are erratic in their movements, and large bands occasionally visit the British Islands during the autumn and winter, the eastern counties being usually the most favoured spots; but on the occasion of one of these immigrations, in the winter of 1872, many were seen in the neighbourhood of the North of London. During the summer they feed on insects, but in autumn and winter on berries and fruit. At this time they become very fat

Photo by J. T. Newman] [*Berkhamsted.*

SONG-THRUSH.

A resident British species, sometimes called the Mavis.

Photo by Scholastic Photo. Co.] *[Parson's Green.*

YOUNG THRUSH.

This photograph shows the mud-lined nest.

and are then captured and sold in large numbers for food in the Russian markets, and occasionally are sent over to London.

Passing over a small group of comparatively uninteresting American birds known as "Greenlets," we come to the WARBLERS, a group which constitutes one of the largest families of birds of the Old World. The species included in this family vary greatly in their characters, so that it is by no means easy to give diagnostic characters, whereby they may be readily distinguished from the Fly-catchers on the one hand or the Thrushes on the other. The Thrushes. however, as a group, may be distinguished from the Warblers by the circumstance that in the former the young have a distinctive spotted plumage, differing from that of the adults, while the young of the Warblers are not so marked, their plumage differing but little from that of their parents.

More than twenty species of warblers are included amongst British birds. Although some of them are but rare and accidental visitors to Britain, others are amongst the commonest of the spring migrants, remaining to nest, and leaving again in the autumn. Some, as the BLACK-CAP, WHITE-THROAT, CHIFF-CHAFF, GARDEN-, WILLOW-, and WOOD-WARBLERS, frequent woods, hedgerows, and gardens; whilst others, as the SEDGE- and REED-WARBLERS, are found only near water affording sufficient shelter in the shape of reed-banks or osier-plantations.

The BLACK-CAP and GARDEN-WARBLER rank as songsters of no mean talent, being held second only to the nightingale. As if by common consent, the two former never clash, so that where black-caps are common there are few garden-warblers, and *vice versâ.*

Most of these birds build a typical cup-shaped nest of dried grasses, lined with finer materials, and placed near the ground; but that of the REED-WARBLER is a most beautiful structure, the dried grass of which it is made being woven around some three or four reed-stems, making it seem as if the latter had, in growing up, pierced the sides of the nest

Photo by J. T. Newman] *[Berkhamsted.*

BLACKBIRD.

The male and female are quite different one from another, and in this respect differ from the Thrushes, in which the sexes are alike.

in their course. The cup-shaped hollow is very deep, so that when the supporting reeds are bowed low in the breeze the eggs rest perfectly safe.

We must pass now to a consideration of the Thrush Tribe, which, as we have already hinted, are very closely allied to the Warblers.

Photo by W. F. Piggott, Leighton Buzzard.

ROBIN.

The young robin wears a distinct livery, quite different from that of its parents.

Birds like the COMMON THRUSH and the BLACKBIRD are so common and so well known that they scarcely need comment here. The same perhaps is true of many other members of this group not popularly associated with the Thrush Tribe; such are the RED-BREAST, or ROBIN RED-BREAST, as it is more generally called, and the NIGHTINGALE. Few birds have inspired so many writers as the nightingale; it even holds a place in classical mythology. Professor Newton gives us one variant of a very common but pretty story: "Procne and Philomela were the daughters of Pandion, King of Attica, who in return for warlike aid rendered him by Tereus, King of Daulis in Thrace, gave him the first-named in marriage. Tereus, however, being enamoured of her sister, feigned that his wife was dead, and induced Philomela to take her place. On her discovering the truth, he cut out her tongue to hinder her from revealing his deceit; but she depicted her sad story on a robe which she sent to Procne, and the two sisters then contrived a horrible revenge for the infidelity of Tereus by killing and serving to him at table his son Itys. Thereupon the gods interposed, changing Tereus into a hoopoe, Procne into a swallow, and Philomela into a nightingale, while Itys was restored to life as a pheasant, and Pandion (who had died of grief at his daughters' dishonour) as a bird of prey [the osprey]."

A not infrequent error with regard to the red-breast may be pointed out here. Many people seem to suppose that the female is less brilliantly coloured than her mate. As a matter of fact this is not so; what are generally regarded as females of this species are the dull, spotted young, which, as we have already pointed out, assume this peculiar livery throughout the tribe.

No less common in Britain, during the summer months at least, are the WHEAT-EARS, STONE-CHATS, WHIN-CHATS, and RED-STARTS. Small and prettily coloured species, these are all insect-eaters, and, with the exception of the wheat-ears, lay blue eggs, deposited in somewhat coarsely constructed nests, placed on or near the ground; or in holes in ruins, trees, or walls, in the case of the red-starts; or in burrows or

Photo by A. S. Rudland & Sons.

NIGHTINGALE.

The sweetest and most renowned of all the British songsters.

Photo by G. Watmough Webster & Son] *[Chester.*

STONE-CHAT.

A resident and generally distributed British bird.

under ledges of rock, as among the wheat-ears, which lay white eggs.

The bird commonly known as the HEDGE-SPARROW is a close ally of the Thrush Family, having nothing to do with the sparrows proper—which are finches—as its name would imply.

Another nearly related form is the DIPPER, or WATER-OUZEL. By no means brilliantly coloured, it is nevertheless an exceedingly interesting bird, and one never met with away from mountain streams. The group has a wide distribution, occurring in suitable localities in Europe, Asia, and the Rocky Mountains of America, and extending from Colombia to Peru and Tucuman. Squat in form, with rounded wings and short tail, the ouzel seeks the greater part of its food on the bottom of swiftly running streams. It is everywhere, writes Dr. Sharpe of the commoner of the two British species, a shy and watchful bird, and, except in the breeding-season, appears to be solitary. By patient watching near the dipper's haunts, however, it is possible to observe the bird scudding over the surface of the water with a rapid flight and a vigorous beating of the wings, something like that of a kingfisher, until it alights on a rock or large stone in the middle of the stream. Its white breast then stands out in bold relief, and, after pausing for a moment, the bird commences to edge to the side of the rock, and either walks deliberately into the water, or disappears suddenly beneath the surface, seeking its food at the bottom of the stream, in the shape of larvæ, caddis-worms, water-beetles, and small snails.

The WRENS are probably near allies of the Dippers. The family includes a number of species of small birds, most largely represented in the New World, but distributed widely over the Old World also. Two occur in the British Islands: of these, one, the COMMON WREN, is found throughout Europe, and occurs also in Northern Africa, Asia Minor, and North Palestine; whilst the other, the ST. KILDA WREN, is only found on the island from which it takes its name.

Considerations of space compel us to pass over three or four families, of comparatively little interest to any save the scientific ornithologist, in favour of the FLY-CATCHERS and SWALLOWS.

The former, in that the young are spotted, appear to evince some affinity to the Thrush Tribe, but they have broad and flatter bills than the latter, whilst the mouth is surrounded by more or less conspicuous bristles. They are entirely Old World forms, having their stronghold in Africa.

Three species of fly-catcher occur in England, though only one, the COMMON or SPOTTED FLY-CATCHER, usually breeds in Great Britain, coming late in the spring from Africa. As its name implies, it feeds upon small insects, capturing them on the wing by sudden sallies, and returning immediately after to some perch, generally a garden-fence, or the bare bough of a tree. As a rule the prey is caught with a sudden dart, but sometimes only after a prolonged flight, when the bird will double and turn, as the necessity arises, with great skill. Its nest, made of dry grass and moss, lined with horse-hair and covered externally with spider-webs and lichens, is usually placed in some sheltered position, such as a crevice in the bark of a tree or in the creepers covering the trellis-work of a house; and owing to the skilful way in which it is covered externally, so as to resemble its surroundings, is difficult to find.

Photo by J. T. Newman] [*Berkhamsted.*

A PAIR OF WRENS.

Known nearly everywhere in England as the "Kitty" or "Jenny" Wren.

The SWALLOWS and MARTINS constitute an exceedingly well-defined group of birds, and one which holds a conspicuously high place in the regard of mankind, finding a welcome everywhere on account of the great benefits they confer by the removal of insect-pests in the shape of the smaller gnats and flies. These, were they not kept in check by the Swallow Tribe, would render most parts of the world uninhabitable. Rarely seen upon the ground, save when procuring mud for the construction of their nests, the birds of this group are all peculiarly strong fliers, turning and twisting with the greatest speed and precision. All have very short beaks and wide mouths, long wings and tails, and small and weak feet.

Photo by Scholastic Photo. Co.] [*Parson's Green.*

COMMON WRENS, WITH NEST BUILT IN PHEASANT'S SKELETON.

In winter wrens have a custom of seeking some hole or other convenient shelter and huddling together in small parties for the sake of warmth.

A large number build their nests of mud, collected in small pellets and held together by the secretion of the salivary glands. These nests are commonly more or less cup-shaped, and fastened under the eaves of dwelling-houses or other buildings, or placed on a convenient beam or other ledge. The RED-RUMPED SWALLOWS and FAIRY MARTINS—species enjoying an enormous distribution, being found in India, Africa, America, and Australia—build very large flask-shaped nests, having the entrance produced into a funnel often eight or nine inches in length. Others, like the SAND-MARTIN, excavate long tunnels, terminating in larger chambers, in the faces of sand-banks—a performance which must certainly be regarded as wonderful, when one realises the feeble tools with which the task of excavating has to be performed. Some species utilise the holes made by other birds, in one species this hole being itself bored within the burrow of the viscacha.

All are more or less migratory in their habits, some covering enormous distances in journeying to and fro between their winter retreats and their summer breeding-places. The COMMON SWALLOW and HOUSE-MARTIN, for example, leave the shores of Africa early in the spring, and distribute themselves over Europe, thousands visiting the British Islands. After rearing in their respective breeding-places from two to three broods, they return with their offspring before the rigours of winter set in to the African Continent. The routes and destinations of the swallow are now well known; but as much cannot be said for the house-martin, whose winter quarters are as yet enshrouded in mystery. That they must be somewhere in Africa is all that can at present be said.

Photo by J. T. Newman] [*Berkhamsted.*

YOUNG SWALLOWS.

For hundreds of years it has been regarded as most unlucky to kill a swallow.

Three species of the Swallow Tribe visit England regularly every year, and remain to breed. These are the COMMON or CHIMNEY-SWALLOW, and the HOUSE-MARTIN just referred to, and the little SAND-MARTIN. In the two first mentioned the upper-parts are of a dark steel-blue colour with a metallic gloss, but they are, nevertheless, easily distinguished one from another,—since the swallow has a deeply forked tail, and a bright chestnut patch on the throat, with a similarly coloured band across the forehead; whilst the martin lacks the chestnut markings, and is pure white beneath, with a large white patch on the lower part of the back, and a less markedly forked tail. Furthermore, the legs of the martin are feathered down to the claws, whilst the feet of the swallow are bare. The sand-martin is a little greyish-brown bird, with white under-parts. It is the earliest of the Swallow Tribe to arrive in Britain, and the first to depart

LYRE-BIRDS AND SCRUB-BIRDS.

At the beginning of the account of the Perching-birds it was stated that the group was divided into two sections, and that each of these was further sub-divided into two. With the Swallows the first sub-division of the first section ended; the second we are to consider now in the very singular LYRE-BIRDS and SCRUB-BIRDS of Australia.

Rendered conspicuous on account of the remarkable lyrate tail, from which the name is derived, the LYRE-BIRDS, on closer acquaintance, prove to be exceedingly interesting forms, though materials for a really complete biography of the three known species are not yet available. The males, it seems, are skilled mimics, reproducing the songs of other birds with great fidelity, this being especially true of the species known as PRINCE ALBERT'S LYRE-BIRD. During the courting-season the males construct hillocks, to which they resort to display their very beautiful and graceful tails, elevating them over the head, and drooping the wings after the fashion of a peacock, accompanying this display with certain spasmodic pecking and scratching actions. They are solitary birds, more than a pair never being seen together, and even these are exceedingly difficult to approach, stratagem always being necessary. But a single egg is laid, which has the appearance of being smeared with ink; whilst the young bird differs from that of all other perching-birds in the thickness of its downy covering and the great length of time in which it remains in the nest. The nest, made of sticks, moss, and fibres skilfully interwoven, and lined inside with the leaf of a tree-fern which resembles horse-hair, is a large domed structure, with a single aperture serving as an entrance.

Lyre-birds are essentially ground-dwellers, feeding upon insects, especially beetles and snails, and keeping to the wilder regions of the country.

The SCRUB-BIRD is an extremely interesting form, scientifically. Only the males are known at the present time, and these are dull-coloured birds of the size of a thrush. Of the female, eggs, and nest, we as yet know absolutely nothing.

CHATTERERS, ANT-THRUSHES, BROAD-BILLS, ETC.

The second major division of the Perching-birds embraces a few forms of considerable interest.

The group of CHATTERERS includes several remarkable forms of very diverse coloration, many representing the most gorgeous of all South American birds.

One of the most remarkable is the UMBRELLA-BIRD. This bird is funereal in appearance, being clothed in a plumage of deep black, with the head surmounted by a large, drooping, flat-topped crest, resembling in shape the familiar crest of certain varieties of the canary, whilst from the throat hangs a long lappet of feathers reaching nearly down to the feet. The female is duller than her mate, and lacks the peculiar plumes. The umbrella-bird is a forest-dwelling

Photo by W. F. Piggott] [*Leighton Buzzard.*

SAND-MARTINS.

This photograph shows a portion of a sand bank, pierced with the tunnel-like nests made by these feeble builders.

species, confined to the Upper Amazons, and dwelling in the tops of the highest trees, where it finds ample sustenance in wild fruits. But few naturalists have ever seen it in a wild state.

Equally wonderful are the BELL-BIRDS, so called on account of their note, which bears an extraordinary resemblance to the sound made by a blacksmith upon an anvil, though it has often been likened to the tolling of a bell. Four species are known, in three of which the males have a pure white plumage, with much naked, vividly coloured skin on the face. One species has a curious pendulous process hanging from the forehead, thinly covered with feathers. By some this is said to be capable of erection during periods of excitement. Like the umbrella-bird, these are forest-dwelling species.

For brilliancy of plumage amongst the Chatterers, the palm must be given to the COCKS-OF-THE-ROCK, in the males of which orange-red predominates, whilst the general effect is heightened by crests and curiously curled and frayed feathers growing from the lower part of the back. The males indulge in remarkable love-displays, the performances being held in some open space, and in the presence of the females. One at a time each male appears to go through a kind of dance, accompanying his peculiar steps and hops with much swaying of the head and extending of the wings. When tired, the performer gives a signal which is understood by his fellows, and retires from the ring, his place being immediately taken by another.

Photo by D. Le Souef] [*Melbourne.*

VICTORIAN LYRE-BIRD.

Lyre-birds, which are also known to the colonists as "Pheasants," are great mimics.

The nesting habits of the Chatterers vary greatly,—some building nests of mud and twigs, which they fasten on projections of rock in damp caves; others simply lining holes in trees with dry grass. Some build a cup-shaped nest of lichens, others a simple platform of sticks, whilst some of the THICK-BILLED CHATTERERS hang large nests of leaves, plant-stalks, and wool from low branches; the entrance to the nest being from a hole in the side. The eggs vary in number among the different species from two to four, and in colour may be white, chocolate, pale salmon-coloured, or greenish blue, and are for the most part spotted.

Closely allied to the Cocks-of-the-rock are the MANAKINS, for the most part small and thick-set birds, and in many instances brilliantly coloured—at least in the case of the males. Some seventy species are known, all of which are confined to South America. They must be sought for, as a rule, in the forests or thick undergrowth of marshy places.

The Manakin Family contains several species of considerable interest, on account of the peculiar modifications which certain of the quill-feathers of the males have undergone. In some species what are known as the secondary quill-feathers are peculiarly twisted, and have the shafts much thickened. With these modified feathers the birds are enabled, probably by clapping the wings and bringing the thickened feathers violently together, to make a sharp sound, which has been likened to the crack of a whip. Other species have the quill-feathers of the hand—the primaries, as they are called—similarly thickened; and they probably are also used to produce sounds.

One species is known as the BAILADOR, or DANCER, on account of a very remarkable habit which the males have of dancing. Two males, choosing some secluded spot, select a bare twig,

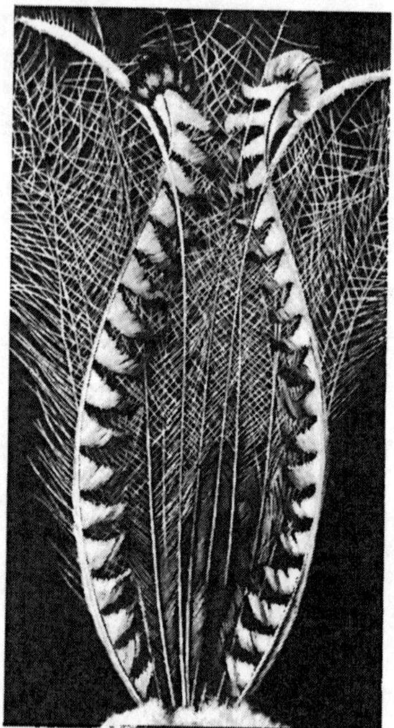

Photo by W. Saville-Kent, F.Z.S.] [*Milford-on-Sea.*

TAIL OF AUSTRALIAN LYRE-BIRD.

This ornamental tail is worn only by the male.

and, taking up a position about a foot and a half apart, alternately jump about two feet in the air, and alight again on exactly the same spot from which they sprang. With the regularity of clockwork one bird jumps up the instant the other alights, each bird performing a musical accompaniment to the tune of "to-le-do—to-le-do—to-le-do," uttering the syllable "to" as he crouches to spring, "le" while in the air, and "do" as he alights; and this performance appears to be kept up till the birds are exhausted.

Some of the manakins are very beautifully coloured. One species, for example, is black, with a blue mantle and a crimson crest; another, black, with orange-coloured cheeks and breast and similarly coloured band round the neck, green rump, and yellow abdomen. The females are generally duller in coloration.

The ANT-THRUSHES, or PITTAS, are long-legged, short-tailed birds, of brilliant coloration, having their headquarters in the Malay Archipelago; but the family is represented in India, Australia, and West Africa.

Photo by A. S. Rudland & Sons.

BELL-BIRD.

So called from its wonderfully clear, bell-like note.

These birds are very shy and exceedingly difficult to approach. One species, the large GROUND-THRUSH, is described by Wallace as one of the most beautiful birds of the East. Velvety black above, relieved by pure white, the shoulders are azure-blue and the belly a vivid crimson. The nest recalls, in the plan of its architecture, that of the Oven-birds, being more or less globular in form, and having a lateral entrance; it is composed of twigs, roots, bark, moss, leaves, and grass, and is frequently cemented with earth. The eggs are usually spotted, and have a creamy-white ground-colour: the spots may be brown, reddish grey, or purplish black.

The curious PLANT-CUTTERS of the temperate regions of South America are nearly related to the Chatterers, though at one time it was believed they were allied to the True Finches. Constituting but a small family, the plant-cutters are remarkable for their strangely serrated beaks, the cutting-edges of which are armed with a series of fine saw-like teeth. This beak is used in cutting down plants; and as these birds appear to cut down a great number in sheer wantonness, they are much disliked in the neighbourhood of gardens and plantations.

Plant-cutters are not conspicuous for the beauty of their plumage, and have a harsh and grating voice.

The WOOD-HEWERS constitute a group of over 200 species, all of which are South American. They are for the most part small and dull-coloured birds, but nevertheless of considerable interest on account of their nest-building habits. The most remarkable members of the family in this respect are three species of OVEN-BIRDS. These construct a massive nest of mud, bearing a more or less fanciful resemblance to a baker's oven; hence the name Oven-bird. Roughly globular in shape, its walls are of great thickness, and to prevent cracking hair and grass-fibres are intermixed with the mud; the interior is gained through a small hole on one side of the nest, which leads into a passage terminating in a chamber containing the eggs, which are laid upon a bed of grass. Strangely enough, the bird seeks the most exposed situations, placing its nest on branches, in the forks of trees, on posts, rocks, or house-tops. Another species, known to the Spaniards as the CASARITA, or LITTLE HOUSE-BUILDER, builds its nest at the bottom of a narrow cylindrical hole, which is said to extend horizontally underground for nearly six feet. Other species build nests of sticks and twigs or of grass, which are divided into chambers after the fashion of the mud nest of the oven-bird, the inner chamber being lined with wool and feathers.

The variation in the form, habits, and coloration of these birds is very great, some recalling the Woodpeckers and Tree-creepers, others the Titmice.

The family of the TYRANT FLY-CATCHERS, though numbering some 400 species, is less interesting, or rather contains fewer peculiar forms, than the Manakin Family. The tyrant fly-catchers are American birds, and represent the fly-catchers of the Old World. One of the best known is the KING-BIRD, which is renowned rather for its pugnacious disposition than for beauty of plumage.

The CRESTED TYRANT-BIRD has a curious habit of lining its nest with the cast-off skins of snakes, a habit which has caused a great deal of discomfort both to juvenile as well as adult egg-collectors, who, recognising the skin by the touch, have hurriedly withdrawn the hand, lest the owner of the cast-off coat should be in the vicinity.

Photo by A. S. Rudland & Sons.

COCK-OF-THE-ROCK.

The cock-of-the-rock is a South American bird, of gorgeous coloration.

All the tyrant-birds are active and restless in their habits, and frequent marshy districts, sitting alone, perched on the dead branches of trees or bushes, whence they dart forth like the Old World fly-catchers on their prey. Some species, however, frequent bare plains; others, also ground-dwellers, associate occasionally in flocks.

Though the prey, which consists chiefly of insects, is, as a rule, captured on the wing, it is not invariably so. One species, for example, pounces down on crawling beetles, grasps them in its claws, and eats them on the ground. Some other species eat mice, young birds, snakes, frogs, fishes, spiders, and worms, the larger victims being beaten on a branch to kill them. One or two species will eat seeds and berries. The nest is often domed, and skilfully felted with moss, lichens, and spider-webs.

The BROAD-BILLS are the sole representatives of the final sub-division of the Perching-birds. After the brilliant coloration, the next most striking feature is the great breadth of the bill. Their range is very limited, extending from the lower spurs of the Himalaya, through Burma and Siam, to Sumatra, Borneo, and Java. They seek the seclusion of forests in the neighbourhood of water, exhibiting great partiality for the banks of rivers and lakes, and feeding on worms and insects, many of the latter being captured on the wing.

The nest of the broad-bill is a large and not very neat structure, oval in shape, with an entrance near the top, which is often protected with an overhanging roof. It is generally suspended from a low branch or plants near the water, and made of twigs, roots, and leaves, and lined with finer materials. From three to five eggs are laid.

With these birds, probably the most primitive of the Perching-birds, this section ends. Many forms have inevitably been crowded out, whilst others have been but briefly noticed; nevertheless, all the really important groups have been more or less completely described, and in the majority of cases well illustrated.

Photo by W. Saville Kent, F.Z.S., Milford-on-Sea.

GREEN AND OCELLATED LIZARDS.

The former species is found in the South of England, as well as on the Continent; the latter is restricted to Southern Europe and North Africa.

BOOK III. REPTILES AND AMPHIBIANS.

BY W. SAVILLE-KENT, F.L.S., F.Z.S.

REPTILES.

CHAPTER I.

CROCODILES AND ALLIGATORS.

THE Reptile Class, as defined by modern scientific limitations, includes among the living animals of the world the several groups of the Crocodiles, the Tortoises and Turtles, the Tuatera, the Lizards, and the Snakes. In the popular mind the Frogs and Toads, and the Newts and Salamanders, are often held to belong to the same main section; but these, as hereafter shown, claim, as Amphibians, an independent position of equivalent rank and value. In bygone geological ages the Reptile Class embraced a considerably larger number of groups; some of the members, such as the extinct Dinosaurs, comprised titanic monsters from 60 to 80 feet in length. The Crocodiles and Alligators of the present day are the only living reptiles which in any way approach the extinct Saurians in their dimensions, or assist us in some small measure to realise their unwieldy forms and bulk.

The members of the Crocodile Order, which, in addition to the Alligators, includes also the Caimans and so-called Gavials or Garials, agree with one another in the more or less ponderous lizard-like shape of their body, supported on well-developed but short and comparatively weak legs, in their special adaptation to an amphibious existence, carnivorous habits, and restriction to tropical and sub-tropical climates.

Photo by W. P. Dando, F.Z.S.] [*Regent's Park.*

YOUNG NILE CROCODILE.

This species was worshipped with divine honours and mummified after death by the ancient Egyptians.

Among the salient characters of the CROCODILE, as the representative of its tribe, which specially adapt it for its aquatic habits, the long, powerful tail is strongly compressed and thus fitted for use as an organ of propulsion, and the feet are more or less webbed. The most striking of its structural adaptations is, however, associated with the formation of the creature's skull. The manner in which a crocodile or alligator contrives to breathe or to save itself from asphyxiation, when opening and shutting its mouth under water, as it may often be observed to do in the Regent's Park Menagerie, is a common source of wonderment to the onlooker. This seemingly difficult feat is compassed by virtue of the posterior nostrils, or breathing-passages, being set so far back in the skull, and being so completely cut off from the mouth-cavity by specially developed bones of the palate, that they have no intercommunication with the mouth. It is this mechanism which enables a crocodile to seize and hold an animal underneath the water between its open jaws until it is drowned. Special valves at the back of the mouth prevent any water running down the creature's throat, while it is able itself to breathe unrestrainedly by allowing just the tip of its elongated snout, with the anterior nostril-apertures, to remain above the water's surface. In many species a conspicuous knob-like bony excrescence is developed at the extremity of the snout, by which the nostril-openings are raised turret-wise above the surface of the water. The eyes also being usually elevated above the level of the creature's head, the crocodile is able to approach its floating or bank-side prey practically unperceived, its huge body, limbs, and even the head, with the exception of the nose and eyes, being totally submerged.

Photo by W. P. Dando, F.Z.S.] [*Regent's Park.*

YOUNG BROAD-SNOUTED CROCODILE.

A native of West Africa, remarkable for the extreme shortness and great breadth of its nozzle.

Although capable of moving with great activity in the water, crocodiles and their allies are usually accounted sluggish and slow movers on the land. Seen basking in the sun, as is their wont, by the hour together on some sand-bank or creeping lazily thereon among their fellows, such a conclusion is natural. The celerity, however, with which

Photo by Norman B. Smith, Esq.

A DEAD CROCODILE.

A man-eating individual. This particular animal has just been shot. The natives in the background give a good idea of its size—little less than 20 feet long.

even a huge 25-footer, as witnessed by the writer in the Norman River, North Queensland, will make tracks for and hurl itself into the water, if disturbed during its midday siesta by the near impact of a rifle-bullet, is a revelation. Crocodiles, moreover, as might be inferred from the slit-like contour of the eye-pupil, as shown by daylight, are to a large extent nocturnal, displaying their greatest activity, and being in the habit of travelling long distances along and away from the river-banks in search of food, or in connection with their migratory or mating instincts, under the cover of darkness.

Of all living animals the crocodile and its allies are probably equipped most efficiently for both defence and aggression. The thick, horny shields, quadrangular on the back, tail, and under-surface, and adapted in shape and size to cover the head, limbs, and sides, constitute an almost impenetrable cuirass. As weapons of offence the formidable array of trenchant teeth, with which the powerful jaws are armed, have not alone to be reckoned with by the victim assailed. The crocodile's limbs and claws are relatively weak, and incapable of aggressive

Photo by Mr. W. Rau] [*Philadelphia.*

A CROCODILE.

Note the massive character of the tail, a weapon wherewith the creature can disable a horse or an ox, or sweep smaller prey into the water.

mischief; but in the long, compressed, muscular tail the reptile possesses a terribly effective weapon, wherewith, with one swift, unexpected side-stroke, it will sweep a smaller animal into the water, or deal a blow of sufficient power to fell or disable a man or bullock. Thus well-nigh invulnerable, and cognisant of its marvellous power of jaw and tail, a full-grown crocodile will not hesitate to try conclusions with even such puissant adversaries as the bear, the tiger, and other large carnivora, when they approach the river's brink to drink. Not infrequently, too, the crocodile comes off the victor in these contests; while, as sometimes happens, both of the well-matched foes are found dead side by side at the water's edge. The dread in which crocodiles are held by the natives of tropical countries, and the heavy toll they levy upon the riverside population, and more especially the women-folk in their accustomed avocations of water-carrying or laundry work, are too familiar to need dissertation. Hence it is that in every country, excepting those particular locations where the creature is a subject of misguided veneration or fetish worship, it may be said that every man's hand is against them, and the enmity most cordially reciprocated.

All the members of the Crocodile Family propagate by egg-production. The eggs are relatively small in size, those of the largest species not exceeding that of a goose in dimensions. In shape they are more or less symmetrically ovate, and encased with a hard, white shell. In the case of the crocodile, the female selects a suitable dry sand-bank near the river's edge, in which it excavates a hole of about 2 feet deep, and, having deposited from twenty to sixty eggs therein, mounts guard over them, sleeping on top of the nest by day, until the young are hatched. With the alligator, the site chosen for the nest is more usually among bushes or reeds at some distance from the water, and the eggs, which may be laid to the number of over 100, are covered over with leaves and vegetable débris, whose decomposition engenders the heat required for their successful incubation. In both instances the parent jealously guards the nest and repels all intruders until the eggs are hatched, and ultimately conducts the young ones to the water, where they soon learn to shift for themselves. Numbers of them, nevertheless, in their young and weak state, fall victims to vultures, hawks, ichneumons, and all manner of birds and beasts of prey. From their birth the little saurians are most vicious and irascible in disposition, hissing and snapping at or laying hold with bull-dog tenacity of a finger or other seizable object that may be held towards them. From their earliest days also they are eminently aggressive and carnivorous. Contenting themselves at first with flies and other insects, they speedily extend their attentions to frogs, lizards, fish, or any small animals which frequent the marshes and river-banks; and finally, with their concurrently increased appetites and dimensions, requisition such larger prey as sheep, goats, deer, horses, and, as before mentioned, even the human species, if they can steal a march on them unawares. Crocodiles are provided with relatively small gullets, and are necessarily incapable of swallowing any prey whole which is of large dimensions. Accordingly any big quarry which is seized and dragged into the river is disposed of piecemeal, the reptile rending the carcase in fragments with the aid of its terrible teeth and side-wrenches of its ponderous body.

Photo by W. Saville-Kent, F.Z.S.] *[Milford-on-Sea.*

A QUEENSLAND CROCODILE.

The specimen referred to in the anecdote on page 550.

Of crocodiles proper, as distinguished from alligators, there are some dozen known species. From their last-named near allies they are distinguished by the entire absence of the supplementary bony armature which in most alligators underlies the outer horny cuirass on the under surface of the body. A more essential distinction is associated with the character of the teeth. The upper and lower teeth of the crocodile interlock, and the fourth lower canine-like tooth is received into a notch in the side of the upper jaw, and is consequently more or less visible when the mouth is closed. In the alligators, on the other hand, this bigger tusk-like tooth fits into a pit-like excavation in the upper jaw, and is invisible when the mouth is shut.

The TRUE CROCODILES are found in the tropical regions of Africa, Asia, Australasia, and Central America. The largest is undoubtedly the estuarine species, ranging from the eastern shores of India, through the Malay region, to North and East Australia, New Guinea, and the Fiji Islands. This wide range is a natural concomitant of their brackish- and salt-water proclivities. Individuals of the species are, in fact, not infrequently met with floating on the sea at some considerable distance from the land. An example of this estuarine species has been recorded which measured no less than 33 feet, while a length of 20 feet and over is by no means of uncommon occurrence.

Photo by J. W. McLellan] [*Highbury*.

CROCODILE, WELL ILLUSTRATING THE CHARACTER OF THE DENTITION.

The lower tusk-like teeth fit into notches in the upper jaw, and are visible when the mouth is closed. In the alligator these teeth fit into pits in the upper jaw, and are hidden from view under the like conditions.

Photo by Scholastic Photo. Co.] *[Parson's Green.*

CROCODILES AND ALLIGATORS, WITH YOUNG.

Notwithstanding their proverbially irascible dispositions, these reptiles, of all ages and dimensions, herd together on the most amiable terms.

The method adopted in Queensland and North Australia for capturing these destructive monsters is that of a running noose, so attached to a suitably flexible mangrove-tree growing in the vicinity of its nocturnal runs as to constitute a gigantic spring-trap. A dead carcase or other suitable bait is added to lure the animal to its doom. The crocodiles thus caught are alive and uninjured, and can be dispatched or reserved for menagerie exhibition. A somewhat amusing incident attended the transport of a "reprieved" captive by steamship from Cairns to Brisbane, Queensland, a few years since. In the dead of night, when all but the watch and engineer had retired to rest (they have to anchor and lay-to at night in the Great Barrier Reef channels), the saurian managed to free himself from his bonds, and started on a voyage of discovery around the decks. Arriving at the stoke-hold, he either incontinently stumbled into it, or descended of *malice prepense*, sniffing the chance of a supper or a good joke at the engineer's expense. Anyway, the engineer was aroused from his peaceful dozings with the impression that the last day of reckoning had arrived, and, rushing up the hatchway, awakened the whole ship's strength with his frantic outcries.

The NILE CROCODILE, the most familiar form in European menageries, and once abundant throughout Egypt to the Nile's delta, has now retired to the upper reaches of that great river. It never attains to the dimensions of the estuarine form. By the ancient Egyptians, as is well known, this species was pampered and worshipped with divine honours while living, and after death embalmed and preserved in the catacombs.

Other noteworthy crocodiles, of which space will allow only of the mention of their names, are the AMERICAN or ORINOCO CROCODILE, and the LONG-SNOUTED CROCODILE of West Africa, which distantly approach to the LONG-SNOUTED GAVIAL or GARIAL of India, in which the snout is elongated in a beak-like manner, and armed with close rows of long, recurved teeth, specially adapted for its ex-

Photo by Robert D. Carson, Esq.] *[Philadelphia.*

A CROCODILE FROM SOUTHERN UNITED STATES.

The teeth of crocodiles, as compared with those of alligators, are much less uniform in size and character.

clusively fish-eating propensities. Full-grown examples of the gavial may attain to a length of 20 feet.

The TYPICAL or MISSISSIPPI ALLIGATOR is, as its name denotes, a North American form, having the modified dental and other structural details previously referred to, but otherwise in size and its aggressively destructive habits nearly corresponding with the Oriental crocodile. A second species of alligator is found in China.

In the tropical South American rivers the place of the alligator is occupied by the CAIMANS, some of which attain to huge proportions, and are distinguished from the former by the greater development of the bony armature of both their back and under-surface, and by certain essential, but to the lay reader obscure, modifications of the skull. An example of the GREAT CAIMAN once did duty as a riding-horse to the naturalist Waterton, as all those familiar with his book of travels will remember.

Photo by Scholastic Photo. Co.] [*Parson's Green.*

MISSISSIPPI AND CHINESE ALLIGATORS.

The Chinese species, which is the smaller of the two, feeds mainly upon fish.

The habits of the caiman differ somewhat locally. From the main stream of the Lower Amazon they are in the habit of migrating in the dry season to the inland pools and flooded forests. In the middle districts of the same river, where the drought is excessive and protracted, the caimans are addicted to burying themselves in the mud till the rains return; while in the upper reaches of the Amazon, where the droughts are not prolonged, the caimans are perennially present. The eggs of these reptiles are much esteemed for food by the natives of Dutch Guiana.

CHAPTER II.

TORTOISES AND TURTLES.

THE order of the Chelonians, including the Tortoises, Turtles, and Terrapins, with their allies, constitutes one of the most distinct and readily defined groups of the Reptile Class. The more or less complete bony shell, or carapace, which encases the body, and into which both head and limbs can in many cases be completely retracted, separates these reptiles very widely from the other orders. In some respects certain details of the skull-structure assimilate them to the Crocodiles; but here again there is an entire absence of the rows of formidable teeth, the upper and lower jaws being sharply pointed, covered with horn, and thus converted into a trenchant beak. The two leading groups of the Tortoises and the Turtles are distinctly separated, by the respective conformation of their limbs, for a terrestrial or aquatic existence. The Tortoises have normal walking-legs, with toes and, in most instances, claws, fitting them for walking on the land or burrowing into the earth. In the True Turtles

Photo by C. N. Mavroyeni] [*Smyrna.*

ASIATIC TORTOISES.

A tortoise, like a turtle, turned over on its back, represents one of the most helpless of living animals.

these limbs take the form of flattened paddles, and in no instance are more than two of the toes provided with claws.

The TORTOISES are sub-divided by zoologists into some six or eight subordinate groups or families, for the most part distinguished by the respective modifications of their protective shells. This shell in all tortoises and turtles consists of two essential elements—the upper or back casing, known as the "carapace," and the under one, or so-called "plastron," which covers the ventral surface. In some forms these two elements are completely welded into one another, forming a continuous box-like shell; in others they are more or less separate; while in yet another series the lower shell is rudimentary. These distinctions have been found to constitute a convenient basis for classification.

In the TRUE LAND-TORTOISES, which invite first attention, the upper and lower shells are completely united in a box-like form, and the neck, bent in the form of the letter S, can be completely retracted within it. The limbs are club-shaped, covered with horny scales or tubercles, and adapted for walking, the toes being unwebbed, and provided with strong claw-like nails.

Pre-eminent among this typical terrestrial series come the huge GIANT or ELEPHANT-TORTOISES, formerly abundant, as their fossil remains indicate, in Southern Europe, India, and North and South America, and now represented only in the isolated oceanic islands of Aldabra, off Madagascar, the Seychelles, and the Galapagos groups. Even within historic times they were very abundant in the islands of Mauritius and Rodrigues; but their huge size and lethargic habits, combined with their esculent qualities, have brought about their extermination. Those remaining in the islands mentioned are now so reduced in numbers that there is a possibility of their becoming extinct at an early date, and this notwithstanding the strenuous endeavours that are being made to save them. A large percentage of the small residue of these giant Chelonians have been transported from their island homes and presented to the London Zoological Gardens, where they are now comfortably housed.

An instructive idea of the aspect and relative dimensions of these giant tortoises may be obtained by a reference to page vii of the First Volume, in which one of these Chelonians is shown to be equal in size and strength to carrying a human rider. It is recorded that these reptiles were so abundant in the island of Rodrigues in 1691 that one might count as many as 3,000 of them in a single flock, and walk for over 100 paces upon their backs. All of these giant tortoises, as obtained from separate island groups, or islets of the groups, exhibit characteristic differences, indicating the length of time they have been separated from one another. The age to which these giant tortoises attain is altogether phenomenal. One example at Port Louis, Mauritius,

Photo by C. N. Mavroyeni] [*Smyrna.*

EUROPEAN TORTOISE.

A tortoise's shell, or carapace, constitutes a portable house, wherein the animal can entirely withdraw for shelter in inclement weather, or when attacked by enemies.

originally brought from the Seychelles, is definitely known to have lived for over 130 years from the date of its transportation. It is stated to have been of large size when imported; and as these animals are notoriously slow growers, another couple of centuries may be safely added to its life-span. The Galapagos Islands down to recent times have produced the greater number of species of these tortoises, the carapace of the largest of these not infrequently measuring as much as 4 feet in direct length, and the weight of such an animal being over 400 lbs.

Highly interesting details concerning the Galapagos giant tortoises and their habits are contained in Darwin's "Voyage of the Beagle." At the time of that illustrious naturalist's visit they were still very abundant in the islands. He remarked that they abounded in both the higher and damper and the lower and arid districts, but gave preference to the former.

Photo by S. G. Payne & Son, Aylesbury, by permission of the Hon. Walter Rothschild.

ELEPHANT-TORTOISES FROM THE GALAPAGOS ISLANDS.

Several species are shown in this photograph.

The old males were invariably the largest, growing to such a size that they required six or eight men to lift them, and yielded as much as 200 lbs. of good, highly nutritious meat. On some of the islands there was no water; and in these cases, as also when they occurred in the dry and arid lowlands, they were observed to feed chiefly on the succulent cactuses. When water was plentiful, the tortoises exhibited a great fondness for it, drinking large quantities and wallowing in the mud. In the larger islands, where wells and springs existed in the higher and damper portions, regular well-beaten paths radiated in every direction, indicating the routes, like sheep-tracks, regularly followed by the tortoises to and from the water-holes. It was these tracks which betrayed their presence and led to their first discovery by the older Spanish navigators. When travelling long distances to the watering-places, it is recorded that they march night and day, pursuing the "even tenor of their way" at the rate of sixty yards an hour—one yard per minute, or four miles per day! During the breeding-season the larger males indulge in hoarse roarings or bellowings that can be heard for a considerable distance. The female deposits her eggs either in the sand, where this is plentiful, covering them up again, or, where the ground is rocky, drops them indiscriminately in any crevice or depression encountered. The eggs are white, spherical, and hard-shelled, as in all tortoises, and somewhat exceed those of a hen in bulk.

The very antithesis of the giant land-tortoises of the Galapagos Islands is the small and familiar GRECIAN TORTOISE, frequently exposed for sale on hand-barrows in the London streets, and acquired by the unsophisticated suburban resident as a quaint but not altogether estimable garden pet. Like the majority of tortoises, this is a vegetarian, and with epicurean tastes that will guide it instinctively to select your choicest lettuces and the gems of your horticultural triumphs for the delectation of its fastidious appetite. The Grecian tortoise rarely exceeds 5½ inches in length, and is abundant throughout South-eastern Europe, Sicily, Italy, and the Grecian Archipelago, extending thence to Syria. In Algeria an almost identical tortoise occurs which grows to the greater length of 9 inches; while Greece produces yet a third form, the so-called MARGINED TORTOISE, which attains the greater length of 11 inches, and is distinguished by the colour of the carapace usually being black, with a small spot of yellow on each shield-like plate. All three of the foregoing species are collectively imported by shiploads for sale in England, and it would be interesting to know what fate befalls them. In Greece and Sicily they are regularly placed on the market as an article of food. When acclimatised in England, and even in their warmer native country, these Grecian tortoises bury them selves in the earth and hibernate during the cold winter months.

Photo by S. G. Payne & Son, Aylesbury, by permission of Hon. Walter Rothschild.

ELEPHANT-TORTOISE.

Note the small size of the head with relation to the huge carapace.

Next to the typical Land-tortoises the so-called HINGED TORTOISES demand brief notice. The several members of this little group are denizens of tropical Africa, and notable for the circumstance that the hinder portion of their carapace is united with the anterior one by a movable ligamentous hinge. As a result of this peculiarity the animal, when retracted within its shell, can entirely close up the hinder aperture. None of these forms exceed a length of 9 inches.

In another group, distinguished by the title of BOX-TORTOISES, a ligamentous hinge is developed across the centre of the lower shell, or plastron, which, being freely movable with relation to the upper shell, enables the animal, when retracted, to completely close up both the anterior and posterior carapace apertures. The box-tortoises are natives of the South-eastern United States and Mexico, and, in addition to the foregoing structural peculiarity, are distinguished by the high or vaulted contour of their carapace. In some the toes are slightly webbed, and their habits are mainly carnivorous, indicating affinity with the flesh-eating and essentially aquatic Terrapins.

Between the two, however, have been intercalated a little group, known as the POND-TORTOISES, one species of which is found in Southern Europe, and a nearly allied one in North America. These pond-tortoises are distinguished by the smooth and depressed form of the carapace; the toes are fully webbed, fitting them for an aquatic life; while a ligamentous hinge, separating the anterior and posterior moieties of the plastron, enables them to cover in and protect their retracted head and limbs, after the manner of the Box-tortoises. The carapace of the European pond-tortoise does not exceed 7½ inches in length, and is usually dark brown or black, ornamented with yellow dots or radiating streaks. This species inhabits both ponds and running water, and during the daytime creeps out on the banks,

Photos by S. G. Payne & Son, Aylesbury, by permission of the Hon. Walter Rothschild.

GIANT OR ELEPHANT-TORTOISES FROM THE GALAPAGOS ISLANDS.

The elephant-like character of their limbs, whence they derive their name, is well exemplified in these examples.

like the Crocodiles, to bask in the sun. As with the Crocodiles, however, the daytime does not represent the period of its greatest activity, this being during the night. The pond-tortoises are highly esteemed for the table in the countries where they are indigenous.

The TRUE TERRAPINS are all tortoises of essentially aquatic habits, differing, however, from the water-frequenting Pond-tortoises, last referred to, in that they have no ligamentous hinge providing for the hermetical closure of the carapace apertures. The carapace and plastron, moreover, are firmly united by bone, so that the two form conjointly a rigid, continuous shell, as in that of the typical Land-tortoises. The terrapins are widely distributed, being found in North America, Japan, China, the Persian Gulf, Spain, and North-west Africa. Terrapin ranks highly as a table delicacy in the United States. The real DIAMOND-BACKED species, however, is now becoming very scarce, the supply not being equal to the demand, and many inferior varieties being substituted in its place. The "fishing" for these terrapins is mainly prosecuted during the autumn months, when the reptiles become dormant, and are easily discovered and secured by probing the mud with sticks. The female terrapin, or "cow," as it is designated, is considered the greater delicacy, the eggs, to the number of twenty or thirty, usually found inside its body, being the *de rigueur* garnishing of the dainty dish. The diamond-terrapin rarely exceeds a length of 7 inches; but some of the inferior varieties, or "Sliders," as they are termed, are of much larger dimensions, and may weigh as much as 4 lbs.

Photo by S. G. Payne & Son, Aylesbury, by permission of the Hon. Walter Rothschild.

GIANT TORTOISE.

The giant tortoises, like the relatively diminutive European varieties, are essentially herbivorous.

From an æsthetic standpoint the PAINTED TERRAPIN undoubtedly bears the palm. Its smooth, depressed carapace is not more than 6 inches long, and its ground-colour is usually a dark olive-green, yellow lines bordering its component central shields; the small marginal shields are sometimes almost crimson with black markings, and the "bridge" uniting the carapace and plastron exhibits the same brilliant coloration. The soft skin of the head, neck, and other exposed parts have yellow and red bands on a brown or blackish ground-colour. This beautiful little terrapin, which is a special favourite for aquariums, is a native of Eastern North America.

Passing the small and not peculiarly conspicuous group of the AMERICAN MUD-TERRAPINS, we arrive at the very distinctly differentiated family of the SNAPPERS, SNAPPING-TURTLES, or ALLIGATOR-TERRAPINS, as they are variously called. These likewise are exclusively confined in their present-day distribution to the New World, though in former ages allied species inhabited Europe. The alligator-terrapins are characterised by the relatively small size of the carapace, within which the animal is unable to completely retract its head and limbs, as in the preceding types. The head is relatively large, and armed with a formidable hooked beak; while the tail greatly exceeds in relative length that of any of the ordinary tortoises or terrapins, and is scaly and crested somewhat like that of a crocodile along its upper ridge, and has horny plates on the under-surface. Their popular name has, in fact, been conferred upon these Chelonians on the strength of their presenting the aspect to no inconsiderable extent of an alligator's body, to which the carapace of an ordinary terrapin has been united. The common alligator-terrapin, or snapping-turtle, is among aquatic Chelonians an animal of considerable size. The carapace alone may be as much or more than 20 inches long, and to this have to be added the thick head and neck and elongated tail, which, taken together, are of almost similar dimensions.

A second closely related member of this family, known by the name of TEMMINCK'S SNAPPER, attains to yet longer proportions, and is the largest known river-tortoise. The carapace in this species may measure over 2 feet in length, and has three strongly marked longitudinal ridges. The head is relatively larger and the tail somewhat shorter than in the preceding species. It is a denizen of the southern districts of the United States, being met with in Texas, Florida, and as far north as the Missouri.

The habits of the two species are stated to be identical. Both of them frequent the rivers and swamps of the areas indicated, preferring the waters that have a muddy bottom, and in some localities occurring in vast numbers. As a rule they prefer lying in deep water near the centre of the river or swamp they inhabit, but they also occasionally ascend to the surface and float in midstream with outstretched necks. Like other water-tortoises, they come on land to find suitable locations for depositing their eggs. The name of Snappers, commonly applied to these tortoises, bears reference to their inveterate habit of snapping and biting viciously at everything placed within their reach. Even from the egg the young of Temminck's species is wont to display this trait. The animals are somewhat esteemed for food, and are consequently caught for the market. They will take almost any bait, but manifest a predilection for fish. Considerable caution has necessarily to be exercised in dealing with them in the boats, and it is a common custom to decapitate them immediately they are hauled on board, otherwise they are capable of inflicting the most terrible wounds with their powerful cutting beaks on the persons of all or any who may remain within their reach. Bathing in waters tenanted by the pugnacious and distinctly aggressive snappers is a risky proceeding, and many cases of serious injuries that have happened to incautious adventurers in this direction have been recorded.

The food of both the alligator and Temminck's snapper consists mainly of fish, and where common these tortoises must be ranked among the most potent agencies in denuding the rivers and lakes of their finny denizens. Not content with fish, the larger examples have been known to drag under water and devour such large water-fowl as ducks, and even geese. It is stated that the snappers exhibit a surprising amount of agility in the water, and swim after and capture the fish on which they feed. Such a feat seems scarcely credible of a bulky adult individual, while, moreover, it is provided with a remarkable and effective adaptation for taking its prey by stratagem. A very fine example of Temminck's snapper was for many years confined in a tank in the Reptile-

Photo by Scholastic Photo. Co.] *[Parson's Green.*

A GIANT TORTOISE WITH A EUROPEAN TORTOISE ON ITS BACK.

Illustrating their comparative dimensions.

house in the Regent's Park Zoological Gardens. It usually lay prone at the bottom of its tank, giving little or no signs of life throughout the day, but was wont to display more activity and to move about its tank at night. At times, when ready for a fresh food-supply, it was observed that it would lie motionless as a stone, as usual, but with its mouth open to its widest gape. This attitude it would maintain for several hours together. The singularity of this action was that the gaping jaws displayed to view two elongate worm-like structures, which sprang close to one another from the floor of the mouth just within its entrance. These worm-like appendages were continually writhing to and fro, and presented in both aspect and movements a most remarkable resemblance to actual living worms. With this naturally provided decoy for fish there can be no need for the snapper to exhaust its energies in the strenuous pursuit of its quarry. To make the delusion complete, the head, neck, and chin of Temminck's snapper are decorated with small lobular or leaf-like membranous appendages resembling sponges or aquatic vegetation. The solid grey-brown triangular head of the animal itself might easily be mistaken for a piece of rock, and thus decorated with seemingly natural growths the unwary fish come browsing along it, rush upon the wriggling worms at the entrance of the cavernous chamber, and are lost. A photograph of this interesting Chelonian is reproduced on page 560, which depicts it with its mouth open, and indicates both the position and the presence of the worm-like decoy-appendages.

Photo by S. G. Payne & Son, Aylesbury, by permission of the Hon. Walter Rothschild.

ELEPHANT-TORTOISE.

Illustrating the ample chamber-like space provided within the carapace for the retraction of the head and limbs.

There are several water-tortoises presenting a considerable external resemblance to the forms already noticed which belong to distinct family groups. Thus the MATAMATA TORTOISE of Northern Brazil has at first sight, except for its short tail and nose-like proboscis, much in common with Temminck's snapper. Fimbriated and foliaceous membranous outgrowths are developed on the head and neck to a much more luxuriant degree, and it would be interesting to ascertain if it possesses similar decoy-appendages inside the mouth.

The so-called SNAKE-NECKED WATER-TORTOISES of South America, and the LONG-NECKED aquatic ones of Australasia, possess modifications of skull-structure and other details that indicate family distinctness. A broad external character that serves to separate this group from the Terrapins and all preceding forms is that the neck, when drawn within the cavity of the carapace, is not flexed in the form of the letter S, but simply bent sideways along the anterior margin of the body. The species belonging to this group, which includes the Matamata, Snake-necked, and Soft-shelled Water-tortoises, and also a few essentially terrestrial species, are distinguished collectively by the appellation of the "SIDE-NECKED" TORTOISES.

TURTLES.

Certain of the Terrapins, or Water-tortoises, belonging to the groups above described frequent saline river-estuaries and salt marshes, but none are strictly marine. With the Turtle Family, however, we arrive at an exclusively pelagic section, in which the animals are specially adapted for life in the high seas, the walking-limbs of the terrestrial and fresh-water species being replaced by long and powerful swimming-flippers. The shell in these marine Chelonians is more or less heart-shaped and flattened, and the carapace and plastron are always separate, and never united in a rigid box-like form, as with the Land-tortoises. In common with those fresh-water tortoises which pass the greater portion of their existence in lakes or rivers, the MARINE TURTLES resort to the land to deposit their eggs. The locations chosen are the sand-beaches or isolated sandy islets in tropical oceans, wherein, after excavating hollows to receive them. the eggs are covered up and left to

By permission of the New York Zoological Society.

SNAPPING-TURTLE.

Also known as the Alligator-terrapin, with reference to its long, alligator-like tail.

hatch with the heat of the sun. The eggs of turtles differ from those of the Land-tortoises and Terrapins in that their external covering is soft or leathery. So soon as the young turtles are hatched, they emerge from the sand, and instinctively make their way to the water. Many, however, are the perils that beset their course, and few there be out of perhaps 80 or 100 turtlets which gain the shore and get through into deep water. Fish-hawks and sea-birds of every description are waiting ready to pounce down upon them immediately they make their appearance, or to thin their ranks as they run the gauntlet of perhaps 100 yards or so to reach the sea in safety. Even at the water's edge the ordeal is by no means passed. Shoals of the smaller sharks and other predatory fish are continually cruising round in the shallow water, and have as high an appreciation of the toothsomeness of tender turtle as the proverbial London alderman. The writer was fortunate on one occasion, among the coral islands on the Australian coasts, to light upon a young turtle brood

Photo by York & Son] *[Notting Hill.*

TEMMINCK'S SNAPPER.

The two white points visible on the lower jaw represent the pair of worm-like appendages which the creature uses as a bait to attract or capture fish.

just emerging from their sandy nest. The majority were assisted to the sea, and a few, reserved in the interests of science, were liberated in a bath of sea-water to have their first swim. Snap-shot photographs were taken, one of which, reproduced on page 561, serves to illustrate the great relative length of the paddle-like limbs at this early stage and the variety of postures assumed during natation.

Of the typical Marine Turtles three distinctly characterised species are recognised by zoologists. These are the GREEN TURTLE, indispensable for soup at aldermanic banquets; the HAWKSBILL, or tortoiseshell-producing turtle; and the LOGGERHEAD. Of these three, the green turtle and the loggerhead more nearly resemble one another, and are apt to be confounded by the uninitiated. Such an error is very readily detected when the Chelonian comes to the table, the flesh of the loggerhead being rank and utterly unfit for food. In order, however, to be wise before the event, and to avoid a grievous misdirection of culinary energy—turtle being a standard dish in the coral seas—it is only necessary to count the number of large shield-like plates that flank each side of the central series in the creature's carapace. In the true green or edible turtle there are only four pairs of these large lateral shields, while in the loggerhead there are never less than five, and sometimes more. The loggerhead-turtle also, as its name implies, has a conspicuously larger and coarser head than the esculent species. The fact that while the green turtle is a strict vegetarian, feeding entirely on seaweeds, the loggerhead is altogether carnivorous, readily accounts for the diametrically diverse gastronomic properties of these two Chelonians. Both species attain to a considerable size, over 3 feet in length (the loggerhead being the larger), and are found inhabiting the same waters throughout the tropics.

The HAWKSBILL, or true tortoiseshell-producing turtle, never attains to quite as large dimensions as the two preceding species, though its carapace may measure as much as 2 feet 6 or 8 inches long. The structural feature that at once distinguishes the hawksbill from either the green or loggerhead species is the character of the horny shields developed on the surface of the carapace. Instead of the edges meeting in juxtaposition, as in those two forms, they overlap one another, like the scales of a fish, and are notable for their thickness and their exceedingly beautiful but variably marbled patterns. It is these marbled horny plates which constitute the tortoise-shell of commerce. In young individuals the substance is thin and very transparent, but thickens with advancing age, until in old individuals the plates may vary from $\frac{1}{8}$ to $\frac{1}{4}$ inch in thickness. Like the two preceding species, the hawksbill, within tropical seas, enjoys a cosmopolitan distribution. Its habits, like the loggerhead's, are essentially carnivorous; but while the flesh is coarse and rank, the eggs are valued for the table.

A remaining member of the Marine Turtle series is the so-called LUTH or LEATHERY TURTLE. This Chelonian differs so materially in structure from the foregoing species as to be referred to a distinct family. The horny plates, so conspicuous in all the other types, are entirely absent, the bony carapace, which is distinctly seven-ridged longitudinally, being covered with a homogeneous leather-like skin. Both jaws are formidably hooked and cutting throughout their edges, and the paddles are destitute of the two rudimentary claws found in the preceding species. The leathery turtle grows to an immense size; specimens have been recorded measuring as much as 8 feet in total length and weighing over 1,600 lbs. Its flesh is not only unfit for food, but is reported to be of a poisonous character. The coasts of Florida and Brazil are among the areas where the leathery turtle is met with in the greatest abundance.

The more ordinary method of capturing turtle for the market or to supply the deficiencies of the larder aboard ship in tropical climates is to land at night, preferably when the moon is full, on the islands to which the females are in the habit of repairing to deposit their eggs. This function is invariably discharged during the night hours, and unless the moon is up the presence of the reptiles is not easily determined. Time is generally given for the turtle to excavate its sand-burrow and lay its eggs, usually over a hundred in number, the proper

Photo by W. Saville-Kent, F.Z.S.] *[Milford-on-Sea.*

NEWLY HATCHED TURTLES ENJOYING THEIR FIRST SWIM.

The limbs at this early stage of their development are of an abnormal length.

moment for the capture being that when, the task accomplished, it sets forth to regain its more accustomed element. The creature is then seized and turned suddenly upon its back, where it is left to struggle and flounder helplessly, being perfectly incapable of righting itself, while other captures are made. On outlying coral islands, such as those of the Lacepedes, off the Western Australian coast, several dozen of the Chelonians may represent one good night's haul, the choice of the fittest examples being left until the return of daylight.

In many places turtles are pursued in the water and speared; while in some locations, notably at Keeling Island, as recorded by Darwin, the animals are chased by the natives in sailing-craft. One man steers the boat, the other one standing in the bows on the look-out for turtle. A Chelonian being sighted, an exciting stern chase ensues, and on coming abreast with the quarry the look-out man plunges into the water straight upon the turtle's back, and

Photo by H. V. Lutkmann.

CUBAN TERRAPINS.

In common with many other water-tortoises, or terrapins, this species is essentially gregarious in its habits.

clings pertinaciously with both hands to the shell of the neck until the creature is exhausted, when it is dragged into the boat.

The most remarkable method of taking turtle, however, is that practised in Torres Straits, as also at Mozambique and formerly in the West Indies. The sucking-fish, or remora, is in this case impressed into the service of the human fishers. Taking advantage of the fish's natural propensity to swim towards and adhere pertinaciously to any larger floating object, fishermen go out with specimens kept alive in a small well in the bottom of their boats. When in pursuit of turtle, a long light line is attached to the fish's tail; and coming within sight of a Chelonian, the fish, with an abundance of slack or pay-out line, is thrown in the direction of the turtle. The remora immediately swims towards and adheres firmly to the under surface of the shell of the turtle, when it will suffer its body to be torn asunder rather than let go its hold of its newly gained sanctuary. Should the turtle be a small one, both fish and turtle are dragged with the line back to the boat. If, on the other hand, it is of large size, one of the natives plunges into the water, and, following the line down, secures the turtle.

In the island of Ascension the cultivation and breeding of turtles for exportation in artificially constructed enclosures have for a considerable time been the subject of an important industry. There are doubtless many other locations on both the Australian coast-line and in the British West Indies where this highly profitable trade could be established. In addition to the green turtle, attention might also be profitably directed at the same locations to the culture of the tortoiseshell-bearing species. Tortoiseshell possesses the singular and useful property of being susceptible of perfect amalgamation. Consequently a number of small-sized pieces can be welded so indistinguishably with one another as to serve the same use as the larger plates for commercial purposes. This amalgamation is effected by bevelling the edges of the two pieces that it is desired to unite along the proposed line of junction, and then, while they are held in juxtaposition in a metallic press, submitting them to the action of boiling water.

CHAPTER III.

LIZARDS.

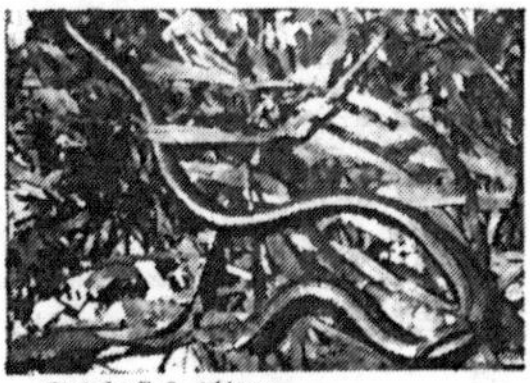

Photo by E. C. Atkinson.

BLIND-WORM.

Notwithstanding its name, the blind-worm possesses small, very bright little eyes.

THE Lizard Tribe or Sub-order is notable as containing a greater number of specific forms than any other of the Reptilian groups, no less than 1,700 distinct species being described in the most recently published catalogues. While formerly regarded as constituting a separate and independent order of the Reptile Class, later investigations have demonstrated that lizards are so intimately related through sundry intermediate types with the Snakes that they cannot be recognised as constituting other than a sub-section of the same order. The two groups of the Lizards and Snakes are consequently, and with reference more particularly to their commonly shared scaly armatures, technically distinguished by the appellation of Scaled Reptiles.

Photo by W. Saville-Kent, F.Z.S.] *[Milford-on-Sea.*

GLASS-SNAKE, OR SCHELTOPUSIK.

The presence of movable eyelids distinguishes this legless lizard from the true snakes.

While the more typical members of the Lizard Tribe are readily distinguished from the Snakes by the possession of well-developed limbs, a no inconsiderable number of species are altogether devoid of these appendages, or possess them only in a partially developed or rudimentary condition. The British BLIND-WORM, or SLOW-WORM, constitutes an example of such a legless lizard, although on account of its outward snake-like appearance it is commonly regarded as a snake by the uneducated. In the South European so-called GLASS-SNAKE, or SCHELTOPUSIK, here figured, the snake-like aspect and creeping habits are still more conspicuous, but yet when examined more critically its lizard affinities become apparent. One of the most readily apprehended external characters that serve to distinguish this and the majority of the legless lizards from snakes is the possession by the former of movable eyelids and conspicuous external ear-openings. Among snakes eyelids are invariably absent, the

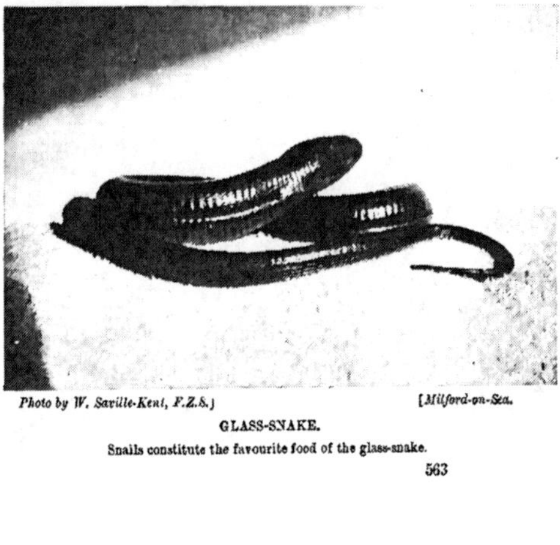

Photo by W. Saville-Kent, F.Z.S.] *[Milford-on-Sea.*

GLASS-SNAKE.

Snails constitute the favourite food of the glass-snake.

Photo by W. Saville-Kent, F.Z.S.] [*Milford-on-Sea.*

BURMESE GECKOS.

One of the largest members of the tribe, measuring 8 or 10 inches in length.

eyes, by way of compensation, being covered by transparent horny plates, which impart to these creatures that peculiar stony stare which undoubtedly constitutes one of the most repulsive features of their tribe. There are, however, a few exceptional lizards devoid of eyelids, though these species do not take a snake-like form.

Lizards, while distributed throughout temperate and tropical regions, attain to the zenith of their representation in size, number, and variety of form and colour in tropical and sub-tropical countries. The majority of species are essentially sun-worshippers, and in temperate climates, such as that of England, where they are but sparsely represented, pass the cheerless winter months in a state of torpid hibernation.

The first position among the Lizard Tribe is usually accorded to the GECKO FAMILY—a group numbering 280 species, which present several somewhat anomalous features and characteristics. In the first place, in contradistinction to the majority of lizard forms, they are for the most part nocturnal in their habits, and have their eyes specially modified to meet them. Geckos, as the exception to the ordinary lizards previously referred to, possess no eyelids, and the pupil of the eye, as seen in broad daylight, is mostly represented by a narrow vertical slit, like that of a cat or a nocturnal dog-fish. As the night approaches, however, the membranous diaphragm is retracted, displaying to view a symmetrically orbicular pupil of abnormal size and luminosity. Another prominent characteristic of the geckos is the peculiar modification of their feet, which in most instances are furnished with adhesive disks or pads, which enable these lizards to run with ease, after the manner of flies, on the smooth surface of a wall or window-pane, or even along the ceiling. It is further noteworthy of the geckos that they are the only lizards which possess the power of emitting

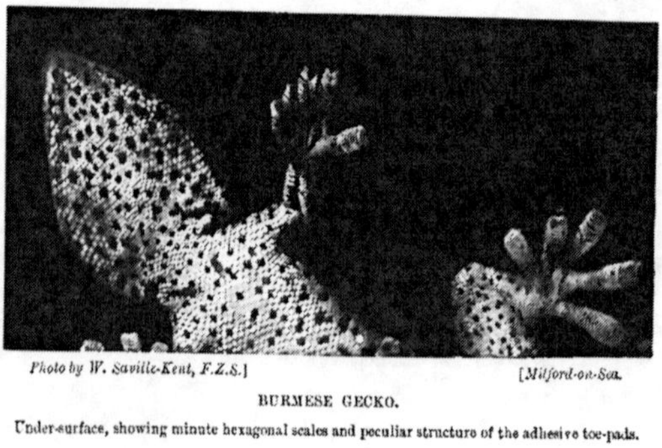

Photo by W. Saville-Kent, F.Z.S.] [*Milford-on-Sea.*

BURMESE GECKO.

Under-surface, showing minute hexagonal scales and peculiar structure of the adhesive toe-pads.

Photo by W. Saville-Kent, F.Z.S.] *[Milford-on-Sea.*

MADEIRAN GECKOS.

Madeiran geckos photographed through a glass window-pane, showing the peculiar formation of their adhesive toe-pads. One example is regrowing its recently amputated tail. These geckos often travel from Madeira to Covent Garden Market among banana bunches.

distinct vocal sounds. The name Gecko is, in point of fact, derived from the fancied resemblance to the word that constitutes the shrill, somewhat bird-like note of one of the most familiar species. "Tok," "toki," "chick, chick," "checko," and "tocktoo" are distinctive call-notes that are respectively associated with other members of the Gecko Family.

The geckos are most numerously represented in the Indian and Australasian regions. None of them attain to large dimensions. They rarely exceed 1 foot in total length, and most frequently measure some 3 or 4 inches only.

Geckos, in common with many other lizards, are notable for the facility with which their tail becomes detached and left in the hands of their would-be captor. In course of time a new tail sprouts out from the truncated stump of the original member, and within a few more months equals it in dimensions. It not infrequently happens that two or even three new tail-sprouts take the place of the original appendage, imparting to the little creature a most bizarre appearance. The above photograph includes an example of the Madeiran species in which a new tail-bud of a normal character has just commenced to grow.

The nearest approach to the phenomenon of flight among lizards occurs in what are known as the FLYING-DRAGONS, belonging to the family of the Agamas, which next invites attention. These lizards are all of relatively small size, not exceeding a few inches in length, and inhabit the Indo-Malayan region. In these singularly specialised forms six or seven of the posterior ribs are abnormally produced on each side of the body, and so united together by thin, semi-transparent membrane as to form a pair of wing-like expansions. When not in use, these structures are folded, after the manner of a fan, closely against the animal's sides, while, when extended, they constitute a most effective parachute, wherewith the little creatures accomplish flying leaps from tree to tree, after the manner of the Flying-squirrels and Phalangers. The

Photo by W. Saville-Kent, F.Z.S.] [Milford-on-Sea.

FLYING-DRAGON OF JAVA.

A lizard with wing-like membranes supported by the abnormally developed ribs. It takes long flights from tree to tree.

colour of these wing-like structures varies among the many different specific forms, being in some instances spotted or reticulated like those of a butterfly.

This same family of the Agamoid Lizards includes a number of species of very dissimilar aspect and habits, which are almost exclusively confined to the Old World or Oriental zoological region. Australia in particular is remarkably rich in representatives of this group, many of them of considerable size. Certain of these have within recent years been found to be endowed with the power of bipedal locomotion. The FRILLED LIZARD of Queensland and the northern territories of Western Australia was the first species in which this bipedal habit was authentically demonstrated in connection with examples observed in Australia and also brought to England by the writer, one of the last-named examples furnishing the photographs reproduced on page 567. In other respects this lizard is one of the most remarkable of its tribe. The peculiar Elizabethan collar-like frill, capable of erection or depression at the creature's will, imparts to it a most singular appearance. When at rest or undisturbed, this membranous frill-like structure is folded down in neat, symmetrical pleats around the lizard's neck. Should the creature be approached by man or dog or other aggressive animal, the mouth springs open to its widest, and simultaneously with this action the frill is erected like the sudden opening of an umbrella, and stands out at right angles around the neck, imparting to it a most formidable and threatening aspect. Dogs, in fact, which will habitually chase and kill larger lizards, such as the Monitors, will frequently halt and retire discomfited when confronted with a frilled lizard at bay with its frill erected. The brilliant colour of this frill, more especially in the male, adds very considerably to the formidable appearance of this lizard. While the body of this lizard is usually of a light brown colour, with more or less distinct darker transverse bars and reticulations, the frill-like membrane has a ground-colour in which orange and chrome-yellow chiefly predominate, and upon which are superimposed splashings and speckles of brilliant scarlet. While the total length of this averages 2 feet, the expanded frill in adult males is not infrequently as much as 8 or 9 inches in diameter. The peculiar, grotesquely human aspect presented by the frilled lizard when running on its hind legs only will be appreciated on reference to the accompanying photographs. This erect attitude is only assumed when the frilled lizard is traversing more or less considerable distances and moving on level ground. Under

Photo by W. Saville-Kent, F.Z.S.] *[Milford-on-Sea.*

FRILLED LIZARD AT BAY WITH EXPANDED FRILL.

Photo by W. Saville-Kent, F.Z.S.] *[Milford-on-Sea.*

FRILLED LIZARD WITH FRILL FOLDED UP.

Photo by W. Saville-Kent, F.Z.S.] *[Milford-on-Sea.*

FRILLED LIZARD RUNNING ON ITS HIND LEGS (VIEW FROM THE REAR).

Photo by W. Saville-Kent, F.Z.S.] *[Milford-on-Sea.*

FRILLED LIZARD RUNNING ON ITS HIND LEGS (BROADSIDE VIEW).

other circumstances it progresses on all-fours, after the manner of the ordinary members of its class.

Several other lizards belonging to the family group of the Agamas have been demonstrated by the writer to move in the same manner as the frilled species. LESEUR'S WATER-LIZARD, also a Queensland form, which attains to a length of 3 or 4 feet, is a notable example in this connection. As implied by its name, it is semi-aquatic in its habits. It frequents scrubs in the neighbourhood of river-banks and backwaters, and passes a considerable portion of its time in shallow water with only its nostrils elevated above the surface. It is a most expert swimmer, sculling itself with grace and rapidity, aided only by its long, laterally compressed tail. Examples brought to England and kept alive for some years by the writer were observed, in hot weather more particularly, to sleep at nights in their water-tanks.

The several instances of bipedal locomotion among living lizards, as here chronicled, are of especial interest in correlation with the circumstance that certain extinct Dinosaurs habitually progressed on their hind limbs only. They, in fact, have left "footprints on the sands of time" which indubitably prove this assumption. There is, however, no relationship between the two groups, and the resemblance is one of pure analogy, just as both bats and birds fly, although they have no kinship.

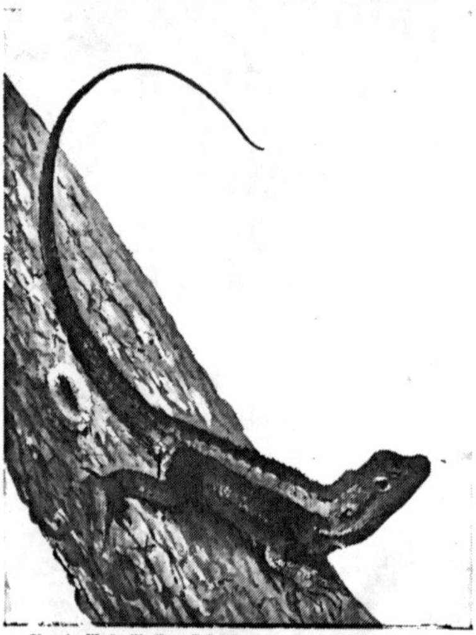

Photo by W. Saville-Kent, F.Z.S.] *[Milford-on-Sea.*

AUSTRALIAN TREE-LIZARD.

This species also runs on its hind legs.

Among other interesting lizards included in the Agama Family, mention may be made of the singular JEW or BEARDED LIZARD of Australia—a flattened, broad-set form, some 14 or 15 inches long, brown in hue, and clothed with rough imbricated scales, but whose chief peculiarity consists of the expansive beard-like development of the cuticle immediately underneath the animal's chin. As in the frilled lizard, this cuticular excrescence is only conspicuous when the creature is excited, at other times being contracted and indistinguishable from an ordinary skin-fold. When retiring to rest, these lizards, in their adult state, almost invariably climb up and cling to the rough bark of a convenient tree, and when young and more slender will also ascend saplings, on which they sleep, clinging by their interlocked claws.

Another member of the Agama Family which invites brief notice is the so-called YORK DEVIL, or MOUNTAIN-DEVIL, of Western and Central Australia. This lizard is of comparatively small size, rarely exceeding 6 or 7 inches in length. Its feeble form and stature, however, are abundantly compensated for by the complex panoply of spines and prickles by which its head and limbs and body are effectually protected. The natural food of this singular lizard consists exclusively of ants, the small black, evil-smelling species which often proves itself a pest by its invasion of the Australian colonists' houses being its prime favourite. These are picked up one by one by the rapid flash-like protrusion and retraction of the little creature's adhesive tongue, and the number of ants which are thus assimilated by a Moloch lizard at a single meal is somewhat astonishing. A number of examples of this species were kept by the writer in Australia, and their gastronomic requirements fully satisfied

Photo by W. Saville-Kent, F.Z.S.] [*Milford-on-Sea.*

AUSTRALIAN WATER-LIZARD.

This lizard is of aquatic habits, and runs on its hind legs when traversing long distances.

every day by taking them into the garden and placing them in communication with a swarming ant-track. By careful observation it was found that no less than from 1,000 to 1,500 ants were devoured by each lizard at a single sitting. The ant-devouring proclivities of these prickly little lizards can no doubt be turned to very useful and effective account in clearing ant-infested domiciles, and were in fact thus utilised by the writer on more than one occasion.

The lizards included in the Agama Family are essentially inhabitants of the Eastern Hemisphere, none occurring in America. In the western continent, however, we find an equally extensive but structurally distinct group which presents many singularly corresponding types. This family comprises the true IGUANAS, many of them of considerable size, and a numerous assemblage of smaller forms. Among those species which present a striking parallel in size and aspect to the peculiarly characteristic Old World Agamas, mention may be made of the little so-called HORNED TOAD, or SPINY LIZARD, of California and other of the North American States. This species might readily be taken by the uninitiated for a near relation of the Australian Moloch Lizard, or Mountain-devil, last described, its flattened diminutive form and bristling spiny armature seemingly justifying such a supposition. The crucial test afforded by the character of the dentition, however, distinctly indicates its true position to be with the Iguanas. In the Agamas the teeth are invariably developed from the apex, or summit, of the jaw. These teeth, moreover, are varied in character. In the Iguanas, on the other hand, the teeth are all more or less uniform in character, and are attached to the outer sides of the jaw.

Photo by W. Saville-Kent, F.Z.S.] [*Milford-on-Sea.*

AUSTRALIAN WATER-LIZARD.

Showing attitude when running.

The larger iguanas are, for the most part, exclusively fruit- and vegetable-feeders, and arboreal in their habits. The thick forest scrubs in the vicinity of streams and rivers are their favourite resort. After the manner of the Australian water-lizards, these iguanas are expert swimmers, and delight in lying along the overhanging branches, whence at the slightest alarm they can precipitate themselves into the water beneath. When swimming, the fore limbs are folded back against the sides, the tail only being used as a means of propulsion. Several of the larger iguanas, such as the common or tuberculated

Photo by W. Saville-Kent, F.Z.S.] *[Milford-on-Sea.*

AUSTRALIAN JEW OR BEARDED LIZARDS.

The scales of the bearded lizard are exceedingly rough and sharp, sometimes cutting the skin of those who handle them incautiously.

Photo by W. Saville-Kent, F.Z.S.] *[Milford-on-Sea.*

BEARDED LIZARD.

With its beard-like throat-membrane fully expanded.

species, attain to a considerable length, 5 or 6 feet; their bodies are proportionably thick, and the white flesh, in this last-named variety more particularly, is highly esteemed as a table delicacy. The common TUBERCULATED IGUANA is an essentially handsome species, its skin being variegated with bands and shadings of brown and green, which are lightest and brightest in the males and younger individuals; the neck and snout and jaws are decorated with projecting, rounded tubercles; a large, baggy, dewlap-like membrane, capable of inflation at the animal's will, depends from the chin and throat; and a deeply serrated crest of elevated scales extends from behind the head, down the centre of the back, nearly to the extremity of the tail.

The Iguana Family includes a species with essentially marine proclivities, this being the GALAPAGOS SEA-LIZARD. This animal was first discovered to science by the late Mr. Charles Darwin, who found it in considerable numbers on the shores of the islands which constitute the Galapagos group. The lizards were observed to spend much of their time swimming in the sea, but at no very great distance from the land. Experiments proved that they could live for a very considerable interval entirely submerged, examples sunk with weights for as much as an hour emerging entirely unaffected from the ordeal.

While the Iguanas may be described as essentially American, one or two exceptional forms are found inhabiting the relatively remote regions of the Fiji Islands and Madagascar. The so-called FIJI BANDED IGUANA (photographs of a pair of which, once in the writer's possession, are reproduced on page 575) is a very beautiful creature. The body is shapely and well proportioned, and terminates in a tail of abnormal length—equal to quite twice that of the body—the entire dimensions measuring some 3 feet. The male is much more bright in hue than the female; for while the latter is usually of a uniform light green throughout, the male is variegated, with broad, alternating bands of brightest

Photo by W. Saville-Kent, F.Z.S., Milford-on-Sea.

A YOUNG BEARDED LIZARD.

Showing its habitual sleeping attitude.

emerald-green and pale French grey. Around the lips and eyes there are lines of brightest yellow, and the throat is almost pure white.

The small group of GIRDLE-TAILED LIZARDS belongs exclusively to the African and Madagascan regions, its typical representative being the Cape and Orange River Colony species, illustrated on page 575. The symmetrical whorls of long, spinous scales encircling the tail in this and the allied forms constitute a prominent feature, and have originated the popular name of Girdle-tails.

Photo by W. Saville-Kent, F.Z.S.] *[Milford-on-Sea.*

AUSTRALIAN YORK OR MOUNTAIN-DEVIL.

A spinous lizard which inhabits the arid plains of Central Australia.

The most aberrant representatives of the Lizard Tribe, with regard to one very important characteristic, are undoubtedly the two species of HELODERM, or "SILATICA," as they are called by the natives. These reptiles (page 576) occupy the unenviable position of being the only known lizards which possess poisonous properties, their bite having been demonstrated to be fatal to smaller mammals, and to be attended by very serious symptoms in the case of human subjects being bitten. The more common MEXICAN HELODERM has been in residence at the Zoo for many years; it attains to a length of from 18 to 20 inches, and its stout, squat body, short limbs, warty skin, and peculiar colouring are calculated at first sight to awaken a feeling of revulsion in the beholder. Like the wasp, the salamander, and other animals whose conspicuous tints indicate their poisonous or other baneful properties, the heloderm is distinguished by a lurid ground-colour, varying in individuals from yellow-orange to flesh-pink, upon which are superimposed bold, network-like markings of blue-black or dark brown tints. Along the tail these reticulations usually take the form of more or less irregular rings.

Although the heloderms possess such deadly properties, those at the Zoo manifest a by no means aggressive disposition, and allow their keeper or even strangers to handle them with impunity. In experiments purposely made to substantiate or refute the previously current rumours as to the poisonous nature of these animals, two guinea-pigs succumbed to bites received in the course of the day. The owner of the reptiles, who was also bitten on one occasion through incautiously handling, suffered very severe, though happily not fatal, effects. In connection with its poison-dealing properties it is found that it possesses certain long and fang-like teeth, which are set loosely in the jaws, and which have grooves before and behind for the transmission of the poison, which is secreted by special glands situated close to their base. The favourite habitat of

Photo by W. Saville-Kent, F.Z.S.] *[Milford-on-Sea.*

SPINOUS LIZARD, OR MOUNTAIN-DEVIL.

This species feeds exclusively upon ants.

Photo by W. Saville-Kent, F.Z.S.] *[Milford-on-Sea.*

A GROUP OF MOUNTAIN-DEVILS OF CENTRAL AUSTRALIA.

The spines of these lizards are so sharp that they will pierce a tender hand.

the heloderm is the arid, sandy, and stony region on the western side of the Cordillera mountain-range. It is at the same time said to be rarely seen in those parts except during the rainy season, and also to be for the most part nocturnal in its habits.

The family group of the MONITORS includes the largest of existing lizards, notably the semi-aquatic form common to North Australia and the Malay Peninsula and adjacent islands, which attains a length of 8 or 10 feet, and is not infrequently mistaken, as it rushes, on being disturbed, through the reeds and other rank herbage to the water, for a young crocodile. An exceedingly fine and well set-up example of these huge water-monitors, shot by Captain Stanley Flower in the neighbourhood of Singapore, is placed in the Reptile Gallery of the Natural History Museum.

Another species, indigenous to the Southern Australian States, and having essentially arboreal habits, commonly attains to a length of 5 or 6 feet. The skin of one example of this species, obtained for the writer from the eucalyptus forests in Gippsland, Victoria, measures no less than 7 feet long. With reference to the elegant lace-like pattern of its skin-markings, this species is frequently associated with the suggestive title of the LACE-LIZARD. Among the more illiterate settlers it is generally known as a Gooana, the name being obviously a corruption of Iguana, and being, as a matter of fact, applied promiscuously, and in all cases incorrectly, to a number of the larger Australian lizards.

All the members of the Monitor Tribe are inveterate egg-eaters. An Egyptian species, the NILE MONITOR, renders service to humanity through the gratification of this propensity in seeking out and devouring the eggs of the crocodile. The larger water-monitor of the North Australian and Malay regions has been reported to the writer to be particularly partial to the eggs of the turtle, digging them out of the sand in which the parent deposits them, and destroying them wholesale. The more strictly arboreal Southern Australian species preys to a very large extent on birds' eggs, climbing to the holes in the trunks and branches in which so many Australian birds build their nests, and not infrequently capturing and devouring also the parent birds and young. In the "bush" settlements this monitor is notorious for its depredations among the hen-roosts, both eggs and young chickens falling victims to its insatiable appetite. It is consequently regarded with but scant favour

Photo by W. Saville-Kent, F.Z.S.] *[Milford-on-Sea.*

HORNED TOAD.

A spiny lizard, somewhat resembling the Australian mountain-devil.

by poultry-farmers, who frequently organise a "gooana" hunt for its special destruction. If surprised out in the open, the quarry at once rushes for a tree, and manifests the most remarkable agility in "swarming" up the smooth, massive trunk, and in dodging round to the side opposite to that on which the sportsman approaches. Not infrequently, trees being remote, the monitor will make for what appears to its apprehension the best substitute for one—*viz.* the upright figure of the nearest sportsman. Should this happen to be a "new chum" enjoying his maiden essay in "gooana" hunting, he will undoubtedly experience a new sensation as the animal, with its sharp cat-like claws, unceremoniously scrambles up to his head and shoulders.

Brought to bay, a monitor possesses a more formidable weapon than its teeth and claws wherewith to repulse the onslaught of the enemy. The long, tough, thong-like tail—not brittle and replaceable, as in many other lizards—is converted, for the time being, into a veritable stock-whip, wherewith it will most severely punish incautious aggressors who venture too near. The potency of this offensive and defensive weapon is fully recognised by the reptile-keepers at the Zoo, who freely admit their reluctance to enter the cage of one of these large, long-tailed, but conversely very short-tempered monitors. All of the monitors, in consonance with their pre-eminently carnivorous habits, are more or less savage and intractable. The several species which have fallen within the writer's cognisance proved no exception to the rule. An Egyptian example, injudiciously introduced to the select society of his extensive miscellaneous collection in a heated greenhouse, proved to be a veritable wolf in the fold, killing several of the choicest specimens before its vindictive propensities were detected and arrested. A comparatively small and rare spiny-tailed monitor, brought by the writer, in company with the frilled lizards, to England from North-west Australia, would harass and bite any other lizard placed with it, and resent every friendly overture on the part of its owner, even after so much as a whole twelvemonth's persistent attempts to tame it. Another, the South Australian monitor, or lace-lizard, was no exception to the rule, and had to be maintained in solitary confinement. This particular specimen, nevertheless, evinced, as the following anecdote will show, a very pronounced affection for its provided quarters. One day it effected its escape from the wire-enclosed cage with which it was accommodated in the writer's Brisbane garden, and after prolonged but unsuccessful searchings it was given up for lost. Considerable astonishment was naturally experienced some ten days later, when the animal was discovered in the garden making frantic attempts to regain access to its former prison-house. During its ten days' absence it had evidently fallen upon evil times, for not only was it in a very emaciated condition, but also bereft of its long and handsome tail. Apparently, after the manner of its tribe, it had been manifesting a too warm

Photo by W. Saville-Kent, F.Z.S.] *[Milford-on-Sea.*

HORNED TOAD.

This species is highly prized for its insect-destroying proclivities.

Photo by W. P. Dando, F.Z.S.] [*Regent's Park.*

TUBERCULATED IGUANA.

This species is esteemed for food by American Indians.

interest in some neighbour's hen-roost, and received across its tail a stroke with a spade or other cutting instrument that was intended for a more vital region. Disgusted by such unfriendly treatment, it evidently determined that free board and lodging at the hands of its former owner, albeit with the sacrifice of freedom, was a pleasanter line of life than liberty and a precarious commissariat, with added bodily risks. An almost identical episode of the voluntary return to captivity of an escaped monitor has been reported to the writer of a species from Borneo by Dr. G. D. Haviland.

The monitors, as a rule, are not distinguished for brilliancy of colouring, shades and mottlings of brown or black being usually dominant. The male of the Australian lace-lizard, after newly changing its coat, is, however, an exception. In addition to the highly ornate lace-like reticulated pattern of its skin-markings, previously referred to, the throat of the animal is resplendent with mingled tints of sky-blue and lemon-yellow. It is necessary, however, to observe that its natural surroundings and the ardent rays of a sub-tropical sun are requisite to bring these brighter tints to their full development. Examples kept in close confinement in the London Zoological Gardens yield little or no indication of their colour potentialities.

Photo by E. C. Atkinson.

SMALL VIVIPAROUS LIZARD.

Occurs on heaths and commons in the South of England.

While the Monitor Family is not represented on the American Continent, we find there another group of lizards whose members are of considerable size, and agree in their carnivorous propensities and general habits in a marked manner with the Monitors. These are the "GREAVED" LIZARDS, named with reference to the peculiar skin-folding on their legs. One of the largest and most familiarly known representatives of this group is the TEGUEXIN, or DIAMOND-LIZARD, indigenous to the greater portion of tropical South America, and also to the West Indies. This lizard attains to a total length of a yard or more, and is of a robust and thick-set build, with the hind limbs much longer and stouter than the front ones. The colour of the teguexin is also notable, the ground-tint being olive or tawny yellow, upon which are superimposed black bands and markings which for the most part take a transverse direction. Like the Monitors, the teguexin in captivity exhibits a sulky and aggressive disposition,

Photo by H. G. F. Spurrell, Esq.] [*Eastbourne.*

WALL-LIZARD.

This species is particularly abundant in Italy.

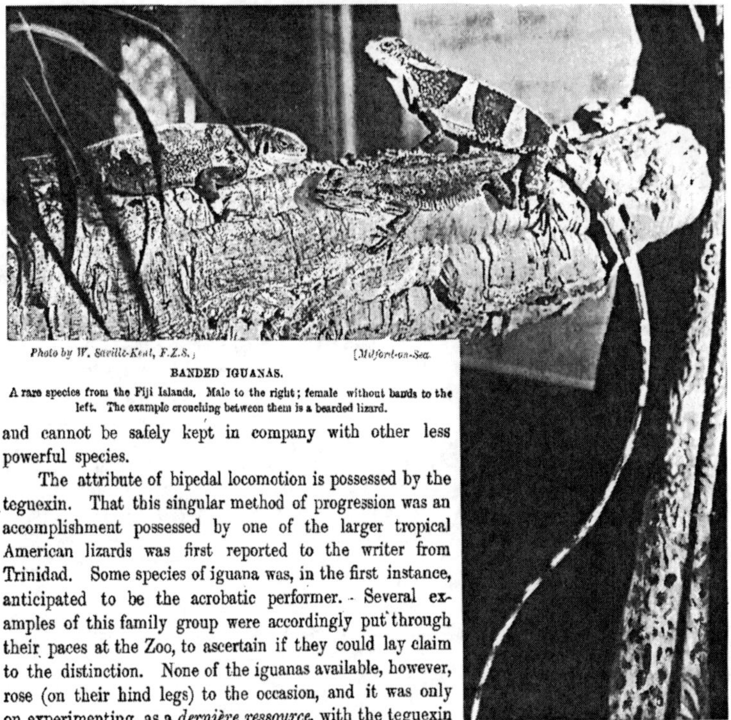

Photo by W. Saville-Kent, F.Z.S.] [Milford-on-Sea.

BANDED IGUANAS.

A rare species from the Fiji Islands. Male to the right; female without bands to the left. The example crouching between them is a bearded lizard.

and cannot be safely kept in company with other less powerful species.

The attribute of bipedal locomotion is possessed by the teguexin. That this singular method of progression was an accomplishment possessed by one of the larger tropical American lizards was first reported to the writer from Trinidad. Some species of iguana was, in the first instance, anticipated to be the acrobatic performer. Several examples of this family group were accordingly put through their paces at the Zoo, to ascertain if they could lay claim to the distinction. None of the iguanas available, however, rose (on their hind legs) to the occasion, and it was only on experimenting, as a *dernière ressource*, with the teguexin that a successful demonstration was accomplished. This lizard was found, in fact, to run bipedally more freely and persistently, when sufficient space was allotted it, than the Agamas. It seems singular that this bipedal power of locomotion should have so long remained undiscovered, and yet is possessed by lizards which have for a number of years been the denizens of many zoological gardens and other menageries. The fact that a comparatively large level area is a *sine qua non* for the exhibition of this phenomenon affords no doubt the explanation of this anomaly; but the anomaly itself at the same time serves to accentuate the desirability, in the interests of both science and the animals' comfort, that exists for providing them in captivity with a more liberal and reasonably sufficient space for their indulgence in those methods of locomotion that are natural to them in their native land.

Photo by W. Saville-Kent, F.Z.S.] [Milford-on-Sea.

SOUTH AFRICAN GIRDLED LIZARD.

Remarkable for the spiny armature, which is arranged in concentric girdles.

The Greaved Lizard Family includes somewhat over one hundred species. While the majority agree with the teguexin in the possession of well-developed limbs, there are a few

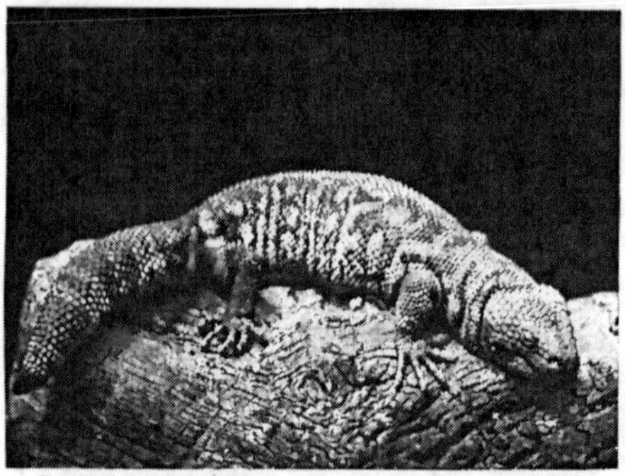

Photo by W. P. Dando, F.Z.S.] *[Regent's Park.*

ARIZONA HELODERM (POISONOUS LIZARD).

In the warted texture of its skin-surface the heloderm differs conspicuously from other lizards.

retrograde forms in which the hinder limbs are entirely absent or the front ones reduced to mere stumps. These exceptional instances pave the way to the family of the Amphisbænas, in which such or a still lower phase of limb development represents the normal condition. The Amphisbænas are remarkable for their worm-like resemblance, and for the circumstances that they live like earth-worms in burrows, that their eyes are functionless (being concealed beneath the skin), and that they are without ears. Other details of structure indicate a most rudimentary condition of development, and they consequently rank as the lowest group in the Lizard series. Another peculiarity of the Amphisbænas is that, in place of scales, the skin of the body is divided into square segments, which form symmetrical rings like those of worms. In addition to this, these retrograde lizards possess the worm-like faculty of being able to move backwards and forwards in their burrows with equal facility. It is from this peculiar property that their title of Amphisbæna, signifying "moving both ways," is derived. The representatives of this family, including between sixty and seventy species, are widely distributed, being found in America, the West Indies, Africa, and also European countries that border the Mediterranean.

While the Teguexins present resemblances in one direction with the Amphisbænas, or Worm-like Lizards, the higher or Monitor-like forms have much in common with the Typical or True Lizards, of which two small but well-known species—the SAND- and VIVIPAROUS LIZARDS—are indigenous to the British Isles. All the members of the True Lizards, numbering some hundred species, are inhabitants of the Old World, becoming scarce, however, towards the far east of the Asiatic Continent. All possess shapely bodies and well-developed limbs with five-toed feet, and are remarkable for the extreme activity of their movements, and in many cases brilliant colouring.

Photo by Scholastic Photo. Co.] *[Parson's Green.*

WHITE MONITOR.

This and other allied species appear to be dead as they lie basking in the sun.

The varying individual shades of the GREEN LIZARD'S brilliant emerald body are almost infinite, no two being quite precisely alike in this respect. In some a yellower, in others a bluer green predominates, while the females and young are more or less mottled or striped with brown. The under surface of the body is usually a more or less bright yellow, and the throat, in the males more particularly, at the breeding-season is frequently brilliant blue. The more conspicuous colour differences exhibited by this lizard are, however, intimately associated with the local habitat of the particular race. Those indigenous to Spain and Portugal, for example, are more or less ornamented with ocellated spots

Photo by the New York Zoological Society.

THE WEST AFRICAN PYTHON.

This splendid snake is said to grow to a length of over twenty feet, although such giants are only occasionally met with.

along the sides of the head and body, while those peculiar to Eastern Europe and Asia Minor are, in the young condition more particularly, marked with longitudinal streaks, but their throat is never blue.

Photo by H. G. F. Spurrell, Esq.] [Eastbourne.

GREEN LIZARD.

The tail of the green lizard is brittle, and breaks off in the hand if the animal is held up by it. A new tail grows from the fractured joint in course of time.

The green lizard is one of the most beautiful of its tribe, and, although not indigenous to Great Britain, is common in the Channel Islands. In Jersey, more especially during the summer months, it is one of the most familiar of the "common objects of the country," as it darts in and out of the hedgerows after flies and other insects, or basks in the bright sunshine on some stone wall, with its emerald-green body flattened out in order to absorb the greatest possible amount of heat. As the colder autumn days advance this lizard is rarely visible, and it finally retires into some rocky cleft or burrow in the hedge-bank, and is no more seen until the return of spring. Green lizards, liberated in suitably mild spots in the South of England, have been known to thrive for brief periods, but succumb to the cold of an extra-severe winter.

The largest representatives of the green lizard are those inhabiting Eastern Europe and Asia Minor, where in size and colour they almost imperceptibly merge into the PEARLY or OCELLATED LIZARD. This very handsome species, which, in company with examples of the green lizard, is frequently imported by London dealers, ranges from 16 inches to close upon 2 feet in length. In form it is stouter and more robust than a typical green lizard, the head in the old males more particularly being exceptionally massive. Whatever may be lacking in grace of form is, however, fully compensated for by brilliancy of colouring, no other lizard, in fact, outrivalling it in this respect. To the brilliant shagreen-patterned emerald-green hues of the Jersey species it has superadded along its sides eye-like spots of brilliant turquoise or ultra-marine, with dark brown or black encircling lines. In the males the green ground-colour has a more distinctly golden hue, while in the young individuals the body is more usually olive-colour, dotted throughout with whitish or pearly-blue, black-edged spots. This beautiful lizard is unfortunately somewhat irascible in temper, and will not as a rule allow itself to

Photo by W. Saville-Kent, F.Z.S.] [Milford-on-Sea.

OCELLATED LIZARDS AT HOME.

The most brilliantly coloured of living lizards. The body is bright emerald-green, decorated on the sides with azure-blue spots.

be handled as freely as the majority of the members of its tribe; when biting, moreover, it has a tendency to fasten itself upon the object seized with bulldog-like tenacity, a grip from a powerful-jawed old male being a somewhat unpleasant experience. In addition to insects the ocellated lizard will prey upon any other small animals it can overpower, including the members of its own species; it is consequently not safe to entrust it in the company of other lizards of less size and strength.

The Skink Family, which next invites attention, contains no less than 400 known species, and, climatic conditions being favourable, enjoys an almost cosmopolitan distribution. The majority of its members have stoutish cylindrical bodies, with relatively short limbs and tail; the legs are sometimes reduced to two only, or altogether aborted, giving the animal a snake-like form.

The COMMON or "MEDICINAL" SKINK—so called since it was regarded in the Middle Ages as an infallible medicinal nostrum—is an inhabitant of North Africa, and notable for its adaptation to a sand-burrowing existence. The body is short, cylindrical, exceedingly smooth through the close apposition of the minute surface-scales, and sharply conical at each extremity. The well-developed toes of all four feet are flattened and serrated at their edges in such a manner that they constitute most effective burrowing-tools in the loose sand these lizards frequent. The length of this skink rarely exceeds 3 or 4 inches. Its colour is rather exceptional for a lizard, but at the same time in keeping with its predominating subterranean habits. The ground-tint in the living examples in the writer's possession, one of which is photographed on page 579, was a light yellowish-white, like that of old polished ivory, with here and there a pale flesh-pink tinge. On the under-surface this light tint was persistent, while the back was traversed by some twelve broadish bands of pale slate-grey. The skink does not, like the mole and the Amphisbænas, obtain its food from subterranean sources. It comes out to bask on the surface of the sand when the sun is at its height, and keeps a brisk look-out for flies or other insects, which, if they approach sufficiently near, are pounced upon with remarkably agility. Should the sky become overcast or any cause for alarm manifest itself, the skink disappears beneath the sand as though by magic, not infrequently burrowing down to a depth of several feet. Even at the present day the skink is esteemed by the Arabs both for medicine and food, and in the latter association, well broiled, has won the commendation of European palates.

Photo by W. Saville-Kent, F.Z.S.] [Milford-on-Sea.

RÖNTGEN RAY PHOTOGRAPH OF OCELLATED LIZARD.

The remarkable length and slenderness of the bones of the hind feet are well illustrated by this photograph.

One of the most bizarre members of the Skink Family hails from Australia, where it is known as the STUMP-TAILED LIZARD. The most remarkable feature in this form is the shortness and roundness of the caudal appendage, the contour and proportions of which, in fact, so nearly correspond with those of the head that it was originally described by its discoverer, Captain William Dampier, just over three centuries ago, as a double-headed animal.

To quote his own quaint description: "The land animals we saw here [Sharks' Bay] included a sort of guanos of the same shape and size with other guanos, but differing from them in three remarkable particulars, for these had a larger and uglier head, and had no tail, and at the rump, instead of a tail there, they had a stump of a tail which appeared like another head, but not really, such being without mouth or eyes; yet this creature seemed by this means to have a head at each end."

Photo by W. Saville-Kent, F.Z.S., Milford-on-Sea.

COMMON SKINK.

Lives and burrows in the sand, coming out when the sun shines.

A specimen of the stump-tailed lizard is usually on view at the Regent's Park Gardens, and will afford visitors an opportunity for its comparison in the flesh with Dampier's description. Fine specimens of the stump-tail will measure as much as 10 inches in length, and are thick in proportion, the legs, however, being very small and weak. The surface of the back is covered with large, overlapping scales, that, in conjunction with its customarily dark brown or blackish hue, convey to it a marked resemblance to a long, imbricated fir-cone. On the under-surface the scales are in comparison very small; the colouring in this region is also usually light grey or yellow, variegated with darker reticulations.

Stump-tails make most good-natured and grotesque household pets. Of two examples which were for some years in the writer's possession a characteristic photograph is reproduced below. When basking in the sun, the tail often becomes distended to enormous proportions. The internal substance of this abnormally dilated organ consists chiefly of fatty tissue, and it seems probable that it fulfils the rôle of a reservoir for the storage of nutrient and heating materials, to be drawn upon during hibernation. The winter months in the southern districts of Western Australia are cold, and this lizard, in common with other local species, retires during that season into the sheltering recess of a hollow tree-stump or rock-crevice until the sun is again in the ascendant. The stump-tail is practically omnivorous in its habits. In captivity fruit, and more especially bananas, constitute a favourite diet, but it will also greedily devour worms, beetles, and garden-snails, and may consequently be turned to good account as a destroyer of garden-pests.

Of other Australian members of the Skink Family, the GREAT CYCLODUS, or BLUE-TONGUED LIZARD, may be mentioned. This species, which is about 18 inches long, presents no abnormal development of head or tail, as in the form last described. The body is smooth and sub-cylindrical, and with its closely set scales resembles that of a snake. The dominant colour is a soft steel or silvery grey, variegated with darker or lighter cross-bands and reticulations that are most strongly marked on the sides; the under-surface, by way of contrast, is most usually pale

Photo by W. Saville-Kent, F.Z.S.] *[Milford-on-Sea.*

AUSTRALIAN STUMP-TAILED LIZARDS.

Two of the author's household pets.

Photo by W. Saville-Kent, F.Z.S.] *[Milford-on-Sea.*

BLUE-TONGUED LIZARDS.

A female with her family of twelve.

salmon-pink. The tongue of this lizard, which gives to it its popular title, is somewhat remarkable. It is large and flat, and of a bright blue tint, resembling nothing so much as a piece of blue flannel. The animal, as it moves about, is in the habit of constantly protruding and retracting its tongue, which consequently constitutes a very conspicuous object. In common with the majority of its allies, the blue-tongued lizard is viviparous; but while the stump-tail only produces one at a time, which is nearly half as large as the parent, the present form gives birth to as many as ten or twelve. An example in the writer's possession on one occasion presented him with a litter embracing the larger number, and afforded the material for the photograph here reproduced.

As a contrast to the two preceding forms, the SPINE-TAILED LIZARDS, with their short, flat, spiky tails, may be cited as a conclusion to this notice of the Skink Family. There are nine known members of the same genus, all inhabitants of Australia. The lower of the two forms here figured is especially abundant on one island of the Abrolhos group, off the Western Australian coast. This example is represented at about two-thirds of its natural size. It is an interesting fact that an allied but considerably larger species monopolises a neighbouring island of the same group, the two species not intermingling: probably the larger one would prey on the smaller. The largest member of the genus, known as CUNNINGHAM'S SPINE-TAIL, of a uniform black hue, peppered white, is not infrequently brought to Europe, and two examples which were for some years in the writer's possession bred regularly, producing eight or ten young at a time for several consecutive years. The fact that these lizards enjoyed full liberty in a heated greenhouse, with a temperature and surrounding conditions closely identical with those to which they were naturally accustomed, no doubt contributed extensively to their fertility.

Photo by W. Saville-Kent, F.Z.S.] *[Milford-on-Sea.*

SPINE-TAILED LIZARDS, WESTERN AUSTRALIA.

These lizards are essentially vegetarian in their habits.

With this group we are compelled by lack of space to close our account of the true lizards, but the reader must understand that only a very few out of an enormous number have been mentioned at all.

CHAPTER IV.

CHAMÆLEONS AND TUATERA.

CHAMÆLEONS.

THE CHAMÆLEONS differ in so many important structural points from the ordinary lizards that they are usually regarded now by scientists as a distinct reptilian sub-order. The essential characters, externally recognisable, that serve to distinguish the chamæleons are:—Firstly, the extraordinary development of their worm-like extensile tongue, the tip of it club-shaped and highly viscous, and the shaft cylindrical and as elastic in texture as india-rubber. Adapted for the special object of catching flies, this organ can be projected from the mouth to a distance of 6 or 8 inches or more with lightning-like rapidity, and rarely misses its quarry. Comparing small things with great, the chamæleon's tongue and its action might be likened to a schoolboy's popgun, having its pellet secured to the barrel by a long elastic ligament. Presuming further that the pellet is covered with a viscid secretion such as bird-lime, and that the object shot at is hit and brought back to the shooter's pocket by virtue of the ligament's intrinsic elasticity, we have an almost veritable replica of the chamæleon's fly-catching apparatus. The second remarkable structural peculiarity of the chamæleon is the independent relationship of the two eyes. The eyes themselves are unlike those of any other lizards; they are large, prominent, skin-covered cones, perforated only at their extreme apex for the minute pupil-opening: while one eye may be fixed on an object in front of it, the other may be rolling around in search of a second quarry. This independent capacity of vision, while peculiar among reptiles to the chamæleon, is common to many fishes, such as blennies and flat-fishes. A third anomaly in the chamæleon's structure is the character of the feet; these resemble those of a parrot, the toes being bound together in two opposable bundles. In the fore foot the inner bundle contains three and the outer one two toes only, while in the hind foot the order

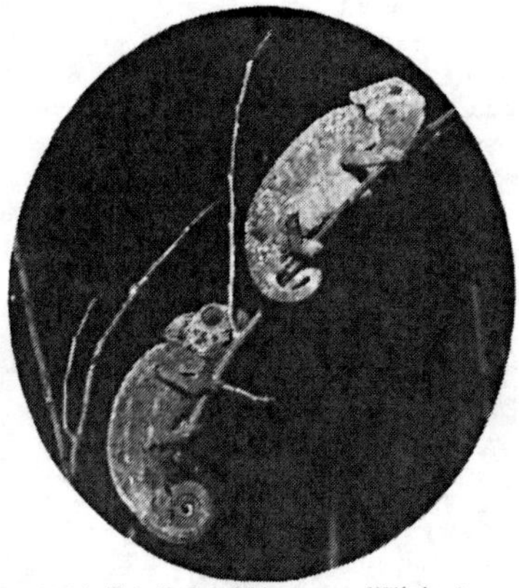

Photo by W. Saville-Kent, F.Z.S. [*Milford-on-Sea.*

CHAMÆLEONS ASLEEP.

The tail of the sleeping chamæleon is frequently coiled spirally like the proboscis of a butterfly.

Photo by W. Saville-Kent, F.Z.S.] [*Milford-on-Sea.*

A CHAMÆLEON IN A RAGE.

Puffing and hissing at an approaching intruder.

of their amalgamation is precisely reversed. In either case these feet subserve, as in parrots and other perching-birds, as most effective organs for maintaining a close grip upon the tree-branches among which they habitually live. The tail of the chamæleon is, finally, highly prehensile, and, as with the New World monkeys, constitutes a veritable fifth hand, wherewith to ensure it against falling off its perch.

The colour-changing properties of the chamæleon have been the subject of enthusiastic but in many instances exaggerated descriptions from the earliest times. As a matter of fact there are other lizard species which share this kaleidoscopic property to an equal or even greater degree. The Indian tree-geckos, referred to on a previous page, as also the calotes from the same region, are cases in point. Chamæleons are undoubtedly possessed of marvellous colour-changing faculties, and it would appear to be scarcely in all instances, as is more usually represented, a case of adapting themselves to the tints of their environment. The assumption of leaf-green, grey, brown, reddish, or yellowish tints, in accordance with their surroundings, is the ordinary record. Some examples which formed the subjects of the writer's experiments exhibited, however, interesting deviations from the beaten track. Male individuals, in particular, were observed to assume tints and decorative patterns that rendered them remarkably conspicuous objects, in spite of their leafy environment. The normal ground-colour of these specimens in full daylight was so dark a green that it might be almost characterised as black. Upon this were superimposed lines and spottings of strongly contrasting tints. The more dominant of these was a brilliant orange, that was distributed in bold lines along the head and cheeks, and formed a radiating pattern on the skin-covered eye-cones. The same colour formed somewhat broken-up bars across all four limbs, and was dispersed in bold spots over the entire remaining body-surface: along the tail these spots were concentrated in threes, giving it a semi-barred appearance. All among these orange limb- and body-spottings were distributed a secondary series of somewhat smaller spots, the tint of which was a pale but very brilliant emerald-green. This chamæleon asleep at night was a very different animal. The ground-colour was transformed from almost black to a bright grass-green. The orange lines became lighter in colour and broken up into patches; many of the orange spots on the body disappeared, but those remaining were of larger size and concentrated in threes in two lines along each side, these triple spots enclosing centrally a larger elongated spot or patch of bright pink or puce. The bright emerald-green secondary spots, as seen in daylight, were almost white. If handled during the daytime, the chamæleon was wont to assume a colour nearly identical with his night garb; the two lines of pink patches, previously invisible, would appear, and, while the orange spotting remained constant, the emerald-green changed to lemon-yellow.

Photo by W. Saville-Kent, F.Z.S.] [*Milford-on-Sea.*

COMMON CHAMÆLEON OF SOUTH EUROPE AND NORTH AFRICA.

A minute or more is often occupied by the chamæleon in making a single forward step.

A chamæleon in a rage is a decidedly grotesque object. The back is arched, the body and more especially the throat-pouch are inflated to their fullest extent, the mouth is opened, the eyes roll, and the creature rocks itself to and fro and hisses in a most threatening manner. When, as often happens, it also simultaneously sits up on its haunches, the effect is doubtless as terrifying as it is intended to be to a rival chamæleon or any small animal which may

Photo by W. Saville-Kent, F.Z.S.] *[Milford-on-Sea.*

A CHAMÆLEON SHOOTING OUT ITS TONGUE TO CAPTURE A FLY.

The tongue is capable of extension to a length of no less than 7 or 8 inches.

Photo by C. M. Martin] *[Beckenham.*

A PHOTOGRAPH OF A CHAMÆLEON IN THE ACT OF CATCHING A BUTTERFLY.

The inflated extremity of the tongue is highly glutinous.

venture to approach it. A number of other lizards, including tree-climbing varieties, were introduced to the company of the examples under observation, and until friendly acquaintanceship had been established their advances towards the chamæleons were always repelled.

The majority of the chamæleons lay eggs, but a small number produce living young, as with skinks and other lizards. Examples of the common European and North African species kept by the writer excavated holes in the earth, in which they laid their eggs, and then carefully covered them up again. Unfortunately these eggs were not fertilised. One South African species has been reported to the writer as being in the habit of placing and separately wrapping and fastening up each egg as deposited in the leaves of the tree in which it resided. While Africa and Madagascar represent the head centres of distribution of the fifty odd known species of chamæleons, they enter Europe through the Spanish Peninsula, and extend eastward to Arabia, India, and Ceylon. The largest known variety, which inhabits Madagascar, attains a length of 15 inches; the smallest pygmy chamæleon of the Cape scarcely measures 2½ inches.

Photo by W. Saville-Kent, F.Z.S.] *[Milford-on-Sea.*

THE TUATERA OF NEW ZEALAND.

Belongs to an ancient reptile race of which it is the only living survivor.

The Tuatera.

That singular reptile found on certain small islands lying to the north-east of New Zealand, and known as the Tuatera, differs in so many structural characters from all other lizards that it is assigned to a separate order. Externally the tuatera does not differ materially in form from an ordinary lizard. The skin, however, is peculiar for its leathery, granulated, and wrinkled texture; there is no trace of external ears; the eyes, adapted for nocturnal vision, have in daylight vertical pupils; and the bases of the toes are united by connecting webs. The deeper internal characteristics include the possession of supplementary so-called abdominal ribs, the presence of which are readily apprehended on handling the living animal. These structures, while absent in ordinary lizards, find their near equivalent in the breastplate of tortoises and turtles. The teeth are not implanted in distinct sockets, but attached to the summits of the jaws, which are developed in a beak-like manner, and in older individuals fulfil, after the manner of a beak, the functions of the worn-out incisor teeth.

Photo by W. Saville-Kent, F.Z.S.] *[Milford-on-Sea.*

A TAME TUATERA.

Is a great acquisition for a greenhouse, feeding on slugs, beetles, and all noxious insects.

Tuateras have been exceedingly scarce of recent years, and in view of their scientific interest, and the risk of their possible extinction, are now protected by the New Zealand Government. Among the multitudinous gifts of which their Royal Highnesses the Prince and Princess of Wales were recipients during their recently accomplished world-embracing tour, a pair of living tuatera lizards formed one of the most singular and highly prized contributions accepted from the loyal New Zealanders.

Photo by H. G. F. Spurrell, Esq.] [Eastbourne.

DARK GREEN SNAKE.

A native of Italy and other countries bordering the Mediterranean. Accredited with a particularly fierce disposition.

CHAPTER V.

SNAKES.

THE characteristic contour of a snake's body is too familiar to need elaborate description; its leading features are, in fact, so nearly approximated by certain of the legless lizards, previously described, that the distinctions between the two can with difficulty be defined. Many of the snake-like lizards, including the Common Blind-worm, are altogether devoid of external limbs. In some snakes, on the other hand, and notably the large terrestrial Pythons, a spur-like development on each side of the base of the tail represents rudimentary hind legs. The Snakes agree essentially with the Lizards in the character of their scaly covering, the scales, however, being larger on their under-surface and specially adapted, as in the legless lizards, for creeping locomotion. The essential distinctions between the two groups have to be sought in the structure of the head. The most notable of these, as it obtains in the Snakes, is the very loose manner in which all the bones connected with the jaws are held together, thus providing for the greatest possible distension in the act of their swallowing their prey whole, as is the custom of all ordinary snakes. To achieve this end, the two halves of the lower jaw are not united together at their extremity or chin, as in lizards, but are merely connected with one another by an elastic ligament. In most snakes the bones of the upper jaw and palate are also attached to one another in a similar way.

The eyes of a snake differ in a very marked manner from those of ordinary lizards. No snake possesses movable eyelids. The eye, in compensation, is protected by a transparent horny disk, continuous with the general epidermis, and is shed with it when the snake casts its skin. This feature imparts to snakes that fixed, stony expression of the eyes which undoubtedly contributes very materially towards increasing the feeling of repulsion with which snakes are commonly regarded. A few exceptional lizards, such as the Geckos, have a similar eye-construction, but it is not met with in any of the limbless or snake-like forms. No snakes, again, show any trace of external ear-openings, such structures, on the other hand, being distinctly developed in almost all lizards. The head itself of the snake is never compressed or elevated, as in most lizards, but flattened down and usually wider than the body, to which, however, it is united without a distinct neck. The tongue of the snake is slender, and terminates in two long, thread-like points; basally it is inserted into a hollow sheath, into or out of which the entire organ can be retracted or exserted at will. The somewhat uncanny, flickering action with which a snake, while moving, displays and as it were feels its way with its long, forked tongue represents another element which adds to the disfavour with which these reptiles are commonly regarded. Among the uneducated even at the present day it is not unusual to hear the tongue, with reference to its peculiar shape and vibrating action, pronounced to be the seat and instrument of the animal's poisonous properties. The swift, silent, stealthy, gliding motions with which, apart from any visible organs of locomotion, a snake slides, as it were, along the ground and over all obstacles fill to the brink the measure for its condemnation in the estimation of all but the snake-devotee or the naturalist.

The locomotion of the snake is, as a matter of fact, one of the most remarkable and beautifully contrived phenomena in animal mechanics. The peculiarly jointed and abnormally mobile ribs constitute the mystic *deus ex machinâ* by which the reptile accomplishes its migration. These ribs articulate in pairs by a single mobile head with their respective segment of the vertebral column. At their opposite extremity they impinge on and are in muscular connection with the broad, slightly overlapping, shield-like scales which clothe the under surface of the body. The rib-muscles, contracting in rhythmical succession, raise the free overlapping edges of the shield-like scales, which, striking against the ground in the same regular order, push the body forward. Adopting an easily comprehensible simile, the snake's body is carried along the ground on the same principle as a paddle-wheel steamer is pushed along the surface of the water, the paddle-boards in the case of the snake being affixed to a long, narrow plane instead of a circular wheel.

Photo by H. G. F. Spurrell, Esq.] [*Eastbourne.*

DARK GREEN SNAKE.

Closely allied to the rat-snake of India, and preys in a similar manner on rats, mice, and birds.

The poison-fangs of snakes are highly specialised structures, and their presence or otherwise was formerly considered sufficiently distinctive for the separation of these reptiles into two sharply defined natural series. More recent investigations have, however, shown that such a system of classification is entirely artificial, both venomous and harmless species occurring among groups which are related to one another by essential structural characters. The teeth in the ordinary or harmless snakes are usually represented by two rows of slender, recurved, sharply pointed teeth in the upper jaw, and a single row of a similar character in the lower one. This recurved character of the dentition effectively assists the snake in gorging its quarry whole, nothing once seized by the hook-like teeth having a chance of retreating, the snake itself being unable to eject the prey upon which the teeth have fastened. In the most poisonous series, such as a rattle-snake, there is but a single row of recurved teeth in the upper jaw, and these are the equivalents of the inner set of the harmless species. Among the most venomous snakes the poison-fangs are tubular in character, the poison being received from the venom-glands at their open base, and discharged at the apex. In other forms the fangs have grooved channels only for the passage of the virus, while in other species there may be an intermediate condition. In all cases the poison-secreting glands are modifications of the ordinary salivary glands of other vertebrate animals. They are situated, one on each side, immediately below and behind the eyes, and are in some instances so abnormally developed as to extend backwards along the sides of the body. Special muscles envelop these glands, and force the poison into the hollow base of the fangs when the mouth is opened to strike.

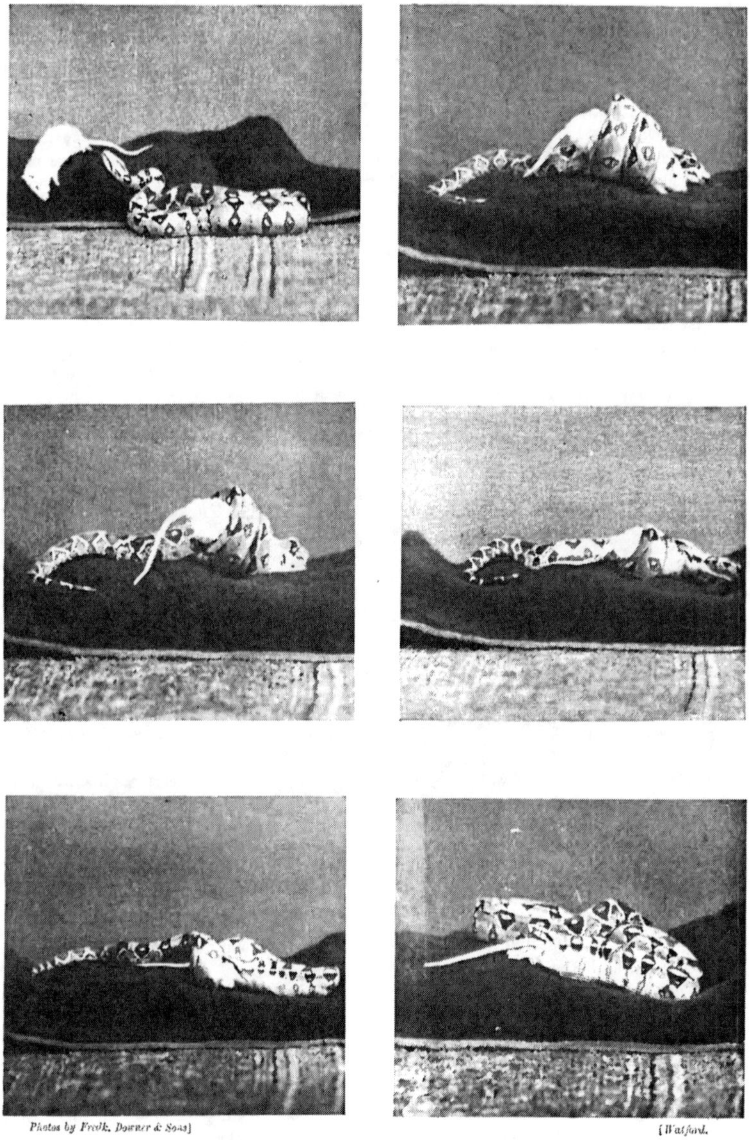

Photos by Fredk. Downer & Sons] *[Watford.*

A SMALL BOA-CONSTRICTOR SEIZING AND DEVOURING A RAT.

Illustrating the consecutive phases of seizing, strangling, and subsequently gorging the prey, as practised by the largest and smallest members of the class.

Snakes, like lizards, are most abundant in tropical countries, the Indian and Malay regions in particular being richest in numbers and varieties. The British Islands support but three representatives of the class—the ADDER, the COMMON RINGED and the SMOOTH SNAKES—this number, by a coincidence, being identical with that of the Lizard Tribe indigenous to the same islands. Many of the smaller species are little over 1 foot long, while the huge Pythons and the Anaconda may attain to or exceed 30 feet. Regarding their habits, some are purely terrestrial, frequenting the rocks or sandy deserts, or even burrowing beneath the earth's surface. Others are essentially arboreal, many amphibious, and some, like the Turtles among the Chelonians, entirely marine. As with the Lizards, the majority of snakes lay eggs enclosed within a white leathery shell, while with a considerable number the young are brought forth alive. The eggs, deposited in the earth, sand, or among vegetable débris, are usually left to be hatched by the heat of the sun. In the case of the Pythons, however, they are incubated by the parent.

A small group of snakes which is usually placed at the head of the series in systematic classifications share the subterranean habits of the Amphisbænas among the Lizards; and the eyes being rudimentary and functionless, they are commonly known as BLIND-SNAKES. A structural peculiarity which separates these singular reptiles from all other members of the Snake Tribe is the entire absence of teeth from either the upper or lower jaw. The food of the blind-snakes consists largely of ants and the larvæ of beetles and other insects which lead a subterranean life. Although spending the greater portion of their existence underground, they occasionally come out upon the surface, such migrations more generally taking place during showery weather. About 100 species of blind-snakes are known, and are mostly confined to tropical countries. One small worm-like form occurs in Greece and the adjacent islands, its range extending through a considerable area of South-western Asia.

Photo by W. P. Dando, F.Z.S.] *[Regent's Park.*

BOA-CONSTRICTOR READY TO STRIKE.

The neck, thrown back in one or more loops, can be projected, with immense force and lightning-like rapidity, to strike or seize an intended victim.

The step from the small worm-like Blind-snakes, with their functionless eyes and underground habits, to the Boas and Pythons, the largest and most highly organised members of the Serpent Tribe, would seem at first sight to be altogether unwarranted. In one essential character, however, they agree very remarkably. In both groups the bony skeleton exhibits a far more generalised structural plan than in any of the succeeding ones, so that they may be regarded as more nearly resembling the primitive stock from which the other more specialised kinds—such as the Vipers, with their death-dealing poison-fangs—have been evolved.

The PYTHONS and BOAS, or BOA-CONSTRICTORS, as they are popularly known, belong entirely to the non-venomous section of the Snake series. The teeth, forming two rows in the upper jaws, gradually decrease in size from before backwards, and none of them are grooved or modified in the form of poison-fangs. The body is usually more or less compressed, and the

Photo by D. Le Souef] [*Melbourne.*

CARPET-SNAKE.

So called with reference to the variegated carpet-like pattern of its skin-ornamentation.

tail prehensile. The TYPICAL PYTHONS, or ROCK-SNAKES, as they are called, with reference to their rock-frequenting habits, are distributed throughout South-eastern Asia, Australia, and Central and South Africa.

The INDIAN PYTHON, which is the largest Old World representative of its race, is known authentically to attain to a length of 30 feet, and in the largest specimens the spinal column may include over 400 vertebræ. In common with other members of its family, this huge snake kills its quarry by compression or strangulation, throwing around it successive coils of its body, which, with their contraction, crush out the life of the victim. The dispatched prey is then swallowed whole, commencing with the head. The previous crushing of the bony framework greatly assists the swallowing process, which is further aided by the snake pouring over the body of its victim a copious discharge of saliva.

The extent to which the jaws and the integument of the body generally can be distended for the passage and reception of the food is remarkable. After partaking of a solid meal in this fashion, pythons remain sluggish and in a state of semi-torpor for several days, not reawakening to active life, in fact, until the digestion of the food has been accomplished. As is well known, these and other snakes can exist for periods of many months' duration between their meals. One of the largest Indian pythons by no means contents itself with such small quarry as hares and rabbits—sheep, young calves, and some of the smaller deer representing its more accustomed food. The human species unarmed is as weak or weaker than the proverbial kitten, pitted against the hydraulic-press-like embrace of these monster serpents; and many an Indian native, and more rarely the white man, has fallen a victim to their attacks.

The RETICULATED PYTHON, so called on account of the bold reticulated pattern of the skin-ornamentation, may equal, if not exceed, the Indian species in dimensions. It is a native of Burma, Siam, and the Malay region generally, and is recorded as occasionally exceeding 30 feet in length. Examples of this species, including one over 20 feet long, have constituted leading attractions at the Reptile-house in the Zoological Society's Gardens for many years past. The gorgeous prismatic tints that play upon the surface-markings of the coils of these huge snakes, as the sun strikes upon them about midday in their cages, form one of the most wonderful sights that the Gardens afford.

The African Continent also produces its large species of pythons. One of these, attaining to a length of 20 feet or more, reaches its maximum on the west coast,

Photo by H. G. F. Spurrell, Esq.] [*Eastbourne.*

ÆSCULAPIAN SNAKE.

A South European species with tree-climbing habits.

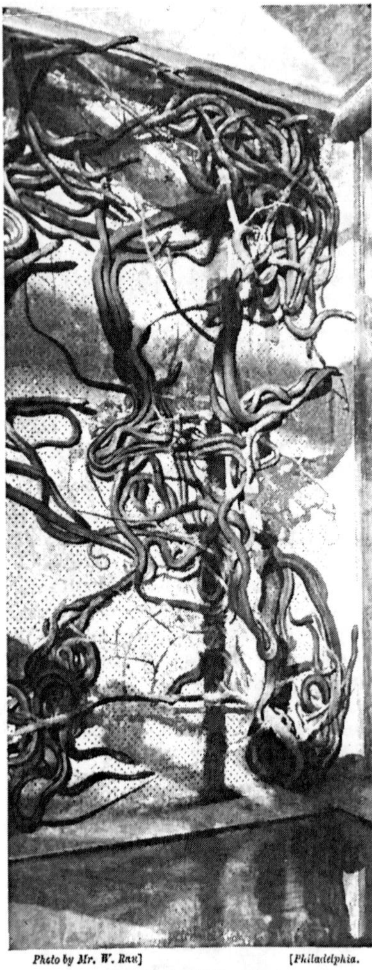

Photo by Mr. W. Rau] [*Philadelphia.*

A GROUP OF GARTER-SNAKES.

An American species which collects together in great numbers.

and occurs with local modifications as far east and south as Natal. In the latter country it is most familiarly known as the NATAL ROCK-SNAKE.

Some rather singular incidents have been recorded illustrating the tenacity with which pythons retain hold of the quarry once seized, or, more correctly, their inability to release it. At the Adelaide Zoological Gardens a specimen, when absorbing a rabbit, managed to entangle its teeth in a corner of its blanket. That blanket had to follow the rodent through the 12-foot-long python. On another occasion two pythons, a Queenslander and Afrikander, happened at the same instant to commandeer respectively the head and hindquarters of an identical rabbit. Inch by inch the portion between the two grew smaller until the two noses met. There was no retreating from this *impasse*, and the momentous question, "Shall I slay my brother boa?" had to be settled affirmatively by one or other of the interested parties without further parley. The somewhat smaller and weaker individual was gradually telescoped, and in due time assimilated. The absorber was decidedly poorly and "off colour" for a considerable period after accomplishing this cannibalistic feat; it ultimately recovered both its appetite and its prismatic tints.

The TRUE BOAS, as distinguished from the Pythons, are more essentially arboreal in their habits, and, with the exception of one or two species found in Madagascar, belong to the tropical American zoological region. The COMMON BOA, or BOA-CONSTRICTOR, which attains to a length of 12 or 14 feet or more, is limited in its distribution to South America. The colours of this snake, which consist mainly of a light brown, with a number of dark brown cross-bars on the back, and light centred, dark brown spots on the sides, so nearly agree with the tint of the tree-branches with their interlacing shadows, among which it usually lies concealed, that, notwithstanding its large size, it readily evades detection, and is unconsciously approached by the animals on which it preys. These, in adult individuals, may be represented by such large-sized quarry as dogs, and even deer; while smaller examples prey largely on birds and their eggs, and the numerous rodents with which the tropical American forests teem. From observations made upon this species in captivity, it would appear that the eggs are usually hatched within the parent's body, though an instance has been recorded in which both eggs and young were produced simultaneously.

A close ally of the typical boas, which shares with them a tropical South American habitat, is the huge ANACONDA, or WATER-BOA, of Brazil and the adjacent countries. This animal, which is undoubtedly the largest living representative of the Serpent Tribe, attains a length little, if any, short of 40 feet. One such monster was specially referred to by Dr. Gardiner, the botanist, in his "Travels in Brazil"; it had devoured a horse, and was found dead, entangled in the branches of a tree overhanging a river, into which it had been carried by a flood. Full-grown cattle, and occasionally human beings, as well as horses, are alleged to fall victims to the destructive prowess of this gigantic snake. The anaconda is essentially amphibious in its habits, the greater part of its life being spent in the water, lying in wait, in the quiet lagoons and backwaters, with only its head above the surface, and prepared to seize any unfortunate animal which may come to the brink to drink. At other times it will coil itself upon the trunks and larger branches of the adjacent trees, and from that point of vantage will dart down its head, with sure aim and lightning rapidity, to seize any suitable quarry which may pass beneath. In some parts of South America where the rivers dry up at certain seasons of the year, the anaconda is recorded to be in the habit of burying itself in the mud and lying torpid, after the manner of crocodiles, until the return of the rains. The ground-colour of the anaconda is usually greyish brown or olive above, the back being ornamented with one or two transversely disposed rows of large, rounded, dark brown or blackish spots, while the sides are decorated with more irregularly scattered, smaller, eye-like spots, having whitish centres and dark margins.

Photo by H. G. F. Spurrell, Esq.] [*Eastbourne.*

LEOPARD-SNAKE.

A harmless and beautifully marked species inhabiting Italy and Sicily.

An interesting little group, connecting the Boas and Pythons with the Common Snakes, is that of the so-called SHIELD-TAILS, or EARTH-SNAKES, of India and Ceylon. These reptiles are earth-burrowers, like the Blind-snakes, previously referred to, but have well-developed eyes, and are further distinguished by the abruptly truncated contour of their posterior extremity, which may be either a naked disk or covered with keeled scales. Their bodies are cylindrical, with the scaly covering very smooth and polished, the scales of the under-surface being but little larger than the upper ones; the jaws, in conformity with the peculiar modification of their skull, are not capable of wide distension. Seven genera and a large number of species are recognised, some being brilliantly coloured with tints of red or yellow. Their main diet is earth-worms.

Photo by H. G. F. Spurrell, Esq.] [*Eastbourne.*

TESSELATED SNAKE.

A European species, similar in size and habits to the British ringed snake, but more handsomely marked.

The family of the COMMON SNAKES

includes the greater number of species, the majority of the most venomous as well as harmless varieties being comprised within its limits. The characters that are made the basis for separating these snakes from the Boas are associated with the structure of the skull, and are not therefore readily recognised without having recourse to dissection. It will suffice to mention that, in this and the remaining groups, there is an entire absence from the lower jaw of the slender supplementary bone known as the "coronoid," which is present in the Boas and Pythons. From succeeding groups, such as the Viperine series, they are distinguished by the circumstance that the upper jaw is firmly fixed in a horizontal position, and is not capable of erection in a vertical plane, or like the lid of a box, as obtains with the Vipers.

These snakes are separated into secondary groups with relation to the structure of their teeth. In one series these teeth are solid throughout, neither grooved nor tubular; and all the snakes thus characterised are harmless. In the second series one or more pairs of the

By permission of the New York Zoological Society.

PINE-SNAKE.

A tree-haunting American species with very bold markings.

hinder upper teeth are longitudinally grooved, and act as poison-fangs; they are consequently distinguished as the "back-fanged" group. In the third series the front teeth of the upper jaw-bone are grooved, and constitute the poison-fangs, and they are known as the "front-fanged" group.

To the first-mentioned solid-toothed and harmless division of the family belongs the British Ringed Snake and some forty other allied species which are collectively known as Water-snakes, with reference to their more or less pronounced aquatic habits. The ringed snake has a stoutish cylindrical body, keeled scales, flat head covered with regular shields, wide mouth-cleft, and numerous teeth, the strongest of which are at the hinder end of the jaw-bone. The colour varies somewhat, being usually grey, brown, or olive above, with darker spots or narrow transverse bands; the under-surface is mottled black and white or grey. The lip-shields are white or yellowish, with black dividing-lines. The neck in the ordinary variety is usually ornamented with a yellow, white, or orange collar-like patch,

Photo by Henry Dixon & Son] [*Albany Street, N.W.*

COBRA (BACK VIEW).

Showing the remarkable pattern on the back of the neck, which has given rise to the name of Spectacled Snake.

behind which is a somewhat broader black collar, which is produced forwards and sub-divides the yellow one in the centre of the upper-surface. In the variety of the ringed snake indigenous to the South of Europe the collar-like markings may be altogether absent, or reduced to a small black patch on each side of the nape of the neck. The maximum length of the ringed snake is some 6½ feet. It is a most expert swimmer, moving swiftly through the water with lateral undulations of its body, and carrying its head and neck well above the surface. Frogs constitute its favourite diet, but it will also capture and devour fish, mice, and young birds.

The VIPERINE and TESSELATED SNAKES, both European forms, as also the GARTER- and MOCASSIN-SNAKES of North America, are all closely allied in structure and habits to the familiar ringed species. The second British species, known as the SMOOTH SNAKE, belongs to the same group, but is more terrestrial in its habits; while comparatively rare in England, and limited to the southern counties, it is plentiful on the Continent. The INDIAN RAT-SNAKE, which is almost as useful as the domestic cat in ridding dwellings of rats and mice, is another representative of the solid-toothed group. This group also includes the so-called PYGMY SNAKES, inhabiting the Malay region, whose habits are mainly arboreal. They are the most diminutive members of their order, some of the thirty known species not exceeding 1 foot in length.

The typical TREE-SNAKES of the Indian and Australian region, with large eyes, somewhat compressed bodies, and colours of green or olive, in harmonious accord with their arboreal surroundings, also belong to the solid-toothed and harmless section. An especially interesting representative of this group is the so-called EGG-EATING SNAKE of South Africa. It does not exceed 2 feet in length, and is for the most part arboreal in its habits, and, as its name implies, would appear to feed exclusively on eggs. As a structural adaptation for this peculiar habit, the spinous processes of a number of the vertebræ project into the throat

Photo by W. Saville-Kent, F.Z.S.] [*Milford-on-Sea.*

QUEENSLAND SEA-SNAKE.

Sea-snakes have compressed tails, which they use for steering.

and are tipped with enamel, thus constituting supplementary throat-teeth. Normally this snake subsists on the eggs of the smaller birds, but when short of this supply has been known to leave the trees and rob hen-roosts, being able, notwithstanding its comparatively small size, to dilate its mouth and throat for the reception of a hen's egg. The egg is split longitudinally by the action of the throat-teeth, the contents swallowed, and the shell ejected.

The second or "back-fanged" group includes many exceedingly poisonous species. Among these may be mentioned the INDIAN WHIP-SNAKES and their allies, comprising many tree-frequenting species, closely resembling in habits and colours the harmless solid-toothed tree-snakes of the preceding section.

It is among the third or "front-fanged" group, however, that the most venomous species occur. To this section belongs the death-dealing COBRA, the yet more formidable HAMADRYAD, the INDIAN CRAITS, the EGYPTIAN ASP, and the AUSTRALIAN BLACK SNAKES and DEATH-ADDERS. The COBRA-DE-CAPELLO, HOODED, or SPECTACLED SNAKE, as it is variously known, is perhaps the most notoriously familiar example of its section, being responsible for the greater moiety of the many thousands of fatalities that annually occur among the natives of India from the bites of venomous serpents. The craits, which resemble the cobras, but do not possess an erectile hood, are accredited a second position in death-dealing. The peculiar feature of the erectile hood that characterises the cobras is due to the circumstance that a certain number of the ribs in this region are independently movable, and can be elevated and depressed at will, the skin-fold that overlies them being loose and elastic. The back of the hood in the ordinary Indian cobra is usually ornamented with two eye-like spots, connected with a loop-like band, which communicate to the complete pattern the fancied resemblance to a pair of spectacles, whence it has derived its appellation of Spectacled Snake. Individuals vary, however, very considerably in this matter of colour-markings; in some instances a single eye-like spot is alone developed, while in others it may be entirely absent. The COMMON COBRA grows to a length of 6 or 7 feet, dimensions greatly exceeded by the GIANT COBRA, or HAMADRYAD, a fortunately rarer form more exclusively confined to jungle and forest districts. This species may attain to a length of 13 feet or more, and on account of its deadly bite and fiercely aggressive disposition is much feared by the natives of the countries it inhabits, which include not only India, but Burma, Siam, and the Malay region. This giant cobra preys almost exclusively on smaller snakes, frequently including the common cobra.

Photo by H. G. F. Spurrell, Esq.] *[Eastbourne.*

ENGLISH VIPER.

The only British venomous reptile.

A third species of cobra, known as the HAJÉ, or SPITTING-SNAKE, inhabits Africa, from Egypt as far south as Natal. It is perhaps the fiercest member of the group, turning readily upon its pursuers, or even commencing the attack. It also possesses the somewhat remarkable and disconcerting habit of ejecting poison from its mouth to a distance of several feet, usually aiming with considerable accuracy at the eyes of its assailant. Although unattended by permanently serious effects, the pain caused by the virus striking the eyes is for the time being excruciatingly painful, placing the recipient of the unwelcome discharge entirely *hors de combat.* The first record of the poison-spitting propensities of this snake, made by Mr. Gordon Cumming, was received with considerable incredulity, but the statement has been confirmed. A relative of the writer's, stationed in Natal, was recently the victim of

By permission of the New York Zoological Society.

AFRICAN PUFF-ADDER.

Horses die within a few hours of being bitten by this serpent.

By permission of the New York Zoological Society.

DIAMOND-BACK RATTLE-SNAKE.

One or more joints are added to the "rattle" each successive year.

such an incident, receiving the poison-discharge in his eyes from one of these snakes, which, in his eagerness to dispatch it, he had imprudently cornered, armed only with a sword. It was some days before the pain entirely abated and the sight regained its normal clearness.

Australia, with its BLACK and TIGER-SNAKES and the DEATH-ADDER, possesses snakes as venomous as the cobra, which the first-named species approach in their capacity to inflate their necks, though to a less degree. The TASMANIAN BLACK SNAKE, as it glides swiftly, as though sailing, across open grass-land, with the midday sun scintillating on its 7-foot stretch of jet-black, highly polished scales, its head and expanded neck threateningly elevated some 18 inches above the ground, is certainly a most impressive sight.

One very distinct group of the front-fanged section which demands brief notice is that of the SEA-SNAKES. These are readily distinguished by their especial adaptation to a marine existence, their much-compressed, oar-like tails constituting powerful propelling organs. In contradistinction to the terrestrial snakes of the same group, the inferior scales, not being required for terrestrial locomotion, are little if any larger than the upper ones. All the species are highly venomous; they feed chiefly upon fish, and are distributed throughout the tropical seas. The larger species rarely exceed 5 or 6 feet in length, and the majority are much smaller. Many species are noted for their conspicuous colouring, which most frequently takes the form of distinctly contrasting bands. All the members of this group are viviparous.

Photo by J. W. McLellan] *[Highbury.*

RATTLE-SNAKE.

The rattle-snake is pre-eminently noted for its power of fascinating birds and the smaller mammals.

The last and most highly specialised section of the Snake Tribe is that of the VIPER and its allies, collectively known as the Viperine Family. In all the representatives of this group the hinder upper jaw-bone is so loosely articulated that it is capable of erection at a right angle to the horizontal plane of the skull, the gape of the mouth being in consequence abnormally wide. The teeth in the upper jaw are reduced to a single anteriorly situated pair of tubular poison-fangs, with which, when striking its prey, the snake deals a direct stab. The head in the majority of the Viperine Snakes is flattened and triangular, nearly resembling in contour the symbolic ace of spades. The body is usually relatively thick, and the tail short and stumpy. The vertical pupil of the eye denotes nocturnal habits. All the members of the section are venomous.

The Viperine Snakes are usually divided into two groups. The first contains the Typical or Old World Vipers, and includes, in addition to the COMMON VIPER, the CERASTES or HORNED VIPER of Egypt, and the large and most repulsive and deadly African PUFF-ADDER. The COMMON VIPER or ADDER, the only poisonous British snake, has a very extensive geographical distribution, extending throughout Europe and Asia as far east as the island of Saghalien, and northwards to the Arctic Circle. The HORNED VIPER of the Sahara and North Africa is one of the most venomous of living serpents. Lying buried beneath the sand, with only its head above, it will spring aggressively at any animal which passes by, and the action of its venom is so rapid that a horse or man bitten by it usually dies within half an hour. In colour the horned viper closely resembles the sand or stony wastes among which it lies. The most remarkable feature in this snake is the presence of two elevated horn-like processes immediately above the eyes, which are most prominent in the male. The species has frequently been on view at the Zoological Society's Gardens. On one occasion an ostensible example was purchased and deposited in the Reptile-house, which proved on nearer investigation to be a base imposition. A common desert-viper had been cleverly manipulated by the deft insertion of suitably shaped splinters of wood into its head, so that it resembled the rarer horned variety. The PUFF-ADDER, the largest member of its tribe, may attain to a length of 6 feet or more, and is distributed throughout the African Continent. Its thick body is almost triangular in section, the head very large, flat, and bluntly rounded anteriorly, while the eyes have a particularly fierce, stony, and repulsive aspect. In colour individuals vary considerably, but there is generally a chequered pattern of reds, browns, and greys, disposed in the form of darker and lighter alternating crescent-shaped bands along the back. The poison of this snake is nearly as virulent as that of the horned viper, and is commonly used by the African bushmen for poisoning their arrows.

The Viperine group is abundantly represented in the New World, where its members differ from the typical Old World species in sundry anatomical points, one of the most conspicuous features being the presence of a distinct depression or pit in the surface of the head between the nostril and the eye on either side. On this account they are distinguished by the title of PIT-VIPERS. Among the more familiar representatives of this group are the RATTLE-SNAKES, the FER-DE-LANCE, the BUSH-MASTER, and the COPPER-HEAD or MOCASSIN-SNAKES. All these are notoriously venomous, fatal effects from bites received by human subjects being of frequent recurrence. The RATTLE-SNAKES are especially distinguished by the peculiar, loosely jointed, horny appendage to their tails, by the rapid vibration of which, when disturbed, they fortunately give timely notice of their presence. In the young individuals this rattle is only represented by a single button-like knob, additional loose, hollow, horny rings being added between it and the scaly termination of the tail as age increases. In full-grown examples the horny rings composing the rattle may number as many as twenty or more, though, owing to the war of extermination incessantly levied against these reptiles in all civilised areas, it is rarely that such elaborate rattle-bearers are now met with. The rattle-snake, in the more northern districts of its distribution, hibernates in the winter, often congregating together in great numbers for the sake of the mutual warmth. In the earlier days certain caves were famous as the retreats into which not only hundreds but thousands of the reptiles would congregate from the country round for their winter's slumber. At such times hunting-parties were specially organised for their wholesale destruction, and accomplished much towards reducing their ranks to their present numbers.

In addition to the common North American rattle-snake there are some four or five other species distributed throughout the Southern States, Mexico, and Panama. None appear to exceed a length of 6 feet. In South America their place is to a large extent taken

By permission of the New York Zoological Society.

FER-DE-LANCE SNAKE.

One of the fiercest and most venomous of American viperine snakes.

Photo by Scholastic Photo. Co.] *[Parson's Green.*

BULL-FROG.

The croaking of this species may be heard at a distance of several miles.

by the so-called BUSH-MASTER, a snake which attains to a length of as much as from 9 to 12 feet, and, in addition to being exceedingly venomous, is of an especially fierce and aggressive disposition. It is devoid of a rattle-like appendage, the tail terminating in a sharp horny spine. The FER-DE-LANCE, or RAT-TAILED PIT-VIPER, is another Central and South American species, held in wholesome dread on account of its death-dealing potentialities. The South American sugar-plantations are an especially favourite resort of this deadly snake, its attraction being the rats which frequent the canes and afford its chief food. Lying concealed among the thick foliage, it will launch itself aggressively at any passer-by, and its bite is usually attended with fatal results within a few hours. The fer-de-lance grows to a length of 6 or 7 or occasionally even 8 feet, with a thickness of a man's arm. Its colours, as with most members of its tribe, are somewhat variable. The ground-colour of the back is usually olive or reddish brown, with dark cross-bands; a black stripe runs backwards from the eye to the neck, and in some instances the sides of the body are bright red.

The American Continent is not wanting in aquatic representatives of the Viperine series. The most notable of these is the fish-eating WATER-VIPER, whose distribution extends from North Carolina in the south over the whole of North America as far westward as the Rocky Mountains. Fish and frogs constitute the main diet of this reptile.

AMPHIBIANS.

CHAPTER VI.

FROGS AND TOADS.

THE Amphibian Class, through the Newts and Salamanders more especially, would appear at first sight to have much in common with and to be most closely allied to the Lizards, previously described. As a matter of fact, however, the group is much more nearly related to the Fishes. Quite the most characteristic feature in the Amphibians that is indicative of the above-mentioned affinity is the circumstance that for a more or less longer period of their existence their respiratory organs take the form of external gills, structures not found in any of the preceding vertebrate classes. Another diagnostic character of the

Photo by W. P. Dando, F.Z.S.] *[Regent's Park.*

AMERICAN BULL-FROG.

Young ducks are a favourite food of this voracious Batrachian.

Amphibia is afforded by the circumstance that they all pass through a transitional or larval condition before arriving at the adult state. The familiar tadpole phase of the common frog or toad typically illustrates this point. During its earliest larval state the fish-like resemblance is especially conspicuous. In addition to possessing gills, the body is limbless, and produced into a long fish-like tail, having superior and inferior fin-like membranes, with which the little animal propels itself through the water. These locomotive fins, however, are never furnished with supporting fin-rays, as obtains among the Fishes. In contradistinction to the Lizards and Snakes, the skin of Amphibians is never covered with spines or scales, but is soft and naked. In many of the Toads and Salamanders the surface of the skin is, however, warted and highly glandular, and capable of emitting an acrid and sometimes poisonous fluid. More or less pronounced conditions of moisture are essential for the well-being of all Amphibians. The eggs are deposited, and the earlier or larval conditions, with but few exceptions, passed, in the water, while the adults remain in its near proximity, and frequently take up their abode in it. Amphibia do not, however, drink water after the manner of lizards and other reptiles, but absorb all the moisture they require through the surface of their skins. The deeper and more essential skeletal elements of the Amphibia differ conspicuously from those of the preceding groups. The vertebræ in the permanently gill-bearing species more particularly are scarcely to be distinguished from those of fishes. In the Frog and Toad Tribe, on the other hand, they are reduced to a less number, seven or eight only, than is found among any other vertebrates, while ribs do not exist or are rudimentary and functionless throughout the class. Many bones of the skull in the Amphibia, as well as its general construction, are more in accord with those of fishes than of ordinary reptiles. The tongue, not always present, is attached immediately inside the front of the lower jaw, its tip pointing down the animal's throat. It is remarkable that, notwithstanding their aquatic proclivities, no Amphibian has been discovered which frequents salt water.

Photo by Scholastic Photo. Co.] *[Parson's Green.*

EDIBLE FROG.

The hind legs only of this species are used for the composition of the famous Parisian dish.

Amphibians amongst themselves constitute two very easily recognised sub-divisions,—the one including the Frogs and Toads, collectively forming the Tailless group; and the other represented by the Newts and Salamanders, or Tailed Amphibians. The former group has an almost world-wide distribution, numbering some thousand species; it is most abundantly represented in the tropics, ranging thence in diminishing numbers to the limits of the Arctic Circle. In colder climates these Amphibia usually hibernate during the winter months; while in tropical countries, where dry seasons intervene, they often bury themselves in the mud, and remain in a state of torpor till the return of the rains. The majority are more or less essentially nocturnal in their habits. Frogs and toads commence life in an aquatic

Photo by W. P. Dando, F.Z.S.] *[Regent's Park.*

TIGER-LIKE FROG.

A species closely allied to the common British frog, but more boldly marked.

tadpole phase. While in the adult state they are strictly carnivorous, the tadpoles are vegetarian feeders.

The section to which the COMMON BRITISH FROG belongs includes nearly 150 species, collectively known as Water-frogs, which present considerable differences in both their aspect and habits. While some are perennially aquatic, others only resort to the water during the breeding-season; some are terrestrial and occasionally earth-burrowers, while yet another series is essentially arboreal.

In addition to the familiar British species the much-esteemed EDIBLE FROG of the Continent has become acclimatised in England. A dark-coloured race of this frog, supposed to have been introduced by the monks centuries since on account of its esculent properties, is plentiful in the fens of Cambridgeshire, while a greener race of the same species was imported to and established in Norfolk somewhere about the year 1840. The edible frog may be distinguished from the common species by the more complete webbing of its hind feet, the absence of the dark so-called temporal spot that extends from the eye to the shoulder, and the presence in the males of a globular sac on each side of the head, which confers upon them louder croaking powers than are possessed by the common species.

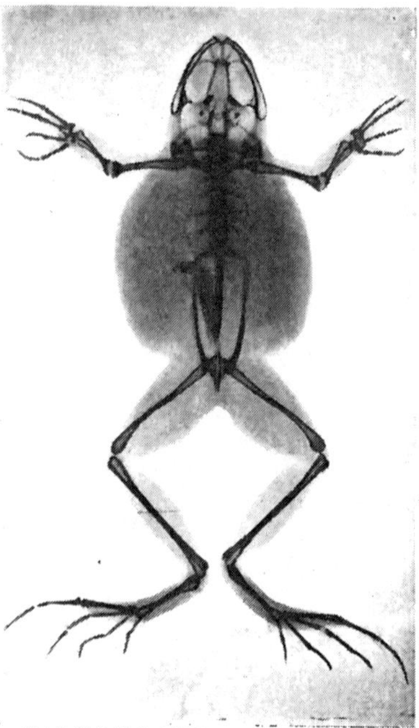

Photo by W. Saville-Kent, F.Z.S.] *[Milford-on-Sea.*

RÖNTGEN RAY PHOTOGRAPH OF COMMON FROG.

The relatively small amount of bone which enters into the structure of the skull is well shown in this photograph.

The loudest-voiced as well as almost the largest member of this group is the BULL-FROG of Canada and the United States. The length of the body in this species may be as much as from 7 to 7½ inches, exclusive of the legs; and its croakings, or more correctly bellowings, are so loud that it may be heard for a distance of several miles. These croakings are most pronounced during the early spring or breeding-season. In the Southern United States, however, they are maintained more or less persistently throughout the year. While the British frog contents itself with a diet of slugs, worms, beetles, and other insects, the bull-frog aspires to larger quarry, and has an especial penchant for young ducklings. As a compensation the flesh of the bull-frog is said to be very delicately flavoured, and the species is so much esteemed in some localities as to be kept in captivity and fattened for the table. It has been recorded that the bull-frog makes leaps of from 8 to 10 feet in length and 5 feet in height.

In point of size the bull-frog is somewhat eclipsed by a species discovered in the Solomon Islands, and known as GUPPY'S FROG. This huge frog has a body no less than 9 inches in length. It has not been recorded whether its vocal powers are proportionately loud. Another large species allied to the Bull-frogs is found in South and East Africa, whose flesh is attested to by Dr. Livingstone as being excellent eating and resembling chicken when cooked. This frog, known to the natives as the MATLAMITLO, is supposed by them to fall from the clouds, on account of its sudden appearance in even the driest parts of the desert immediately after a thunder-storm. The species, however, is in the habit of making holes at the roots of bushes, into which it retires during the months of drought, rushing out into the hollows filled by the thunder-showers while the rain is still actually falling. Even during the long drought these frogs continue their croakings from their retreats at night, and are very misleading to travellers, who customarily associate their presence with the immediate neighbourhood of water.

Photo by Scholastic Photo. Co.] *[Parson's Green.*

ORNAMENTED HORNED TOAD.

The bite of this toad is highly venomous.

There is a remarkable difference in the voice-timbre of the various species of frogs. In England, with its one indigenous variety, comparisons cannot be instituted. In countries, however, like Australia, where numbers of species live in close proximity, the phenomenon is very marked. Some only give voice in the evening or night, while others keep up their clamour throughout the day; with some the note is metallic and almost bell-like, while one diurnal croaking species, which congregates in great numbers in the eastern Tasmanian coast district, emits a loud percussive note closely resembling that of a stone-breaker's hammer. On several occasions, in fact, when driving through the areas these frogs frequented, the impression produced by their croaking was so realistic that the next turn in the road was expected to reveal the presence of a large gang of road-makers engaged in negotiating a wayside stone-heap.

One of the most remarkable species is the Flying-frog of Java. The power of flight is simulated in this instance on a different principle to that which obtains in any other group. It is not accomplished through the medium of abnormally produced ribs with connecting membrane, as occurs in the Flying-lizards; nor by means of a flap of skin stretched between the fore and hind limbs, as in the Flying-squirrels and Phalangers. In place of these the toes of all four feet are abnormally prolonged, and their interspaces bridged over to their tips by webbing. The body of this frog is about 4 inches long, while the webs of the feet, when fully expanded, cover collectively an area of fully 12 square inches; they thus constitute aerial floats, which enable their owner to make prodigiously long flying leaps among the trees in which it takes up its abode. The colours of this singular species are striking; the back and limbs are a deep shining green, the under-surface and inner toes yellow, and the webs black rayed with yellow. In common with the typical Tree-frogs, the toes of this Javan flying variety all terminate in a dilated adhesive disk.

Photo by W. P. Dando, F.Z.S.] *[Regent's Park*

ORNAMENTED HORNED TOAD.

Is accustomed to prowl round farmyards to pick up stray chicks and ducklings.

Among the oddities of the Frog Tribe prominence may be given to the singular Short-headed Frogs of East Africa. In these the head is so short, and the body, when puffed out, so nearly globular, that they have been aptly described as more nearly resembling india-rubber balls than frogs. Another notable form, inhabiting Chili, is remarkable for the circumstance that the throat-sac of the male is so enlarged and modified as to form a chamber on the under surface of the body. In this sac the eggs laid by the female are deposited and pass through their tadpole phases.

The HORNED FROGS, or HORNED TOADS, of South America constitute a distinct and interesting group. They are of large size, stout and rotund, gorgeously apparelled, and truculent in bearing. There are nearly a dozen known species, the distinctive feature from which they take their name having reference to the stiff, horn-like development of their upper eyelids. The largest species is a native of Brazil, whose body may be as much as 8 inches long. This species has the horn-like processes of the eyelids most prominently developed. A somewhat smaller but conspicuously handsome species, plentiful in the Argentine Republic, is at the present time represented by several individuals at the Regent's Park Gardens. In this animal the body is relatively more obese and toad-like than in the Brazilian form, but the horn-like angle of the upper eyelid is only slightly produced. The colours vary somewhat, the general ground-tint of the upper-surface is bronze-green or yellow, upon which are distributed large spots and blotches of dark olive or chocolate, having light yellow or golden margins. The spots on the limbs are the widest, and almost take the character of cross-bands. Bright claret-red lines are sometimes developed in and among the body-spots.

Photo by Scholastic Photo. Co.] [*Parson's Green.*

EUROPEAN GREEN TREE-FROG.

Indigenous to Southern Europe.

A very interesting account of the habits of this frog appears in Mr. W. H. Hudson's "The Naturalist in La Plata." Mr. Hudson reports it as being common on the pampas as far south as the Rio Colorado, in Patagonia. In the breeding-season it congregates in pools, and displays extraordinary vocal powers, which are exercised at night. The notes uttered are long, resembling those of a wind instrument, and are so powerful that on still evenings they may be heard distinctly a mile off. After the pairing-season the frogs disperse, and, retiring to moist places, bury themselves just deep enough to leave their broad green backs on a level with the surface. The eyes, under these conditions, look out as from a couple of watch-towers, and are on the *qui vive* for any approaching prey. This consists of any moving creature which they can capture, such as other frogs and toads, birds, and small mammals. In very wet seasons they will frequent the neighbourhood of houses, and lie in wait for chickens and ducklings, often capturing and attempting to swallow objects much too large for them. In disposition they are exceedingly pugnacious, savagely biting at anything that comes near them. When teased, the creature swells itself out to such an extent that one expects to see it burst. It follows its tormentors about with slow, awkward leaps, its vast mouth wide open, and uttering an incessant harsh croaking sound. When they bite, these frogs hold on with the tenacity of a bull-dog, poisoning the blood of the creature seized with their glandular secretion. Mr. Hudson records two instances in which to his knowledge horses were killed through being bitten by a horned frog. One of them, while lying down, had been seized by a fold in the skin near the belly; the other had been grasped by the nose while cropping grass. In both instances the vicious frog was found dead, with jaws tightly closed, still hanging to the dead horse. "It would seem," Mr. Hudson remarks, "that they are sometimes incapable of letting go at will, and, like honey-bees, destroy themselves in these savage attacks."

The TREE-FROGS represent one of the most distinct groups of the tribe. All its members are more or less arboreal in their habits, repairing to the water only during the breeding-season, or leaving the trees to seek shelter in the earth or underneath stones or timber for the purposes of hibernation. As an adaptation for their special habits, the toes of the tree-frogs are provided at their tips with suctorial disks, so that they can walk on perpendicular or smoothly glazed surfaces after the manner of the Geckos among the Lizards. Another characteristic feature is the development on the under surface of their bodies of peculiar granular glands pierced by numerous pores, through the medium of which they rapidly absorb the moisture deposited by dew or rain on the surfaces of the leaves among which they live. The colours of the tree-frogs harmonise, as a rule, so completely with those of their leafy environments that their presence very readily escapes detection. Many of the species, moreover, rival the chamæleon in their capacity of quickly adapting their tints to that of a newly occupied surrounding. Green is naturally the dominant ground-tint of these frogs. Often, however, it is intermixed with stripes and bands of other colours, while sometimes the green hue is entirely replaced, as in the BLUE or BICOLOURED TREE-FROG of South America, which is brilliant azure above and pure white beneath. A very beautiful Australian species, abundant in Tasmania and Victoria, and appropriately named the GOLDEN TREE-FROG, has its grass-green overcoat thickly overlaid and embroidered with, as it were, the purest beaten gold.

Photo by W. Saville-Kent, F.Z.S., Milford-on-Sea.

QUEENSLAND TREE-FROGS.

This species is in the habit of making itself at home in chamber water-jugs.

One small species of tree-frog is common on the European Continent, its distribution extending to North Africa and eastward throughout Asia north of the Himalaya to Japan. The species is imported into England in considerable numbers, and readily becomes acclimatised in a conservatory. Green above and whitish beneath constitute the prevailing tints of this species, such uniformity being, however, varied by the presence of a darker, often nearly black, light-edged streak, that extends from the snout through the eye and ear along each side of the body, and sends a branch upwards and forwards on the loins. The male of this European species shares with many others of its tribe the possession of a large external vocal sac, which when inflated bulges out from the throat in a spherical form to dimensions little inferior to those of the creature's body. It may be

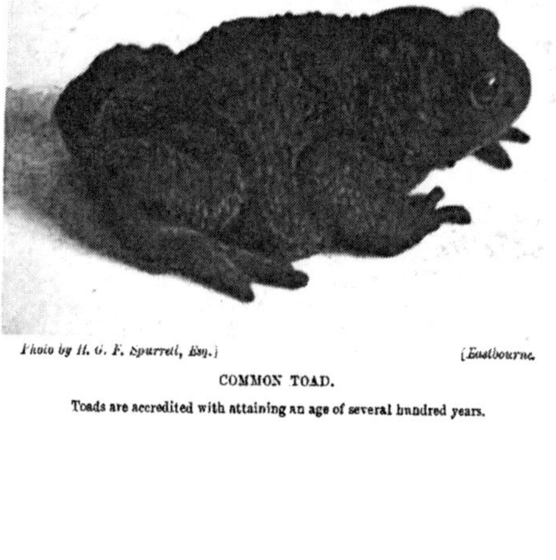

Photo by H. G. F. Spurrell, Esq.] [Eastbourne.

COMMON TOAD.

Toads are accredited with attaining an age of several hundred years.

observed of examples of these frogs acclimatised in a conservatory that the falling of heavy rain on the roof is an almost certain incentive to their croakings. By pouring water resonantly from a little height into another vessel, the writer also found that he could produce a frog chorus at command.

The European and other tree-frogs deposit their eggs in the water, some species constructing a symmetrical crater-like nest of mud for the reception of the eggs and tadpoles. Certain kinds, however, never leave the trees, having adapted their requirements to the naturally provided environments. Thus one Brazilian species deposits its eggs in the water almost invariably contained in the central cup of a tree, while another allied frog chooses for the same purpose the moist interstices at the bases of decaying banana leaves. A step further, resulting in complete independence of external water, is arrived at by the MARSUPIAL or POUCHED TREE-FROG of Central America. In this species the female develops a capacious pouch on her back, which opens backward, and wherein both the eggs—primarily assisted to their position by the male — and tadpoles undergo their characteristic transformations.

Photo by Scholastic Photo. Co.] [*Parson's Green.*

COMMON TOAD.

The toad is highly appreciated by the horticulturist on account of its utility in destroying insect-pests.

As a contrast to the foregoing exclusively tree-dwelling forms, one very fine species common in Queensland has pronounced social proclivities. He is a fine fellow, with a bright pea-green coat and large, lustrous black eyes, and either with or without your leave invades your bedroom from the adjoining verandah, and makes the lip of your water-jug his headquarters. Here he will "lie low" the livelong day. With the approach of night, however, this lethargy is thrown aside, and he hops forth, making excursions through every room in search of black-beetles, spiders, moths, or other acceptable quarry. In this vermin-destroying capacity he is a welcome guest to all except perhaps the ultra-squeamish housekeeper, his occasional offence of an upset glass or cup during his excited chase of the wily cockroach being readily condoned. He has a playful habit too, during his midnight wanderings, of climbing up walls and ceilings, to which he readily clings with his adhesive toes, and mayhap drops down on the recumbent form of some peaceful sleeper, who, if a stranger, possibly wakes with an alarming apprehension of snakes or other uncanny intruders. When once this QUEENSLAND GREEN FROG has determined upon his camping-ground, he clings to it with remarkable pertinacity. You may deport him time after time, and even carry him half a day's journey into the wilderness, but he turns up again the next morning or the following one.

Toads are distinguished from frogs by their sluggish creeping movements and by their non-possession of teeth. There are over eighty species, having collectively an almost cosmopolitan range, though they are not found in Australia, New Guinea, Madagascar, or the Pacific Islands. The common British species enjoys a wide distribution, being found throughout Europe, Asia excepting India, and North-west Africa. Its somewhat clumsy, brown, wrinkled, and warted body, with darker spots and markings on the upper-surface and white-speckled under-surface, will be familiar to every reader. With many it is an unwarranted object of aversion, and in country districts is not infrequently accredited with venomous properties. Toad-spawn is plentiful in ponds and ditches in the early spring, and may be distinguished from that of the frog by the fact of its being deposited in chain-like strings, the eggs being arranged in a double alternating row, instead of in irregular masses, as obtains with the last-named species. The individual eggs are, moreover, smaller, and deposited two or three weeks later in the season than those of the frog. A second and somewhat rarer British toad is known as the NATTERJACK. It may be distinguished from the ordinary species by the shorter hind limbs, the more prominent eyes, and the conspicuous yellow line down the middle of its back. It is also somewhat more active than the common species.

The last member of the group which demands brief notice is the singular WATER-TOAD of Surinam. This animal, also known as the PIPA, is an inhabitant of the moist forest regions of the Guianas and Central America, and remarkable on account of the singular phenomena connected with its breeding habits. The eggs, from 60 to over 100 in number, are deposited by the female in the water in the ordinary manner, but at this stage they are taken in hand by the male and literally planted in the back of the female, whose skin in this region becomes abnormally soft and thickened at this season. The young toads undergo their complete development in the parental integument, each egg and its resulting embryo occupying a separate primarily cylindrical chamber, which by lateral pressure becomes hexagonal, resembling a honeycomb-cell. Eighty-two days are occupied from the time of the deposition of the eggs until the young toads emerge into the outer world, their appearance as they make their *début*, with here a head and there one or it may be two limbs thrust out from the surface of the parent's back, being highly grotesque.

CHAPTER VII.

NEWTS AND SALAMANDERS.

THE Newts and Salamanders, or Tailed Amphibians, are distinguished from the preceding group of the Frogs and Toads by the retention of a tail throughout life. In this manner they very nearly resemble the advanced larval or tadpole phases of the latter. In some instances, in fact, the earlier or externally gill-bearing tadpole phase is persistent. The geographical distribution of the Salamander Tribe is much less extensive than that of the Frogs and Toads, but few are found south of the Equator, and they are entirely unknown in Australia or in Africa south of the Sahara.

Two members of the group are indigenous to the British Islands, where they are familiarly known as NEWTS, ASKERS, EFFETS, or EFTS. The larger and handsomer of the two, the CRESTED NEWT, occurs in ponds and ditches throughout the warmer months of the year. It grows to a length of nearly 6 inches, of which the tail constitutes about one moiety. Its

Photo by James B. Corr, Esq.] *[Dundee.*

COMMON OR SMOOTH NEWT.

This harmless little creature is accredited by many country people with venomous properties.

colour is more usually blackish or olive-brown with darker circular spots above, and yellow or orange-red with black spots or marbling beneath, while the sides are speckled white. In the breeding-season the colours are more especially brilliant, and it is at this time that the male develops the serrated crest along the middle of its back, from which it takes its title.

The eggs, or spawn, of the newt are deposited in a different fashion to those of the frog and toad. In place of being aggregated together in an irregular or ribbon-like mass, each is deposited separately and attached to the leaves of water-plants. By the dexterous use of its feet, the female newt twists or folds the leaf, or a portion of it, around the egg, its viscid envelope allowing it to readily adhere, and it is thus effectually concealed or protected from injury. When about a quarter of a inch long, the tadpole escapes from the egg. At this early stage the gills are quite simple and the front limbs represented by mere knobs. Immediately in front of the gills are two fleshy lobes, by means of which the tadpole can temporarily adhere to the surfaces of water-plants. Within a fortnight the little animal has grown to double the size. The gills are now elegantly branched and the fore limbs well developed. The latter are, however, only bifurcated at their extremities, and it is some little time later that four distinct toes are possessed by each fore limb and that the hind limbs make their appearance. The gills, which have at this stage reached their most complex state of development, now begin to diminish in size, and are gradually absorbed, the lungs in the meantime acquiring their full functional proportions. The newt, having now passed from the fish-like to a reptilian stage, is unable to live entirely beneath the water, and is obliged to come up to the surface at intervals to breathe, or is adapted for living entirely upon land. Newts in their fully matured state, except during the breeding-season, pass much of their time on land, and wander to considerable distances from the water. They at all times, however, exhibit a preference for moist situations, such as a shady wood or damp cellar.

Photo by James D. Corr, Esq.] *[Dundee.*

SMOOTH NEWT.

This species often travels long distances from water, taking up its residence in damp cellars and vaults.

Like the toad and blind-worm, the feeble, inoffensive newt has from the earliest time to the present day been the victim of the most unmerited dread and persecution among the uneducated. In some country districts it is not only accredited with the property of biting venomously, but of spitting fire into the bitten wound. A property that is actually possessed by these creatures is that of reproducing lost parts. The Geckos and other lizards, as already recorded, are in the habit of reproducing their mutilated tails. The newt, however, beats that record to the extent of reproducing lost legs, and, it has been affirmed, eyes also.

A second species of British newt, of somewhat smaller size and even more common than the crested one, is the Common or Smooth Newt. It scarcely exceeds 3 inches in length, and is distinguished by its smooth skin and relatively less conspicuous crest. In habits it is less addicted to a prolonged aquatic residence than the crested form, and wanders to more considerable distances from water. One of the largest and handsomest representatives of the family is the Marbled Newt of Southern France and the Spanish Peninsula, which attains a length of 8 or 9 inches. The upper-parts of the male at the breeding-season are bright bronze-green with irregular black markings; its crest is ornamented with black and white vertical bars, and a silvery white band is developed along the sides of the tail. The crestless female has a distinctive orange streak running down the centre of the back.

The True Salamanders have no British representative, though the common or spotted species is abundant throughout Central and Southern Europe. Its conspicuous livery—in which bold markings of black and brilliant yellow are somewhat equally balanced, no two individuals, however, precisely corresponding—distinguishes it broadly from all other members of the group. The surface of the skin is very smooth and shining, and thickly set on the surface with glands and pores, from which a viscid and undoubtedly poisonous secretion is exuded. In common with that of other salamanders, the tail is cylindrical, instead of compressed and oar-shaped, as in the Newts, and there is no crest down the back. The SPOTTED SALAMANDER frequents moist situations in mountain and forest districts. It is essentially nocturnal in its habits, lying up during the day in some suitable rock or mossy crevice, exposure of its sensitive skin to the direct rays of the sun speedily having a fatal effect. Large numbers of this salamander are sold as suitable and curious additions to the fernery and vivarium, and will survive for long periods, appropriate food and the necessary conditions of moisture being provided. Snails, worms, and beetles and other insects constituting its natural food, it fulfils as useful a rôle as the toad in the extermination of insect-pests, and may be as strongly recommended for introduction to the greenhouse.

Photo by W. Saville-Kent, F.Z.S.] *[Milford-on-Sea.*

SPOTTED SALAMANDERS.

Natives of Central Europe.

Salamanders repair to the water to breed, after the manner of newts, but the young are usually brought forth alive, though occasionally eggs are deposited, from which the young tadpoles almost immediately emerge. The number usually produced at a birth ranges from sixteen to thirty, but instances are recorded where there have been as many as fifty.

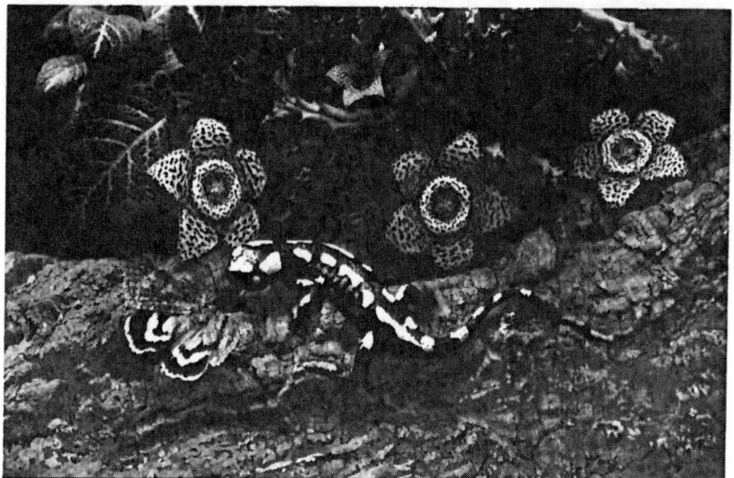

Photo by W. Saville-Kent, F.Z.S.] *[Milford-on-Sea.*

SPOTTED SALAMANDER.

The skin of the salamander exudes a poisonous secretion, and its bright colours advertise its non-edible properties to carnivorous birds and mammals.

The colossus of the tailed Amphibian race is the GIANT SALAMANDER of China and Japan, which may attain to a length of from 3 to 3½ feet. The body, like that of the ordinary salamanders, is broad and depressed; but the eyes are very small, and have no eyelids; and the tail, which is relatively short, is compressed, and has a fin both above and beneath. This salamander lives entirely in the water, and is adapted for such an aquatic life by the possession of both lungs and gills. In its native habitat it is most usually found in small, clear mountain-streams, at elevations of from 700 to 5,000 feet above the sea-level, such streams being often not more than a foot in width, and more or less overgrown with grasses; in these the adults are usually found curled round the larger stones, while the smaller ones occupy holes and crevices among them.

A representative of the tribe now commonly kept in aquaria is the Mexican AXOLOTL. It has usually a velvety black skin, and grows to a length of 9 or 10 inches. As generally known it presents a very newt-like aspect, or, more correctly, that advanced tadpole state of

Photo by James B. Corr, Esq.] [Dundee.

YELLOW PHASE OF SPOTTED SALAMANDERS.

The first four or five months of the young salamander's life are passed in the water.

the newt in which the external gills are most highly developed. The animals breed freely in the water, eggs being laid, which pass through the earlier tadpole to the adult phase. Up to within comparatively recent times the foregoing matamorphoses were supposed to represent the Alpha and Omega of the animal's existence. Some exceptional examples, however, bred in an aquarium in which rocks projected out of the water, surprised their owners by gradually absorbing their supposed persistent gills, also their fin-like tail-membranes, and, crawling out on the rocks, were transformed into ordinary salamanders.

The OLM, or BLIND PROTEUS, of the subterranean caves of Dalmatia and Carniola is a form with persistent external gills. Nearly allied is the North American form known as the FURROWED SALAMANDER. The latter, however, living under more normal conditions, has well-developed eyes. While possessing the customary number of limbs, the number of toes in the American type is four to each foot. In the European Proteus there are but three toes to the front and two toes to the hinder limb. In a yet lower form, the SIREN SALAMANDER of the South-eastern United States, a yet more primitive persistently gill-bearing condition is presented.

Photographed and coloured by W. Saville-Kent, F.Z.S.

WESTERN AUSTRALIAN SCARLET ROCK-COD.

A member of the Sea-Perch family not infrequently exposed for sale in the Freemantle fish market having excellent edible qualities.

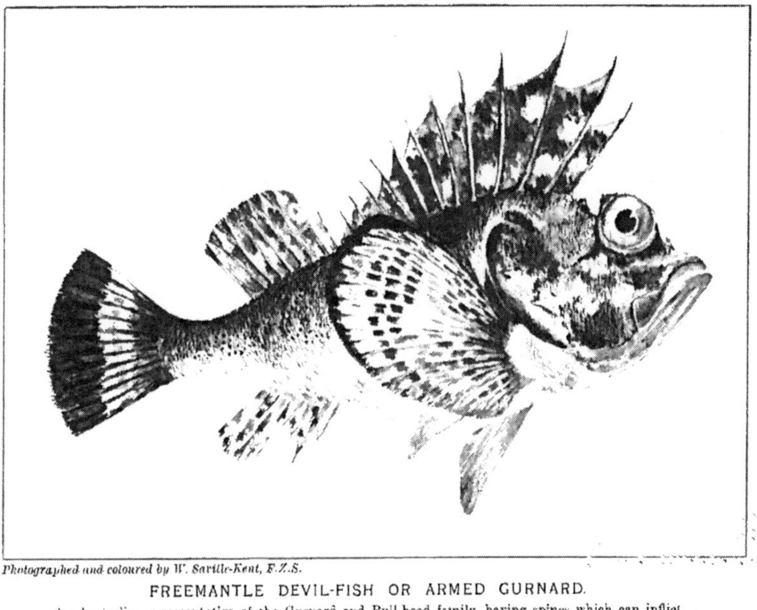

Photographed and coloured by W. Saville-Kent, F.Z.S.

FREEMANTLE DEVIL-FISH OR ARMED GURNARD.

An Australian representative of the Gurnard and Bull-head family, having spines which can inflict exceedingly painful wounds.

Photo by W. Saville-Kent, F.Z.S.] [Milford-on-Sea.

AUSTRALIAN LUNG-FISH.

This fish is also known as the Burnett River Salmon.

BOOK IV. FISHES.

CHAPTER I.

LUNG-FISHES AND CHIMÆRAS.

BY W. P. PYCRAFT, A.L.S., F.Z.S.

THOUGH amongst the lowest of the backboned animals, the Fishes are nevertheless an exceedingly interesting group, distinguished from all others by the possession of fins, which are divisible into two series,—an unpaired, ranged along the middle of the back and abdomen, and including the tail-fin; and a paired series, representing the fore and hind limbs of land animals. The body is either clothed with scales or naked, and, being perfectly sustained by the water, needs no support from the fins, which serve as balancing-organs.

In the brilliancy and beauty of their coloration fishes display a variety that cannot be excelled by any other animals. Furthermore, the coloration is often rendered still more beautiful from the fact that it can undergo rapid changes of hue. Frequently this coloration is of a protective character, causing the fish to harmonise with its surroundings, and so escape the observation of its enemies. The colours of living fishes can only, for the most part, be indicated in the present pages when a pattern exists by the formation of stripes or spots; but the wonderful variations in the form of the body will probably prove a revelation to many.

LUNG-FISHES.

The LUNG-FISHES are a peculiarly important group, inasmuch as they form a connecting-link between the class Fishes and the land-dwelling Amphibians—the class containing the Frogs and Toads and their allies. They are accorded this position mainly because, like Amphibians, they possess true lungs, which almost entirely replace the gills, the breathing-organs of other fishes.

One of the best known of the lung-fishes is the AUSTRALIAN BARRAMUNDI, or LUNG-FISH OF QUEENSLAND—the BURNETT or DAWSON SALMON of the settlers. It lives among the weeds at the bottom of muddy rivers, rising frequently to the surface to take in atmospheric air by the lungs, the gills alone being insufficient for breathing purposes. The flesh, which is salmon-coloured, is much esteemed as food. The adult fish is said to attain to a weight of 20 lbs. and a length of 6 feet.

Other lung-fishes, eel-like in form, occur in the rivers of Africa and South America. The

African species is perhaps the better known of the two. On the approach of the dry season it buries itself in the mud at the bottom of the river, and when the latter becomes dry the mud hardens, holding the fish a prisoner till the return of the wet season several months later. A considerable number of these fishes have from time to time been dug out and sent to England enclosed in the mud into which they had retreated. The writer remembers assisting in the liberation of some during the last meeting of the British Association at Oxford. So hard had the prison-walls become that the mass had to be plunged into tepid water; this soon brought about a dissolution of the soil, and in a short time the fishes were swimming about as if in their native rivers. The African lung-fish is known also as the MUD-FISH; its American relative as the LEPIDOSIREN, or SOUTH AMERICAN MUD-FISH. In the American species, as in its African relative, the fins are whip-like in form; but the hinder or ventral pair, which correspond to the hind limbs of the higher vertebrated animals, are remarkable in that in the male they develop during the breeding-season numerous thread-like processes, richly supplied with blood, the function of which is as yet unknown.

The young, both of the African and South American mud-fishes, bear external gills closely resembling those of the tadpoles of the frog and other Amphibia; traces of these gills remain throughout life in the African form.

Photo by A. S. Rudland & Sons.

BOTTLE-NOSED CHIMÆRA.

The remarkable structure in front of the mouth is probably an organ of touch.

CHIMÆRAS.

Shark-like in their general characters, the CHIMÆRAS, now briefly considered, are nevertheless regarded as constituting a very distinct group of great antiquity.

The modern representatives of the group are few in number—five species in all. Of these, the species shown in the accompanying photograph and the SEA-CAT are remarkable for the possession of a movable tentacle on the snout. The under surface of this tentacle is armed with small spines, and fits into a hollow in the head. The first back-fin is supported in front by a strong spine, and can be depressed into a sheath in the body-walls. The teeth take the form of large plates closely united with the jaws, and studded with hardened points, or "tritors."

One species widely distributed in the Mediterranean and Atlantic is taken usually in deep water; it is the largest living species, often attaining a yard in length. Its occurrence is, however, very erratic, months elapsing without any being taken; at other times several will be caught in a few days. A closely allied fish is often exposed for sale in the Lisbon markets, where it ranks with the Sharks as a food-fish.

The egg of the BOTTLE-NOSED CHIMÆRA is perhaps the only egg with a mimetic resemblance to a foreign object. It is elliptical in form, and bordered by a fringe, so as to present a close resemblance to a piece of seaweed.

In the next chapter we begin the description of the great group of Fan- and Fringe-finned Fishes, which, briefly, embrace all fishes not grouped among the Lung-fishes, Chimæras, or Sharks. The anatomical characters used for the purpose of classifying this great group are not discussed here, save only in a few cases of prime importance, when features such as can readily be observed, without demanding an intimate knowledge of anatomy, are selected.

Photo by Dr. R. W. Shufeldt] [*Washington.*

WHITE PERCH.

The so-called white perch is a species of bass, found in the rivers of the United States of America.

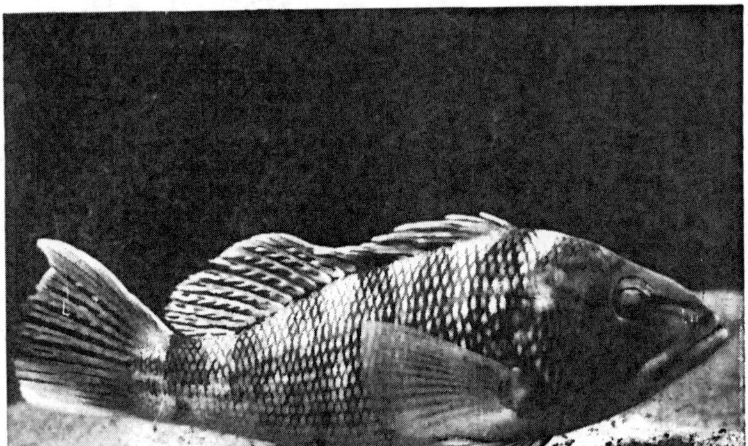

Photo by Dr. R. W. Shufeldt] [*Washington.*

SEA-BASS.

This is another American member of the Perch Tribe.

CHAPTER II.

THE PERCH FAMILY.

BY JOHN BICKERDYKE, M.A.

Photo by Dr. R. W. Shufeldt] [*Washington.*

LARGE-MOUTHED BLACK BASS.

The introduction of this fish into the fresh-waters of Great Britain has been frequently urged.

THE thick-set, golden-bronze, dark-barred, hog-backed fish known as the PERCH has many striking characteristics, and is remarkable, among other things, for the vast number of its relations scattered all over the world. So numerous, indeed, are its cousins that ichthyologists have had to divide the Perch Family into a large number of groups. There are various species of perch found, as a matter of fact, in the fresh-waters and on all the coasts of the temperate and tropical regions.

The COMMON PERCH, which is widely distributed over Europe, Northern Asia, and North America, is properly an inhabitant of rivers, lakes, and ponds, but sometimes descends to brackish water. It runs up to about 5 lbs. in weight, and is carnivorous, eating most kinds of fish small enough for its swallow, including the fry of its own species, which are, in some waters, an excellent bait.

In England perch spawn in the spring, the eggs being held in a band-like mass of gelatinous matter deposited on weeds or the roots of trees not far below the surface of the water. The spawn, as a matter of fact, is often collected by fish-culturists and hatched out. Swans and water-fowl generally eat the eggs by the million, and wherever perch are preserved these birds should, so far as possible, be kept from the water during the spawning-season. At Henley and other places on the Thames those interested in fishery preservation place wire netting round the boughs and weeds where perch have spawned, to prevent the eggs being eaten by swans and ducks.

Photo by W. Saville-Kent, F.Z.S.] [*Milford-on-Sea.*

BUTTER-FISH.

A native of the tropical parts of the Indo-Pacific Ocean

Perch are usually termed voracious fish, but when large are extremely shy and difficult of capture. There is a story told of a hungry little lake-perch which had its eye hooked out by accident. The angler, leaving the eye on the hook, lowered it into the water again, and a moment after hauled out a one-eyed perch!

Photo by Dr. R. W. Shufeldt] [*Washington.*

AMERICAN "SUN-FISH."

Not to be confounded with the true Sun-fishes described in Chapter VII.

Among the species of perch found in British waters are the RUFFE, or POPE, a very small and common river-fish of no great value; the BASS, a fine sporting sea-fish, which comes up the estuaries of rivers to spawn, and is much sought after by the amateur sea-fisher; the COMBER, or GAPER, a fairly common fish on the coasts of the West of England; a rare sea-fish known as the DUSKY PERCH, caught occasionally off the South of England; the STONE-BASS, also called the WRECK-FISH, from its habit of following wreckage in the sea; and, lastly, the DENTEX, a rare species, not often caught off the British coasts, which attains the weight of about 70 lbs.

On the Continent there is the PIKE-PERCH, a fish having the appearance of a cross between a pike and a perch, and growing to 25 or 30 lbs.; this voracious species is found in the lakes and rivers of the temperate northern zones, and is much esteemed for food. In the tropics there are a number of true SEA-PERCHES, which rarely enter fresh-water; they include the ANTHIAS, most beautifully coloured with pink and yellow, of which there are between 100 and 200 species. Some of the tropical sea-perches grow to an enormous size, and there are instances recorded of bathers having been attacked by them at Aden. Several monsters are stuffed in the Natural History Museum at South Kensington. Among the coral-islands live many very beautifully coloured sea-perches of various species. Perhaps the most remarkable of all is the BOAR-FISH, or BASTARD DORY, which has a prolonged snout, no doubt used for getting out its food from the crannies among rocks and other awkward places.

CHAPTER III.

SCALY-FINS, RED MULLETS, SEA-BREAMS, SCORPION-FISHES, SLIME-HEADS, TASSEL-FISH, MEAGRES, AND SWORD-FISHES.

BY W. P. PYCRAFT, A.L.S., F.Z.S.

FOR quaintness of shape, combined with beauty of coloration, the family of Scaly-finned Fishes has no rivals. The name by which they are collectively known refers to the scaly covering which invests the bases of what are called the median fins—the fins seated along the middle of the back and abdomen. A large number of distinct species have been described, the majority of which occur in tropical seas, and especially in the neighbourhood of coral-reefs; but some frequent the mouths of rivers, which they occasionally ascend for a short distance. All are of relatively small size, of carnivorous habits, and but little used for food.

The pattern of coloration commonly takes the form of bands or stripes, those in which this pattern is most marked being known as ZEBRA-FISH. One of the most beautiful is the

Photo by W. Saville-Kent, F.Z.S.] *[Milford-on-Sea.*

THE MISCALLED ARCHER-FISH.

So named on account of its supposed habit of shooting water at insects.

EMPEROR-FISH, which ranges from the east coast of Africa to the Indian and Malayan seas. The ground-colour of the body is deep blue, relieved by some thirty golden-yellow stripes running from the shoulder backwards to the tail. Crossing the head is a crescent-shaped bar of black edged with yellow, whilst a similarly coloured patch runs upward from the pectoral fins to within a short distance of the top of the back. This species, which attains a length of 15 inches, is highly esteemed for food in India. The most beautiful of all, perhaps, is the zebra-fish of the Indo-Malayan seas, which has the ground-colour of yellow, striped with vertical bars of blue edged with brown, a yellow tail, and an anal fin barred with narrow blue lines.

A tubed-shaped mouth is a common feature of the fishes of this group, and two Indian species in which this character is especially well developed have acquired the habit of shooting therefrom a drop of water at insects resting on overhanging foliage fringing the sea or along the banks of rivers. Having sighted its quarry, it would seem the fish moves upwards to the surface of the water, and with careful aim ejects its liquid bullet with such unerring precision that its prey is invariably knocked down and speedily seized. On this account these fishes are commonly known as ARCHER-FISHES. The archer-fishes are sometimes kept in tubs of water, for the purpose of affording amusement to their captors. Somehow the shooting prowess of these fishes has been accredited to an allied form, shown in the above photograph.

The peculiar shape of these fishes is sufficiently indicated by the photograph already mentioned, but a large series would be necessary to show the numerous variations, some of which are quite remarkable. The brilliancy of the coloration is probably protective, since the most brightly coloured forms live amongst coral-reefs built by gorgeous polyps, or coral-animals, so that amidst such surroundings the fishes are quite inconspicuous.

The RED MULLETS occur chiefly in tropical seas, but one species inhabits European waters, and occur sparsely around the British Islands. Occasionally, however, these fishes visit the British coasts in vast shoals, more than 5,000 having been taken in a single night in August, 1819, in Weymouth Bay, whilst in May, 1851, 10,000 were taken off Yarmouth in one week.

Although about forty species of red mullet are

Photo by W. Saville-Kent, F.Z.S.] *[Milford-on-Sea.*

STRIPED RED MULLET.

The head is ornamented with brilliant blue and violet stripes.

known, the European species is the most prized as a food-fish. Its fame, indeed, extends backwards to the time of the ancient Romans, who sought far and wide for large specimens, paying ruinous prices for them. "Then, as nowadays," writes Dr. Günther, "it was considered essential for the enjoyment of this delicacy that the fish should exhibit the red colour of its integument. The Romans brought it, for that purpose, living into the banqueting-room, and allowed it to die in the hands of the guests, the red colour appearing in all its brilliancy during the death-struggle of the fish. The fishermen of our times attain the same object by scaling the fish immediately after its capture, thus causing a permanent contraction of the chromatophores containing the red pigment."

Photo by W. Saville-Kent, F.Z.S.] *[Milford-on-Sea.*

BROWN SNAPPER.

The snappers are esteemed for the table.

Beneath the chin of the red mullets will be noticed two long finger-like processes; these can be thrust forward and moved about, or laid back in a groove between the sides of the lower jaw, and are used to rake about in the sand and gravel at the bottom of the sea to discover burrowing shrimps or worms. Even dead food they are said to feel with these barbels, as they are called, before biting. The red colour has been observed in the Marine Aquarium at Plymouth to become darker when the fish rise from the ground, and to pale away when they descend.

Two forms of red mullet occur in European waters, but it is not yet finally settled whether they represent distinct species. The one is the plain RED MULLET, of a rich carmine-red above and silvery white below; the other the STRIPED MULLET, or SUR-MULLET, which has a beautiful red colour on the back and sides, and from three to five bright yellow bands passing from head to tail. Till recently the striped form was regarded as the female of the plain red mullet, but many authorities incline to the view that the two are distinct species.

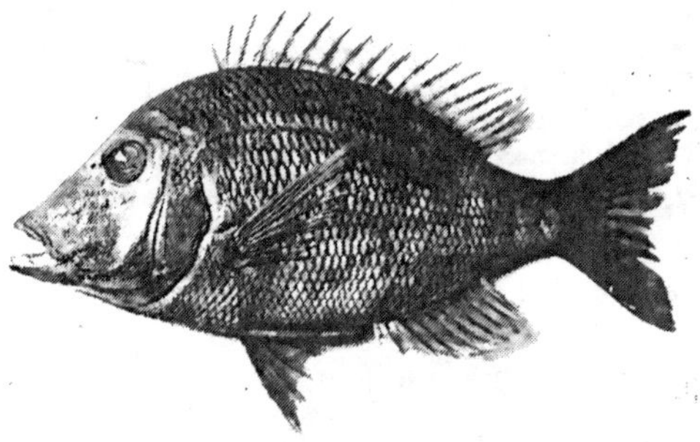

Photo by W. Saville-Kent, F.Z.S.] *[Milford-on-Sea.*

RED SEA-BREAM.

Some species of sea-bream occasionally enter fresh-water.

The SEA-BREAMS are fishes of the tropical and temperate regions, represented by a considerable number of species. Only one is at all abundant on the British coasts, and this

Photo by W. Saville-Kent, F.Z.S.] *[Milford-on-Sea.*

SNAPPER.

An Australian species of Sea-bream.

occurs especially on the south and south-west coasts of England and Ireland. It is of an orange-scarlet colour above, and somewhat silvery on the sides, with a large black spot on the shoulder.

Several species of sea-bream occur in Australia, where they are known as SNAPPERS. One of the largest of these, which attains a length of more than 3 feet and a weight of over 40 lbs., is not only considered excellent eating, but is also the most popular sport-yielding fish of that colony.

The ancient Romans kept a species of sea-bream, the GILT-HEAD, in their vivariums, where it grew extremely fat. This species is said to stir up the sand with its tail, to discover buried shell-fish. It is particularly fond of mussels, and the noise it makes in crunching them between its jaws is loud enough to be heard by the fishermen.

Nearly allied to the Sea-breams are a group known, for want of a better name, as the THICK-RAYED FISHES, some of which rank as of prime importance among the food-fishes of the British Colonies. A general idea of the shape of the members of this family may be gathered from the photograph of an Australian GROPER. The name of LONG-FIN, given to one species, is bestowed on account of the fact that one or more of the rays of the breast-fin on each side is drawn out into a filament, often of very considerable length, which is used as an organ of touch. In other species, where the elongation is less, and more rays have undergone modification, an auxiliary organ of locomotion is the result. At the Cape of Good Hope species of long-fin are very abundant, and preserved in large quantities for export.

Other members of this family lack the elongated fin-rays altogether. The fishes known as the TUMPETERS of New Zealand and Tasmania belong to this section. They are considered by the colonists the best flavoured of any native fishes, and are eaten smoked as well as fresh. But two species are known, one ranging from 30 to 60 lbs. in weight, and the other, a much smaller form, scarcely attaining a weight of 20 lbs.; the latter is the more abundant of the two, though confined to the coast of New Zealand.

Photo by W. Saville-Kent, F.Z.S.] *[Milford-on-Sea.*

KING-SNAPPER.

A member of the group of Slime-beads.

In the SCORPION-FISHES we have a small group including several forms remarkable for their ugliness, having added to an uncouth shape skinny appendages, which, projecting from the body, resemble rather leaves of seaweed than parts of the fish. These appendages, by their waving motion, serve either to attract other fishes or to afford concealment by their resemblance to the surrounding weeds. The ground-dwelling forms have some of the rays of the breast-fin modified into finger-like processes, like those of the Gurnards, by which they both crawl and feel. Some members of the family bear a rather close resemblance to the Sea-perches. In addition to their ugliness, some have become especially offensive by the transformation of certain of the fin-spines into poison-organs.

One of the ugliest, and at the same time most dreaded, of the family is the STONE-FISH figured on page 619. Each spine of the back fin is grooved. At the lower end of these grooves lies a pear-shaped bag containing a milky poison, which is conveyed to the point of the spine by ducts lying in the grooves. The native fishermen carefully avoid handling these fish; but persons walking with bare feet in the sea step upon the spines, and, receiving the poison into the wound, are killed.

All the scorpion-fish are carnivorous, and differ from the majority of fishes in that

Photo by W. Saville-Kent, F.Z.S.] *[Milford-on-Sea.*

AUSTRALIAN GROPER.

Highly esteemed as a food-fish.

they produce their young alive. The smallest of the Spiny-finned fishes are members of this group, some scarcely exceeding 1½ inch in length. They are common amid the coral-reefs of the Pacific.

Passing over some comparatively unimportant members of this family, we come to a small group of vegetable-feeders from the Indo-Pacific, of which the TEUTHIS is one of the best known representatives. They are chiefly remarkable for the fact that the abdominal cavity is surrounded by a complete ring of bones, and that the air-bladder is forked at both ends. Some are rather brilliantly coloured.

The SLIME-HEADS, which constitute the next family, derive their name from the presence on the head of large mucus-bearing cavities covered with a thin skin. The eyes are always of great size, indicating a deep-sea habitat, or at least a depth only dimly lighted. All indeed, save two species, descend considerably below the surface, one species having been found in 345 fathoms. The species of one genus are believed to inhabit still greater depths, for their eyes are extremely small, indicating degeneration through disuse. The copious supply of slime is also an indication of a deep-sea habitat. The members of this family vary much in size and shape, but the most remarkable of all is a small and rare species

Photo by A. S. Rudland & Sons.

INDIAN WEAVER-FISH.

One of the group of scorpion-fishes.

found off Japan, in which the scales have joined together to form a perfectly solid armour, whilst the paired fins of the abdomen have been reduced to a single spine, with a few vestiges of other rays.

The next family, a comparatively small one, includes the TASSEL-FISH, so called from the long and delicate feelers springing from the base of the breast-fins, of which they originally formed a part. Varying in number from three to fourteen, these feelers can be moved independently of the fins. As these fishes all live in muddy water, and have the eyes obscured by films, such tactile organs are necessary, in order to enable them to procure their food. In some species they attain an enormous length. The flesh is highly esteemed. Some species have an air-bladder, which yields a good kind of isinglass, and forms an article of commerce in the East Indies. The majority are small species, but some attain to a length of 4 feet.

No less important than the preceding group, from an economic point of view, are the MEAGRES, a family of coast-haunting species of the tropical and sub-tropical Atlantic and Indian Oceans, exhibiting a special preference for the mouths of large rivers, into which they freely enter. Some, indeed, have become entirely fresh-water species.

One of the most interesting of the family is the species to which the name of DRUM has been given, from the extraordinary noise which it produces—though some other kinds emit similar noises. "These sounds," Dr. Günther writes, "can better be expressed by the word 'drumming' than any other. They appear to be very frequently heard by persons in vessels lying at anchor off the coasts of the United States, where these fishes are very common. The precise method by which these sounds are produced is not known. Since they are accompanied by a tremulous motion of the vessel, it seems more probable that they are due to the beating of the tails of the fish against the bottom of the ship to get rid of the parasites with which that part of their body is infested." The drum attains a length of more than 4 feet and a weight of over 100 lbs.

Though forming but a single small family, the SWORD-FISHES are nevertheless to be reckoned amongst the most interesting of living fishes. Attaining a length of from 12 to 15 feet, exceeding vigilant, pugnacious, and powerful, they are amongst the most formidable of all fishes. They derive their name from the great development of the upper jaw, which forms a huge, tapering, sword-like weapon, covered along its under-surface with numerous small teeth. They attack, apparently without provocation, whales and other large

Photo by A. S. Rudland & Sons.

RAGGED SEA-SCORPION.

A second representative of the scorpion-fishes.

Photo by W. Saville-Kent, F.Z.S.] *[Milford-on-Sea.*

STONE-FISH.

A species of scorpion-fish dreaded on account of its poisonous spines.

Photo by W. Saville-Kent, F.Z.S.] *[Milford-on-Sea.*

TASSEL-FISH.

Valued for the isinglass it yields.

Photo by A. S. Rudland & Sons.

SWORD-FISH.

The huge back-fin is said to be often used as a sail when the fish is floating near the surface of the water.

cetaceans, which they invariably succeed in killing by repeated thrusts of the sword. It appears that occasionally sword-fishes make a mistake, and, after the fashion of Don Quixote, tilt at windmills, in the shape of large vessels, under the impression that they are whales. But this most grave error of judgment brings with it a heavy penalty, in that, having no power to make effective backward movements, the sword remains fixed, and is eventually broken off in the struggle for freedom. Frank Buckland reminds us that in the Museum of the Royal College of Surgeons, London, is a section of the bow of a whaler impaled by one of these swords. That portion of the sword which remains is 1 foot long and 5 inches in circumference. "At one single blow," he writes, "the fish had plunged his sword through, and completely transfixed 13½ inches of solid timber. The sword had of course broken off and prevented a dangerous leak in the ship." In the British Museum is a second specimen of a ship's side in which the sword of a sword-fish is fixed.

CHAPTER IV.

HAIR-TAILS, HORSE-MACKERELS, SEA-BATS, DORIES, MACKERELS, SUCKING-FISHES, WEAVERS, FROG-FISHES, ANGLER-FISHES, BULL-HEADS, AND GURNARDS.

BY W. P. PYCRAFT, A.L.S., F.Z.S.

Of the family of Hair-tails perhaps the most important members are the Scabbard- or Frost-fish and the Snoek. The first is common in the Mediterranean and the warmer parts of the Atlantic, extending northwards to the south coast of England, where it occurs at rare intervals. It is also known in New Zealand, where it is called the Frost-fish, and furthermore is regarded as one of the most delicious fish of the colony, its flesh being fine, tender, and of delicate flavour. On this account it is much in demand, but the supply is very uncertain. The conditions of capture, indeed, of this fish are unparalleled in the annals of fishing, for it can be taken neither with the rod nor the net. The would-be captor has to wait patiently under favourable conditions on the seashore for the fish to come

Photo by Percy Ashenden.] *[Cape Town.*

SNOEK.

This fish is also known as the Barracuda.

and cast itself up on the beach. This happens with tolerable certainty during the autumn and winter months, when the sea is calm and the nights frosty. Then the frost-fish come ashore alive, wriggling through the surf on to the beach. Two explanations have been offered for this extraordinary conduct. One is that the fish commits suicide; being pursued by a shark or other enemy, it prefers uncertain life on land to certain death at sea! The other and more probable hypothesis has it that the air-bladder of the fish becomes distended to enable it to reach the surface for food —for it is a deep-sea fish—and that the keen, frosty air prevents it from compressing the bladder and returning to the depths; thus it gradually drifts into shallow water, is hurled shorewards by the surf, and finally wriggles itself on to the beach to die. The long stretches of sandy beach a few miles from Dunedin are a favourite resort for frost-fish catching. Two or three men camp out at the foot of the cliffs overhanging the beach, pitching a tent and lighting a huge fire, so as to render life bearable during the long vigils. The "fishing" consists in perambulating the beach up and down shortly before dawn, and keeping a sharp look-out in the surf for the silver streak which betokens the approach of a victim. As soon as a fish is

Photo by W. Saville-Kent, F.Z.S.] *[Milford-on-Sea.*

FRINGED HORSE-MACKEREL.

Note the great length of the fin-rays.

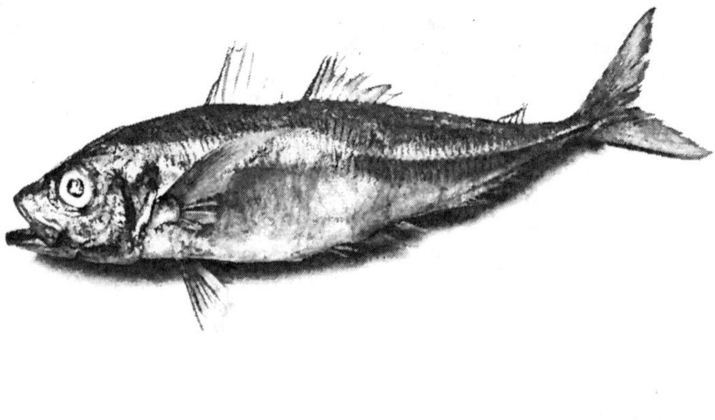

Photo by Reinhold Thiele & Co.] *[Chancery Lane, W.C.*

HORSE-MACKEREL.

The strong keel formed by ridged scales running down each side of the tail is a characteristic feature.

descried, all that remains to be done is to seize hold of it and drag it ashore, if it has not already stranded itself, and then dispatch it.

The BARRACUDA, or SNOEK, is likewise a New Zealand species, attaining a length of 5 feet. It is found also at the Cape and South Australia. In New Zealand the flesh is exported to Mauritius and Batavia as a regular article of commerce, being worth £17 per ton.

The HORSE-MACKERELS, or SCADS, are represented by some very bizarre-looking forms. It is a large family, belonging to tropical and temperate seas. One species, the COMMON HORSE

Photos by W. Saville-Kent, F.Z.S.] *[Milford-on-Sea.*

JOHN DORIES.

These two photographs show the difference in the jaws when protruded and when at rest.

MACKEREL, is common in British seas. Many members of the family have the hinder portion of the body on each side armed with large plates, well seen in the accompanying photographs; others have the median fins produced into long filamentous processes. All are eatable, and some highly esteemed as food. One of the most remarkable is the PILOT-FISH of tropical and temperate seas, occurring occasionally off the British coasts. It derives its name from its habit of accompanying ships and large sharks. From this habit of accompanying ships it was regarded by the ancients as a sacred fish, since they considered it pointed out the way to embarrassed sailors, and announced the vicinity of land by suddenly disappearing. The close companionship between the pilot-fish and the shark has excited much comment, many observers believing that the former was of great use to the latter in guiding it to its food. How this is done is graphically described by Dr. Meyer, who writes: "The pilot swims constantly in front of the shark; we ourselves have seen three instances in which the shark was led by the pilot. When the shark neared the ship, the pilot swam close to the snout or near one of the pectoral fins of the animal. Sometimes he darted rapidly forwards or sidewards, as if looking for something, and constantly went back again to the shark. When we threw overboard a piece of bacon fastened on a great hook, the shark was about twenty paces from the ship; with the quickness of lightning the pilot came up, smelt at the dainty, and instantly swam back again to the shark, swimming many times round his snout and splashing, as if to give him exact information as to the bacon. The shark now began to put himself in motion, the pilot showing him the way, and in a moment he was fast upon the hook." As Dr. Günther remarks, commenting on this account, one may entertain reasonable doubts as to the usefulness of the pilot to the shark in this instance! It is probable that the pilots follow the sharks for the sake of feeding on fragments scattered by the latter, and also for the sake of picking off the parasites with which sharks, in common with other large fish, are infested; furthermore, the pilot, being but a small fish, obtains greater security from enemies when in the company of its giant friend. The habit of seeking the company of more powerful or otherwise offensive animals is apparent also in other members of this family, the young of the horse-mackerel seeking shelter beneath the "umbrella" of a jelly-fish till they are big enough to defend themselves.

But the most remarkable members of this family are the SEA-BATS. Few in species and confined to the Red Sea, Indian Ocean, and Western Pacific, they are nevertheless in those regions very common. Although not used as food-fishes, they are of extreme interest on account of their shape, which is nearly oval and much compressed from side to side, and the form of their fins, which in some species are excessively developed. Young sea-bats differ markedly from the adults in the much greater length of the fin-rays, so much so that they have frequently been described as distinct species.

We pass now to the DORIES, which recall the Sea-bats in the oval and compressed form of the body. The resemblance to sea-bats is, indeed, so close that the latter are frequently described as dories. The mouth of the members of this family is so constructed that, when opened, the upper jaw is thrust forward, and the whole mouth forms a kind of long tube. Dories inhabit the seas of the temperate regions, two species being fairly common in British waters. The best known of these two is perhaps the JOHN DORY, the largest specimens of which attain to a weight of 18 lbs. Mr. Cunningham has described the very peculiar way in which the dory captures its prey. "It does not," he writes, "overtake it by superior speed like the mackerel, or lie in wait for it like the angler, but stalks it and approaches it by stealth. It is able to do this in consequence of the extreme thinness of its body and the peculiar movement of its hinder dorsal and ventral fins. The dory places itself end on towards the fish it desires to devour, and in this position it is evident that it excites no alarm on the part of its prey. The appearance of the dory, seen in this way, is a mere line in the water, to which no particular significance can be attached. I have not particularly noticed the effect of the ribbons of membrane which project from the dorsal fin. But I have observed that the movements of the dory are very gradual, except in turning; it alters the position of its body by a turn of the tail or side-fins, and then swims forward by vibrating the second dorsal

Photo by W. Saville-Kent, F.Z.S.] [*Milford-on-Sea.*

LONG-FINNED DORY.

This species closely resembles a fossil form. It has nothing to do with the True Dories, but is one of the Coral-fishes, and is placed here for the sake of contrast.

and ventral, a movement which causes very slight disturbance of the water. The appearance of the dory in these actions is suggestive of suppressed excitement, his eyes being fixed on his prey. I do not recollect seeing him actually swallow another fish, but have no doubt that he gets near enough to a sprat, for example, without alarming it, to seize it by the sudden elongation of his curious jaws." The way in which these jaws are elongated is admirably shown in the photograph on page 622.

Passing now to the Mackerel Family, we arrive at a group of considerable importance from an economic point of view. Extremely active, migrating, and predaceous, mackerel swim in shoals and seize their prey with great voracity, hunting merely by sight, and snapping at anything moving through the water, especially if it is silvery, like a small surface-fish. The various species differ greatly in size, ranging from the Common Mackerel of about 18 inches long to the giant Tunny weighing nearly half a ton.

COMMON MACKEREL swim in vast shoals, or "schools," as they are called, and one half a mile wide and at least twenty miles long is on record. Mackerel feed on the young of other fish and small fish generally, and, when these are not to be had, on minute crabs and shrimps. They are very prolific, a single mackerel laying from 430,000 to 540,000 eggs.

Photo by Reinhold Thiele & Co.] *[Chancery Lane, W.C.*

JOHN DORY.

In the centre of each side is a round black spot surrounded by a pale yellow ring.

The TUNNIES are amongst the largest of the surface-fishes of the ocean. Abundant in the Mediterranean Sea, they occur occasionally in British waters. For centuries the flesh of the tunny has been held in high regard as food, and it is frequently seen in the Lisbon markets at the present day. The flesh, which is as red as beef, is cut up and sold by weight. The BONITO closely resembles the tunny, but is a much smaller fish, which preys largely upon flying-fishes, which it follows for long distances.

Peculiarly interesting are the SUCKING-FISHES. The name by which they are commonly known is bestowed on account of the presence of a large oval sucker, placed on the top of the head and extending backwards over the shoulders—an organ formed by modification of the back-fin. By means of this sucking-disk these fishes are enabled to attach themselves to sharks, turtles, ships, or any large object floating in the sea. The hold which they obtain is so strong that it is almost impossible to remove them by force. Being poor swimmers, this method of transportation enables them to pass rapidly to fresh feeding-grounds.

The natives of Zanzibar, Cuba, and Torres Straits are said to employ sucking-fishes in the capture of sleeping turtles, the fish being secured by a ring round the tail, and liberated as soon as a sufficiently near approach to the quarry has been made. About ten different species are known, the bulkiest of which attains a length of 2 feet and a weight of about 8 lbs., a longer but more slender species measuring 3 feet.

Carnivorous, of small size, and feeble swimming-powers, the family of the WEAVERS are remarkable rather for their disagreeable qualities than anything else, though at least one

Photo by W. Saville-Kent, F.Z.S.] [Milford-on-Sea.

SUCKING-FISH.

By means of the sucker on the top of its head this fish attaches itself to ships and larger fishes.

species is declared to be excellent eating. The STAR-GAZER is a particularly ugly-looking fish, especially noteworthy in that the eyes, which are on the top of the head, can be raised and depressed at pleasure, whilst the heavy jaw is armed with a freely moving tentacle, which, waving about in the current of water drawn in at the mouth, serves as a lure to attract small fishes, the rest of the body being concealed between stones at the bottom of the sea.

The COMMON WEAVER is a well-known British fish, much dreaded on account of the poisonous wounds which it inflicts unless most carefully handled, the poison being introduced by the spines of the back-fin and gill-cover. No special poison-organs seem to be developed, but the mucous secretion around the spines has poisonous properties. As the flesh of this fish is extremely palatable, fishermen remove the spines at once directly after capture. Should a wound be inflicted, great suffering and occasionally death follows.

Passing over one or two unimportant groups, we come to the family of the FROG-FISHES, which, but for the fact that many of its members are poisonous, calls for no special comment here. One species, however, from the coasts of Central America, possesses the distinction of having the most highly developed poison-organs of any fishes, being equalled only by the

Photo by Reinhold Thiele & Co.] [Chancery Lane, W.C.

LARGER WEAVER.

The spines of the first back-fin and of the gill-cover are highly poisonous.

Venomous Snakes. The poison-weapons are a spine on the gill-cover and two spines of the back-fin. The former is of the same shape as the hollow venom-fang of a snake, perforated at both ends. A little bag containing the poison lies at the base of the spine, and when pressed by the spine as it makes its puncture ejects its contents into the body of the latter, whence it escapes from the hole in the top. The structure of the back-spines is similar.

The family of the ANGLER-FISHES contain more strange forms than any other. Living on the sea-bottom and seeking their prey by stealth, angler-fishes do not need powerful swimming-muscles; consequently the size of the body and tail has become considerably reduced, so that the head, relatively to the rest of the body, is unusually large. The head, jaws, and belly are indeed of great size and capacity. The side or paired fins are not used for swimming, but have become modified to serve as feet, enabling the fish to shuffle along the ground. A further remarkable feature of these fishes is seen in the back-fin, the rays of which are very long, the foremost being provided with a flag-like flap of skin at

Photo by Reinhold Thiele & Co.] *[Chancery Lane, W.C.*

ANGLER-FISH.

This hideous species is also called the Frog-fish.

the top, extremely sensitive to touch, and playing a very important part in the capture of food. It seems that the fish commonly lies concealed on the sea-bottom, with this "flag" erected. From its general resemblance to the surrounding seaweed it is quite inconspicuous, so that passing fishes take no trouble to avoid it. If by any chance they should touch it, however, the jaws beneath open instantly, and the unfortunate trespasser is suddenly engulfed. This elaborate and sensitive mechanism has been likened to a spring-trap, which is always set, and never betrays its presence. It seems probable, however, that this flag serves also as a lure, passing fishes being occasionally attracted by the waving flap of skin. Should they become sufficiently curious as to proceed to touch it, capture in the manner above described is certain. Certain deep-sea forms have a luminous organ in the place of the flap of skin, and this certainly seems to act only as a lure.

Angler-fishes are found all over the world; some, as we have seen, are bottom-fishes, some inhabit deep sea, whilst others lie hidden amongst floating seaweed, to which they cling by means of their arm-like fins. Only one species occurs in British waters. Its method of spawning is remarkable, in that the eggs are laid in the form of large raft-like sheets, which float on the surface of the sea. The number of eggs laid by a single fish has been computed to be 1,345,000. A single sheet of spawn may measure from 2 to 3 feet in breadth and from 25 to 30 feet long.

Photo by W. Saville-Kent, F.Z.S.] [*Milford-on-Sea.*

BUTTERFLY-GURNARD.

The head of all gurnards is encased in an armour of bony plates.

The BULL-HEADS and GURNARDS, constituting the next family, are characterised by the spiny armature of the head and the great size of the breast-fins. The former are represented in British waters by four species, one of which, the MILLER'S-THUMB, inhabits fresh-water. The marine species include the SEA-SCORPION and FATHER-LASHER.

The BULL-HEADS on the Indian and Australian coasts are represented by the closely allied FLAT-HEADS, or CROCODILE-FISHES, in which the head, as its name implies, is much depressed, and fully armed with spines, which are highly poisonous, and cause a violent irritation. These fishes live in shallow water, lying on the bottom, with which their colours harmonise so completely that they are practically invisible. The very large ventral fins—those seen in the photograph immediately behind the breast-fins—are of great use in locomotion.

Photo by Reinhold Thiele & Co.] [*Chancery Lane, W.C.*

REEL-GURNARD.

The curious finger-like processes are used as organs of touch as well as locomotion.

The GURNARDS are well-known fishes, common on the

Photo by W. Saville-Kent, F.Z.S.] [*Milford-on-Sea.*

BAR-TAILED FLAT-HEAD.

A shallow-water fish.

Photo by W. Saville-Kent, F.Z.S.] [*Milford-on-Sea.*

ROCK FLAT-HEAD.

About forty species of flat-heads are known.

coasts of Britain, and extending from tropical to arctic seas. Their curiously shaped heads give them a very quaint appearance. One of the most remarkable peculiarities of these fishes is the separate condition of some of the rays of the breast-fins, which form finger-like organs, used to feel the ground and rake over loose stones, to discover small shrimps and other animals hidden underneath. Furthermore, the gurnards are peculiar in that they are enabled to communicate one with another by means of sounds produced by the expulsion of air from one compartment of the air-bladder to another. The females are much more common than the males, and also slightly larger. The young are remarkable for the enormous size of the breast-fins, though even in the adult these are unusually large.

Close allies of the Gurnards are the FLYING-GURNARDS, which, by reason of the extreme development of the breast-fins, are enabled to take flying leaps out of the water. One species is common in the Mediterranean. The flying-gurnard is not to be mistaken for the true "flying-fish," or flying-herring, described later.

The curious mail-clad ARMED BULL-HEAD, or POGGE, commonly taken in shrimp-nets, is an ally of the flying-gurnard.

CHAPTER V.

LUMP-SUCKERS, GOBIES, BLENNIES, BARRACUDAS, GREY MULLETS, STICKLEBACKS AND THEIR ALLIES, GARPIKE, AND FLYING-FISHES.

BY W. P. PYCRAFT, A.L.S., F.Z.S.

UGLY in appearance and carnivorous in habits, the Sucker-fish Family are distinguished by the presence of a large round sucker on the belly, with which they adhere to rocks. Furthermore, the sucker-fishes are remarkable for the softness of their skeleton, which may be cut through at any point with an ordinary knife. The male lump-sucker is smaller than the female, but much more brightly coloured, especially during the breeding-season, when he dons a livery of blue, scarlet, and yellow. He is also a model parent, always remaining near the eggs and keeping a constant stream of fresh water running over them by the action of his breast-fins. A single female may produce as many as 136,000 eggs in a single season. In Scotland the male is known as the COCK and the female as the HEN PADDLE. The species is more common off the coasts of Scotland than elsewhere in the British Islands.

Like the Lump-suckers, the GOBIES, which form the next family, have the ventral fins modified so as to form a sucking-disk, which is used as an anchor. But the gobies are easily distinguished by their smaller size, elongated bodies, hard skeleton, and the disposition and structure of the fins, characters which need not be discussed further.

One species, the SPOTTED GOBY, or POLE-WING, found in the Thames, is noteworthy on account of its nest-building habits. The male chooses the empty shell of a cockle or mussel, selecting one with its concave surface downwards. Beneath this the sand is cleared away and cemented by a special glue-like secretion formed by the skin of the fish. A cylindrical tunnel is then built to give access to the nest, and the whole is covered over with loose stones. In the nest-chamber formed by the shell the eggs are laid, the male immediately after mounting guard over them till they hatch, which they do in about nine days.

Another species, the PELLUCID GOBY, is remarkable in that its whole life's course is run

Photo by Reinhold Thiele & Co.] *[Chancery Lane, W.C.*

LUMP-SUCKER.

Known also as the Cock and Hen Paddle.

in a single year. In June and July the eggs are laid; they are hatched in August; by the time winter has arrived the fish have reached maturity, and die off in the following July and August, so that in September only the fry are to be met with.

One of the strangest of all fishes is a member of the Goby Family. This is the WALKING-FISH, so called from its habit of spending most of its time on the mud-banks of rivers, or on the roots of trees growing in the neighbourhood. The late Surgeon-General Day, describing these fishes as he saw them along the side of the Burmese rivers, writes that at first sight they look like large tadpoles. When suddenly startled by something, away they go with a hop, skip, and a jump inland among the trees, or on the water like a flat stone or piece of slate sent skimming by a schoolboy. When climbing, the breast-fins are used, as if they were arms, to grasp the boughs. If placed in deep water, these fishes are speedily drowned!

The BLENNIES are fishes whose skins are soft, slimy, and quite scaleless, or at most covered with very tiny and degenerate scales. The general form of the body may be seen in the photograph below. They are shore-fishes, lurking about in the crevices of rocks, among seaweed, or under stones, and occurring generally along the coasts of temperate and tropical regions. The species known as the SEA-CAT or WOLF-FISH is, however, a deep-water form.

As a rule the eggs are deposited in hollow places between stones or rocks; but in the BUTTER-FISH, or GUNNEL, the eggs are adhesive, and the parents roll them into a ball by coiling their bodies round them. Furthermore, since the parents are frequently found, under natural conditions, coiled round these masses of spawn, it appears that they adopt this method of guarding their treasures. Some species bring forth their young alive.

The largest of the family is the WOLF-FISH, whose jaws are armed with very powerful teeth, able to crush the hardest shells, such as those of the whelk. Sea-urchins and crabs are also eaten.

We pass on to a group comprising three families—the BARRACUDAS, SAND-SMELTS, and GREY MULLETS.

It should be mentioned that two very distinct fishes are known as BARRACUDAS, one of which we have already described under the name of Snoek. The forms described here as barracudas are large, voracious fishes living in tropical and sub-tropical seas, and evincing a preference for the coast rather than the open sea. Attaining a length of 8 feet and a weight of 40 lbs., they are a source of danger to bathers. They are very frequently used as food, though in the West Indies such food is attended with some danger, as the flesh is often poisonous, from the fish having fed on smaller poisonous fishes.

Photo by Reinhold Thiele & Co.] *[Chancery Lane, W.C.*

BLENNY.

Blennies have soft, shiny, scaleless skins.

The SAND-SMELTS are small carnivorous species inhabiting the seas of temperate and tropical regions. Many enter fresh-water, and some have become entirely acclimatised there. Some species bear a very close resemblance to the true smelt, from which, however, they may be readily distinguished by their small, spinous, first back-fin. The young of at least one small group or genus of this family are remarkable for their habit of clinging together for some time after they are hatched in dense masses and almost incredible numbers.

The GREY MULLETS are brackish-water fishes, feeding on vegetable growths and minute shell-fish. They also suck up large quantities of sand into the mouth for the sake of the minute organisms contained therein; much of this is passed on into the stomach, which is thick and muscular, like that of many birds. Altogether some seventy species of grey mullets are known, the majority of which attain a weight of about 4 lbs., but there are many which grow to 10 or 12 lbs. All are eaten, and some highly esteemed.

The FLUTE-MOUTHS, STICKLEBACKS, and TORTOISE-FISHES are three closely allied and extremely interesting families. The first are really gigantic marine sticklebacks, in which the jaws are produced into a long tube. They are shore-fishes, entering brackish water, and confined to sub-tropical and tropical parts of the Atlantic and Indo-Pacific.

Of the STICKLEBACKS there are several species, some of which are entirely salt-water fishes,

Photo by W. Saville-Kent, F.Z.S.] [*Milford-on-Sea.*

NORTHERN MULLET.

A member of the family of Grey Mullets.

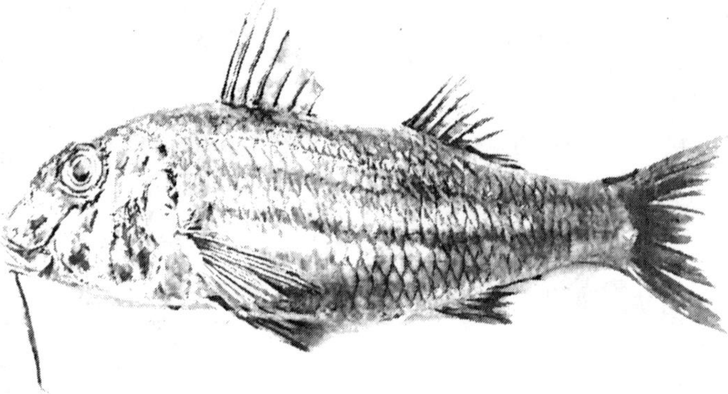

Photo by Reinhold Thiele & Co.] [*Chancery Lane, W.C.*

RED MULLET.

Not related to the Grey Mullets, this species is placed here for the sake of contrast.

Photo by W. Saville-Kent, F.Z.S.] [*Milford-on-Sea.*

GARPIKES.

Frequently called Guard-fishes.

whilst others enjoy the rather unusual distinction of being able to live in either fresh or salt water, even when rapidly transferred from one to the other. The small species commonly inhabiting ponds and ditches can sustain changes of this kind with impunity. These last are very ferocious. One kept in an aquarium devoured in five hours seventy-four young dace about a quarter of an inch long. They occasionally occur in vast shoals, and, according to the naturalist Pennant, appear in the river Welland, in Lincolnshire, once in seven years in amazing shoals, so that a man employed in collecting them earned four shillings a day by selling them at the rate of a halfpenny a bushel!

The salt-water species, or FIFTEEN-SPINED STICKLEBACK, is less well known. Like its fresh-water relative, it is a nest-builder, and the male defends the eggs and young with great courage.

The TORTOISE-FISHES may serve as the representatives of the last family of this group. They are very remarkable fishes, being invested in a wonderful bony cuirass, formed by a modification of the skeleton, similar to what has taken place among the Tortoises and Turtles. The body is so thin that it looks as if it had been artificially compressed, and is semi-transparent. Three species are known from the tropical Indo-Pacific and three from other seas; besides these are four smaller and less perfectly armed forms, one of which, the TRUMPET-FISH, or BELLOWS-FISH, occurs rarely off the south coast of England.

The GARPIKE and FLYING-FISHES are both interesting, especially the latter. The garpike is represented by several species, easily recognised by the long, pointed jaws. These fishes are furthermore peculiar in that the bones are green, a colour which remains even after cooking, and on this account some object to eating them, supposing the unusual colour to indicate unsoundness. The elongated jaws are not developed in the young fish, and, strangely enough, as this character is acquired, the lower jaw grows faster than the upper. In some species the lower jaw remains permanently the longer; hence they are known as HALF-BEAKS.

Photo by W. Saville-Kent, F.Z.S.] [*Milford-on-Sea.*

PIPE-FISH.

The Flute-mouth, as this fish is often called, is really a gigantic stickleback.

The FLYING-FISHES, or FLYING-HERRINGS, like the Flying-gurnards already

Photo by Dr. Robert T. Morris, New York.

A SALMON LEAPING.

The height to which salmon will leap in ascending a waterfall is little short of marvellous. When the fall is very high the ascent is often accomplished in a series of leaps, the fish resting in pools of comparatively still water.

noticed, are enabled, by reason of the great development of the breast-fins, to take extended journeys through the air. The flight of these fishes is, however, not quite the same as true flight, inasmuch as the fins serve mainly as a parachute, and do not, by sustained vigorous movements, propel the body through the air, like the wings of bats and birds. Darting out of the water when pursued by an enemy or frightened by a passing vessel, these fish are borne along by the wind, the speed at first being very considerable, exceeding indeed that of a ship going ten miles an hour. At a single flight they may cover as much as 500 feet, but are quite unable to steer themselves, except when, during their course, the tail-fin is immersed in the water, when by a stroke from one side to the other the direction may be changed from left to right, or *vice versâ*, as the case may be. By day they will avoid ships, but by night, when they are unable to see, "they frequently fly," writes Dr. Günther, "against the weather-board, where they are caught by the current of air and carried upwards to a height of 20 feet above the surface of the water, while under ordinary circumstances they keep close to it."

Photo by A. S. Rudland & Sons.

FLYING-FISH.

More than forty distinct species of this family are known.

CHAPTER VI.

THE WRASSE-LIKE FISHES.

BY W. P. PYCRAFT, A.L.S. F.Z.S.

THE members of the four families noticed in this chapter are remarkable for their wonderful coloration. The species of the first family, from their peculiarly striking resemblance to the Scaly-finned group, share with them the name of CORAL-FISHES. This resemblance is a very remarkable one. Occurring, like the Scaly-fins, more abundantly in the neighbourhood of coral-reefs, they also resemble the latter not only in shape, but also in coloration, the same pattern being often common to members of both families.

To this family belongs the remarkable fish known as the AMPHIPRION, which makes its home in the interior of an enormous species of sea-anemone measuring 2 feet across. When first discovered by Mr. Saville-Kent, it was believed that the fish had been swallowed—a view, however, which was speedily rejected, when it was found that, if ejected by means of a stick, it invariably returned. Thus the anemone is obviously to be regarded as host, and not as captor. More than this, from the facts so far to hand, it appears that this strangely assorted pair are mutually dependent on one another, at least to a large extent—the fish undertaking to supply the larder, whilst the anemone in return affords shelter from enemies. The part played by each is as follows:—The fish, which is very conspicuous, wearing a livery of vermilion crossed by three bands of white, sallies forth and swims about till it attracts the attention of some other carnivorous member of its class, on which, if it gives chase, the amphiprion returns with all speed to its living cave, and quickly disappears down its mouth. The pursuer, blundering against the outspread tentacles, is immediately paralysed by a shower

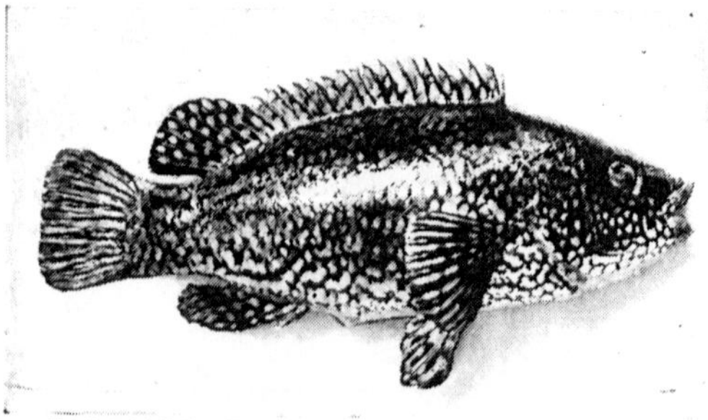

Photo by Reinhold Thiele & Co.] *[Chancery Lane, W.C.*

SPOTTED WRASSE.

On account of their greatly thickened lips wrasses are also known as Lip-fishes.

of stinging-darts which proceed therefrom as a result of the shock, and, rendered insensible, becomes the spoil of both. Thus the active fish plays the part of a lure, and in return is afforded shelter.

The WRASSES proper may be distinguished, amongst other things, by their thickened lips—hence the name Lip-fishes given them by German naturalists—by the greatly extended back-fin, the greater part of which is spinous, and the arrangement of the teeth, which need not be discussed here. They are shore-fishes, living in the neighbourhood of weed-covered rocks, or in tropical seas, where they are most abundant, amid coral-reefs. Most are brilliantly, many gaudily coloured, iridescent hues frequently adding to the beauty formed by the permanent deposit of coloured pigments in the scales. Some grow to a large size, specimens not seldom exceeding a weight of 50 lbs., and these are the most esteemed as food-fishes, the smaller species, as a rule, being regarded as of inferior quality.

A well-known British species is the STRIPED or RED WRASSE, the sexes of which exhibit a remarkable variation in colour, the male having the body marked with blue streaks or a blackish band, whilst the female has two or three large black blotches across the tail. A second British species, the BALLAN WRASSE, is bluish green in colour, with the scales and fin-rays reddish orange. It may be found hiding in the deep gullies among rocks, sheltering in the dense clusters of seaweed, and feeding on crabs and shrimps. It takes a bait freely, and fishermen have remarked that at first they catch few but large fish; some days later a great number may be caught, but all will be of small size, indicating that the larger fish assume the dominion of a district and keep the smaller at bay.

Amongst the most brilliantly coloured of the wrasses are the PARROT-FISH. Mr. Saville-Kent, writing of the species which inhabit the waters of the Great Barrier Reef of Australia, remarks that to stand up to your knees or higher in water, with such a shoal of magnificent fishes swimming round you, is an experience well worth a journey to the tropics. The coloration of these fishes, which is extremely transient, fading almost immediately after death, nearly defies description. One of the most beautiful is perhaps the GOLD-FINNED CORAL-FISH, in which the body is of an intense ultramarine, whilst the fins are bright golden. Others have the most amazing combinations of green, vermilion, blue, and yellow, in endless variety. It was one of the parrot-fishes which found such favour with the ancients. "In the time of Pliny," writes Dr. Günther, "it was considered to be the first of fishes . . . and the

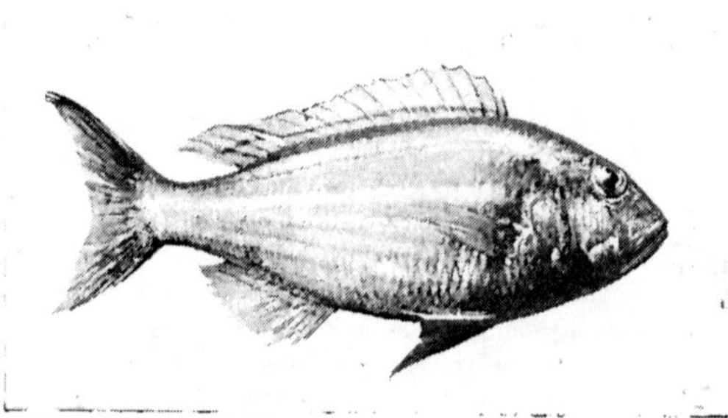

Photo by W. Saville-Kent, F.Z.S.] *[Milford-on-Sea.*

SATIN PARROT-FISH.

The Parrot-fishes, or Parrot-wrasses, are so called on account of the peculiar structure of the teeth in the front of the jaws, which form a sharp-edged beak.

expense incurred by Elipentius was justified, in the opinion of the Roman gourmands, by the extreme delicacy of the flesh. It was a fish, said the poet, whose very excrement the gods themselves were unwilling to reject. Its flesh was tender, agreeable, sweet, easy of digestion, and quickly assimilated; yet, if it happened to have eaten an aplysia, it produced violent diarrhœa." To this day the Greeks hold it in high regard, and eat it with sauce made of its liver and intestines. It feeds on seaweed, and from its habit of thoroughly chewing its food, and moving it backwards and forwards in the mouth, it was at one time believed that this fish chewed the cud after the fashion of the ruminating mammals!

Photo by W. Saville-Kent, F.Z.S.] *[Milford-on-Sea.*

BLACK-SPOTTED PARROT-FISH.

The flesh of some of the Parrot-wrasses is of great delicacy.

One of the most interesting of all the wrasses is a small species from King George's Sound, which, while retaining the principal characters common to the group, has assumed the general shape and proportions of the pipe-fish.

The third family of the wrasses are remarkable chiefly on account of the fact that they produce their young alive. These fishes are confined to the temperate regions of the North Pacific.

The CHROMIDS constitute the last family of the wrasse-like group. Numerous in species, they are all dwellers in fresh-water. One species occurs in amazing numbers in the Lake of Galilee, shoals over an acre in extent, and so closely packed that movement seemed almost impossible, having been recorded. They are taken in such enormous numbers that the nets in which they are caught often break. Occasionally shoals are carried down the Jordan into the Dead Sea; but the fish never get farther than a few yards, becoming stupefied almost at once, and, turning over on their backs, fall an easy prey to flocks of cormorants and kingfishers. Heaps of putrefying carcases are washed ashore, poisoning the atmosphere, in spite of the presence of flocks of ravens and vultures which have gathered to the feast.

Another species is remarkable for its peculiar method of protecting the eggs and young. The female deposits the eggs, over 200 in number, in a small hole worked out among the roots of reeds and rushes. There they are taken into the mouth of the male one by one, and retained till hatched a few days later. The young fry remain in this nursery for some considerable time, increasing rapidly in size, so that the father-nurse is unable to close his mouth. Some of the young develop among the gills; others lie, closely packed, with their heads turned towards the mouth of the parent, remaining in this position till nearly 4 inches long, when they are ejected or wriggle out to forage for themselves.

Photo by H. V. Letkmann] *[New York.*

A WRASSE.

The majority of the Wrasses are brilliantly coloured.

CHAPTER VII.

PIPE-FISHES, SEA-HORSES, GLOBE-FISHES, SUN-FISHES, AND THEIR ALLIES.

BY W. P. PYCRAFT, F.L.S., F.Z.S.

THE fishes described in the present chapter form two well-marked groups, known as the TUFT-GILLED and the COMB-GILLED FISHES, on account of the peculiar arrangement of the gills, or breathing-organs; they are also remarkable for their peculiar shapes. The breast-fins are present in all; but in three of the families the second pair of fins, corresponding to the hind limbs of the higher animals, are wanting.

Photo by A. S. Rudland & Sons.

GLOBE-FISH.

From the formidable armature of spines, known also as the Sea-hedgehog.

The TUFT-GILLED FISHES are represented by two families—the MAILED TUBE-MOUTHS and the PIPE-FISHES and SEA-HORSES, all of which have undergone very considerable modification of form, the body being encased in mail-like armour, whilst the jaws are toothless and produced into a long tube.

The first family is composed of a few small fishes from the Indian Ocean. Grotesque in appearance, they are remarkable also for the fact that the female takes sole charge not only of the eggs, which are exceedingly minute, but the young fry also. Only one other fish is known in which the care of the eggs and young is undertaken by the female: this is one of the Cat-fishes, described in a later chapter. The eggs in the TUBE-MOUTHS are carried in a pouch formed by the union of the inner borders of the ventral fins, which are long and broad. For the retention of the eggs within the pouch its wall develops long filaments, which serve the purpose of slender fingers.

The second of these families contains the PIPE-FISHES and SEA-HORSES. They are small marine fishes, inhabiting the seas of tropical and temperate regions wherever there is sufficient vegetation to offer shelter, for they are peculiarly defenceless creatures. They possess but feeble powers of swimming, and consequently are not seldom borne away by strong currents far out to sea or on to distant shores. Their method of locomotion is, indeed, quite different from that of other fishes, as they progress neither by undulatory motions of the body nor by powerful strokes of the tail, but by wriggling in the case of the pipe-fishes, or vibrating motions of the back-fin in the sea-horses.

The long, semi-cylindrical PIPE-FISHES, partly on account of their peculiar form and colour, and partly on account of their swaying motions, so closely resemble the fronds of seaweed

Photo by A. S. Rudland & Sons.

BLACK-SPOTTED GLOBE-FISH.

Globe-fishes possess the power of inflating the body with air, when they float at the surface, and thus escape enemies.

amongst which they dwell as to pass unnoticed by their enemies. Unlike the Tube-mouths, just described, the care of the eggs and young devolves upon the males. The young are borne in a pouch, but, ventral fins being wanting, this is formed by a fold of skin developed from each side of the trunk and tail, the free margins being united in the middle line. Here the eggs remain till they are hatched. But the pouch is by no means done with after this event, for the young continue to occupy it for some time, returning when danger threatens—a habit which recalls the custom of the young of the kangaroo. Mr. Yarrell relates a curious fact which he gleaned from some fishermen—to wit, that if they take a pipe-fish, open the pouch, and drop the young into the sea, they will not disperse, but hover around the spot, as if waiting for their parent. Then, if the newly opened fish be held in the water, the young immediately return and enter the pouch. In another species of pipe-fish the eggs, instead of being carried in a pouch, are held by a sticky secretion to a groove in the under surface of the parent. This groove would seem to indicate the beginning from which the complete pouch has been developed. The pipe-fishes swim in a very peculiar manner, holding the body now in a vertical, and now in a horizontal position, accompanied by contortions of every conceivable kind, poking their long snouts into bunches of seaweed in search of food as they go.

Photo by N. Lazarnick] [*New York.*

TRIGGER-FISH.

A well-known member of the File-fishes.

The SEA-HORSES have a still more eccentrically modified form, inasmuch as the body is thrown into a series of curves, the head being bent upon the trunk in a manner suggestive of the head and neck of the horse; hence the name of the group. The tail, which lacks the membranous portion, or fin, can be spirally coiled, and is used as an organ of prehension, and on this account is unique amongst fishes. Gripping the stems of seaweeds with this tail, and swaying the body to and fro among the vegetation, the fish is rendered comparatively inconspicuous, the lines of the body being broken up by numerous more or less filamentous processes, which in one species, the FUCUS-LIKE SEA-HORSE, become excessively developed, forming long, frond-like blades. These, streaming in the water, both by their shape and coloration render the resemblance to the vegetable growths in which the animal hides so perfect that detection is almost impossible. Thus they furnish one of the most remarkable examples of adaptation to the environment amongst living animals. The males of most sea-horses, like the pipe-fishes, carry the eggs and young in a pouch on the abdomen, but in the species just mentioned the eggs are embedded in the soft skin on the under surface of the tail.

Sea-horses swim with the body more or less vertical, the motive power being supplied by rapid vibration of the back-fin. Both pipe-fishes and sea-horses occur in British seas, the first being the more common.

Photo by H. V. Lehmann] *[New York.*

COFFER-FISHES.

Coffer-fishes have the body encased in a hard shell of closely fitting plates, leaving only the tail and fins free to move.

The COMB-GILLED FISHES, to which we come next, are divided into two families, whose members are as remarkable for their extraordinary shape as are the tuft-gilled forms just discussed. The abnormal shapes which mark out certain fishes so conspicuously from the more normal and typical forms are generally regarded as adaptations, serving to ensure concealment, to ward off attack, or to effect the capture of prey otherwise unattainable. Instances illustrating all three of these ends are furnished by these two groups of the tuft- and comb-gilled fishes.

The FILE-FISHES and COFFER-FISHES, which form the first of the two families, present considerable variation in shape as well as in the covering of the body, which may be naked, covered with rough scales or bony spines, or invested in a complete bony cuirass.

The file-fishes are represented by numerous species, the typical one being known also as the TRIGGER-FISH, on account of an armature of spines on the top of the back. These spines are three in number; the first is very strong, roughened like a file—hence the name File-fish—and hollowed out behind to receive the second much smaller spine, which has a projection in front at its base, fitting into a notch in the first. Thus these two spines can only be raised or depressed simultaneously, and the first cannot be forced down unless the second has been previously depressed. These fishes have very powerful teeth, to break off pieces of coral, which form a large part of their diet. They also destroy a large number of shell-fish, and work great destruction amongst pearl-oysters. Frequently these fishes, when eaten, prove highly poisonous, from having fed on poisonous corals, jelly-fish, or decomposing substances.

Photo by W. Saville-Kent, F.Z.S.] *[Milford-on-Sea.*

LACE-FINNED LEATHER-JACKET.

Another species of File-fish.

Photo by W. Saville-Kent, F.Z.S.] *[Milford-on-Sea.*

SPOTTED BOX- OR TRUNK-FISH.

In this species of Coffer-fish the arrangement of the plates forming the hard cuirass can be plainly seen.

Photo by W. Saville-Kent, F.Z.S.] [*Milford-on-Sea.*

SEA-HORSES.

The species on the right is remarkable for the development of long leaf-like processes all over the body, causing the fish to bear a very close resemblance to the seaweed amongst which it dwells.

As a rule file-fishes are of small size, but some attain a length of 2 feet, and many are beautifully and symmetrically marked.

The COFFER-FISHES derive their name from the box-like cuirass in which they are invested. This is formed by numerous closely fitting, hexagonal bony plates, forming a mosaic, and leaving only the fins and hind part of the tail free. This bony case varies greatly in form, in some species being three-ridged, in others four- or even five-ridged; while in some long horns are developed, making the defensive armature still more complex. More than twenty species are known, all confined to tropical and sub-tropical seas.

The GLOBE-FISHES and SUN-FISHES constitute the last family of this really extraordinary assemblage. The covering of the body consists either of minute scales or large spines, which can frequently be raised or depressed at will. All the members inhabit tropical or sub-tropical seas, and a few occur in the fresh-waters of the same regions.

The GLOBE-FISHES have short, thick bodies, covered either with small spines, as in the TOAD-FISH, or very large ones, as in the PORCUPINE-FISH, or SEA-HEDGEHOG. They are remarkable for their habit of filling the gullet with air, and then distending the body to an enormous size. This device enables the fish to escape its enemies; for when so inflated it rises to the surface and floats belly-upwards, and, the inflated portion projecting above the water, the fish is blown along by the wind to more secure regions. The more heavily armed species become still more formidable when inflated, as the spines are then fully erected. Escaping from enemies below by flight, they are thus secure from enemies above by reason of their armature. Globe-fishes have been found floating alive and unhurt within the stomachs of sharks which had swallowed them, and one has even been known to eat its way out through its captor's side, and so killing its would-be devourer! When a globe-fish desires to return to its normal elongated shape, it expels the air from the gullet through the mouth and gills, the expulsion causing a curious hissing sound.

Extremely unlike the foregoing members of the group of comb-gilled fishes, the SUN-FISH is nevertheless quite as remarkable in form, looking as if it had undergone the amputation of its hind parts. The singular shape of the other members of the comb- and tuft-gilled fishes are undoubtedly adaptations to avoid enemies, either by rendering the animal inconspicuous, or hurtful by reason of its powerful armature. The form of the sun-fish appears to be an adaptation for the capture of food, as this fish preys largely upon the fry of other fishes which inhabit enormous depths, and consequently can only be obtained by diving. Sun-fishes inhabit the surface-waters, but as divers have few equals.

Photo by W. Saville-Kent, F.Z.S.] [*Milford-on-Sea*

SEA-HORSES.

Attaching themselves to marine plants by twisting their tails around them.

CHAPTER VIII.

THE COD FAMILY.

BY JOHN BICKERDYKE, M.A.

THE large and important Cod Family belongs to the order of Spineless Fishes and the group in which both sides of the head are symmetrical. The Common Cod, the Whiting, the Haddock, the Pollack, the Coal-fish, the Hake, the Ling, and the little Rocklings, all belong to this important family, which has one representative in fresh-water, the Burbot, or Eel-pout, found in various rivers in Central and Northern Europe and North America.

Perhaps the most remarkable member of the Cod Family is the CHIASMODUS, which has huge jaws lined with large pointed teeth, and a distensible stomach and abdomen. During the *Challenger* Expedition a specimen was taken 1,500 fathoms down in the North Atlantic. It had swallowed another fish, a kind of scopelus, more than twice its own size. The stomach of the chiasmodus had swelled to an enormous extent, and had become so thin from distension that the fish inside could be clearly seen through its walls. The scopelus, it is interesting to mention, is a fish brought up sometimes by the dredge from 2,500 fathoms. It occasionally comes to the surface at night, and has phosphorescent spots along its sides, giving out a dim light, which has its uses in the dark depths of the sea.

To come back to the head of the family, the COD is a fairly plentiful fish all around the British and Irish coasts, but appears to be decreasing in some waters as time goes on, owing to the over-trawling of the North Sea. Off the coasts of Norway, in the neighbourhood of the Lofoden Islands, the cod are sometimes so thickly packed in shoals that as the fishermen

Photo by A. S. Rudland & Sons.

WHITING.

Easily distinguished from the cod by the absence of a barbel on the chin.

lower their tackle they can feel the leads hitting the backs of the fishes. Both there and off the Faröe Islands and Iceland it is common practice to fish with a hook bearing a little piece of polished lead on its shank, no other bait being required, owing to the cod being so numerous that food is scarce.

About the commencement of the fifteenth century the English began to go to Iceland for cod, and since the sixteenth century English cod-fishing vessels have visited Newfoundland and other far northern waters, which produce fish superior to English cod. It should be mentioned that the Cod Family is not found to any extent in tropical seas.

While the BURBOT is one of the few species of the group inhabiting fresh-water, and is peculiar in living there permanently, there are instances recorded of POLLACK having ascended from the salt water of the Norwegian fiords into fresh-water lakes, and it is an undoubted fact that many other species of sea-fish can accustom themselves to a residence in fresh-water.

All through the year cod frequent the British coasts; but it is two or three months before

Photo by W. Saville-Kent, F.Z.S.] *[Milford-on-Sea.*

POLLACK-WHITING.

A British representative of the group in which the lower jaw is the longer and all the teeth of the upper jaw are of equal size.

the spawning-season, which commences in January or later according to the locality, that they gather in vast shoals and come close inshore. First come the small codling of a pound or so, and as the winter approaches the longshore fish are found gradually to increase in size, until by Christmas-time it is no uncommon thing on the east coast of England and Scotland for fish of from 10 to 20 lbs. to be caught from the beach.

As a rule the eggs of cod float, owing to a little globule of oil which each one contains, but in water which lacks salinity they sink. The quantities of eggs shed by each fish are enormous; nearly two millions were counted in a cod of a little under 12 lbs. It is fairly certain, however, that not more than two or three, if so many, mature fish are the product of the two million eggs; for if each fish even doubled itself in numbers (if we may use the expression) every year, the sea would soon contain more fish than water. Millions upon millions of eggs are destroyed when there is an on-shore wind during the spawning-season. Sometimes the shore on which they have been wafted has been seen to glisten with them.

By the end of summer such of the young cod-fish as have escaped their many dangers attain about 1 inch in length. They are very varied in colour, which depends on that of the seaweed and their other surroundings. The parent fish, too, vary somewhat in appearance, those round the English coast as a rule having brown backs with irregular spotty markings on the sides, while those from more northern waters usually have darker backs and are less often spotted. Cod are most enormous feeders, and in consequence grow very rapidly. At the Southport Aquarium codling of only ¾ lb. increased in weight to 6 or 7 lbs. in about sixteen months.

So voracious is the cod that it is very apt to swallow anything it sees moving, without considering whether it is wholesome. In 1879 a black guillemot in perfect condition was removed from the stomach of one of these fish; while among other strange finds by cod-fishermen from the same receptacle was a piece of tallow candle 7 inches long, a hare, a partridge, a white turnip, and, going back to the year 1626, a "work in three treatises," which was found in the stomach of a fish captured in Lynn Deeps on midsummer eve, and brought to the Vice-Chancellor of Cambridge. The usual food of cod is, however, small fish of various kinds—herrings, pilchards, sprats, crabs, and sea-worms; but the species is not particular what it seizes when shoaling before the spawning-season and food is scarce owing to the number of mouths.

CHAPTER IX.

CAVE-FISHES, SAND-EELS AND THEIR ALLIES, AND FLAT-FISHES.

BY W. P. PYCRAFT, A.L.S., F.Z.S.

THE subterranean fresh-water caves of Cuba furnish the most interesting and most remarkable members of the family in certain small fishes known as CAVE-FISHES. Living in complete darkness, the eyes have degenerated so as to be no longer useful as organs of sight; indeed, in many species they are entirely wanting. By way of compensation delicate organs of touch have been developed, taking the form, in different species, of barbels, hair-like processes, or tubercles. These blind fishes are closely allied to certain marine forms found in the tropical Atlantic and Indian Oceans, and it is curious to note that amongst these about seven very rare species are found at great depths in the southern oceans, so great that light fails to reach them, and they too are blind.

The SAND-EELS, or LAUNCES, are extremely common on the sandy shores of Europe and North America, living in vast shoals, and displaying a wonderful unison in their movements, rising and falling as with one accord. They burrow in the sand with amazing rapidity, forcing

Photo by W. Saville-Kent, F.Z.S.] [*Milford-on-Sea.*

SPOTTED SOLE.

A larger and coarser fish than the common sole.

their way by means of a horny projection on the lower jaw, and remaining buried at ebb-tide some 5 or 6 inches under the sand, when they are captured by fishermen, armed with rakes, for bait. When swimming in shoals, their presence is often betrayed by schools of porpoises, which feed greedily upon them, preventing their return to the bottom by getting under the shoal, whilst others swim round it. Mackerel also make large raids upon the ranks of such shoals.

FLAT-FISHES may be reckoned among the most important of food-fishes, and besides are of quite peculiar interest, on account of the remarkable modifications of structure which they have undergone. They differ from all other vertebrates in that, save for the first few weeks of existence, they spend the whole of their lives with one side of the body uppermost—the right or left, according to the species. Whether resting or swimming, this position holds good. The newly hatched fish, however, maintains the normal poise of the body, the back being uppermost. Of the many changes which the organs of the body undergo during this strange transformation from a "round" to a "flat" fish, one of the most interesting is that which concerns the eyes. These, in the very young fish, lie one on either side of the head; but as the fish grows older it begins to lie on its side on the ground, and ultimately, when it is two or three months old, loses the power of sustaining itself in an upright position altogether. The most remarkable feature in this very strange mode of development is, that as the fish comes to lie more and more on its side, so the eye which is undermost begins to move round to the other side, till eventually the two eyes lie side by side on the upper-surface. Strangely enough, in some species the eye moves *round* the head, passing over its edge, and so to its place beside the stationary eye, whilst in others it acquires its ultimate position by moving *through* the head, sinking in on one side and appearing again on the other. The coloration of these fishes is also peculiar, in that the two sides are quite differently coloured, the upper side resembling in tone that of the sea-bottom, whilst the under side is pure white. In the young fish, before the habit of lying on one side has been acquired, both sides are coloured alike. The difference in coloration between the two sides of the adult fish appears to be due to the effect of light, since in flat-fishes kept in a tank with

Photo by W. Saville-Kent, F.Z.S.] [*Milford-on-Sea.*

HALIBUT.

The largest member of the Flat-fish Family. The back-fin usually commences much farther forward.

a mirror at the bottom the under-surface was found in many cases to be very largely coloured. But the colour of the upper-surface is by no means constant. On the contrary, the flat-fish appears to possess the power, in common with all other fishes, of changing its colour so as to harmonise with the tone of its surroundings. Thus on a light sandy ground the exposed surface of the body becomes pale, while on a dark muddy bottom it is almost black. By this power of changing the colour of the exposed portion of the body so as to harmonise with the surroundings, the fish is enabled to become in a large measure invisible, and in proportion to the effectiveness of the change to escape its enemies. Some soles are quite invisible.

Photo by W. Saville-Kent, F.Z.S.] *[Milford-on-Sea.*

BRILL.

As in the turbot, the eyes are on the left side of the head, instead of on the right side, as in the halibut.

The most important of the flat-fishes are the PLAICE, FLOUNDER, DAB, HALIBUT, SOLE, TURBOT, and BRILL.

The PLAICE is one of the commonest of the British flat-fishes, and may be distinguished by the numerous orange or red spots which are scattered over the upper surface of the body. From 15 to 18 inches in length, specimens are occasionally captured which have attained a length of 28 inches. Plaice feed on shell-fish, such as mussels or scallops, which they crush by means of strong, blunt teeth in the throat; but worms are also eaten.

The eggs of the plaice are amongst the largest fish-eggs known.

The FLOUNDER is a smaller fish than the plaice, and lacks the red spots. It differs from the other flat-fishes in the preference it shows for the mouths of rivers, ascending these, indeed, so far as to enter fresh-water.

The HALIBUT is the largest of the flat-fishes, specimens of as much as 20 feet in length being on record, while examples of from 6 to 7 feet long are not uncommon in Grimsby market. This fish has a wide distribution, occurring on both sides of the North Atlantic and North Pacific, being most abundant in deep water. The halibut which are brought into the markets of Grimsby and Hull are chiefly caught off the coasts of Iceland and the Faröes with long lines.

The SOLE is a shallow-water fish, feeding chiefly upon worms, crabs, and shrimps. These it apparently hunts by smell, gliding over the sea-bottom, and tapping with the lower side of its head, which is provided with sensitive organs of touch in the shape of filaments. By day it conceals itself by burrowing in the sand, coming out after dark to feed.

The TURBOT resembles the brill, from which it may be distinguished by the greater breadth of the body in proportion to the length, the absence of scales, and the presence of large bony tubercles scattered over the surface. In Great Britain the turbot is most abundant in the English Channel.

The BRILL closely resembles the turbot not only in general form, but in the numerical superiority of the females, and in the habits of the young, which, like the turbot, are surface-feeders and possess an air-bladder.

CHAPTER X.

EELS AND CAT-FISHES.

BY W. P. PYCRAFT, A.L.S., F.Z.S.

EELS, like flat-fishes, show plainly, in the shape of their bodies, a remarkably perfect adaptation to their environment. They are burrowing fishes, passing much of their time buried in the mud, and leaving little more than the head exposed. In accordance with this habit, the body is very long and round, and lacks both the hinder paired fins, and scales. When swimming, the body is propelled by rapid undulations, the movement being from side to side, it may be remarked, instead of up and down, as in the "serpentine" movements of snakes.

Whether all the fishes commonly regarded as eels really belong to this family or not is a moot-point. It is possible that the eel shape has been independently acquired by unrelated forms as a result of adaptation to a similar mode of life. But as the group now stands it embraces several distinct types,—the COMMON FRESH-WATER EELS; numerous marine species, such as CONGERS, SERPENT-EELS, DEEP-SEA EELS, and PAINTED EELS; and the fresh-water ELECTRIC EELS.

The RIVER-EELS and CONGERS are perhaps the best known, and are also highly important food-fishes. That they are fishes of comparatively slow growth seems to be shown by the

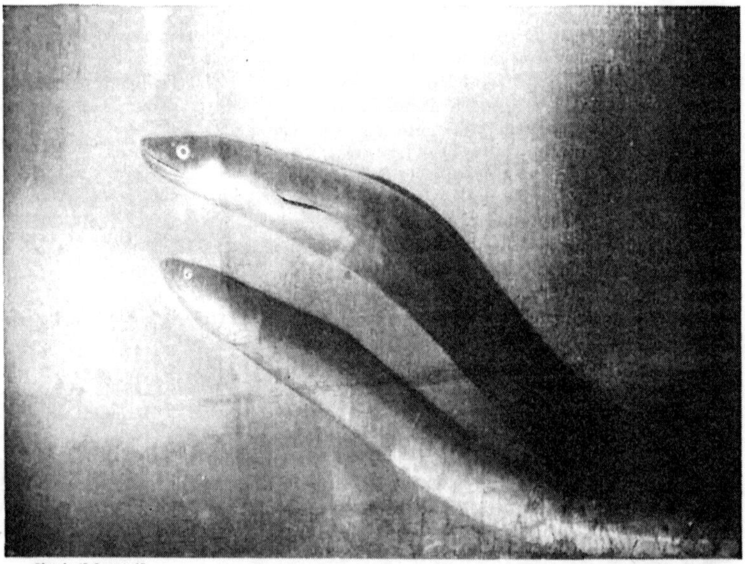

Photo by N. Lazarnick] [*New York.*

EELS.

Two species are shown in this photograph.

Photo by W. Saville-Kent, F.Z.S.] *[Milford-on-Sea.*

CONGER-EEL.

The females of this species often swallow the males.

fact that the common eel takes about four or five years to attain a weight of between 5 and 6 lbs. The males are smaller than the females, the greatest length attained by the former being a little over 1 foot 7 inches, whilst the latter may attain a length of nearly 4 feet. For a long while what is now known to be the female river-eel was regarded as a distinct species—the SHARP-NOSED EEL. The two sexes have quite different habits, the smaller males being found mostly in the brackish water of river-mouths, and rarely above the reach of the tides, whilst the females ascend the rivers for great distances, thousands finding their way into isolated ponds, which they reach by travelling overland. Here they appear to remain till they have reached maturity, when they migrate with one accord to the sea. Coming down the rivers during the months of October and November, hundreds are taken in large niches with traps, the mouths of which are directed up-stream.

The migration of eels to the sea is for the sole purpose of spawning and fertilising the eggs, which done, they die. The spawning appears to take place in extremely deep water, where the young eels pass the earlier stages of their development. Like the majority of young fishes, the fry are at first very different in form from the adults, and many have from time to time been described as distinct species, no suspicion of their true nature having been aroused. And this is not to be wondered at, for at this stage they are perfectly transparent and compressed from side to side, so as to be but little thicker than a sheet of stout paper; the head is ridiculously small, and only median fins are present. As development proceeds, having reached a certain maximum size, they, strangely enough, begin to slowly diminish, growing shorter and at the same time rounder, so that eventually, by the time the characteristic eel form is attained, they are considerably shorter than they were at the maximum period of larval life.

By the time the adult eel form has been attained, the larvæ have made their way to the mouths of various rivers, preparatory to making their ascent, which takes place between

February and May. They are then from 2 to 5 inches long, and perfectly transparent save for a black line inside the body, running along the spinal cord. The numbers passing up a single river during this ascent are almost beyond belief. In one of these migrations, or "eel-fares," upwards of three tons were captured in a single day in the Gloucester district in 1886, and it has been calculated that more than 14,000 go to make a pound weight. In the previous year the annual consumption of eels was estimated at a minimum of 1,650 tons, with a total value of £130,000. Few obstacles seem too great to be overcome in their ascent, for they will ascend the flood-gates of locks, or even travel overland if the ground be wet, till a desirable resting-place is found. In some parts of England these young eels, or "elvers," as they are called, are salted and made into cakes.

The CONGER-EEL is a marine species, differing from the river-eel, amongst other things, in its larger head and eyes, and in the arrangement of its teeth and the large size of the gill-openings. The conger is also greatly superior in size, examples of between 6 and 7 feet

Photo by Dr. R. W. Shufeldt] [*Washington.*

CAT-FISH.

Note the presence of barbels, or "feelers," round the mouth

in length and 60 lbs. in weight being common. The females are larger than the males, and an instance is on record of a female which was over 8 feet in length and weighed 128 lbs. Congers feed on other fishes, cuttle-fishes, and lobsters, as well as upon one another, the larger females eating the smaller males.

SERPENT-EELS are confined to tropical and sub-tropical seas, and are remarkable for their extreme voracity. More than eighty species are known, some of which are brilliantly coloured.

The DEEP-SEA EELS are represented by numerous species, and dwell at depths varying from 340 to 2,000 fathoms. In some species the body is remarkably modified, the mouth being of enormous size, and the stomach capable of marvellous distension, so much so that eels of this family have been captured which had swallowed fishes several times their own weight. The tail in many of the deep-sea eels tapers to a fine hair-like point.

The PAINTED EELS are remarkable for their bright spotted or mottled coloration, and are of large size, ranging from 6 to 8 feet in length. Armed with formidable teeth, the larger

Photo by N. Lazarnick] [*New York.*

PAINTED EELS FROM BERMUDA.

More than eighty species of these fishes are known.

Photo by N. Lazarnick] [*New York.*

CAT-FISHES.

These belong to the unarmoured group.

species are held in no little fear by fishermen and bathers, attacks from these fishes being by no means rare. Their distribution is closely similar to that of the Serpent-eels.

The ELECTRIC EEL is an extremely abundant fish in the rivers and lagoons of Brazil and the Guianas. It is the most powerful of the electric fishes, and attains a length of 6 feet. The electric organs of this fish are sufficiently strong to kill by their shock other fishes and even mammals. The traveller Humboldt is responsible for the statement, now generally discredited, that the Indians procured this fish by driving horses into the water, and so provoking such violent discharges from the fish that they became exhausted and fell an easy prey.

The CAT-FISHES, or SHEATH-FISHES, are an extremely interesting group, one of the principal characteristics of which is the total absence of scales, the body being either entirely naked or armed with bony tubercles or overlapping plates. Another peculiarity of these fishes is the presence of feelers round the mouth; these, by their delicate sense of touch, enable the fish to procure its food in extremely muddy water, when the eyes would be useless. The latter, indeed, in many species are extremely reduced in size. Many cat-fishes are armed with powerful spines, attached to the body by a very complicated mechanism. Such spines are capable of inflicting dangerous wounds, either by the introduction of poison or the violent inflammation following on the laceration of the wounded part. Some species have elaborate accessory breathing-organs, enabling them to travel overland for short distances from one piece of water to another. Other members of the group possess electrical organs of considerable power; one species inhabiting the Nile attains a length of 4 feet.

The nesting-habits of the group are exceedingly interesting, some building nests in which to deposit the eggs; others carry the eggs in the mouth till they hatch. In one species the care of the eggs is undertaken by the female, which carries them about embedded in the skin of the under surface of the body, which at this season becomes very soft and spongy. When the eggs are laid, she presses them into the spongy skin by lying on them.

The cat-fishes are of world-wide distribution, but only one species, the WELS, occurs in European waters. It commonly attains a length of from 6 to 9 feet, and occasionally as much as 13 feet. The majority of cat-fishes inhabit fresh-water, but some are marine.

CHAPTER XI.

THE CARP FAMILY.

BY JOHN BICKERDYKE, M.A.

THE Carp Family, like the Perch group, is one of the largest among fishes. It includes the Rudd, Roach, Tench, Bream, Minnow, etc., and is divided into many groups, which again include numerous species found chiefly in the temperate and tropical parts of the world. Included among these are the Barbels, of which there are about 200 species, varying from little fishes of 2 inches

Photo by A. S. Rudland & Sons.

CARP.

The members of the Carp Tribe are vegetable-feeders. They have teeth in the throat, but none in the jaws.

to monsters of 6 feet or more in length. Some of the largest are found in the Tigris; but the Mahseer of India must be regarded as the king of all the species. In some of the rivers flowing from the Himalaya Mountains are curious Barbel which have their vent and anal fin in a sheath covered with large scales. Roach are important members of the Carp Family, and the Roach group is a very large one, including the various fishes coming under the term of "white fish" in Germany. The Roach proper is common all over Europe north of the Alps. In this group is the Ide of the central and northern parts of Europe, which when domesticated becomes golden in hue, and is then called the Golden Orf, a pretty fish kept in many English aquariums. Rudd are found all over Europe and Asia Minor. Of Tench, only one species is known, the Golden Tench being merely a variety differing in the matter of colour. The Bream group consists of the Common Bream, Bream-flat, and the American Bream, or Shiner. Lastly, we may mention the Bleak group, of which there are fifteen known species in Europe, East Africa, and the temperate parts of Asia. This list by no means exhausts the numerous members of the Carp Family.

The COMMON CARP is one of the most remarkable fishes which swim. In early times in England it was extensively cultivated as a food-fish, and in Germany at the present day is as much domesticated as the sheep, pig, or ox. The fish-culturists have indeed done extraordinary things with it, having, for instance, produced a variety with a single row of scales down each side and sometimes on the back only, called the MIRROR-CARP, or KING-CARP. There is also the LEATHER-CARP, with no scales at all, which is much esteemed in Germany.

Photo by W. Saville-Kent, F.Z.S.] *[Milford-on-Sea.*

GOLD-FISH.

A native of China and the warmer parts of Japan.

There is reason to believe that the common carp was originally a native of the East, and it certainly has been domesticated in China for many hundreds of years. Thence it is supposed to have been imported to Germany and Sweden, reaching England some time in the early years of the fifteenth century. In that curious work the "Boke of St. Albans," published in 1496, it is said that the carp is a "dayntous fysshe, but there ben fewe in Englonde, and therefore I wryte the lesse of hym."

China is the home of the GOLD-FISH, a pretty little carp common in that country and the warmer parts of Japan. The Chinese have distorted Nature with regard to this fish even more than the Germans have the common carp. Their most extraordinary monstrosity is, perhaps, the TELESCOPE-FISH, which has a huge tail and projecting eyes. It is believed that gold-fish were not known in England before the year 1691.

The carp has many interesting peculiarities. It is an extraordinarily fertile fish, and one of the most rapid growers in fresh-water. Under the most favourable conditions it attains a weight of from 3 to 3½ lbs. in three years. In a pond which is overstocked, carp hardly increase in weight at all; while, on the other hand, their growth in hot countries is very much greater than above stated. A fish of from 4 to 5 lbs. may contain, on an average, from 400,000 to 500,000 eggs; these are spawned in May or June, and hatched in from twelve to sixteen days, according to the temperature.

The life of this curious fish may be one of extraordinary duration, carp having been known to attain an age of a hundred years or more. When very old, they are apt to go blind and develop white marks, due to the growth of funguses.

In the winter carp either bury themselves in the mud, or lie among the water-weeds or roots of trees at the bottom. They are vegetarians for the most part, with no teeth in their mouths, but strong, powerful grinding-teeth in their throats; they are believed to regurgitate their food and chew it, somewhat as a cow chews the cud.

With regard to the weight which this fish attains, one of 19 lbs. was taken at Sheffield Park in 1882. This was exceptionally large; but one still larger, weighing 21 lbs. 10 ozs., was caught at Bayham Abbey, near Lamberhurst, in 1870; while one of 22 lbs. was exhibited many years ago to the Zoological Society. In the German lakes these fish reach a weight of 40 lbs., or even more.

Carp will, however, occasionally eat small fish, and have even been caught with a salmon-fly.

CHAPTER XII.

PIKES, ARAPAIMAS, BEAKED SALMON, AND SCOPELIDS.

BY W. P. PYCRAFT, A.L.S., F.Z.S.

THE PIKES are strictly fresh-water fishes, which are extremely voracious, and grow to a large size. They are met with in most of the fresh-waters of Europe, Asia, and America; yet they must be regarded rather as a Western than an Eastern type, since all the known species occur in America, whilst only one—the COMMON PIKE—is known outside that country. These fishes capture their prey by stealth—practised, however, not so much by concealment as by lying suspended in the water, perfectly motionless save for the movement of the gills, which is barely perceptible. When the victim comes within reach, it is seized by a sudden rush. The form of the body is admirably adapted to this manner of feeding, resembling rather a submerged log than a fish. It is, furthermore, on account of this shape that the name Pike has been bestowed, since it recalls the "pike" borne by the soldiers of bygone days.

When on the feed, nothing comes amiss to pike, and the havoc they commit in trout-streams is enormous. Not only other fishes are devoured, but both the young and adults of water-birds are frequently seized, and instances are on record where boys have been attacked while bathing. The mouth of a pike bristles with teeth, even the roof being thickly covered. These are all attached by hinges, moving readily backwards towards the throat, so as to assist the swallowing operation, but preventing any possibility of the victim's escape.

In Great Britain the pike is held in high esteem by anglers, though as an article of food it does not find much favour. The females are larger than the males. The largest specimens attain a length of about 4 feet, sometimes a little more, and a weight of from 36 to 37 lbs.

About six species of pike are known, five of which are confined to American waters. Of these, the one known as the MUSKET-LUNGE, or MUSKINONGE, attains the same large size as the common

Photo by Dr. R. W. Shufeldt] [*Washington.*

PIKE.

The most voracious of British fresh-water fishes.

Photo by N. Lazarnick] [New York.

PIKEREL.

This is an American species.

Photo by W. Saville-Kent, F.Z.S.] [Milford-on-Sea.

"SERGEANT BAKER."

An edible Australian representative of the group of fishes which, for want of an English name, are here called Scopelids.

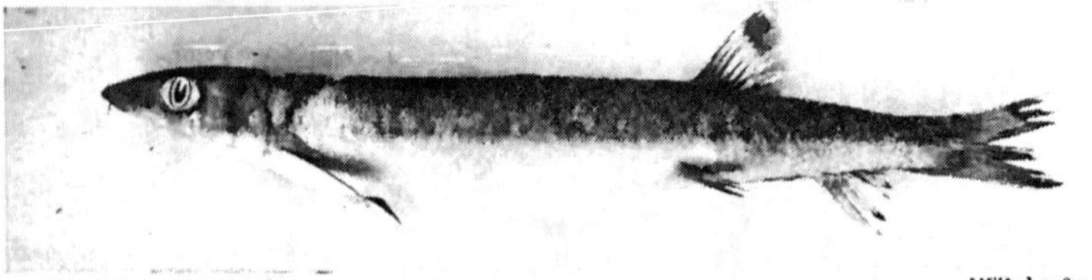

Photo by W. Saville-Kent, F.Z.S.) [*Milford-on-Sea.*

BEAKED SALMON.

Known in New Zealand as the Sand-eel.

pike; the other species are known as PIKEREL. The immature pike is commonly called a JACK.

The ARAPAIMAS are large fresh-water fishes, confined to the tropics, their distribution being practically the same as that of the Lung-fishes; they are represented in America, Australia, and Africa, but one species occurs in the East Indian Archipelago. The largest species of all—which is also the largest fresh-water bony fish known—is found in the rivers of Brazil and the Guianas, attaining a length of 15 feet and a weight of 400 lbs. It is highly esteemed as an article of food, being salted and exported from the inland fisheries to the sea-ports. The natives take it either with a rod and line, or with a bow and arrow, a line being fastened to the arrow, thus converting it into a harpoon.

Four species of arapaimas are distinguished by the presence of "barbels" on the chin; of these, two are Australian, one American, and one occurs in Sumatra and Borneo. Yet another species is found in the Nile and the rivers of West Africa. The Australian species, like the large Brazilian form, are highly esteemed as food; one of these, known as the DAWSON RIVER SALMON, is confined to the rivers of Queensland, the other to the rivers emptying into the Gulf of Carpentaria.

The BEAKED SALMON occurs in the open seas of the Cape, Japan, and Australia; but in New Zealand, where it is known as the SAND-EEL, it is found in bays with a sandy bottom.

The group of fishes known as SCOPELIDS is one of particular interest, on account of the number of remarkable forms which it contains. For the most part they are inhabitants of the open sea, many being found only at great depths. Of the latter, some apparently come to the surface to feed at night, whilst others are entirely confined to the abysses of the ocean. As with the members of other groups which have adopted a deep-sea habitat, certain modifications of the body have become necessary in these fishes. Many of them have a direct relation to the absence of light, which has rendered normal eyes of little use; consequently the eyes of these fishes have become either greatly reduced or enormously enlarged, or sometimes lost altogether. As a rule the large-eyed forms are those which come to the surface at night or do not live beyond the reach of daylight; whilst those in which the eyes are small or reduced live in the very lowest depths, far beyond the limit of daylight. In all these forms compensation for the loss of light has taken place, generally by the development of phosphorescent organs. These may take the form of a number of luminous areas distributed down each side of the body, as in the PHOSPHORESCENT SARDINE; or of a pair of lens-like light-producing organs, occupying the place of the eyes of other fishes. Another eyeless member of the group, instead of developing light-producing organs, has increased the length of the rays of the paired fins to an enormous extent, so that they serve as delicate feelers either for the discovery of food or the detection of enemies. Many of the fishes of this group have extremely large mouths, armed with a formidable array of tusk-like teeth, between which are numerous smaller ones.

As food-fishes the majority of the Scopelids are not of much value. The species known as the QUEENSLAND SMELT, shown in the adjoining photograph, is an edible species, occurring off the north-west coast of Australia. Its near ally, the BUMMALOE, or BOMBAY DUCK, however, enjoys a quite exceptional notoriety. Salted and dried, it is exported in large quantities from Bombay and the coast of Malabar, and forms an indispensable adjunct to an Indian curry. This fish apparently inhabits considerable depths, and when freshly taken is brilliantly phosphorescent. Another edible species is the "SERGEANT BAKER" of Australia, of which a photograph is given on page 653.

With regard to the deep-sea Scopelids, it is interesting to note that, in addition to very remarkable modifications of the eyes and fins, and the production of phosphorescent light, certain of the body-cavities are characterised by an intensely black coloration. The inside of the mouth, the gills, and the lining of the abdomen, for example, are always so coloured in those fishes which inhabit the deepest abysses. This coloration is difficult to account for, but

Photo by W. Saville-Kent, F.Z.S.] *[Milford-on-Sea.*

QUEENSLAND SMELT.

A near ally of the Bummaloe, or Bombay Duck, that indispensable adjunct to an Indian curry.

it is generally supposed to be due to excretory products. Another interesting point concerns the air-bladder. Whenever this organ is present in the fishes of this or any other family inhabiting the abysses of the ocean, it bursts before the unfortunate victim is brought to the surface, owing to the enormous differences in pressure which obtain between the depths of the sea and the surface.

CHAPTER XIII.

THE SALMON FAMILY.

BY SIR HERBERT MAXWELL, BART., F.R.S.

ALTHOUGH the Salmon Family occupies a low place in the classification of fishes, yet every member thereof is possessed of singular beauty of form and colour. The ATLANTIC SALMON, which is the species frequenting European rivers and those of the eastern coast of North America, may be considered the type of the family, and certainly it would be difficult to name any animal more perfectly adapted to its peculiar mode of life, which is one of constant activity. A native of fresh-water, hatched in early spring from eggs laid in rivers during the winter months, it spends from fifteen to twenty-seven months in the shallows of the river, almost indistinguishable in habits and appearance from a small common trout. Sometimes in the second spring after its birth, and failing that, always in the third spring, the fish, having attained the length of 5 or 6 inches, undergoes a wonderful change: its prevailing tints of olive and gold become overspread with a glittering coat of silver, known

Photo by A. S. Rudland & Sons.

SALMON-TROUT.

Known also as the Sea-trout, and in Ireland as the White Trout.

to anglers as the "sea-jacket," and shoals of "smolts," as they are called in this stage, begin descending to the sea. In about fifteen or eighteen months, perhaps in some instances longer, they return to the inland waters as "grilse"—small salmon from 2 to 5 lbs. in weight. Grilse and mature salmon spawn chiefly in November and December, undergoing, before they do so, another strange metamorphosis. Their brilliant silvery scales become darkly discoloured, the males turning copper-colour, the females blackish and dull purple; their elegant form becoming distorted to such a degree as to render them hardly recognisable as the same fish which left the tide in the perfection of beauty. In their efforts to reach the higher waters where they spawn, salmon display extraordinary perseverance and activity in surmounting weirs, waterfalls, and other obstacles which bar their way. After spawning, the fish are emaciated and lanky, but speedily regain the bright silver hue so characteristic of the species. In this state they are usually known as "kelts"; they are worthless either for food or for sport, and make their way back to the sea, where abundant provender soon restores their condition. Their chief food consists of herrings, haddocks, and other small fishes. Dr. Kingston Barton recently recorded finding five full-grown herrings in the stomach of one salmon. Although the excellence of their flesh exposes salmon to the attacks of innumerable foes, including man, predacious fishes, seals, and cetaceans, a few survive for many years and attain to great size. Fish weighing from 30 to 40 lbs. are far from uncommon; one of 60 lbs. has been taken in the Tay with rod and line, and the same river has yielded one of upwards of 70 lbs. to the nets. The fine sport afforded to anglers by the salmon causes a good beat on a prolific river to be a very valuable property. Two thousand pounds was the season's rent paid a few years ago for less than three miles of the Tweed, and the season happened to be such a bad one that the lessee only killed thirteen fish!

Closely resembling the true salmon in habits and appearance, and sometimes rivalling it even in size, are two kinds of sea-trout—the SALMON-TROUT, greatly prized both for its sporting qualities and for the excellence of its flesh, and the BULL-TROUT, a very inferior fish in both respects. Bull-trout are not infrequently taken in the Tay weighing upwards of 40 lbs.

The Pacific Ocean has its counterpart to the Atlantic salmon and sea-trout in several closely allied species, whereof the QUINNAT and the STEELHEAD are the most notable. These ascend the great rivers of Western North America in prodigious shoals, penetrating more than 2,000 miles inland to deposit their spawn. Few of these fish survive to return to the sea. In their emaciated condition they succumb to exhaustion and starvation; their corpses, piled to the height of several feet, line the banks of the river for miles, and contribute nothing to the traveller's comfort. Although Pacific salmon are of no value to the sportsman, as they are said to refuse any bait in fresh-water, yet they are the staple of an important trade, tens of thousands of tons being taken and canned for export.

If we could peer far enough back into the course of time, we should no doubt be able to identify a common stock from which all the Salmon Family are descended. That they are all natives of fresh-water is proved by the fact that they cannot reproduce their kind in the sea. Those that resort to the ocean for food must be the descendants of vigorous, roving members of the family, which, having to choose between starvation and migration, braved the perils of travel, and became so much altered in constitution by the liberal diet they found as to establish themselves as separate species.

Among the stay-at-homes there are many interesting and beautiful fishes. None of them exhibit the variable nature of the family more than the common BROOK-TROUT of British waters, and not long since men of science dignified each of these varieties by a separate title, treating them as distinct species. However, experiment and observation have now led to the almost unanimous conclusion that the pygmy denizens of some hungry Highland burn, whereof the weight must be reckoned in fractions of ounces, are of precisely the same species as the lordly trout of deep lakes, which sometimes scales as much as 25 lbs., and as all the other innumerable varieties, such as the trout of the Thames, of the English chalk-streams, and of the Irish loughs. The quality of the soil affects the food-supply, which in turn regulates the size and appearance of the fish. Moreover, Nature seems indifferent to the number of individuals composing the population which the water is to sustain. If there are no pike, and spawning-ground is abundant, there will be many and small fish; if the contrary is the case, there will be few and large ones; the aggregate weight per acre of water will remain the same, proportioned to the food-supply. The American equivalent of the British brook-trout is the RAINBOW-TROUT, a beautiful creature which has lately been widely distributed in European waters. What is known as the brook-trout in America really belongs to the CHAR group, fish of the Salmon Family, closely resembling trout, but distinguished from them by extraordinary brilliancy of colour. Common trout, like salmon, lose all their beauty as the spawning-season approaches. Char, on the other hand, take gaudy colouring at that time, the whole of the under-parts becoming clear red or flame-colour. Unlike trout, British char never enter rivers, but spawn in lakes. In Norway, however, char descend to the sea. The distribution of char is indeed mysterious, nor has any explanation been offered why they inhabit certain waters, while other lakes in the neighbourhood, apparently equally suitable, contain none.

The GRAYLING is an elegant member of the Salmon Family, and a deserved favourite with fly-fishers. Instead of the golden tints and scarlet spots of the brook-trout, this fish displays the silvery colouring of the salmon-trout. It is not at all uncommon to meet with grayling in the chalk-streams of Southern England weighing 3 lbs. and upwards.

The POWAN is the type of another large group of salmon-like fishes, inhabiting lakes in the temperate and sub-arctic regions of both hemispheres. There are four species in Great Britain, among which may be mentioned the mysterious VENDACE of Lochmaben, unknown to exist elsewhere.

Lastly, the Salmon Family is closed by the delicate SMELT, called in Scotland the SPARLING, which is netted in vast numbers in the estuaries of suitable rivers. It never ascends beyond the highest point of the

Photo by W. Reid] [*Wishaw, N.B.*

AMERICAN SALMON-TROUT FROM DIAMOND LAKE, NEW ZEALAND.

These fish were taken out of the water to be photographed, and then put back again.

tide, where it deposits its spawn in the spring months. It is a gratifying tribute to the good work done of late years by the local authorities in purifying the Thames that, after a long absence, this valuable fish has reappeared in that river, which it now ascends in considerable numbers as high as Teddington Weir.

Much discussion has taken place recently with regard to the question whether salmon feed while in fresh-water. Not long ago it was announced that they suffered from a diseased condition of the stomach during this period, and were consequently quite unable to feed. Subsequently it was found that the supposed diseased condition of the stomach was due to the fishes not being perfectly fresh when they were examined. It is now known that although salmon do not feed freely in fresh-water, yet they take a certain amount of nutriment, such as an occasional shrimp, fly, or even small fish, while there.

Photo by A. S. Rudland & Sons.

SMELT.

This fish is remarkable for its peculiar smell when freshly caught, which resembles that of the cucumber.

CHAPTER XIV.

THE HERRING AND ITS KINDRED.

BY F. G. AFLALO, F.Z.S.

"KING HERRING," as the trade-paper of the fishing industry rightly calls it, is one of the chief commercial fishes of the British seas, and the enormous North Sea herring fisheries probably support more boats and men from all parts than any other. Europe has no very large herring; but the TARPON of the Mexican coast, as well as another giant which occurs in the northern waters of Australia, grows to an enormous size. All the members of the Herring Family feed and travel near the surface of the sea, and are therefore caught in drift-nets, miles of which are "shot" a few fathoms from the top of the water, catching the shoaling-fish in their meshes. All of them, too, are wanderers, most capricious in their goings and comings. Hence the uncertainty of the fisherman's wage.

The principal kinsmen of the herring in British seas are the SPRAT and PILCHARD, though the two kinds of SHAD, which, like the salmon, ascend certain rivers for spawning purposes, also support a number fishermen; and the ANCHOVY is, authorities have lately suspected, sufficiently numerous on the British coasts to repay a regular fishery, if the men could be induced to try the experiment and use a sufficiently fine-meshed net for this little fish.

The HERRING of the more northern waters is larger than that of the English Channel, 17 inches being recorded as its maximum size in the former, as against only 12¼ inches farther south. In the Baltic, however, the writer found the herrings still smaller than those of the English Channel. The herring lacks the lateral line, already alluded to in other fishes; its scales are large and thin; its under-edge is smooth and keeled; and the male is slightly the larger of the two sexes. The SPRAT, on the other hand, is a smaller species. It has no teeth; its belly is saw-edged; its back-fin starts nearer the tail than that of the herring. The herring, moreover, differs from the sprat, and indeed from all our most important fishes, in that its eggs sink to the bottom. The eggs of almost all other sea-fish float at or near the surface of the sea, so that the herring's spawn alone can be damaged by the operations of the ground-

Photo by W. Saville-Kent, F.Z.S.] *[Milford-on-Sea.*

OX-EYED HERRING.

This species attains a length of several feet.

sweeping trawl-net. The shad's eggs also sink to the bottom, but are deposited in the less buoyant waters of rivers.

The PILCHARD, the all-important fish (together with mackerel) on the south-west coast of England, is of a more decided green hue than either of the foregoing. Its scales are large and coarse, and its back-fin starts closer to the head than in the rest. The pilchard of Cornwall and the sardine of the Mediterranean are one and the same fish in different stages of growth—that is to say, the pilchard is a grown-up sardine. The late Matthias Dunn of Mevagissey was one of the first practical fishermen to accept this identity, and the flourishing sardine factory at his native town bears lasting witness to his enterprise. Although, from the economic standpoint, we associate the pilchard with the extreme south-west of the English Channel, the fish finds its way to more eastern counties. The writer has found it at both Bournemouth and Ventnor; and it is taken, though sparsely, in the herring-nets of the North Sea fleets.

The ANCHOVY, smaller than any of the foregoing, may be distinguished by its projecting, shark-like snout and deeply cleft mouth. It is seen in England only pickled for table purposes, but the writer used fresh anchovies for bait almost daily during a stay of four months on the shores of the Mediterranean.

The two shads—the ALLIS SHAD and TWAITE SHAD—are in some respects, though less important commercially, the most interesting of the family. Their habit of coming up rivers to spawn, like salmon, has been already noticed, but they appear to be more difficult to please than the other fish. The Severn used to be a noted shad-river, but the fishery has fallen off of late years. The ALLIS SHAD grows to a weight of 7 or 8 lbs., and its pale green and silver scales are varied by some darker spots at irregular intervals on the shoulders and sides. The edge of the belly is serrated, like that of the sprat. The fish has a curious transparent eyelid, and its other peculiarities include an abnormally large number of gill-rakers, through which the water filters much as it does through the "whalebone" of whales. Its food is said to consist of small fishes and shrimps, as well as of vegetable substances. Though usually caught, for market purposes, in a seine-net, which is slipped round the shoal in shallow water, the shad is now and then taken on the hook, and instances of this are on record in the neighbourhood of Deal. The rivers of Morocco are very productive of shad, particularly the BOUREGREG at Rabat, and the UM ERBEYA at Azimur. At the latter town the writer has bought newly caught shad weighing 5 or 6 lbs. for native money equivalent to as many pence, and very excellent fish they proved in camp. The TWAITE SHAD is a somewhat smaller fish, attaining to a maximum weight of perhaps a couple of pounds. It is not known to differ materially in habits from the larger species.

Reverting for a moment to the herring as a type of the family, a few words may be said on some very interesting facts in connection with its life-history and commercial uses. In the first place, the fact that the spawn sinks to the bottom is of more importance than would at first sight appear, since it not only exposes this spawn to disturbance by the trawl, but also subjects it to the voracity of cod, haddock, and other ground-feeding fishes. Some little protection is afforded by a natural provision which enables the eggs to adhere to stones and weeds, but this cannot in the long-run be of much service against prowling fishes. The eggs of the shad, which likewise sink (in fresh-water), do not adhere in this way.

The migrations of the herring, again, have furnished almost as much material for argument to marine biologists as the migrations of birds in ornithological circles. Older naturalists described marvellous Arctic journeyings with careful attention to detail, much of which is now repudiated. Later theories hold that the shoals of herrings simply move, according to

Photo by W. Saville-Kent, F.Z.S.] [*Milford-on-Sea.*

QUEENSLAND LUNG-FISH.

Known also as the Dawson River Salmon, on account of the colour and flavour of its flesh.

changes in the weather and temperature, backwards and forwards between the shore and the deeper water outside; and so far as the fishermen are concerned, the mere fact of the fish moving at any season of the year beyond reach of their drift-nets, which work at only moderate distances from the land, would be quite sufficient to convince them that the absent fish had departed on world-wide travels. Much of the former acceptance of these extensive migrations may have been due to confusion between the goings and comings of the different races of herrings now recognised by biologists. It is also probable that, when the identity and movements of these different "races" are more firmly established, we shall be able to clear up many of the difficulties at present surrounding the spawning-time of the herring, and to show that it does not, as sometimes alleged, deposit its spawn at every season of the year indiscriminately, but that some herrings spawn at one season, some at another. Although the herring is not, individually and by comparison with some other sea-fish, an enormously fertile fish, its numbers must be fairly large, when we bear in mind that something like 50,000 crans a week are, in good seasons, packed in Shetland alone. Taking, as an average, 750 fish to the cran, this gives a weekly curing of not far short of 40,000,000 of herrings in a single fishery. Owing indeed to the property, already noted, of adhering to stones and rocks, it is improbable that even the trawl troubles the eggs to any appreciable extent, as the stony ground on which the herrings generally spawn is not suited to the operations of the trawler. The spawning and life-history of the herring are, in fact, the converse of those of the plaice. The former deposits its eggs on the ground close inshore, and the young herrings, almost as soon as they are hatched, steer for the open sea and live near the surface of the water. The flat-fishes, on the other hand, deposit eggs that float at the surface some distance from the shore; and the young plaice and soles, when hatched, come inshore and take up their residence close to the bed of the sea.

It would be improper to conclude this account of the Herring Family without a passing reference to the commercial mixture known as "WHITEBAIT." Until comparatively late in the

Photo by W. Saville-Kent, F.Z.S.] [*Milford-on-Sea.*

AUSTRALIAN PILCHARDS.

Distinct from the British species.

last century whitebait was regarded, even by scientific men, as a distinct species, and there were even some who declared that they had identified peculiar characters. It is now, however, common knowledge that the so-called "whitebait" is neither more nor less than a mixture of young herrings and sprats, the former predominating in summer, the latter in winter. Other fishes are also found in the dish, and, appropriately enough, at a recent banquet given by the Worshipful Company of Fishmongers, at which the writer had the pleasure of "assisting," a plate of whitebait was found to include no sprats, but the fry of herrings, gurnards, and sand-eels: this was in the month of July. Whitebait are caught in special fine-meshed nets in river-estuaries; and although they make a capital dish for the epicure, the large supplies needed for the restaurants probably entail a most regrettable sacrifice of valuable food-fishes, which, if left a year or two, would provide food for ten times the number of consumers. It would, however, be too much to expect that epicures should give up such an unrivalled dish for this cause. Moreover, if these little fishes were not captured by man, it is highly probable that a large proportion would fall victims to birds or other fishes.

CHAPTER XV.

BONY PIKE, BOW-FIN, STURGEON, REED-FISH, AND BICHIR.

BY W. P. PYCRAFT, A.L.S., F.Z.S.

THE present chapter deals with the remaining forms belonging to that great assemblage of fishes known as the Bony-mouthed group, which includes all the members of the class save the Lung-fishes on the one hand and the Shark Tribe on the other.

This great assemblage, as we have already remarked, is divided into two sections—the Fan- and Fringe-finned Fishes. The fishes presently to be described belong partly to the one and partly to the other of these divisions, and were at one time, together with the Lung-fishes, regarded as nearly allied, and as forming but a single group, which, on account of the structure of the scales, was known as the Enamel-scaled group.

The BONY PIKE, the BOW-FIN, and the STURGEON are the last of the Fan-finned Fishes.

The BONY PIKE, or GAR-PIKE, is an inhabitant of the fresh-waters of North America, and has the most completely ossified skeleton and the most perfectly jointed backbone of all the fishes, whilst externally it is covered with a complete armour of thick, quadrangular scales coated with enamel. Three distinct species of this family are known, all of which are of large size, attaining a length of 6 feet. They are carnivorous in their habits, lying in wait among the reeds, and rushing out to seize their prey as soon as within range. In the Mississippi, great lakes, and rivers of South Carolina bony pike are especially abundant, occurring at times in such numbers as to fill the shad-nets and render the fishery for many days impossible. The larger members are said to be as aggressive as sharks, and remarkably tenacious of life.

The geographical distribution of the BOW-FIN closely corresponds with that of the bony pike. It is an extremely common fish, and, though worthless for food purposes, has yet been deemed worthy of a number of different names, such as GRINDLE, DOG-FISH, SAWYER, MUD-FISH, and LAWYER-FISH. At one time it was regarded as a near ally of the Herring Tribe, but modern research has shown this view to be erroneous. The bow-fin attains a length of about 2 feet, and is very voracious, preying both upon other fishes and aquatic insects and shrimps. It has a habit of coming frequently to the surface to breathe, especially when the water is foul, taking in large mouthfuls of air. When near the surface, it is said to utter a bell-like note.

Photo by A. S. Rudland & Sons. *Photo by Scholastic Photo. Co.] [Parson's Green.*

BONY PIKE.

One of the very few survivors of the ancient group of Enamel-scaled Fishes.

Photo by A. S. Rudland & Sons.

STURGEON.

The air-bladder of the sturgeon is used for making isinglass, its roe for caviare.

probably caused by the escape of air from the air-bladder. During the breeding-season the male takes entire charge of the eggs.

The STURGEONS differ from the other fan-finned fishes in many particulars. To begin with, the skeleton is almost entirely cartilaginous instead of bony, whilst externally the body is either naked or covered with bony bucklers, arranged symmetrically. The snout is prolonged into a more or less shovel-shaped beak, used for turning over the mud at the bottom of the water in search of prey, and in some forms this becomes further developed into a spoon-shaped paddle, constituting one of the most remarkable appendages of fishes.

Sturgeons grow to a large size, and are the largest of the fresh-water fishes of the northern hemisphere. The GIANT STURGEON of the Black and Caspian Seas and the Sea of Azoff attains a length of 24 feet, and sometimes more, specimens of 3,200 lbs. weight having been recorded.

Photo by A. S. Rudland & Sons.

STERLET.

A smaller species of the Sturgeon group.

On account of the wholesomeness of their flesh, sturgeons are highly esteemed wherever they are found. In Russian rivers they are very abundant, regular fishing-stations being established for their capture. The approach of a shoal of fish is announced by a watchman, and it is said as many as 15,000 sturgeon have been captured at one of these stations in a single day. Should the fishing be suspended for a short time, the fish assemble in such numbers as to form a solid mass, completely blocking a river 400 feet in width and 25 feet in depth.

From the roe of these fishes caviare is made, and isinglass from the inner lining

Photo by A. S. Rudland & Sons.

BICHIR.

A second representative of the Enamel-scaled group.

Photo by Scholastic Photo. Co.] [*Parson's Green.*

BICHIR.

Note the remarkable finlets on the back and the peculiar structure of the breast-fins.

of the air-bladder. But the best-flavoured flesh and the finest caviare are obtained from a comparatively small form, the STERLET, a species which does not exceed a yard in length. It is common in the Black and Caspian Seas, the Siberian rivers, and the Danube as far as Vienna.

With the Sturgeons we come to the end of the Fan-finned Fishes. The Fringe-finned group are represented to-day only by the BICHIR and the REED-FISH. These are extremely interesting forms, if only because they are the sole survivors of a once numerous tribe, the remains of which occur as fossils in some of the oldest geological formations. They are known as Fringe-finned on account of the fact that the rays which support the fin-membrane in the paired fins are ranged round a lobe-shaped base, instead of running directly backwards to the body. As in the bony pike, the body is clothed externally by large quadrangular bony plates of considerable thickness, and coated with a layer of enamel.

The BICHIR, which is found in the Nile and other tropical rivers of Africa, is easily recognised by the peculiar structure of the back-fin, which takes the form of a series of detached finlets, varying in number from eight to eighteen. The length attained by the bichir is about 4 feet. Gill-breathing is supplemented by the air-bladder, which is used as a respiratory organ, the expired air escaping by a slit, known as the "spiracle." The young bichir breathes, like a tadpole, by means of large external gills, projecting backwards on each side of the head; later these are replaced by the more efficiently protected internal gills.

The only surviving relative of the bichir is the REED-FISH of Old Calabar, which differs by its eel-like form and the absence of the hinder paired fins.

CHAPTER XVI.

SHARKS AND RAYS.

BY F. G. AFLALO, F.Z.S.

TWO prevalent errors with reference to sharks continually recur in England. The first is local, and has reference to the absence of "proper" sharks, whatever that may mean, from British waters. The second, of wider application, holds that all sharks are dangerous to man. When, some few years ago, the writer addressed a letter to the *Times* newspaper, warning yachting-men against summer bathing in deep water in Cornwall, a host of critics accused him of a tendency to pose as an alarmist, and insisted that he was confusing sharks with dog-fish. Apart from the fact that the distinction between the two groups is in some cases extremely slight—it does not even rely on size, for there are dog-fishes which attain to larger dimensions than the smallest sharks—these gentlemen were wholly in error, since four sharks at any rate are very common in Cornish seas, and even occur in lesser numbers on other parts of the British coasts. The largest of these, the great BASKING-

Photo by W. Saville-Kent, F.Z.S.] *[Milford-on-Sea.*

WOLLIBONG, OR CARPET-SHARK.

The leaf-like processes surrounding the head serve to attract prey, while the shark lies concealed on the sea-bottom.

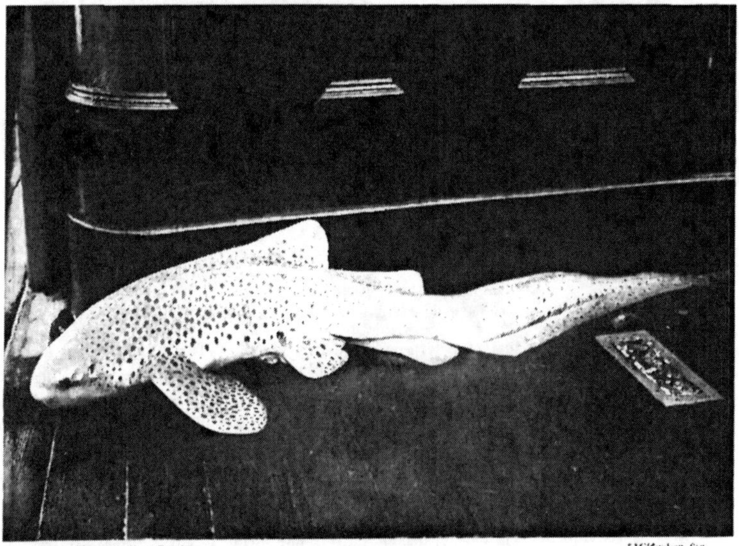

Photo by W. Saville-Kent, F.Z.S.] *[Milford-on-Sea.*

SPOTTED SHARK.

Note the peculiar shape of the tail, and the aperture behind the eye, known as the "spiracle."

SHARK (of which a photograph, taken at Mevagissey, is given below), illustrates in its harmless person the fallacy of condemning all sharks as man-eaters, since in this, the largest of its race, we have an absolutely innocuous fish. From its habit of lying at the surface with the large back-fin erect, it is also known as the Sail-fish, while the equally appropriate name of Sun-fish sometimes causes confusion with other British fishes properly so called.

A commoner British shark (in the limited space allotted, British species must be allowed prior claims) is the BLUE SHARK, small examples of which, weighing 30 or 40 lbs., the writer has often killed with the rod at Mevagissey. When thus hooked, this fish has a curious and very trying habit of revolving rapidly in the water, scoring its own granulated skin with the line. The PORBEAGLE-SHARK, another Cornish species, is of thicker build than the last, and swims with far less graceful movements. It is a deep brown colour above, and its general

Photo by S. Dalby Smith] [*Mevagissey.*

BASKING-SHARK.

Regularly hunted on the west coast of Ireland for the sake of the oil obtainable from its liver. Note the keel by the side of the tail.

outline may be likened to that of a torpedo. The FOX-SHARK, or THRESHER, so often seen on hot summer days leaping out of water among the pilchard-shoals, is easily recognised, even at considerable distances, by the disproportionately long upper lobe of the tail-fin. This is the shark which attacks certain of the Whale Tribe. Many who stay at home find it agreeable to cast doubt on the story; but the writer has, in Australian seas, witnessed the sight of two of these sharks flinging themselves on the back of an apparently exhausted whale in such unmistakable circumstances that the only alternative (which the reader may accept, if preferred) is to suppose that they were all congenial playmates.

Before specifying some general characters of this interesting group of predatory fishes, it may be as well briefly to summarise the BRITISH DOG-FISHES; for the HAMMERHEAD-SHARK, very common in southern seas, is so rare a visitor to Britain as to be negligible in an epitome of the group. The dog-fishes, then, which trouble fishermen are the SMOOTH HOUND

Photo by W. Saville-Kent, F.Z.S.] *[Milford-on-Sea.*

OCELLATED DOG-FISH.

So called from the presence of the eye-like spots on the body, two of which can be seen above the breast-fins.

and ROUGH HOUND, the NURSE, the PICKED DOG, and the SILVER DOG, or TOPE. The NURSE and ROUGH HOUND are spotted leopards of the sea, and the latter has a very curious property. If a fresh-caught "row-hound," as the fishermen pronounce the name, be put in a basket or boat's well with pollack and other fishes, the points of contact will be marked by discoloration of its neighbours. This is probably due to some acrid and bleaching secretion of the row-hound's skin, for which some economic use might possibly be found. The PICKED DOG, or SPUR-DOG, has very sharp spines in front of both back-fins, and has therefore to be handled by the fishermen very cautiously, often punishing their hands badly when entangled at night in the nets. Of SMOOTH HOUNDS there are two species or varieties, between which there is some confusion, and in one at any rate there are interesting anatomical peculiarities in the unborn fish (like many other sharks and dog-fishes, the smooth hound bears living young instead of depositing eggs), any account of which would obviously be out of place in so short a description.

Generally speaking, then, the sharks are cartilaginous fishes, having the upper lobe of the tail larger than the lower, a shovel-shaped snout, and the crescent-shaped mouth beneath the head. Another peculiar feature of the group is the presence of breathing-spiracles behind the eyes; while the latter have a manner of blinking not found in other fishes. Of the teeth, which differ in structure from those of other kinds of fishes, there are several rows. The gill-openings are lateral, and usually number five, though one species has six and another seven. With the exception of the afore-mentioned BASKING-SHARK and the PORT JACKSON SHARK, which the writer met with in Australia, they are all more or less dangerous; and when of insufficient size to be harmful to man, do great damage among the lines and nets of the fishermen. Indeed, the

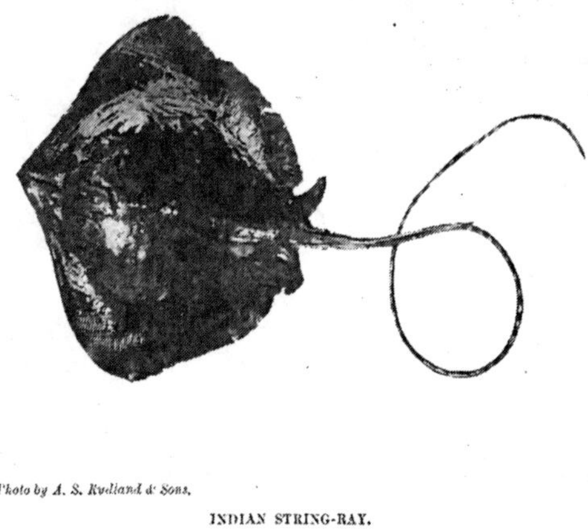

Photo by A. S. Rudland & Sons.

INDIAN STRING-RAY.

The tail is armed with a powerful poison-spine.

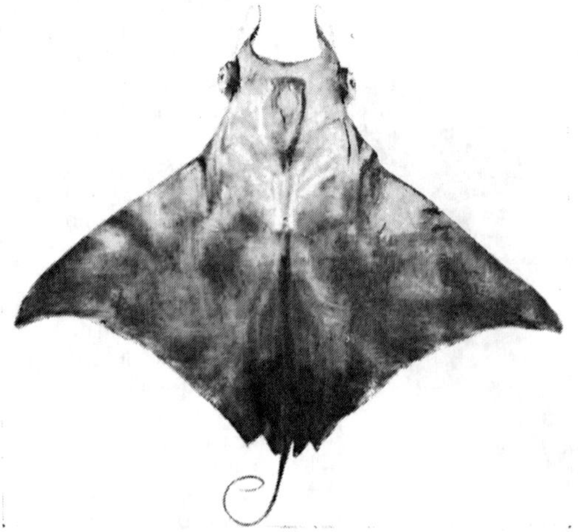

Photo by W. Saville-Kent, F.Z.S.] *[Milford-on-Sea.*

HORNED OX-RAY, OR DEVIL-FISH.

This species and its allies attain enormous proportions. One taken at Barbadoes required seven yoke of oxen to draw it.

late Matthias Dunn of Mevagissey seriously urged on the Admiralty to dynamite them in the interests of the fishing industry. Most of the sharks deposit their eggs in the curious oblong vessels known by those who pick up the disused cases on the foreshore as "purses"; and these attach themselves to rocks and stones by long tendrils that cling to every support. A number of species (the PORBEAGLE and TOPE among British kinds), however, bring forth their young alive.

Between the Sharks and Rays there is a curious and interesting link in the form of the MONK-FISH, or ANGEL-FISH, which is common on all sandy shores, and a frequent victim of the trawl. Such local names as Mongrel-skate and Shark-ray indicate a widespread acceptance of its intermediate position between the two groups under notice. Like some of the sharks already noticed, it produces living young, and its maximum size may be set down as at any rate over 7 feet. The writer measured and weighed one trawled in Bournemouth Bay during the summer of 1896. Its length was nearly 4½ feet, and its weight rather less than 50 lbs. Like many of the rays, this species feeds to a great extent on flat-fishes.

In outward form the monk-fish, though it is in reality more nearly allied to the sharks, brings us by an easy transition to the flattened RAYS, with their long whip-like tails and pointed snouts. There are a dozen, or rather more if we count casual visitors, of these skates and rays in British seas, the largest being the great EAGLE-RAY, examples of which have been recorded of the enormous weight of 1,000 lbs. Many of the smaller kinds are studded with sharp spines, curved in some species, and the THORNBACK owes to these

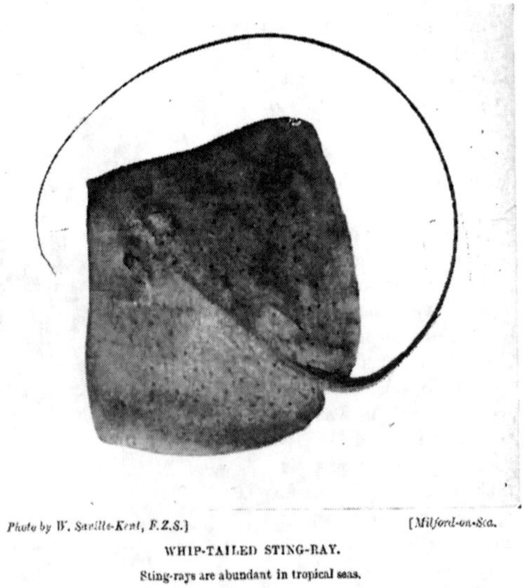

Photo by W. Saville-Kent, F.Z.S.] *[Milford-on-Sea.*

WHIP-TAILED STING-RAY.

Sting-rays are abundant in tropical seas.

its trivial name. All these rays, in fact, have some form or other of formidable offensive and defensive apparatus. The STING-RAY has on its tail a fearful serrated dagger, 6 or 8 inches long in large examples; while the TORPEDO- or NUMB-FISH has electric organs in the head, with the aid of which it can give a shock sufficiently strong to paralyse the fishes on which it feeds.

Photo by W. Saville-Kent, F.Z.S.] [Milford-on-Sea.

SHOVEL-NOSED SKATE.

Known also as the Halavi Ray.

Two interesting peculiarities of the rays deserve notice in concluding this chapter. The first is that their egg-purses, instead of attaching themselves with filaments to weeds and rocks, like those of the sharks, are provided with a sticky secretion which answers the same purpose of anchoring them in security from currents that would carry them out into deep, cold water. The second is the sexual difference in the teeth, which are pointed in the male and flat in the female. Whether this difference in the teeth (which may be likened to that between the bills of the male and female Huia-bird of New Zealand) indicates a corresponding difference in food, or, on the other hand, some co-operation between the sexes in procuring it, is an interesting question that our present slight knowledge of the habits of these fishes does not enable us to answer.

Finally, attention must be drawn to the remarkable transformation which the breast-fins and tail have undergone. The former have developed into powerful swimming-organs, locomotion being effected by their undulatory movements, instead of by similar movements of the whole body, or by side-to-side motions of the tail, as in other fishes. Whilst the latter, no longer used in swimming, has either been reduced to a mere vestige, as in the HORNED OX-RAY, or has become developed into a long and tapering "whip-lash," provided with a poison-spine. In such cases the long tail is used to encircle prey, and at the same time to force the victim on to the deadly spine.

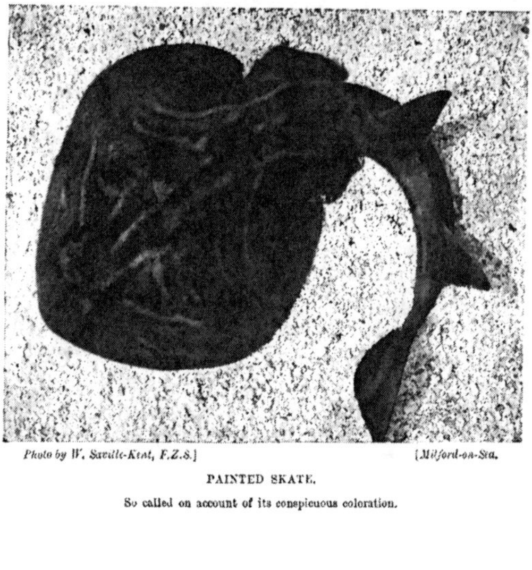

Photo by W. Saville-Kent, F.Z.S.] [Milford-on-Sea.

PAINTED SKATE.

So called on account of its conspicuous coloration.

BOOK V. JOINTED ANIMALS.

CHAPTER I.

THE CRAB AND SCORPION GROUPS.

BY W. F. KIRBY, F.L.S.

Photo by E. Connold.

BARNACLES.

A species which commonly attaches itself to ships' bottoms and floating wreckage.

THIS section of animals is often called a "sub-kingdom," and differs from back-boned animals in having the framework of the body outside. That is, instead of a skeleton, Crabs, Spiders, Centipedes, and Insects are protected either by a hard shelly casing, or by a tough skin, to which the muscles are attached; and this arrangement renders them much stronger and much less susceptible to injury, in proportion to their size, than vertebrate animals. They have cold blood, generally of a white colour; and their bodies and limbs are usually composed of a considerable number of separate joints.

The group is a very large one, and it is probable that there are at least 300,000 different kinds of insects already known, while the total number of species now existing is estimated by different entomologists as from two to ten millions. It is, therefore, no exaggeration to say that every word of our brief account of the Insects represents from ten to twenty known species at least. The other classes of the group are also very numerous. Our account must necessarily be very short; the characters of the principal classes of the Jointed Animals are referred to in their places.

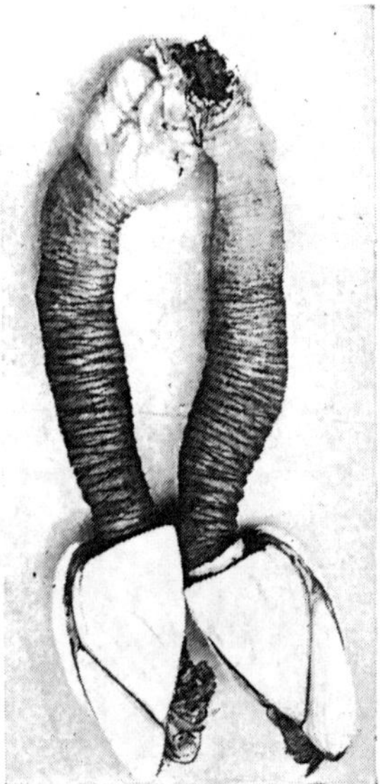

Photo by W. P. Dando, F.Z.S., Regent's Park.

A PAIR OF BARNACLES.

The larger size of this photograph exhibits more structural details than the last.

CRABS, LOBSTERS, SHRIMPS, WOOD-LICE, BARNACLES, ETC.

Jointed animals are generally provided with one pair of long jointed organs, called "antennæ," a naturalised word derived from the Latin, in which language *antenna* means a sail-yard. They are often called "feelers," and usually fulfil this function at least; but they are also frequently organs of smell, and sometimes probably of hearing and other senses. One peculiarity of the CRAB and LOBSTER group is that they are generally furnished with two pairs instead of one pair of these organs.

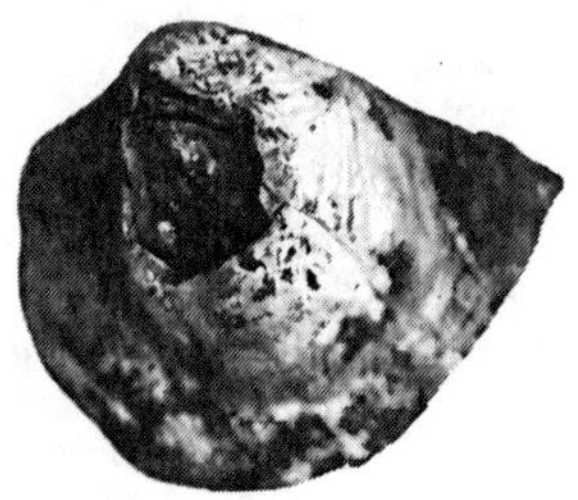

Photo by W. P. Dando, F.Z.S.] *[Regent's Park.*

ACORN-BARNACLE.

The general appearance is so different from the Stalked Barnacle that it is difficult to believe the two belong to the same group.

They are nearly all aquatic animals, by far the larger portion being marine, and they breathe with gills. They are provided with a hard calcareous or horny covering. The head is not separated from the trunk, as in insects; and they are provided with a number of jointed organs, usually classified as three pairs of jaws, three pairs of foot-jaws, and five pairs of legs in the more typical families; but in the smaller and more aberrant species the number is more variable. In their early stages they frequently pass through very extraordinary changes of form, but after assuming their adult shape they grow by casting their shells at intervals.

We will now notice a few typical examples of the different groups of these creatures.

The BRINE-SHRIMP is a little reddish creature about half an inch long, which prefers the concentrated solution of brine-pits to sea-water. It has eleven pairs of legs, and, notwithstanding its name, the front portion of its body is considerably broader and flatter in proportion than that of a real shrimp, the other half consisting of a jointed tail.

BARNACLES were formerly considered to be shell-fish, but are now usually classed with the crabs and lobsters, because, when they are young, they appear as freely swimming creatures, with one eye, two antennæ, and six pairs of jointed limbs. When they grow larger, they fix themselves to a rock or some other object by the head, and develop a shell, usually composed of several pieces. The commonest is the ACORN-BARNACLE, the white shell of which, measuring rather less than an inch across, swarms on rocks at the seaside. It is shaped like a limpet, but open at the top. The GOOSE-BARNACLES hang down by a stalk, and their jointed shells more resemble those of a mussel than that of a limpet, though they are composed of several pieces. Various species similar to both those mentioned are found on piers, rocks, the bottoms of ships, and even sometimes on the skin of whales.

In dark cellars in the country, under loose bark, or under pieces of wood which have been left in the fields, we often see creeping about brown creatures about half an inch long, with jointed bodies and antennæ, and short jointed legs. They are called WOOD-LICE, and several species roll themselves up into a ball when alarmed. These creatures feed chiefly on decaying vegetable substances; and there is a larger marine species much like them, which is common in holes and crannies in the rocks on the seashore.

There are other curious creatures, called WHALE-LICE and FISH-LICE, which are parasitic in their habits. Some of these look like spiders, and one or two have enormously long legs; but others are of strange and almost indescribable forms, and sometimes without legs at all. One species, found on the sprat, has two long appendages at the end of its body not unlike a pair of compasses.

SHRIMPS and PRAWNS are red when cooked, but when alive are very pretty semi-transparent objects, which may be seen swimming about through the glass of aquariums placed against the wall. Prawns are larger than shrimps, and have a strong

Photo by W. P. Dando, F.Z.S. Regent's Park.

WOOD-LOUSE.

A land representative of a numerous marine group.

Photo by W. P. Dando, F.Z.S.] *[Regent's Park.*

SHRIMP.

A species which plays an important part in the food-supply of London.

serrated spine in front of the head. Shrimps and prawns, of which several kinds are found off the British coasts, generally prefer shallow water, with a sandy bottom. In most of these the first two pairs of feet are divided to form a pair of pincers at the extremity; but in such small creatures this is easily overlooked, unless special attention is directed to it. It is different with the LOBSTERS and CRAYFISH, which much resemble shrimps in form, but are very much larger, and armed with a pair of very large pincer-like claws, in addition to the other legs. Lobsters live in the sea, in holes in the rocks, into which they dart backwards, and there protect themselves with only the head and claws projecting at the opening, ready to face any intruder. Crayfish, which are smaller, live in holes in the banks of brooks and rivers. There are many species, some of large size and bright colours. The COMMON LOBSTER is black when living, but other species are red, blue, or variegated.

Sometimes, if we pick up a whelk-shell on the beach, we shall find it inhabited, not by a mollusc, but by a crab, with its legs and claws wedged together, so as to fill the aperture completely—one claw, much larger than the other, resting in front; and if we pull it out, we shall find that, though the front of its body and the legs and claws are hard, like those of an ordinary crab, it has a long, soft, fleshy tail, absolutely defenceless and unprotected. Crabs belonging to this curious section are called HERMIT-CRABS, and protect themselves by taking possession of shells which they have either found empty or appropriated by the easy and economical process of devouring the owners. The few species found on the British coasts are all small, and more frequently noticed in whelk-shells than in any others; but tropical species attain to a considerable size, and may sometimes be found in shells measuring 3 or 4 inches across at the opening.

Crabs are distinguished from the lobsters by their compact form, and by having the short tail turned in under the body. There are a great number of species, differing much in size, shape, and appearance. One of the best known in England is the large EDIBLE CRAB, which may often be seen in fishmongers' shops, and, unlike the lobster, does not change much in colour when boiled. Every visitor to the seaside must

Photo by C. N. Macrogeni] *[Smyrna.*

FRESH-WATER CRAB.

In general appearance very similar to the common shore-crab.

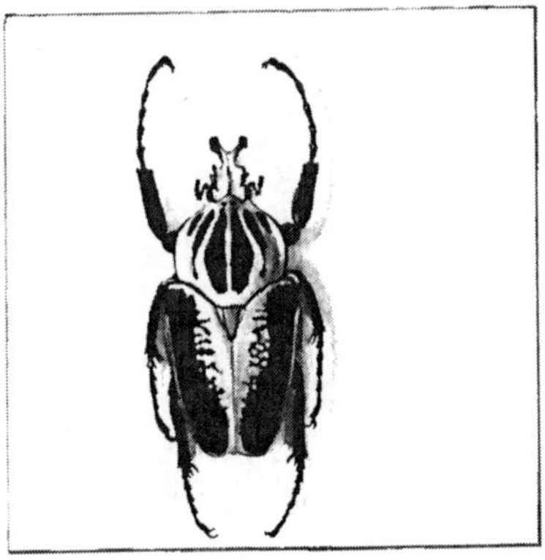

GOLIATH BEETLE
West Africa (Half natural size)

BRAZILIAN BEE
(Enlarged [illegible])

GRASSHOPPER
From [illegible] (Slightly reduced.)

CANDLE FLY
From Ceylon. (Slightly reduced.)

AUSTRALIAN ROBBER-FLY
(Slightly reduced.)

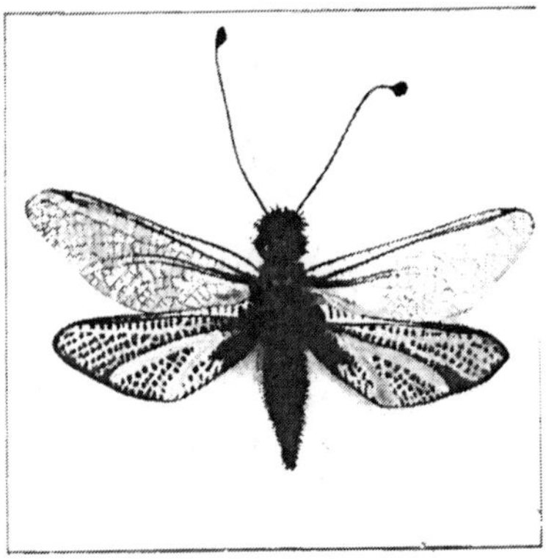

JAPANESE ASCALAPHUS
([illegible])

Photos by W. P. Dando, F.Z.S., Regent's Park.

Photo by W. Saville-Kent, F.Z.S.] [*Milford-on-Sea.*

SPIDER-CRAB.

An active sea-scavenger.

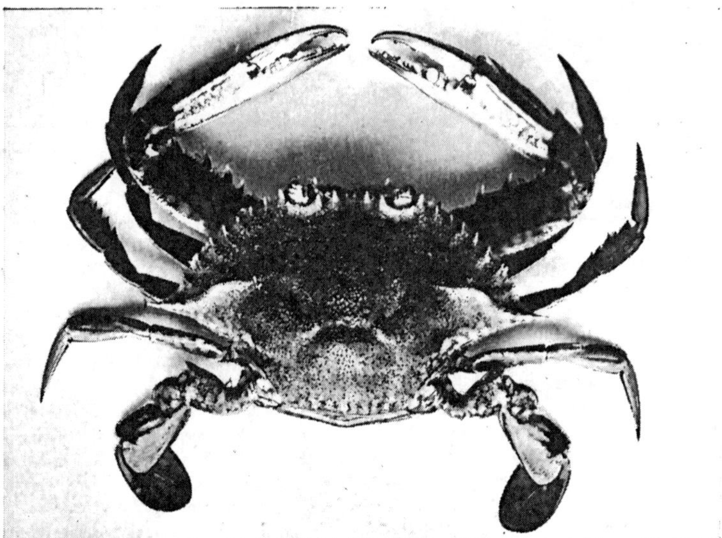

Photo by W. Saville-Kent, F.Z.S.] [*Milford-on-Sea.*

BLUE CRAB.

Much esteemed for the table.

have seen numbers of the little greenish SHORE-CRABS, running about on the sand, or over seaweed-covered rocks, at low tide. These small crabs are harmless, but large kinds are able to give a very severe pinch. It is related that when the great chemist Sir Humphry Davy was a boy he used to maintain that pain was no evil, until a large crab gripped his toe one day when he was bathing, after which he changed his opinion.

Some crabs are smooth and shining, but others are covered with bosses, excrescences, and spines, which give them a very formidable appearance, and must be a useful protection against any enemies to whose attacks they are exposed. In many species one of the two great claws is always much larger than the other. Some have round bodies, others are oval or nearly square; some have short legs, and others very long ones. The species differ much in their habits; and in tropical countries there are land-crabs which live entirely on shore, and others which are amphibious, and climb cocoanut-trees, to get at the nuts. As a general rule, however, crabs are carnivorous and marine, and play the part of sea-scavengers.

The KING-CRABS differ very much from any now living in the British seas, but are generally considered to be allied to the Trilobites, an extinct family which appears to have been extremely numerous in very ancient seas. King-crabs are 2 or 3 feet long from the front of the body to the end of the tail. The front part of the body is entirely covered by a curved oval shield, while the hinder part of the body is much narrower, and armed at the sides with strong teeth directed backwards, and also with a long and strong spear, something like that of a sword-fish on a small scale, as long as the rest of the body. The few species known exhibit an instance of what is called "discontinuous distribution," since they are found only on the coasts of the Moluccas, East Indies, and the Southern United States and West Indies.

Photo by W. Saville-Kent, F.Z.S.] *[Milford-on-Sea.*

FIGHTING CRABS.

The males are remarkable for having one large scarlet claw, the other being rudimentary (the females possess two small claws only). The eyes also are seated at the end of long stalks.

SCORPIONS, SPIDERS, AND MITES.

These creatures form a peculiar group in which there are only two principal divisions of the body, the head and thorax being fused into one mass, and the abdomen forming a separate division. In the Mites, however, the body forms a single round or oval mass, even the division between the thorax and the abdomen having disappeared. The members of the group have no antennæ, but two pairs of jaws and a pair of palpi, frequently very long, and armed with a pincer-like arrangement at the end, in which case they are called "foot-jaws." Except in some of the mites, which have only four or six, all the group have eight legs. They pass through no metamorphosis, but moult several times after quitting the egg before attaining their full growth. They have frequently several pairs of simple eyes, but no compound eyes like the large pair on the head of most insects.

In the SCORPIONS, of which there is a considerable variety in different parts of the world.

Photo by Highley.

EGYPTIAN SCORPION.

A fairly large and venomous representative of the group.

the united head and thorax are comparatively short; but the abdomen is very long, and divided into a broad half, consisting of seven segments, and a narrow tail of five very movable segments, besides a sharp, curved sting at the extremity. There are from three to six pairs of eyes on the head and thorax, and in front of the body projects a pair of very large pincer-bearing foot-jaws. Scorpions are generally of a yellowish or black colour; and the largest black scorpions of Africa and India sometimes measure as much as 9 inches in length. They are nocturnal creatures, hiding under stones, or in holes in the ground, or in crevices in walls during the day. They kill the insects and other small animals on which they feed with their stings, the sting of one of the large black scorpions, like that of the large tropical centipedes, being as painful and dangerous as that of a snake. There are a few small and comparatively harmless species found on the shores of the Mediterranean, but most of the scorpions inhabit warmer countries.

The JOINTED SPIDERS are creatures 1 or 2 inches long, remarkable for having the head and the segments of the thorax separated from each other, so as to form distinct divisions of the body. They have rather long and very hairy legs, and only one pair of well-developed eyes, another pair being rudimentary. Some species are diurnal and others nocturnal in their habits. They feed on insects, and sometimes on small birds, etc., and can inflict a very painful bite. They are found in South-eastern Europe, Africa, Southern Asia, and from the Southern States of North America south to Chili and Argentina.

Photo by Highley.

EGYPTIAN SCORPION.

Shows the sting uplifted for attack.

The FALSE SCORPIONS, or BOOK-SCORPIONS, are

small animals resembling scorpions in shape, but with no sting, and the abdomen not narrowed into a tail. They are sometimes found in houses among dusty old books, as well as out of doors among moss, or under stones or bark. Sometimes they cling to the legs of flies; they are believed to feed on mites and other small creatures, but not to injure the flies, only employing them as a convenient method of being conveyed from one place to another.

Photo by Highley.

TREE TRAP-DOOR SPIDER OF BRAZIL.

Trap-door spiders are plentiful in some parts of Europe, but there is only one British representative of the family.

The WHIP-SCORPIONS are not unlike scorpions, and have large claws, but the front legs are very long, slender, and whip-like, and there is either no tail, or else a long, slender, whip-like one without a sting. They are inhabitants of warm countries, and, rightly or wrongly, are reputed to be venomous. Different species measure from 1 inch to 4 or 5 inches in length.

The curious HARVEST-MEN have two eyes, a small, compact, oval body, large pincers, and very long, slender legs, longer and more slender in proportion to their size than those of crane-flies, and equally liable to be broken off, if the owner is roughly handled. They feed on plant-lice and other small insects.

We now come to the large and important group of SPIDERS, which more frequently attract attention in England than any others of the group. The abdomen is not usually divided into distinct segments, and is connected with the thorax by a short stalk. Spiders have strong, poisonous jaws, which make some of the larger species formidable even to man, and several pairs of eyes; while many possess an apparatus for spinning a strong silken web, in which they entangle their prey, consisting in England chiefly of flies and other winged insects.

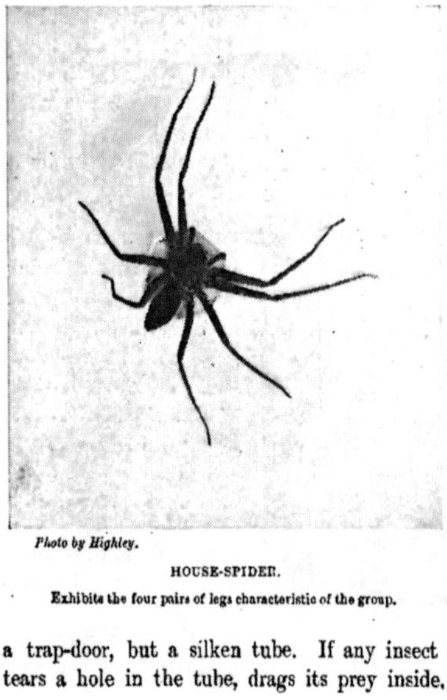

Photo by Highley.

HOUSE-SPIDER.

Exhibits the four pairs of legs characteristic of the group.

The largest known spiders are usually placed first in the series. These are the great BIRD-CATCHING SPIDERS of South America, some of which have bodies 3 inches long, and strong, hairy legs. These large spiders have now been proved not only to feed on insects, but occasionally on humming-birds, and even sometimes on larger birds, such as finches.

The TRAP-DOOR SPIDERS are allied, but smaller, perhaps averaging about an inch in length. They construct a silken gallery in the ground, with a round door, which they shut behind them when they enter. There is only one species in England, which does not form a trap-door, but a silken tube. If any insect settles on it, the spider clutches it from within, tears a hole in the tube, drags its prey inside, and then repairs the rent.

Different spiders have many curious methods of capturing their insect-prey. Some catch insects by running after them, and others by leaping on them, while those which spin webs are also very dissimilar in their habits and in their abodes. The brown HOUSE-SPIDERS spin webs in any room left undisturbed long enough to allow them to construct them. On the other hand, the ORB-SPINNERS, or GARDEN-SPIDERS, construct elaborate webs out of doors. One of the most beautiful of these is the DIADEM-SPIDER, which is nearly an inch long, and of a green or reddish colour, with a white cross bordered with black on the back. The web is very regularly constructed, the principal threads radiating in all directions from a common centre, where the spider generally sits in fine weather, ready to rush out upon any insect which may become entangled in the web.

The GOSSAMER-SPIDERS spin light webs, which are easily carried up into the air, and upon which the spiders are borne from one place to another. Sometimes on an autumn morning the air may be seen to be full of these floating webs, which also cover the grass and bushes where they have settled. The WATER-SPIDERS, again, construct a habitation of water-tight silk under water, like a diving-bell, and inflate it by carrying down bubbles of air from the surface, entangled in the hairs of the body.

The nesting-habits of many spiders are very curious. The eggs are usually laid in a silken case, and the RUNNING-SPIDERS may often be seen with the egg-cases attached to the end of the body, as in the female cockroach.

The males of many spiders are much smaller than the females, and are very liable to be devoured by their partners.

Among the most curious of the group are the SPINY SPIDERS, strange, horny, semicircular

Photo by B. H. Bentley] *[Sheffield.*

GARDEN-SPIDER IN WEB.

A beautiful example of the structure of the web.

creatures, studded with strong spines. They are allied to the Garden-spiders, but confined to the tropics.

The SPOTTED SPIDER is a very beautiful species, often seen among cases of mixed insects, etc., sent from India. It is black, with brown abdomen and numerous yellow spots, and about 1½ inch long; the body is much longer than broad, and the legs are about twice as long as the body.

Attempts have been made to turn spider-silk to commercial purposes, but the great difficulty is that spiders are so voracious and cannibalistic in their propensities that they cannot be kept in captivity, for they will kill and eat each other as long as there are any left, to the very last spider. The silk of some of the large tropical spiders is sometimes strong enough to cause a man much annoyance when riding through the woods, striking up against his face, and sometimes knocking off his hat.

The last section includes the MITES and TICKS, most of which are small or microscopic. The whole body forms one round or oval mass, with scattered hairs, and eight legs, though most mites have only six legs when young, while the PLANT-MITES have only four. The largest mites are those called TICKS. There are one or two small British species which are sometimes sufficiently troublesome; but in many warm countries they are a far more serious nuisance, lurking on the herbage, and fixing their proboscis in the skin of any passing man or animal, and retaining their hold till they are gorged with blood, and allow themselves to drop off by their own weight.

Photo by Highley.

SPANISH TARANTULA.

So called because the bite of an Italian species was supposed to produce a fit of melancholia, which could only be cured by the tune known as the "tarentella."

Among the smaller mites some species are parasitic on warm-blooded animals, causing itch, mange, and other diseases; while many infest insects, especially humble-bees and dung-beetles. These are of considerable size for mites; and there are other bright scarlet species which are sometimes found on saw-flies, dragon-flies, etc. Many feed on decaying animal or vegetable matter, such as the CHEESE-MITE and the SUGAR-MITE, the former being a very familiar and interesting microscopic object; and others, again, are very destructive to plants, like the small scarlet mite known in greenhouses as the RED SPIDER.

Among the plant-feeding mites are the four-legged GALL-MITES, which produce galls or other excrescences on the plants which they infest.

Mites are probably almost as varied in their forms and habits and as interesting objects of study as insects or spiders; but the group is somewhat neglected by naturalists, owing to the small size of most of the species, and the consequent difficulty of collecting and preserving them.

CENTIPEDES AND MILLIPEDES.

These are creatures with long, worm-like bodies, composed of a number of rings or segments, each provided with one or two pairs of legs. They have one pair of antennæ, like insects, but they pass through no metamorphoses, nor do they moult. Instead of this, they begin their existence, on quitting the egg, without legs, or with only three pairs of legs, and continue to add to the number of their segments and legs until they have attained their full growth. They are called Centipedes, or Hundred-legs, and Millipedes, or Thousand-legs; but in the majority of species the number of legs is considerably below 100, though in some few it may exceed 300.

The CENTIPEDES have only one pair of legs attached to each segment of the body, and are carnivorous, being armed with a pair of strong mandibles, which are perforated poison-fangs. The British species are all small and harmless, but the bite of the large tropical centipedes is more painful and almost as dangerous as that of a snake. Centipedes are long, broad, flattened creatures, with about twenty-one pairs of legs, and sometimes measure more than a foot in length. A reddish centipede, belonging to an allied family, is common in England under stones and in loose mould. It has long antennæ and fifteen pairs of legs, and feeds chiefly on worms. It is about an inch long.

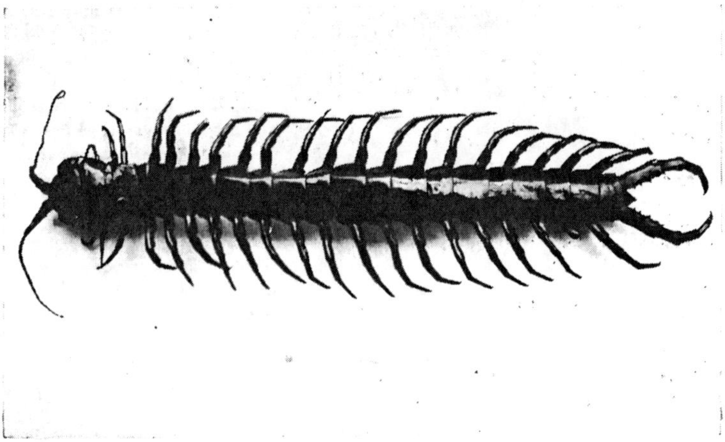

Photo by W. P. Dando, F.Z.S.] *[Regent's Park.*

GIANT CENTIPEDE.

Most centipedes have considerably fewer than a hundred legs.

The ELECTRIC CENTIPEDES are much longer and more slender than the others in proportion to their length, with rather short antennæ, and short and very numerous legs. They are of a white or yellow colour, and 2 or 3 inches long. All are nocturnal in their habits, and feed on decaying animal or vegetable matter, and are fond of ripe fruit. They emit a pale phosphorescence, visible in the dark along the track over which they have crawled.

MILLIPEDES are not venomous, and feed chiefly on soft vegetable matter. Except the first three behind the head, which are provided with only one pair each, every segment bears two pairs instead of one pair of legs. The COMMON SNAKE-MILLIPEDE is about an inch and a half long, and is brown, with yellow rings and ninety-nine pairs of short white legs. It is nearly as destructive as the Wire-worms, which it resembles in its habits, and may often be seen clinging to a partly eaten potato. Millipedes are able to roll themselves up into a spiral. Many foreign kinds grow to a much larger size, measuring nearly a foot in length. They are more frequently sent to Europe from foreign countries than centipedes, probably because they are sluggish, harmless creatures which do not bite.

The members of one family of millipedes, called PILL-MILLIPEDES, are so similar to wood-lice

Photo by W. P. Dando, F.Z.S.] [*Regent's Park.*

GIANT MILLIPEDE.

Shows the absence of jaws, which distinguishes these creatures from the predatory centipedes.

in shape and appearance that they might easily be mistaken for them, and they exhibit the same habit of rolling themselves up into a ball. One species is not uncommon in England.

A curious genus, generally placed in a distinct class by itself, includes a few species which may be called SLIMY MILLIPEDES. The species are found in widely separated parts of the world, chiefly in the most southern regions, such as South America, South Africa, Australia, and New Zealand, though one or two are known from Ceylon and the West Indies. They resemble slimy caterpillars, with conspicuous antennæ, and from thirteen to forty pairs of legs. The body is not distinctly divided into segments, and it exudes a very viscous slime, which acts like bird-lime in capturing the small insects which form at least a part of the food of these creatures, but which will not adhere to their own bodies. These creatures are found among decaying vegetable matter.

INJURIOUS CREATURES.

We are sometimes inclined to complain of our English climate, but we have cause to congratulate ourselves that it is far less prolific of noxious creatures than many others. We have no venomous scorpions or centipedes, and are not obliged to shake such intruders out of our boots before we can venture to put them on. Since the country has been so well drained, we are very little troubled with gnats, which breed in standing water, and are equally troublesome in cold countries like Lapland, and warm countries like South America. Nevertheless, several very troublesome creatures, not native to this country, have taken up their abode with us permanently, and more care should perhaps be exercised in preventing the possible introduction of others. Among the most troublesome of our household insects are bugs, cockroaches, and house-ants, all of which have been introduced from abroad. Among field- and garden-pests, the American Blight (which destroys our apple- and pear-trees) and the Hessian Fly are probably invaders from abroad; but the latter does not seem to have committed great ravages in this country. Among pests which have not succeeded in establishing themselves here, but which we should be specially on our guard against, are the White Ants, which are found as far north as Bordeaux, and are terribly destructive to woodwork, wherever they are met with; the Gypsy-moth, very destructive on the Continent and in North America, but extinct as a British species, perhaps because there is something inimical to its constitution in our climate; and the Colorado Potato-beetle, which is only kept out of Europe by incessant vigilance. But apart from actually injurious insects, it is remarkable how many species which are common everywhere on the Continent are either absent from Britain, or are only met with in very restricted localities. Let us hope that we may long enjoy our comparative immunity from noxious insects in Britain.

CHAPTER II.

INSECTS.

INSECTS are easily distinguished from the other jointed animals by many salient characters. They have one pair of antennæ, two large compound eyes, composed of a great number of facets, and sometimes one, two, or three simple eyes placed on the crown or front of the head. In its adult condition an insect is composed of three different parts, which can be most readily noticed in a wasp. There is the head, with the antennæ and mouth-parts; the thorax, to which one or two pairs of wings are attached above, and three pairs of legs below; and the abdomen. Insects breathe through openings, called "stigmata," in the sides of the thorax and abdomen. They never possess more than six legs in the perfect state, the abdominal legs present in caterpillars, etc., disappearing in the adult condition. They generally pass through what is called a "metamorphosis,"—four different stages of life, called respectively egg; larva or caterpillar; pupa, nymph, or chrysalis; and imago, or perfect insect.

Insects are divided into several large sections, of which the following seven are the most important, and many entomologists prefer to include all insects under them:—

Sheath-winged Insects, or Beetles; Straight-winged Insects, or Earwigs, Cockroaches, Soothsayers, Stick-insects, Crickets, Grasshoppers, and Locusts; Nerve-winged or Lace-winged Insects, or Dragon-flies and their relatives; Stinging Four-winged Insects, or Ants, Bees and Wasps, and their allies; Scale-winged Insects, or Butterflies and Moths; Half-winged Insects, or Bugs and Frog-hoppers; Two-winged Insects, or Flies.

We proceed to notice these orders separately.

SHEATH-WINGED INSECTS, OR BEETLES.

BY THE REV. THEODORE WOOD, F.E.S.

BEETLES are distinguished from most other insects by the fact that the front wings are not employed in flight, but are modified into horny sheaths, which cover and protect the lower pair while not in use. This arrangement, however, is also found in the Earwigs as well as in the so-called "Black-beetle" and its allies, and it is to be noted that the wing-cases of beetles lie evenly side by side together when the wings are folded, while the folding of the wings themselves is transverse as well as longitudinal. The number of species is very great, upwards of 100,000 having already been described, of which about 3,400 have been taken in the British Islands.

The order is again divided into several smaller groups, first among which stand the predaceous beetles of the land. Of these the common English TIGER-BEETLE is a familiar example. It is found on sandy and peaty heaths, and may be known at once by its bright green wing-cases, marked with white spots, and the metallic blue of the abdomen. The legs are coppery. It flies with great swiftness in the hot sunshine, taking to wing as readily as a blue-bottle fly, and feeds entirely upon other insects.

Photo by W. P. Dando, F.Z.S., Regent's Park.

TIGER-BEETLE.

The colouring of this insect is bright green with white markings and coppery legs.

Another representative of the group is rich golden green in colour, with coppery reflections. It is only an occasional visitor to Britain, but abounds in France and Germany, where it feeds upon the caterpillars of the famous Processionary Moth, and is largely instrumental in checking their ravages in the great oak forests.

Familiar to almost all is the PURPLE GROUND-BEETLE, so plentiful in gardens, and easily recognisable by the violet margin to the black wing-cases. It pours out an evil-smelling liquid from the end of the body when handled.

The curious red-and-blue BOMBARDIER, which, when interfered with, discharges a little puff of bluish-white smoke from the tip of the abdomen, accompanied by a distinct report, is also a member of this group. It is found under stones on river-banks, and also on the coast.

Photo by W. P. Dando, F.Z.S., Regent's Park.

GROUND-BEETLE.

The beetles of this group are generally of a black or bronzy colour, some species being beautifully metallic.

Next come the predaceous beetles of the water, of which we have a well-known British representative in the GREAT BROWN WATER-BEETLE. This insect, which is plentiful in weedy ponds, swims by means of its hind limbs, which are modified into broad, flat oars, with a mechanical arrangement for "feathering" as they are drawn back after making each stroke. It flies by night, often travelling for a long distance from one pond to another, and regains the water by suddenly folding its wings and allowing itself to fall from a height. In the female insect the wing-cases are grooved for about two-thirds of their length.

Photo by W. P. Dando, F.Z.S., Regent's Park.

GREAT BROWN WATER-BEETLE (MALE).

A large olive-brown species, about an inch in length, and nearly half as broad. The wing-cases of the female are grooved.

This beetle must not be confounded with the still larger BLACK WATER-BEETLE, which belongs to another group. This fine insect, which is not predaceous in the perfect state, is locally plentiful in ditches, and is in great request as an inmate of the fresh-water aquarium. The hind limbs are not modified for swimming purposes.

Next in order come the COCKTAILS, so called from their curious habit of turning up the end of the body when alarmed. To this group belong most of the tiny "flies" which cause such severe pain when they find their way into the eyes. Some species, however, attain to a considerable size, the well-known DEVIL'S COACH-HORSE being fully an inch in length. The great majority are scavengers, being found in carrion, manure, and decaying vegetable matter. A few, however, are lodgers in the nests of ants, by whom they appear to be regarded as pets and treated with the utmost kindness.

The next group includes the curious insects popularly known as BURYING-BEETLES, which inter the bodies of small animals in the ground, scooping out the earth from underneath them by means of their broad and powerful heads, and shovelling it back when the carcases have sunk to a sufficient depth. The eggs are laid in the carrion thus buried. Most of these beetles are distinguished by broad blotches or bars of orange on the wing-cases, but one common British species is entirely black.

Allied to these, and very similar in habits, are the FLAT BURYING-BEETLES, of which there are about a dozen British species. In the best known of these the thorax is dull red in colour, and the black wing-cases are curiously wrinkled. Another species is reddish yellow in colour, with two round black spots on each wing-case. It is found on oak-trees, and feeds upon caterpillars.

Photo by W. P. Dando, F.Z.S., Regent's Park.

BLACK WATER-BEETLE.

A shining black species, longer, narrower, and more convex than the Great Brown Water-beetle.

The LEAF-HORNED BEETLES are distinguished by the fact that the terminal joints of the antennæ lie one upon another like the leaves of a book. In many cases they can be expanded at will into a broad fan-like club. The well-known STAG-BEETLE of Great Britain is a representative of this group. It is a somewhat local species, being plentiful in some parts of the country, and entirely unknown in others. The grub lives for several years in the trunks of elm-trees, feeding upon the solid wood. When fully grown, it buries itself in the earth, and constructs a large cocoon, in which it passes the chrysalis stage of its existence. The perfect beetle emerges in November, but remains within the cocoon until the following June. In the female the jaws are very much smaller than in the male, but are nevertheless more formidable as weapons. The insect may often be seen flying on warm summer evenings.

A still larger insect belonging to the same group is the HERCULES BEETLE, found in the West Indies and tropical America, a male of average size being nearly 5 inches in length. In this beetle the thorax is prolonged into a horn, which is curved downwards, while the head is produced into a similar horn curved upwards, so that the two look like a pair of enormous jaws. It has been stated that these horns, both of which are furnished with tooth-like projections, are employed in sawing off the smaller branches of trees, the beetle grasping

Photos by W. P. Dando, F.Z.S.] *[Regent's Park.*

TWO BURYING-BEETLES.

These insects are about an inch in length; many are black, but others have orange-red bands on the wing-cases.

a bough firmly, and flying round and round in a circle, till the wood is completely cut through. This assertion, however, is totally unworthy of credit. An example of the beetle—evidently imported—was recently found crawling on a hedge near Biggleswade.

One of the largest of all known beetles is DRURY'S GOLIATH BEETLE, a native of the Gaboon, whose body is almost as big as the closed fist of a man. It appears to feed, while a grub, on the wood of decaying trees, and undergoes its transformation to the chrysalis state in an earthen cocoon, the peculiarity of which is that a thick belt, or ridge, runs round the middle. How this belt is formed is a mystery, as it lies upon the outside, while the grub necessarily constructs the cocoon from the inside. Several living examples of this beetle were exhibited in the summer of 1898 in the Insect-house of the Zoological Gardens in the Regent's Park, where they remained for five or six weeks, feeding on the flesh of melons. A photograph of this beetle will be found in the Coloured Plate.

The common COCKCHAFER belongs to another division of the same group. This insect is extremely injurious, as the grub lives for three years or more underground, feeding on the roots of various cultivated plants. The perfect beetle appears in May and June, and is only too plentiful almost everywhere. A month or so later its place is taken by the SUMMER CHAFER, or JUNE BUG, which may often be seen flying in hundreds round the tops of

Photo by W. P. Dando, F.Z.S.] *[Regent's Park.*

MALE STAG-BEETLE.

The males are often 2 inches long; the females have comparatively small jaws.

low trees soon after sunset, while the smaller COCH-Y-BONDDHU—the "Cocker-bundy" of the angler—often appears about the same time in hundreds of thousands. The beautiful ROSE-BEETLE, too, with its bright golden-green wing-cases marked with wavy whitish lines, may often be seen sunning itself in roses or on the blossoms of pinks.

Photo by W. P. Dando, F.Z.S., Regent's Park.

SKIPJACK BEETLE.

The larvæ of this family are known as Wire-worms.

The famous EGYPTIAN SCARABÆUS is also a member of this group. It is remarkable not only for the sacred character attributed to it by the ancient Egyptians, but also for its curious habit of rolling along balls of dung until it can find a soft spot in which to bury them. When the egg hatches, the grub feeds upon the dung, the quantity provided being exactly sufficient for its requirements. The common DOR BEETLE of Great Britain is allied to this insect; it tunnels down to a depth of 14 or 15 inches beneath a patch of excrement, and lays its egg at the bottom of the burrow.

The SKIPJACK BEETLES, parents of the well-known Wire-worms, which cause so much mischief by feeding upon the roots of cultivated crops, represent another group. These beetles owe their popular title to their singular method of regaining their feet when they happen to roll over upon their backs. Their bodies being very smooth and polished, and their legs very short, they cannot recover their footing in the ordinary manner. On the lower part of the body, however, is a highly elastic spine, known as

Photo by L. H. Joutel] *[New York.*

HERCULES BEETLE FLYING.

The most remarkable feature about this insect is its huge horn-like projection from the thorax, which is nearly as long as the rest of its body.

the "mucro," which lies in a sheath. When the beetle falls over, it arches its body into the form of a bow, resting only upon the head and the extreme tip of the abdomen, removes the spine from its sheath, and then drives it sharply back again. The result is that the central part of the body strikes the ground with such force that the insect springs into the air to a height of 2 or 3 inches. Then, turning half over as it falls, it alights on its feet.

The FIRE-FLY of the tropics belongs to the same group. The luminosity of this insect proceeds from two different parts of the body, a brilliant yellowish-green light shining out through two transparent window-like spots on the thorax, while an orange glow is visible on the lower surface of the abdomen. The exact cause of the light is unknown, as is also the manner of its control by the insect.

The same may be said of the common English GLOW-WORM, in which the light proceeds from the lower surface of the hind part of the body. The male of this insect is winged; the female is grub-like in appearance and wingless. The grub itself, which may be found in autumn, is also luminous, and feeds upon snails.

Another group includes a very large number of beetles of very varying character and appearance. Among these are the OIL-BEETLES, so called from their habit of exuding small drops of an oily liquid from the joints of their limbs when handled. The eggs are laid in batches of several thousand in holes in the ground, and the little long-legged grubs, on emerging, clamber up the stems of flowers, and hide themselves among the petals to await the coming of a bee. When one of the latter appears, two or three of the grubs cling to its hairy body, and are carried back to the nest, in which they live as parasites. One of these beetles may be seen commonly upon grassy banks in early spring.

Photo by B. H. Bentley] [*Sheffield.*

COCKCHAFER ON DAISY.

A very destructive insect which feeds on the leaves of trees. The larva devours the roots of plants, and is often so plentiful as to cause very serious mischief.

Allied to these insects is the BLISTER-BEETLE, or SPANISH FLY, so well known from its use in medicine. It is a very handsome species, of a bright golden-green colour, occasionally found in Great Britain on the foliage of ash-trees. In many parts of Southern Europe it is extremely abundant.

The beetles belonging to the large and important group of WEEVILS are characterised, as a rule, by the fact that the head is prolonged into a more or less long and slender snout, or "rostrum," at the end of which the jaws are situated. The number of species already known is above 20,000.

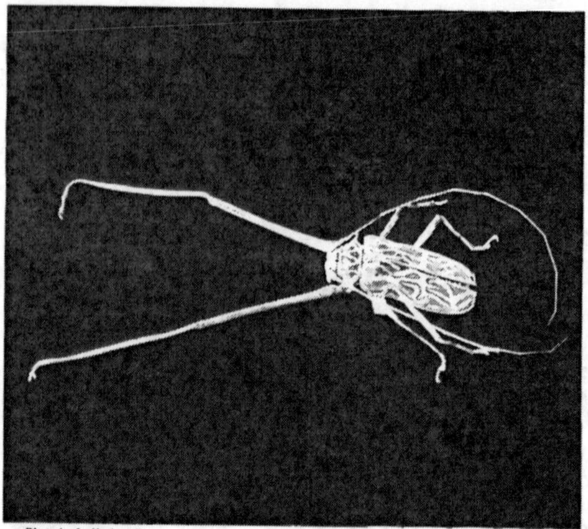

Photo by L. H. Joutel] *[New York.*

HARLEQUIN BEETLE.

Notice the enormous length of the front legs.

One of the largest and most famous of these insects is the DIAMOND-BEETLE of Brazil, the scales from whose wing-cases are so frequently mounted as microscopic objects. When viewed through a good instrument under a powerful light, the beauty of these scales is simply indescribable. All that one can say of them is that they seem to be composed of diamonds, rubies, topazes, and emeralds massed together in rich profusion, while diamonds are transformed into rubies, rubies into topazes, and topazes into emeralds at every change of light.

The OSIER-WEEVIL, a black-and-white species about three-eighths of an inch long, is found on osiers in Great Britain, the grub boring galleries in the stems, and often causing considerable damage. The well-known CORN-WEEVIL is still more destructive in granaries, the walls of which are often completely blackened by its crawling multitudes. The grub lives inside the grain, eating out the whole of the interior, and a single pair of the weevils are said to be capable of producing a family of more than 6,000 individuals in the course of a single season. The RICE-WEEVIL is equally destructive to rice, and may be recognised by the two red spots on each wing-case.

The famous "GRU-GRU" of the West Indies, which is regarded as so great a dainty both by the negroes and by many of the white colonists, is the grub of the PALM-WEEVIL. It lives in the stems of palm-trees, and also in those of sugar-canes, causing a great deal of mischief by its burrowings. When fully fed, it constructs a cocoon by tearing off strips of bark and weaving them neatly together. The SUGAR-WEEVIL is still more troublesome, feeding upon the juice of the sugar-cane, and affecting the entire plant in such a manner that sugar can no longer be manufactured from it.

Photo by J. Edwards] *[Colesborne.*

JUMPING-BEETLE, ALLIED TO THE TURNIP-FLEA.

It is about one-tenth of an inch in length.

"Bad" nuts are also due to one of these insects, the common NUT-WEEVIL, which introduces its egg into the kernel during the earlier stages of its development. When the grub hatches, it proceeds to devour the kernel, leaving a quantity of bad-flavoured "frass" behind it, while the shell is left untouched until the perfect insect emerges. An allied species attacks acorns in a similar manner.

Among the finest and largest of all beetles are many of those belonging to the great Long-horn group, of which the common BRITISH MUSK-BEETLE is a familiar example. This insect owes both its popular and scientific titles to its powerful odour, which perhaps resembles that of sweetbriar rather than musk, and can often be detected at a distance of twenty or thirty yards. The beetle, which is rich metallic green in colour, with long, slender antennæ, may be found in July sunning itself on the trunks or foliage of willow-trees. It varies considerably in size.

Still more plentiful is the WASP-BEETLE, with its black wing-cases banded with bright yellow. While flying, it may easily be mistaken for the insect whose name it bears. The grub lives in old posts, rails, hop-poles, etc., feeding upon the solid wood.

The TIMBERMAN is remarkable for the extreme length of the antennæ, which, in the male insect, are three or four times as long as the body, and trail out far behind it during flight. It is found, not uncommonly, in fir woods in Scotland.

The beautiful HARLEQUIN BEETLE of tropical America is one of the largest members of the group, and is remarkable for the great length of the front legs as well as for the singular colouring of the wing-cases. It lives almost entirely in the trees, swinging itself from branch to branch somewhat after the manner of a spider-monkey. When it ventures into the air, it is greatly incommoded by the size of its limbs and the length of its antennæ, and seems to have but little power of directing its course.

Another great group of beetles is that of the PLANT-EATERS, many of which are exceedingly beautiful. The REED-BEETLES of Britain, for example, are resplendent in crimson and green and purple and blue, while the metallic radiance of others has gained for them the title of GOLDEN APPLES.

Photo by J. Edwards, Colesborne.

REED-BEETLE.

Among the group to which this insect belongs are many of the most brilliantly coloured British beetles.

The notorious COLORADO BEETLE is a member of this group. It may be recognised at once by the five black streaks running down each of the yellow wing-cases. On the havoc which it causes among potato-plants in North America it is unnecessary to dilate. On a smaller scale, the TURNIP-FLEA is very mischievous in Britain, perforating the leaves of turnip-plants, or —worse still—eating off the seed-leaves as soon as they appear above the surface of the ground. Of only too many of these exquisite beetles, in fact, it must be said that their beauty is only equalled by their destructiveness.

The LADYBIRDS include a very large number of species. Some of these, such as the common TWO-SPOT LADYBIRD, are exceedingly variable, a long series being easily obtained in which no two specimens resemble one another. Both as grubs and as perfect insects they feed upon the "Green Fly" of the farmer, combining with the grubs of the Lace-wing and Hoverer Flies to keep its numbers within due limits.

Almost equally common is the SEVEN-SPOT LADYBIRD, a considerably larger insect, with seven round black spots on its scarlet wing-cases, which may be seen on almost any grassy bank in spring. Both this and the preceding species sometimes visit the Kentish coast in vast swarms, the beach being reddened by their bodies for miles. The last immigration of this description took place in 1886, in the summer of which year the hops in East Kent were almost destroyed by blight, and the ladybirds made their way at once to the hop-fields and cleared them of the pest in a wonderfully short space of time. A much smaller species, known as the TWENTY-TWO SPOT, is yellow in colour and has eleven black spots on each wing-case. It is generally found crawling about on nettle-leaves in the early part of the summer.

Allied to the Ladybirds are the very curious TORTOISE-BEETLES. In these insects the wing-cases project to a considerable distance beyond the sides of the body, and the legs are so short that only the feet can be seen from above, so that the appearance is very much like

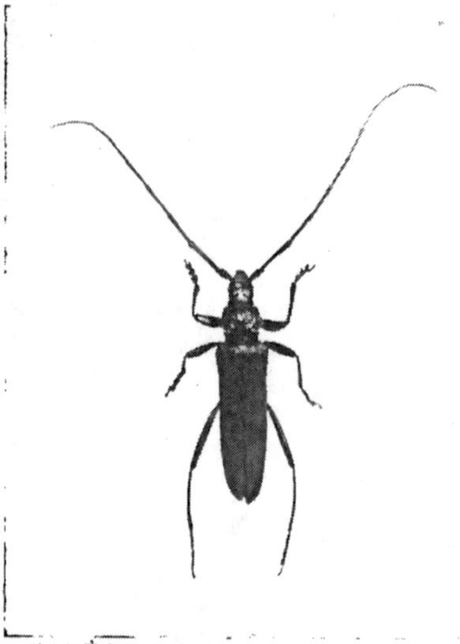

Photo by W. P. Dando, F.Z.S.] *[Regent's Park.*

MUSK-BEETLE.

The odour of this beetle may often be detected at a distance of twenty or thirty yards.

that of a tortoise with the limbs partly withdrawn into the shell. Many different species are known, in some of which the wing-cases are streaked with brilliant metallic silver, which, however, fades away very shortly after death. The commonest of the British tortoise-beetles is found on thistles.

Another very large group of beetles is represented by the CELLAR-BEETLE, which is generally very common in old houses. This insect must not be confused with the so-called "Black-beetle," from which it may easily be distinguished by its deep black colour, its very much shorter feelers, and the curious point into which the end of its body is produced. It hides away in dark corners by day, and crawls slowly about by night. Related to it is the MEAL-WORM, so much in request for the food of cage-birds, which is usually very plentiful in granaries.

Very different in appearance, yet belonging to the same group, is the handsome CARDINAL BEETLE, a bright scarlet insect which is not uncommon in summer. It may sometimes be found lurking behind pieces of loose bark, and is also fond of resting upon the flowers of umbelliferous plants in the hot sunshine. A second species, which is not nearly so plentiful, may be distinguished by the fact that the head is entirely black.

Still more curious is the RHIPIPHORUS BEETLE, which is parasitic within the nests of wasps. Where the egg is laid, or how the grub first finds its way into the nest, no one has yet succeeded in discovering; but having made its entry, the insect proceeds to burrow into the body of a wasp-grub, and lives within it for several days, feeding upon its flesh meanwhile. After increasing considerably in size, it creeps out of the carcase of its victim and changes its skin, after which it resumes its interrupted meal, and continues to feed until the last vestige of the wasp-grub has been devoured. It then changes to a chrysalis in the cell, and the perfect insect appears a few days later. Oddly enough, the wasps appear to take no notice of its presence, and never attempt to molest it. The two sexes of this beetle are quite unlike one another, the male having the wing-cases yellow and the feelers heavily plumed, while the female is black, with the feelers only slightly toothed.

Most singular of all the insects belonging to this order, however, is the strange little STALK-EYED BEETLE, which spends the greater part of its life half buried in the body of a bee. In this insect the feelers are branched, somewhat like the antennules, or lesser feelers, of a lobster, and the eyes, which are comparatively few in number, are set at the ends of short foot-stalks. The male has very narrow wing-cases, but extremely large wings, which have a milky appearance during flight that can hardly be mistaken. The female has no wings at all, and in general aspect is nothing more than a grub. In early spring a great number of solitary bees are infested by this extraordinary parasite, which burrows into their bodies under cover of the projecting edges of the segments, and there remains feeding upon their internal juices for several weeks, with only just the tip of its tail protruding. When fully fed, it emerges from the body of its involuntary host, leaving a large round hole behind it, which frequently closes up and heals. In any case, strange to say, the ravages of the parasite appear to have but little effect upon the health of the bee.

STRAIGHT-WINGED INSECTS, OR EARWIGS, COCKROACHES, SOOTHSAYERS, STICK-INSECTS, CRICKETS, GRASSHOPPERS, AND LOCUSTS.

BY W. F. KIRBY, F.L.S.

THE insects of this order are less numerous in species than those of any other but the next, and are easily recognised. The fore wings are usually of a leathery consistency, and the hind wings are folded beneath them like a fan in the more typical families, though in the Earwigs and Cockroaches a somewhat different arrangement prevails. In the Earwigs, indeed, the wings are doubled back at the ends, and in the Cockroaches the wing-cases, or "tegmina," as they are technically called, overlap. As a rule these insects feed entirely on vegetable substances. The "Soothsayers" form an exception, being carnivorous, though they are not parasitic, like the Ichneumon-flies, but feed on fresh food; and several species of Earwigs, Cockroaches, and Crickets, especially those which are semi-domesticated, are omnivorous, and will eat animal as well as vegetable food. These insects have an imperfect metamorphosis—that is, there is no inactive pupa-state; but the young, on emerging from the egg, already possess a recognisable resemblance to their full-grown parents, and their metamorphosis consists of a series of moults, before the last of which rudimentary wings appear in those species which ultimately acquire these appendages. A considerable number of species never have wings, a circumstance which frequently renders it difficult to determine whether a specimen is fully developed. The antennæ are usually long, and the joints distinctly separated, but are very rarely feathered. At the other end of the body we often find two long jointed organs, called "cerci." The jaws are always furnished with strong mandibles. Many Grasshoppers and Locusts have a curious arrangement on the shank of the front leg, consisting either of a round or an oval cavity on each side, closed by a membrane, or of two long parallel slits in front. These are considered to be organs of hearing. The largest known insects belong to this order; the proportion of large or moderate-sized species is considerable; and the smallest are probably considerably larger than the smallest members of any other group. They are not numerous in temperate climates; there are only about fifty British species, and most of the larger of these are either naturalised species, or merely casual visitors from abroad.

Photo by W. P. Dando, F.Z.S., Regent's Park.

EARWIG.

The forceps-like appendage at the end of this insect's body is said to be used for folding and unfolding the wings.

The EARWIGS form the first family. Some are wingless, but most have very short wing-cases, under which very large wings, forming the most beautiful feature of these otherwise unattractive insects, are doubled and folded into a very small compass. Some of the smaller species fly readily; but others, such as the COMMON EARWIG, though furnished with ample wings, are rarely seen to use them. The most conspicuous organ of the earwigs is the curious forceps at the extremity of the body, the use of which does not seem to be well made out, though it has been suggested that it is used for folding and unfolding the wings. The forceps differs very much in size and shape in different species; it is always larger in the male than in the female, and often differently shaped. In the common earwig the male forceps is flattened and contiguous at the base, and rounded and

Photo by W. P. Dando, F.Z.S.] *[Regent's Park.*

AMERICAN COCKROACH.

Common in many warehouses in England, and now found in most parts of the world.

Photo by Highley.

STICK-INSECT.

The largest insect known is a species of stick-insect; it is a native of Borneo, and measures 13 inches.

Photo by Scholastic Photo Co.] [*Parson's Green.*

WALKING LEAF-INSECTS.

Natives of the East Indies, and remarkable for their resemblance to green leaves.

incurved at the extremity. There are two varieties, in one of which the forceps is twice as long as in the other; but intermediate gradations do not seem to be met with. In the female the forceps is narrow, nearly straight, and approximating. The earwig is a nocturnal insect, and hides itself during the day in large-headed flowers, like dahlias, to which it is very destructive, or in any convenient dark and narrow crevice, especially among decaying vegetable matter. It derives its name from its occasionally entering the human ear, but it may be easily driven out by dropping in a little olive oil. In most books it is denied that earwigs enter the ear at all, but it is, nevertheless, an undoubted fact; and the fanciful derivation that has been suggested of *earwing* in the place of *earwig* cannot be entertained respecting an insect which seldom shows its wings at all. It should be noted that the female earwig is said to tend her young very much as a hen tends her chickens—an uncommon habit in insects.

The COMMON COCKROACH is too well known to need description. The individuals with half-developed wings are the perfect females; but there are other species in which the wings are fully developed in both sexes, others in which the male is winged and the female wingless, and others again in which both sexes are wingless. In warm countries and on ship-board cockroaches are far more troublesome than in cold climes; and the large brown ones, with a mark on the back of the thorax resembling a crown, and very broad wing-cases and wings, are called DRUMMERS in the West Indies, from the loud noise they keep up during the night.

Lady Burton has given an amusing account of her introduction to cockroaches abroad: "After two days we were given a very pleasant suite of rooms — bedroom, dining- and drawing-room—with wide windows overlooking the Tagus and a great part of Lisbon. These quarters were, however, not without drawbacks, for here occurred an incident which gave me a foretaste of the sort of thing I was to expect in Brazil. Our bedroom was a large whitewashed place; there were three holes in the wall, one at the bedside bristling with horns, and these were cockroaches some three inches long. The drawing-room was gorgeous with yellow satin, and the magnificent yellow curtains were sprinkled with these crawling things. The consequence was that I used to stand on a chair and scream. This annoyed Richard very much. 'A nice sort of traveller and companion *you* are going to make,' he said; 'I suppose you think you look very pretty and interesting standing on that chair and howling at those innocent creatures.' This hurt me so much that, without descending from the chair, I stopped screaming, and made a meditation like St. Simon Stylites on his pillar; and it was, 'That if I was going to live in a country always in contact with these and worse things, though I had a perfect horror of anything black and crawling, it would never do to go on like that.' So I got down, fetched a basin of water and a slipper, and in two hours by the watch I had knocked ninety-seven of them into it. It cured me. From that day I had no more fear of vermin and reptiles, which is just as well in a country where Nature is over-luxuriant. A little while after we changed our rooms we were succeeded by Lord and Lady Lytton, and, to my infinite delight, I heard the same screams coming from the same room a little while after. 'There,' I said in triumph, 'you see I am not the *only* woman who does not like cockroaches.'"

Photo by W. P. Dando, F.Z.S., Regent's Park.

HOUSE-CRICKET.

Very similar in its habits to the cockroach.

The dimensions of the insects are not so much exaggerated; for I believe this story refers to the large reddish American cockroach, which is common in many English cities, although only in warehouses. It does not usually much exceed an inch in length; but the antennæ are very long, and the wing-cases expand nearly 3 inches. (See photograph on page 689.)

The SOOTHSAYERS, or PRAYING-INSECTS, are not British, though one or two species are found in the south of Europe. They have long fore legs, the shanks of which are set with a double row of long, curving, sabre-like spines, and when at rest they hold them up as if in the attitude of prayer; but they are really on the look-out for prey, and the long spines are admirably adapted for wounding or grasping the insects which form their food. They also fight fiercely among themselves, and it is no uncommon occurrence for a female to tear to pieces and devour her mate, either during or after their courtship. The soothsayers are often of a green colour, so as to match the grass and leaves among which they live, and thus conceal them from their prey.

Photo by W. P. Dando, F.Z.S., Regent's Park.

MOLE-CRICKET.

A brown insect about 2 inches long. The very broad and flat front legs are used for burrowing.

The STICK-INSECTS, or SPECTRE-INSECTS, have some resemblance to the Soothsayers, but are exclusively vegetable-feeders, and have long, sprawling legs, or shorter ones, sometimes more or less lobate; but they never possess prehensile fore legs for seizing prey. The wing-cases are generally quite small; but some species have beautiful large green or pink wings, folded fan-wise, and covered by the stout front border of the wing. Many species are wingless, and of a grey or brown colour, which renders them scarcely distinguishable from dry bits of stick; and among these is the largest living insect known, a grey stick-like species from Borneo, measuring nearly 13 inches from head to tail. Other species have curious excrescences on the legs and body, which make them look like bits of wood overgrown with moss or lichen; while others possess large flat lobes growing from the legs and body, which cause them to be almost indistinguishable from green leaves; and, indeed, these insects are frequently called "Walking Leaves."

Photo by L. H. Joutel] [*New York.*

LONG-HORNED GRASSHOPPER.

This insect belongs to the same family as the well-known British species. The specimen from which this photograph was taken had unfortunately (as is often the case) broken antennæ; they should be twice as long as the wings.

With the CRICKETS we commence the last three families of the group, which are distinguished from the others by their power of leaping. The hind legs are very long, with very thick thighs, and generally a double row of strong teeth or spines on the shanks. The feet are generally three-jointed, and there is usually a long ovipositor in the females. There are very few true crickets in England, but three of these are very conspicuous species. The first is the MOLE-CRICKET, a large light brown insect nearly 2 inches long, with broad, short front legs rather like those of a mole, which it uses in a similar way. Though common and destructive in fields and gardens, it is not often seen; but if water be thrown on the ground overnight, and a board laid over it, one or two mole-crickets are likely to be found underneath in the morning. The HOUSE-CRICKET resembles this insect in colour, but is not much more than half an inch long, and there is nothing remarkable in the structure of its legs. It is almost the only noisy insect found in English houses, and is very similar to the common cockroach in its habits, although free from the disagreeable smell which adds to the disgust the latter insect often inspires. The third species, the FIELD-CRICKET, is a smooth black insect, larger and stouter than the house-cricket. It constructs burrows in grassy places, but is not now a very common species in England. In the last two species, and many others, there is a bare space on one of the wing-cases of the male, crossed by ribs in a manner varying according to the species, which helps to produce the loud chirping for which these insects are remarkable.

The LONG-HORNED GRASSHOPPERS, which form the next family, are distinguished by having four joints to their feet, a long ovipositor in the female, and very long, slender antennæ. The commonest species inhabiting England, and one of the largest grasshoppers, is the GREAT GREEN GRASSHOPPER, which is found leaping about among long

Photo by J. Edwards] [*Colesborne.*

CAPE GRASSHOPPER (FEMALE).

This insect, which is remarkable for the inflated bladder-like appearance of the male, is an object of superstition among the Boers. Colour, bright apple-green with white stripes.

Photo by Highley.

EGYPTIAN LOCUST.

A common North African species, of which specimens occasionally visit England.

Photo by Highley.

EGYPTIAN LOCUST.

This figure shows the upper surface of the specimen represented in the preceding photograph.

grass and low bushes, especially in the south of England. It is about 2 inches in length. Among the foreign species of this rather extensive family, we may mention some green or reddish South American species, with a large round spot on the hind wings, not unlike those seen in the peacock-butterfly.

The last family includes the SHORT-HORNED GRASSHOPPERS, or TRUE LOCUSTS, so very destructive in many countries, though the real MIGRATORY LOCUSTS are only casual visitors to England, the native British species being all small insects, found among grass, and doing but little damage. The commonest of the Migratory Locusts visiting Britain is the RED-LEGGED LOCUST, which expands from 2 to 4 inches, and has grey wing-cases varied with brown, pale green hind wings, and red hind shanks, with white black-tipped spines. Another species, the EGYPTIAN LOCUST, more rarely met with, has brown fore wings, and grey hind wings, crossed by a broad blackish band. Two photographs are given on page 693 of a specimen brought to England among vegetables in the spring of 1901. Many foreign locusts, large and small, have beautiful red or blue hind wings, and some of these are common on the Continent, though not in England; those found in Europe are comparatively small, measuring only 1 or 2 inches across the wing-cases; but some of the great South American locusts measure as much as 7 or 8 inches in expanse. However, some of the smaller species, such as the CYPRIAN LOCUST and the ROCKY MOUNTAIN LOCUST, which measure less than 2 inches across the wing-cases, are much more destructive than the large species.

Photos by W. L. H. Duckworth] *[Cambridge.*

WART-EATING GRASSHOPPER (TWO VIEWS).

Used by Swedish peasants to bite off their warts.

A real invasion of locusts is a terrible calamity, for the insects fly like birds, but in vast flocks, and devour every scrap of vegetation where they settle. Sometimes a flight, two or three miles broad, continues to fly steadily over the same spot for hours together. Sometimes flocks perish at sea, and are cast up on the beach in heaps like sand-hills, extending for a distance of forty or fifty miles. Nor are the young locusts less destructive before they acquire wings; for they march across a district in such numbers as to extinguish fires, fill up trenches, and overcome all similar obstacles placed in their way by sheer force of numbers; and it is well said of a visitation of locusts, "The land is as the Garden of Eden before them, and behind is a desolate wilderness."

NERVE-WINGED OR LACE-WINGED INSECTS, OR DRAGON-FLIES AND THEIR RELATIVES.

BY THE REV. THEODORE WOOD, F.E.S.

THE Nerve-winged Insects owe their title to the peculiar character of their wings, the horny veins which form the framework of those organs being multiplied and sub-divided to such an extent that they assume the appearance of exceedingly delicate network.

These insects fall naturally into two great groups, in one of which the chrysalis, or pupa, is active, and continues to take food like the grub, while in the other it is passive and helpless, like that of a butterfly or a moth.

Prominent among the members of the first division are the Dragon-flies, which owe their title partly to their extreme voracity, and partly to the fact that they feed entirely upon living insects, which they pursue through the air. They are exceedingly swift of wing, and may be seen hawking over ponds and streams on any fine day throughout the summer and early autumn.

The earlier part of their lives is spent in the water, in which the eggs are laid by the parent insect. The grubs are usually of a dull grey or brownish-green colour, and are remarkable for a curious organ known as the "mask," which partly covers the lower surface of the head. This apparatus consists of two joints, which fold upon one another, but can be extended at will, the one farthest from the head terminating in a pair of large and powerful jaws. When the grub perceives an insect-victim, it swims cautiously beneath, and seizes it by means of these jaws. The "mask" is then folded, and the prisoner drawn down within reach of the mandibles, by means of which it is speedily devoured.

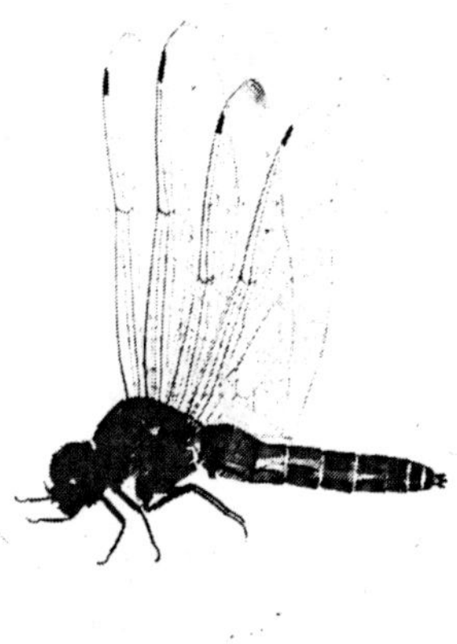

Photo by W. P. Dando, F.Z.S.] *[Regent's Park.*

DRAGON-FLY.

These insects are often known as "Horse-stingers," although they do not sting horses; in fact, they are perfectly harmless, except to insects smaller and weaker than themselves.

The method of swimming practised by the dragon-fly grub is also very curious. Through the centre of the body runs a longitudinal tube, terminating in a circular orifice, closed by means of five tightly fitting valves. These valves, which together form a sharp spike when closed, can be separated at will. When the insect wishes to swim, it fills the tube with water, and then squirts the contents forcibly out, the result being that it is driven swiftly forwards by the reaction.

The pupa of the dragon-fly is very much like the grub, with the exception that the rudiments of the future wings may be seen on the back.

About forty species of these insects are found in the British Islands, of which the GREAT DRAGON-FLY is a well-known example. The body is 3 inches in length, while the extended wings measure about 4 inches from tip to tip. In colour it is light rusty brown, with a few pale markings. The "HORSE-STINGER"—which is perfectly harmless, notwithstanding its popular title—is also common, and may be recognised at once by its flat dull yellow body, which becomes blue in the fully developed male. In the graceful and beautiful DEMOISELLE the male is deep blue, with black patches on the wings, while the female is entirely green.

Allied to these insects is the COMMON MAY-FLY, popularly supposed to live for one day only. As a matter of fact, however, it spends a couple of years in the grub and pupa states, inhabiting burrows in the banks of ponds and streams. These burrows are curved, and have

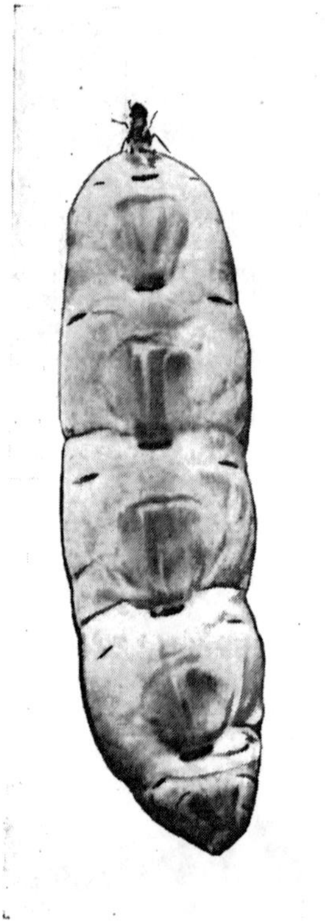

Photo by W. P. Dando, F.Z.S., Regent's Park.
QUEEN TERMITE.
Her huge white body is full of eggs, of which she lays thousands every day.

two entrances, one above the other, so that the insect can pass in and out with perfect ease.

The May-fly is also remarkable for the fact that the perfect insect changes its skin shortly after reaching maturity. Before this change takes place the female insect is the "Green Drake" of the angler; afterwards, the "Grey Drake."

To this group belong also the TERMITES, or "White Ants," so exceedingly numerous in almost all the warmer parts of the world. These are social insects, living together in vast colonies, and making most wonderful nests, which consist of a vast and complicated series of chambers and passages, sheltered beneath a turreted dome of clay. In the centre is the "royal cell," inhabited by the "king" and "queen," as the perfect male and female are called. These are winged when first they leave the pupal shell. But after taking a single flight, they snap off their wings at the base, just as ants do; while for the rest of their lives they are absolute prisoners in the cell built around them by the workers.

Shortly after this strange incarceration takes place, the body of the queen swells to a huge size, so that, to quote Professor Drummond, she becomes "a large, loathsome, cylindrical package, 2 or 3 inches long, in shape like a sausage, and as white as a bolster." She now begins to deposit eggs at the rate of several thousands in a day, which are at once carried off by the workers, to whom is entrusted the entire care of the helpless young. These workers, which are exceedingly numerous, also enlarge the nest from time to time, and construct tunnels of clay up the trunks and along the branches of trees, through which they may convey to the nurseries in security the gums and decaying wood for the nutriment of the young.

A fourth form of insect is also found in the termites' nest, known as the "Soldier." The head is much larger and the jaws are much longer and stronger than those of the worker, and the sole function appears to be to defend the nest when attacked. Both soldier and worker, apparently, proceed from the same eggs which produce the king and queen, the difference in development being probably due—as in the hive-bee—to the character of the food with which the young are supplied.

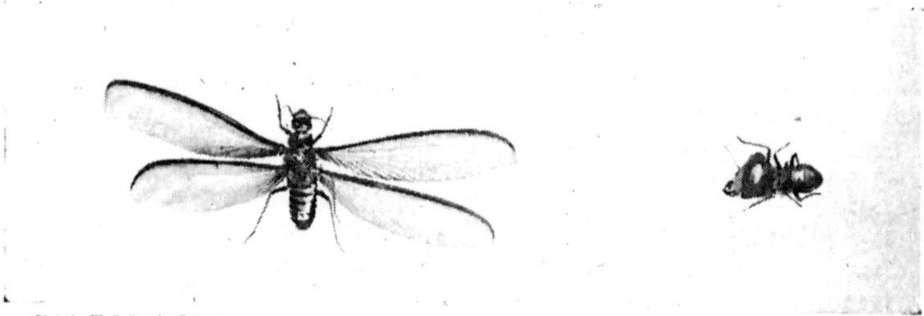

Photo by W. P. Dando, F.Z.S.] *[Regent's Park.*
TERMITES.
The perfect male and female are winged, the "worker" and the "soldier" being more like grubs than perfect insects.

Photo by W. Saville-Kent, F.Z.S.] [*Milford-on-Sea.*

TERMITES' NESTS IN QUEENSLAND.

These nests are sometimes 14 or 15 feet high.

Photo by W. Saville-Kent, F.Z.S.] [*Milford-on-Sea.*

TERMITES' NEST IN QUEENSLAND.

The smaller nests, when opened and emptied, are used by the natives as ovens.

Photo by W. Saville-Kent, F.Z.S.] *[Milford-on-Sea.*

TERMITES AT WORK.

This shows one of the most destructive of wood-eating insects, nearly of the natural size.

In a state of nature termites are undoubtedly beneficial. They are scavengers, in fact, whose duty it is to remove the dead and decaying wood which would otherwise encumber the ground for many years. But in civilised districts they are extremely mischievous, books, furniture, and all the woodwork of houses being often completely destroyed by them before their presence is even suspected.

The second division of the order also forms two well-marked groups—namely, the Flat-winged Insects, in which the wings are fully spread, horizontally or obliquely, even in repose, and the Hairy-winged Insects, in which those organs can be folded longitudinally, like the joints of a fan.

Of the former group, the ANT-LION of Southern Europe is a familiar example. The perfect insect is seldom seen, owing to its nocturnal habits. In appearance it is not unlike a small and delicately built dragon-fly, with a yellowish head, a black body, and transparent wings marbled with brownish spots. The larva, however, is terrestrial, and lives in a funnel-shaped pitfall which it scoops out in the sand, always working backwards in a spiral direction, and jerking out the sand with its broad head in an almost continuous shower. Having completed the excavation, it buries itself at the bottom with merely the tips of its jaws appearing above the surface, and there waits for ants or other small creatures to fall down the sloping sides, accelerating their descent, if need be, by flinging sand upon them. The size of the pit varies with that of the insect, the fully grown grub digging down to the depth of about 2 inches, while the cavity is about 3 inches in diameter.

The mouth of the ant-lion grub is very curiously constructed, the jaws lying in a groove on the inner margin of the mandibles, or jaws proper; so that while an insect is held prisoner by the latter, the former can be employed in sucking its juices. When the body of the victim has been completely drained, the empty skin is thrown out of the pit by a jerk of the head.

The chrysalis, too, is remarkable for possessing jaws, by means of which it cuts its way out of the cocoon which it made, when a larva, by spinning grains of sand together with silken threads.

In some South European and African insects allied to the ant-lions the hind wings are modified into extremely long and slender shafts, slightly expanded at the extremities. In an Indian species belonging to a related genus these wings are scarcely more than threads, and bear a superficial resemblance to the attenuated limbs of certain gnats. One group, of which a Japanese species is a well-known representative, is characterised by the long, slender, and clubbed antennæ.

Photo by W. Saville-Kent, F.Z.S.] [Milford-on-Sea.

TERMITES' NEST.

Showing one year's reconstruction to nest, of which the photographer made a section.

The MANTIS-FLIES are remarkable for the structure of the fore limbs, which are almost exactly similar in character to those of the praying-mantis. The upper segment of the leg is so lengthened as to look like an additional joint; the lower surface of the thigh is armed with a number of long, sharp spines; and the tibia, or lower part of the leg, folds closely down upon it, after the manner of the blade of a clasp-knife. These limbs are used for seizing, an insect which is once grasped being effectually prevented by the spines from breaking away.

The larvæ of these insects are parasitic in the nests of tree-wasps and spiders, and have the peculiarity of practically losing their limbs as they approach maturity; so that while at first they are free and active, they afterwards become almost as helpless as those of many beetles. One species is found in Southern Europe, the remainder being widely distributed over the hotter regions of the globe.

Photo by W. P. Dando, F.Z.S., Regent's Park.

SCORPION-FLY.

Remarkable for the curious structure of the end of the body.

Allied to the Mantis-flies are the curious SNAKE-FLIES, or CAMEL-FLIES. In these insects the head is very large, and is attached to the thorax, or central division of the body, by a long and distinct neck, which allows it great freedom of motion. The neck is usually raised and the head bent down, giving to the insect a remarkably snake-like appearance.

These flies are predaceous in their habits, and the four British species may be found on the banks of ponds and small streams, where they can obtain insect-victims in plenty. The larvæ live beneath the bark of trees, and wriggle about in a singularly serpentine fashion.

Equally curious in a different way are the SCORPION-FLIES, in which the body is prolonged into a slender three-jointed process, the extremity of which, in the male, is furnished with a pair of curved forceps. In spite of their somewhat formidable appearance these insects are perfectly harmless. They are very plentiful almost everywhere, and may be found in numbers on any sunny summer morning resting on the herbage on hedge-banks, or running actively about on the leaves of low bushes. Like the Snake-flies, they are predaceous, feeding entirely upon other insects, and often attacking those which are bigger and apparently stronger than themselves. The eggs are laid underground, and the grubs, which are entirely subterranean in their habits, feed upon decomposing vegetable matter. When fully fed, they burrow still deeper into the ground, and there change into pupæ, from which the perfect insects emerge about a fortnight later. In the common English species the body is shining black, and the legs are yellow, while the transparent wings are marked with brown spots, which generally form three broken transverse bands. The insect is about half an inch in length.

Certain allied insects have very slender bodies and long legs, and might easily be mistaken for "daddy-long-legs" by any one who failed to notice the presence of two pairs of wings. A species found in Southern Europe is reddish yellow in colour, with a brown thorax and yellowish wings. It has a curious habit of suspending itself from a twig by its fore legs, and seizing any flying insect which may come within reach with the middle and hinder pairs.

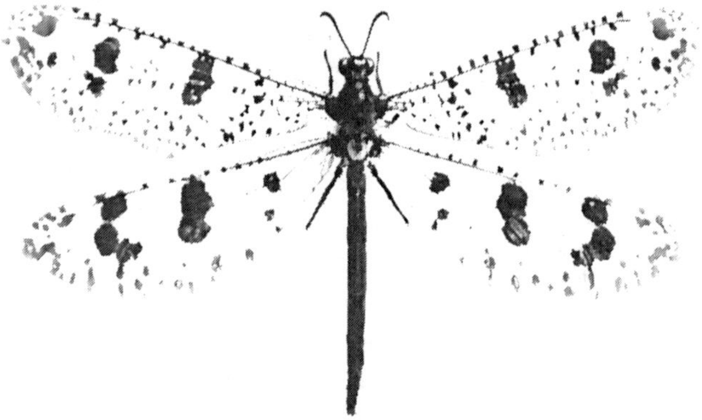

Photo by W. P. Dando, F.Z.S.] *[Regent's Park.*

ADULT FORM OF ANT-LION.

The grub of this insect lives in small pits in sandy places, and feeds upon the ants, etc., which roll down the sloping sides.

Allied to the foregoing is the extraordinary little snow-insect, which makes its appearance in mid-winter, and may even be found crawling on the surface of snow. In general appearance it is not unlike a larval grasshopper, with very long, slender legs, and antennæ of about the same length as the body. There is also a well-developed beak. The wings are quite rudimentary in the female, while even in the male they are so short as to be perfectly useless for flight. The insect is remarkably active, nevertheless, and possesses the power of leaping, although the hinder thighs are not developed in any great degree. In colour it is metallic green, with the beak, antennæ, legs, wings, and ovipositor rusty red. It is not uncommon in the north of England and Scotland.

Far more generally distributed is the LACEWING-FLY, or GOLDEN-EYE, which may be seen almost anywhere on warm summer evenings flitting slowly to and fro in the twilight. During the daytime it may often be found resting upon fences, or sitting on the leaves of low plants. In colour it is pale green, with a peculiar milky appearance, and the eyes glow as though lighted by an inward fire. The wings are so closely and elaborately veined that they look like a piece of the most delicate lace-work. It is not advisable to handle the insect, for, although perfectly harmless, it possesses the power of pouring out from its body a liquid of the most horrible odour, which clings to the fingers in spite of repeated ablutions.

The life-history of the lacewing-fly is very curious. When the maternal insect lays her eggs, she first deposits a drop of a highly glutinous fluid upon a leaf or slender twig, and then, with an upward jerk of her long body, draws it out into a slender thread. On contact with the air this thread immediately hardens, and just as she releases her hold the fly attaches a single egg to the tip. In this way 200 or 300 eggs are laid together in a little cluster, which looks just like a tiny patch of moss. In the earlier botanical manuals, indeed, it was actually named, figured, and described as a moss.

The grubs which hatch out from these eggs feed upon plant-lice, of which they devour vast numbers, draining the juices by means of their hollow jaws, and then fastening the empty skins on their own backs, as an American Indian might decorate himself with the scalps of his victims. Owing to this singular habit, the grub becomes perfectly unrecognisable after the first few days of its life, only the jaws and feet being visible beneath the pile of dry skins. When fully fed, it changes to the pupal condition in a silken cocoon, which it attaches to a leaf, and the perfect insect makes its appearance in the course of a few days.

Photo by W. P. Dando, F.Z.S., Regent's Park.

LARGE CADDIS-FLY.

The largest British species measures about an inch and a half across the wings.

The ALDER-FLIES, in general appearance, are not unlike caddis-flies, but may easily be distinguished by the fact that the wings are not longitudinally folded while at rest. They are very abundant in the neighbourhood of ponds and small streams, where they may be seen flying slowly and heavily, or resting on low herbage or the foliage of trees and bushes. The female insect lays her eggs in clusters of 300 or 400 on the leaves of water-plants, and the little grubs make their way down into the water immediately on hatching out, where they creep about on the mud at the bottom in search of the tiny creatures on which they feed. When full-grown, they are about an inch in length. They then leave the water and bury themselves in the earth, where they change to pupæ, the perfect insects emerging in June or July.

The CADDIS-FLIES, of which there are many British representatives, belong to the Hairy-winged group. The larvæ of these insects are entirely aquatic, and remind one of hermit-crabs, the front part of the body being clothed with horny armour, while the hinder part is entirely unprotected. In order to escape the attacks of predaceous insects these grubs construct cases round their bodies, which they drag about wherever they go. In one or two instances, however, the case is attached to the lower surface of a stone.

The materials of which these cases are made vary in accordance with the species. In one group, for instance, they consist of pieces of twigs and leaves, cut into short lengths, and arranged side by side in such a manner as to form a spiral band. The larva of another kind uses entire leaves, gluing them firmly together and living between them. A third species employs grains of sand and tiny stones, which it arranges in the form of a cow's horn. Most curious of all, however, is the case of a caddis-fly which is made entirely of the shells of water-snails. As these shells are, as a rule, still tenanted by their owners, the snails may sometimes be seen attempting to crawl simultaneously in half a dozen different directions, while the grub is dragging them in a seventh.

All the grubs retain tight hold of their cases by means of a pincer-like organ at the end of the body. When fully fed, they close the aperture at each end of the tube, and assume the chrysalis state, the perfect insects emerging a few weeks later. Although the wings are large and broad, they fly very slowly, and never seem to take more than a short journey through the air. They may often be seen in numbers resting upon the herbage on the banks of streams and ponds, or crawling down into the water in order to deposit their eggs.

STINGING FOUR-WINGED INSECTS, OR ANTS, BEES AND WASPS, AND THEIR ALLIES

BY W. F. KIRBY, F.L.S.

Photo by W. P. Dando, F.Z.S., Regent's Park.

SAW-FLY.

One of the commonest of the larger British species is a blackish hairy insect, measuring rather more than an inch in expanse, with transparent wings bordered with brown.

THE order of insects to which the Ants, Bees, and Wasps belong includes a very large number of species. All these are provided with four membranous wings, alike in consistency, and provided with comparatively few nervures. The wings are usually of small size, as compared with the dimensions of the insects, but are very powerful, owing to the fore and hind pair being connected together during flight by a series of little links; and the flight of the insects is usually very rapid. These insects pass through a perfect metamorphosis, the pupa being always inactive; the jaws are provided with mandibles, though a proboscis, or sucking-tube, is also present, and the abdomen of the female is armed with an ovipositor, or boring instrument, which is frequently modified into a powerful sting, used to deposit the eggs in their proper position. One peculiarity is that several species of ants, bees, and wasps live in large communities, in which the bulk of the inhabitants, on whom most of the work of the nest falls, are imperfectly developed and usually sterile females, called neuters, or workers. This arrangement is also met with in the White Ants, which belong to the order of Lace-winged Insects. Among both the Ants and White Ants the neuters are unprovided with wings; but these organs are present in the fully developed males and females, though soon cast.

A great variety of other insects also belong to this order, such as Saw-flies, Gall-flies, and an immense number of parasitic species, generally called Ichneumon-flies, among which are some of the smallest insects known.

This extensive order of insects is divided into two principal sections—those in which the ovipositor is used as a saw or an auger, and those in which it is modified into a sting. One of the most interesting sections of the Borers includes the SAW-FLIES, in which the boring instrument is modified into a pair of toothed saws, which are used for cutting incisions in leaves, or in the tender bark of twigs, in which to deposit the eggs. These flies have four transparent wings, sometimes stained with yellow or purple, and their bodies are moderately stout and obtuse, and generally black, red, or yellow. The antennæ are very variable in form, and are sometimes knobbed at the end like those of a butterfly; sometimes they are formed of a number of long, slender joints; some-

Photo by W. P. Dando, F.Z.S., Regent's Park.

MARBLE GALL-FLY AND GALL.

Found on oak, and not unlike the foreign gall used for making ink.

Photo by W. P. Dando, F.Z.S., Regent's Park.

TREE-WASP.

Very similar to the common wasp, but builds its nest in trees instead of in the ground.

times of only three—a moderately long basal one, a short middle one, and a long terminal one, composed of a number of joints united into one; and rarely, as in the case of the males of some small species about half an inch long which feed on fir and pine, the antennæ are feathered. The grubs are very like caterpillars, and are sometimes called "false caterpillars"; but a true caterpillar (except in one or two very rare exceptions among foreign species) has never more than sixteen legs, while these "false caterpillars" have more, often as many as twenty-two. They also resemble caterpillars in another way, for the pupæ are enclosed in cocoons. One interesting Australian species, which feeds on gum-trees, proceeds from a black caterpillar with only six legs. The perfect insect has a blackish head and thorax, with three large yellow spots on the latter, yellowish antennæ and wings, and a green abdomen; it measures about an inch and a half across the wings, and has knobbed antennæ. An allied species, found in Tasmania, is said to tend its young larvæ—an unusual habit, except among social insects like bees, wasps, and ants. Among the commonest and the most destructive saw-flies in England are those feeding upon the currant, gooseberry, and pear, of which there are several species, measuring about half an inch across the wings. The commonest flies which lay their eggs on the gooseberry and currant are yellow, with the head, antennæ, and three long spots on the back black, and the wings transparent, with black veins. The grubs are bluish green, with twenty legs, and numerous black dots; and several may often be seen on one leaf. The best-known of the PEAR SAW-FLIES is black, with the wings transparent, except the veins; the grub is very like a slug, and is green or yellow, very slimy, with the front of the body much thickened.

The WOOD-WASPS include only a few species, the grubs of which live in the stems of plants, or in the solid wood of trees. One of the largest feeds on fir- or pine-trees, and the fly measures from half an inch to an inch and a half in length, and varies much in size, though the male is generally much smaller than the female. The female is yellow, with two black bands, and a stout ovipositor half as long as the abdomen. In the male the tip of the abdomen is black, and ends in a rectangular point. The wings are transparent, with yellow nervures.

Next to these insects come the GALL-FLIES, most of which produce round galls on oaks; and in some species we meet with a wingless brood, living alternately with the winged broods, but at the roots of the trees instead of in the open air. The veining of the wings is reduced to one or two veins; the antennæ are rather long, and not angulated; and the abdomen is

Photo by Scholastic Photo. Co.] [Parson's Green.

TREE-WASP'S NEST.

Generally built in a thick bush.

short, and constricted at the base. The flies seldom measure more than half an inch across the wings. Some galls are hard, like the one found on the Turkey oak, from which ink is made; while others are large and juicy, resembling cherries, or small apples, among which is the so-called apple of Sodom. Others, like the Bedeguar, which is found on roses, have a mossy appearance. The latter are produced by a small black saw-fly, with part of the legs, and, in the female, the base of the abdomen, red beneath.

Photo by W. P. Dando, F.Z.S.] *[Regent's Park.*

PINE-BORING WASP (FEMALE).

Formidable in appearance, but quite harmless.

Some of the smaller gall-flies do not produce galls, but are parasitic on other insects; but galls are very liable to the parasitic attacks of other insects, especially to those of small brilliant metallic green four-winged flies, belonging to an allied family, with very few nervures, but with a black membranous spot on the front edge of the fore wings, and angulated antennæ. Many galls do not begin to grow until the larva is hatched and begins to eat.

We now come to five or six families of parasitic species, popularly called ICHNEUMON-FLIES, and immensely numerous and varied. There are probably considerably over 2,000 species in England alone; but they are comparatively little known or studied. Some of these have beautifully delicate wings, fringed with long bristles, and are among the smallest insects known, being of quite microscopic dimensions. These are parasitic on the eggs of various insects, and some are aquatic. But the more typical ichneumon-flies are of larger size, often measuring more than an inch across the wings. Their bodies are usually black or yellow, and there is often an irregularly shaped space in the middle of the fore wing, where the veins of the wing converge. In these flies the ovipositor is very short; but in others it is of great length, especially in the case of the largest British insect of this group, which is parasitic on the larvæ of the great black-and-yellow wood-wasp, of which we have already spoken. This parasite is as large as the wood-wasp, but much more slender; it is black, with red legs, and two white dots on each segment of the abdomen. The ovipositor, which looks like three black threads, is as long as the whole body.

The numerous parasites of which we have spoken usually deposit their eggs in punctures in the bodies of caterpillars or other immature insects, which the grubs devour from within during the life of their victim, leaving it to die when they themselves have reached their full growth.

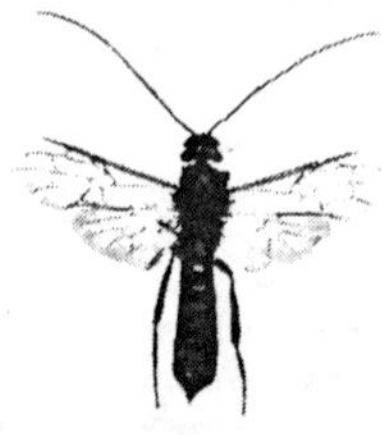

Photo by W. P. Dando, F.Z.S., Regent's Park.

PINE-BORING WASP (MALE).

Smaller than the female, and very different in appearance.

Intermediate between the boring and stinging insects of this order comes the small family of the RUBY-TAILED FLIES. These are brilliantly coloured bronze-red, blue, or green metallic four-winged flies, with the thorax covered with large depressions, and the abdomen smooth, and usually composed, as seen from above, of one large, smooth joint, and one or two much smaller coarsely punctured ones beyond it, the last ending in a variable number of short teeth. They roll themselves up in a ball when alarmed, and are parasites, depositing their eggs in the nests of other insects. An entomologist once saw a ruby-tailed

CRŒSUS BUTTERFLY OF BATCHIAN.

Male, natural size.

Photos by W. P. Dando, F.Z.S., Regent's Park.

CRŒSUS BUTTERFLY OF BATCHIAN.

Female, slightly reduced.

Photo by W. P. Dando, F.Z.S., [*Regent's Park.*

ICHNEUMON-FLY.

One of the largest British species of a very extensive group of parasitic insects.

fly hurled to the ground by a mason-bee which had built her nest in a hole in a wall. The fly rolled herself up into a ball, when the bee bit off her wings, and then flew away. But as soon as she was gone the wingless fly stretched herself out again, and climbed up the wall to the bee's nest to deposit her eggs.

The group of stinging insects begins with the ANTS, which are probably the most intelligent animals now living in the world. Different species, however, differ very much in their manners and customs, and in the grade of civilisation to which they have attained. Some of the more industrious among them keep other insects as cattle, and even as pets; others harvest grain, while a few species cultivate grain for their own use; and others make large mushroom-beds of comminuted leaves, and thus do great harm to cultivated trees in many parts of tropical America. When the industrious ants are not too busy, they sometimes indulge in sports and pastimes. But there are some species which live in idle communities. Such ants are only energetic as marauders, and are so degraded that they cannot even feed themselves, and starve to death if they are deprived of the services of their black slaves, which have been carried off as pupæ by the others in piratical raids, and brought up by other slaves, which do all the work in the nests of their captors.

Quitting the Ants, we arrive at a rather extensive series of insects of moderate or considerable size, and with very spiny legs, called BURROWING-WASPS. They are brightly coloured, active insects, and generally dig holes in the ground, which they provision with caterpillars, grasshoppers, or spiders, which they paralyse with their stings, and leave in a moribund condition to form the food of their progeny. They are generally winged in both sexes, but in one family the females are stout and very hairy, and look like large hairy ants, while the males are slender winged insects, very unlike their partners. In the burrowing-wasps the front of the thorax, or second division of the body, is usually transverse, and often narrow; but in the TRUE WASPS it bends back to the wings. Among these latter it is only the small group of the SOCIAL WASPS which are gregarious, and among which we find workers as well as males and females. The largest of the British wasps is the HORNET; but there are several much larger species in the East Indies, some of which are black and yellow, like the Chinese MANDARIN-WASP, the largest of all, which often measures 2 inches across the wings. Others are black, with one large reddish band on the abdomen. Their nests, which they construct of a kind of paper, are formed in a hole in the ground, in a hollow tree, or in a bush, or under the eaves of a house. A nest is commenced by a single female which has survived the winter, and is afterwards enlarged by the exertions of her progeny.

The last group in this order are the BEES. They may generally be easily recognised by their shaggy bodies and legs. As with the Wasps, most species are solitary, or live in very small communities. Some few are smooth,

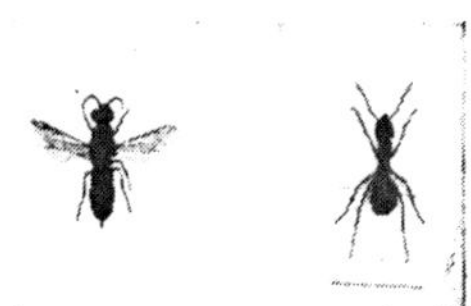

Photos by W. P. Dando, F.Z.S., Regent's Park.

RUBY-TAILED FLY. — Generally of a brilliant metallic green or blue.

WOOD-ANT. — The largest species found in Britain.

Photos by W. P. Dando, F.Z.S., Regent's Park.
SOLITARY ANT.
(MALE.) (FEMALE.)
Not a true ant, but a burrowing-wasp, believed to be parasitic in the nests of humble-bees.

and more or less metallic. A photograph of a large and beautiful South American species appears in the Coloured Plate. The largest British bees are the stout-bodied HUMBLE-BEES, or BUMBLE-BEES, which are generally yellow, more or less banded with black, or else black with a red tail. They form a small nest of cells just beneath the surface of the ground in meadows. A common European species, not found in England, is the large black, violet-winged CARPENTER-BEE, which makes its nest in a gallery burrowed in a post, where there is a separate compartment for each grub.

There are only a few species belonging to the TRUE HIVE-BEES found in different parts of the world. They can always be distinguished from any of the SOLITARY BEES, some of which much resemble them, by having a single long, narrow cell, about four times as long as broad, running along the front edge of the fore wing. In the solitary bees the corresponding cell is much broader and shorter, rarely more than one and a half times as long as broad, and only occupying a small portion of the front edge of the wing.

Hive-bees have always been looked upon with more interest than most other insects, both on account of the valuable products of honey and wax which they produce, and because of their remarkable habits. They are probably less intelligent than ants, but they are larger; and as all classes of their adult population are winged insects, and have been kept in a domesticated or semi-domesticated state for many centuries, they have lent themselves more readily to observation.

The hive-bees live in very large communities, and in a state of nature they make their nests in hollow trees or in crevices of rocks, where they build their waxen cells, store their honey, and rear their young. There are three classes among them,—the queen-bee, the female and the mother of the hive; the male, or drone; and the neuter, or worker, which is really an imperfectly developed and usually sterile female. Like other insects, bees pass through a metamorphosis, which in their case is of the description called "complete," for the immature forms of the bee show no resemblance whatever to the winged insect which will finally be perfected. Every bee commences its life in the form of an egg. Each egg is laid by the queen-bee in a separate cell, and in a few days the egg hatches into a white footless maggot, which is carefully tended by the workers, and fed by them with a preparation secreted by the bees, which is carefully graduated, not only according to the age of the grub, but is differently constituted according to the sex and status of the bee; for it is well known that it is in the power of the workers to develop a young grub which would otherwise become a sterile worker into a perfect queen-bee, by placing it in a large cell, and rearing it on the same nourishing food which is supplied to those grubs which are intended to become perfect queens. When the grub is full-grown, it spins itself a small silken cocoon, and becomes a pupa, or nymph, as it is called. The pupa somewhat resembles a swathed mummy, for all the external portions of the future bee can be seen outlined in the hard casing which encloses it. As soon as it arrives at maturity, it makes its way out through the upper end, when the cell is at

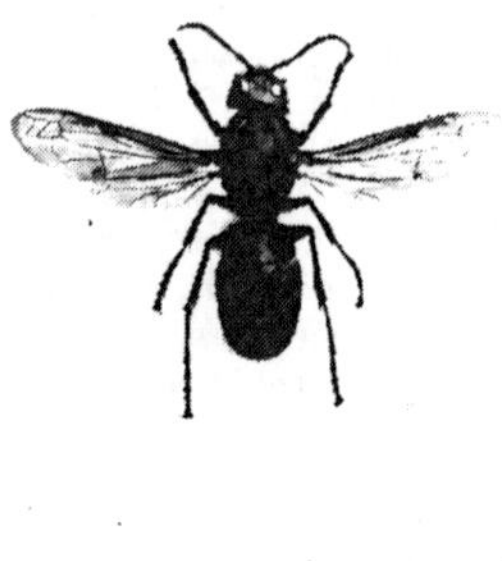

Photo by W. P. Dando, F.Z.S.] *[Regent's Park.*
HORNET.
The largest species of true wasp found in Britain.

Photo by W. P. Dando, F.Z.S., Regent's Park.

HIVE-BEE.
(QUEEN, WORKER, AND DRONE.)

There are only about ten or twelve kinds of true hive-bees known.

once prepared by the other bees for a fresh occupant. The newly born bee is at first moist, flabby, and pale-coloured; but in a few hours her skin dries and hardens, when she at once commences her life-long labours, at first tending the young bees and doing other necessary duties in the hive, and then, a fortnight later, going forth with her companions to collect honey and pollen in the meadows and gardens.

There is never room for more than one queen-bee in a hive; and the queens, which may be recognised by their longer bodies and shorter wings, have such a mortal hatred of each other that, whenever two of them meet, they will fight, if permitted, until one is killed. But in summer, when young bees are hatching daily in large numbers, and the hive is getting over-populated, the workers do not permit the queens to fight; and finally one of them (usually the old queen in the first instance) works herself up into a great flurry, and rushes out of the hive, attended by several hundred followers, to seek for fresh fields and pastures new. This is called "swarming"; and a strong hive will often throw off as many as four or five swarms in the course of the summer. It is then the object of the bee-keeper to get the queen to enter a new hive, for otherwise the swarm may fly to a distance and be lost; but wherever the queen-bee takes up her abode, her companions will assemble round her, and at once commence the work of building combs and storing up honey.

The drone, or male bee, is rather larger than the worker, and has a more obtuse body. He may be at once distinguished by his long thirteen-jointed antennæ, or feelers, for the antennæ are shorter and only twelve-jointed in the queen and worker. There are several hundred drones in a hive; but the queen only pairs once in her life, on the wing, and the ceremony is immediately followed by the death of the drone. The drones have no sting, for the sting of the female and worker is really a modified ovipositor, or egg-laying apparatus, analogous to the organ which is so conspicuous in many ichneumons and other insects belonging to the same order as the bees. In the autumn the unfortunate drones are all massacred or else driven forth from the hive by the workers, when they speedily perish. The workers are by far the most numerous of the inhabitants of a bee-hive; there may be many thousands of them, and their number appears to be only limited by the dimensions of the hive itself.

Photo by B. H. Bentley] *[Sheffield.*

BUMBLE-BEE ON EVERLASTING-PEA.

Bumble-bees make their nests in the ground, and live in smaller communities than the hive-bee.

The ancients had observed something of the economy of bees, but many of their ideas on the subject were strangely fantastic. It was perhaps natural to suppose that the leader of the bees was a king rather than a queen; but it was also supposed that a swarm of bees could be obtained by killing an ox and leaving the carcase to rot. This notion appears to have originated in swarms of flies, more or less resembling bees, having been noticed flying round or near putrefying carcases.

Among all the truly social insects—*i.e.* hive-bees, wasps, ants, and termites, or so-called white ants—we find that the bulk of the community consists of sterile females, and the number of fertile females is very small, even in those cases where more than one female is permitted to live in a nest, as among wasps.

HUMBLE-BEES live in small communities, consisting of males, females, and workers; but

Photo by C. Reid] [*Wishaw, N.B.*

BEES.

Swarming from the hive after the queen.

their economy is very simple compared with that of the hive-bee, and they do not confine themselves to a single female to a nest.

The SOLITARY BEES are very numerous in species, and consist only of males and females. They do not live in communities, but each female constructs a dwelling for her own young. Many of them burrow in the ground, and they are so far gregarious that a large number of females will sometimes form their burrows near each other in the same bank. There are about two hundred different kinds of bees known to inhabit the British Isles. The solitary bees are very varied in their habits, and some of them are parasitic on other species.

The large CARPENTER-BEES, which form their nests in wood, are not British; but there are some small British species which make theirs in the interior of bramble-sticks. Some are very hairy; others are smooth, and look at first sight like small wasps, being banded with black and yellow. But one of the handsomest and most conspicuous of the solitary species is the FULVOUS BEE, which is a hairy species much resembling a small humble-bee, and is one often seen in abundance along with other bees, flying round sallow blossoms in spring.

SCALE-WINGED INSECTS, OR BUTTERFLIES AND MOTHS.

BY W. F. KIRBY, F.L.S.

BUTTERFLIES and MOTHS are easily distinguished from other insects by many very obvious characters, and a considerable number are remarkable for the beautiful and varied colours of their wings. These are, as it were, tiled with overlapping scales, attached to the membrane by a slender stem; hence their name, Scale-winged Insects. These scales differ very much in shape, sometimes being long and slender, and almost hair-like, while at other times they are widened at the extremity, like a battledore, or they may be short and broad, like a fan or a shovel. Different forms of scales are found on different parts of the wings of the same insect; and some forms of scale are peculiar to the male, as are usually the dense tufts of scales found on the fore wings of the Skipper Butterflies, and on the hind wings of the Chrysippus Butterfly. The varied colours of these scales are due partly to pigment, interposed between the extremely delicate double or triple tissues of which the scales are composed; or, more rarely, to the refraction of light from the surface of the scales themselves, or, as has recently been stated, to different coloured scales alternating so that the varying colours are visible at different angles, as in the metallic "shot" colour of the Purple Emperor Butterfly, and in various species found in South America and other countries. In the case of the Purple Emperor, and in many other butterflies, this "shot" colouring is confined to the males. Indeed, as a rule, female butterflies and moths are larger than the males, but far less brilliantly coloured than their mates. There are, however, many species in which the sexes differ little in size or colour; but it only rarely happens that the female is more brightly coloured than the male.

The bodies of butterflies and moths, the legs, and often more or less of the base or borders of the wings are clothed with hair or hair-like scales. These insects have a long or short proboscis, through which they imbibe their food, which consists of the honey of flowers, the sap of trees, or moisture from the ground. Like other insects, they have six legs in the perfect state; but in some species either the front or hind pair becomes more or less rudimentary, especially in the males.

Butterflies and moths pass through four stages. The egg is laid by the female on some plant which will provide suitable nourishment for the caterpillar. A caterpillar, which is the next stage, is a jointed, worm-like creature with sixteen legs; those corresponding with the legs of the perfect insect are horny, and a pair is placed on each of the first three joints behind the head. The next four pairs, called "pro-legs," are thick and fleshy, and a pair is placed under each of joints seven to ten (reckoning the head as joint one), the last joint of all being provided with a pair slightly differing from the others, and called "claspers." In many young caterpillars, however, and also in the full-grown caterpillars of a considerable number of moths (especially among those with slender

Photo by J. Edwards] [*Colesborne.*

LEAF-BUTTERFLY.

These butterflies are so remarkably like certain leaves that it is almost impossible to distinguish the difference even at close quarters.

Photo by L. H. Jouteli] [*New York.*

SOUTH AMERICAN LONG-WINGED BUTTERFLIES.

Showing external resemblance between two butterflies of different families.

Photo by L. H. Jouteli] [*New York.*

DIANA FRITILLARY.

The male is dark brown, with a broad orange border spotted with black. The female has green marginal markings.

Photo by J. Edwards] [*Colesborne.*

QUEEN OF SPAIN FRITILLARY.

Brown above, with plush spots; spotted with silver beneath.

bodies), one or more of the first three pairs of pro-legs may be rudimentary or absent, and the caterpillar walks by arching its back at every step, in a way that must be seen to be appreciated, though such caterpillars (popularly called Loopers, on account of the way they loop up their bodies in walking) are often very active, and cover the ground much more rapidly than one might imagine. Sometimes the claspers, or last pair of legs, are modified into tentacles, which, in the caterpillars of the Puss-moth and its allies, contain retractile whips, used as weapons of defence.

Caterpillars are very voracious, and increase in size with great rapidity; and whenever their skin gets too tight, after splitting it, they slip it off (along with the lining of the stomach and intestines), and after a few hours' lethargy, necessary to recover from the debilitating effects of such a serious operation, and to give the new skin time to dry and harden, they begin to feed again as voraciously as ever. The number of these moults varies according to the species; when the caterpillar has attained its full growth, it enters upon the third stage of its life as a pupa, or chrysalis.

A pupa means a doll, or swaddled baby, and is a very appropriate name for the dark-coloured object, cased in a horny skin, with no detached organs visible, except the sheath for the proboscis in some of the Hawk-moths, in which this organ is unusually long, but with the separate cases of the wings, legs, etc., of the future butterfly or moth plainly visible in the sutures on its surface. The pupæ of some butterflies have more or less metallic colours; and to these only is the term "chrysalis" applicable.

Some pupæ are naked, and those of most butterflies are either suspended by the tail, or attached to a branch by a belt of silk round the body. Those of moths are generally formed either in an earthen cell under the surface of the ground, or else are enclosed in an oval case called a "cocoon," chiefly composed of silk, though sometimes moss or chips of wood are worked into it. Other pupæ are found between leaves, or, in the case of caterpillars which feed in the wood of trees, or in the stems of plants, in the galleries where they have lived.

When the perfect butterfly or moth is ready to emerge, the pupa splits, and the insect works its way to the open air. Its body is limp and heavy, and the wings are like little flaps of wet rag; but it discharges a quantity of superfluous fluid, generally of a red colour, and fixes itself on a branch, or other convenient foothold, where its wings can hang downwards.

Photo by Highley.

TAWNY ADMIRAL.

A North American butterfly.

The expansion and contraction of the muscles pump air into the hollow tubes which form the framework of the wings; these rapidly expand to their full size, and become dry and firm at the same time. After this, the insect flies about with its companions, pairs, lays its eggs, and then dies, after enjoying its life for a period, varying according to the species and the season, from a few hours to several months.

We have not yet spoken of the feelers, or antennæ, of butterflies and moths. They are two long, jointed organs, nearly always knobbed at the end in butterflies, or at least the terminal joints are thicker than the rest. But in moths the antennæ are of different shapes, and generally end in a point. Sometimes they are simple and thread-like; sometimes they are thickest in the middle, and thinner at both ends, as in the Hawk-moths; and they are often comb-like, especially in the males, as in the Silk-moths.

BUTTERFLIES.

As already mentioned, butterflies may be distinguished from moths by their antennæ being thickened at the extremities. There are comparatively few species in Europe—only about three hundred, of which between sixty and seventy are met with in the British Islands; but in tropical countries they are much more numerous and varied. It is a mistake to suppose that butterflies are always bright-coloured insects, and moths the reverse; for though many butterflies are brightly coloured, others are very dingy. On the other hand, although it is equally true that many moths are dull-coloured, others, especially among those with slender bodies, or those which fly by day, are quite as brilliantly coloured as any butterflies.

Photo by L. H. Joutel] *[New York.*

CATERPILLAR OF TAWNY ADMIRAL.

Remarkable for the sharply contrasted black and pale markings.

Photo by E. C. Atkinson.

BLUE BUTTERFLY.

Among the most conspicuous of the smaller European butterflies.

Butterflies are divided into several groups, the first of which includes the BRUSH-FOOTED BUTTERFLIES, so called because the front pair of legs is converted into hairy paws, useless for walking, and only employed for toilet purposes. This is a very extensive group, including about half the butterflies known, and is divided into several smaller sections. The most interesting species among the DANAIDS is the MONARCH, one of the largest and commonest butterflies found in North America. It is migratory in its habits, and has succeeded in acclimatising itself throughout the Pacific islands as far as Australia and New Zealand, as well as in the Canaries; and so many specimens have been taken recently in the south of England that it seems not unlikely to take up its residence there also. It is a tawny butterfly, not unlike the one represented on the preceding page, but much larger, measuring about 5 inches across the wings. The caterpillar is yellow, with transverse black bands, and a pair of long, black slender filaments near each extremity of the body. The pupa is pale green, with golden spots, and is suspended by the tail, as is the case with most of those of the Brush-footed Butterflies.

The next group, the LONG-WINGED BUTTERFLIES, includes a considerable number of species with long rounded wings, found in tropical and sub-tropical America. A species with black and transparent markings is shown on page 710, but many have wholly transparent wings, except for a narrow black or brown border.

Turning to more familiar insects, there are several kinds of large or moderate-sized tawny butterflies, marked with black spots and lines, called FRITILLARIES in England. The caterpillars are spiny, and feed on violets and other low-growing plants. The photograph on page 710 shows the DIANA FRITILLARY, a large and handsome species, which is somewhat of a rarity in the Southern States of America; it measures 4 inches in expanse, and the sexes are very dissimilar. It is dark brown, with a broad orange border spotted with black in the male, and rows of more or less connected green or white spots in the female.

Photo by W. Saville-Kent, F.Z.S.] *[Milford-on-Sea.*

BLUE MORPHO BUTTERFLY AND HUMMING-BIRD.

Note proportionate sizes.

The ANGLE-WINGED BUTTERFLIES include several of the best known and most brightly coloured British species, such as the RED ADMIRAL, a velvety black butterfly, with a transverse red band on the fore wings, and several white spots between this and the tip, the hind wings having a red border, spotted with black and blue. It measures about 2½ inches across

Photos by J. Edwards]

LARGE BLUE BUTTERFLY (MALE, FEMALE, AND UNDERSIDE).

Scarce and nearly extinct in England.

[*Colsborne.*

MAZARINE BLUE BUTTERFLY (MALE, FEMALE, AND UNDERSIDE).

Practically extinct in England.

Photos by J. Edwards]

LONG-TAILED BLUE BUTTERFLY (MALE, FEMALE, AND UNDERSIDE).

An occasional immigrant on the south coast of England.

[*Colsborne.*

BLOXWORTH BLUE BUTTERFLY (MALE, FEMALE, AND UNDERSIDE).

Probably a casual visitor in England.

the wings, and is common in gardens and orchards in summer and autumn. The caterpillar, which feeds on nettle, is brown or black, with yellow stripes and spines. The TAWNY ADMIRAL is a North American butterfly, remarkable for its resemblance to the larger butterfly called the Monarch, of which we have already spoken. The Danaids and Long-winged Butterflies have tough integuments and a disagreeable odour, which more or less protects them from birds. Many other butterflies belonging to other families have a superficial resemblance to these, and are believed to share in their immunity. This phenomenon is technically called "mimicry." The caterpillar of the tawny admiral is grey and black, with curious spiny tufts.

Photos by J. Edwards]

LARGE COPPER BUTTERFLY (MALE, FEMALE, AND UNDERSIDE).

Extinct in England since 1860.

[Colesborne.

DUSKY COPPER BUTTERFLY (MALE, FEMALE, AND UNDERSIDE).

Taken near Ilfracombe, August, 1857.

The group of the SATYRS contains a great variety of moderate-sized brown or tawny butterflies, usually with round spots centred with white towards the margins of the wings. Many species are common in meadows; others, which are dark brown or black, with red, white-centred marginal spots, are numerous in mountainous countries, and two species are found in the north of England and Scotland. The caterpillars of the Satyrs are usually smooth and green, with a forked tail, and the pupæ are formed on the surface of the ground.

The great BLUE BUTTERFLIES of South America form another group of Brush-footed Butterflies.

The second family is almost entirely American, and is only represented in England by a brown butterfly about an inch in expanse, called the DUKE OF BURGUNDY FRITILLARY. The caterpillar is reddish, and feeds on primroses. It is not a very abundant species in England.

The third family is represented in Britain by three very distinct sections of rather small butterflies, the largest of which scarcely measures more than an inch and a half across the wings. These are the HAIR-STREAKS (brown, with light lines on the under surface of the wings, and a short tail on the hind wings, except in the GREEN HAIR-STREAK, so named from the green under surface of the wings); the small BLUE BUTTERFLIES, which generally have brown females; and the COPPERS, the only common species of which measures about an inch across the wings. The fore wings are bright coppery red, with dark brown spots and borders, and the hind wings are dark brown, with a coppery red border, spotted outside with black. The small copper butterfly and some of the blues are common in meadows and gardens.

Photo by W. Saville-Kent, F.Z.S., Milford-on-Sea.

NEW GUINEA GOLDEN BUTTERFLY.

A remarkable and recently discovered swallow-tailed butterfly.

Many of the members of the fourth family are of a white or yellow colour, among which are the destructive WHITE CABBAGE-BUTTERFLIES, three species of which are very common in England, where they may be seen in every garden throughout the summer. The photograph on page 716 represents one of these at rest. A prettier species is the ORANGE-TIP, which is common in spring. The underside of the hind wings is mottled with green; and there is a bright orange spot before the tip of the fore wing, both above and below. Some of the South American butterflies of this family much resemble the Long-winged Butterflies of the same country.

Photo by W. Saville-Kent, F.Z.S., Milford-on-Sea.

AUSTRALIAN BUTTERFLIES.

Emerging from their pupæ.

The family of the SWALLOW-TAILED BUTTERFLIES includes a considerable number of large and handsome species, but they are not numerous in Europe, and only one black-and-yellow species, measuring 3 inches across the wings, is found in England, where it is now almost confined to the fens of the south-eastern counties; its green caterpillar, with transverse black bands spotted with orange, feeds on carrot, fennel, and other similar plants. All the caterpillars of this family are remarkable for possessing a retractile fork on the neck; but the butterflies do not all possess the long appendage to the hind wings which has given some of them the name of Swallow-tails. Thus it is wanting in most of the great BIRD-WINGED BUTTERFLIES of the Eastern Islands, one of which, the CRŒSUS BUTTERFLY, is represented in the Coloured Plate. The great difference between the sexes is well worth noting. The female is considerably larger than the male, but in the coloured figure the former has been reduced, owing to the exigencies of space. Mr. A. R. Wallace writes as follows of the capture of the first specimen:—

"One day about the beginning of January, I found a beautiful shrub with large white leafy bracts and yellow flowers, a species of Mussænda, and saw one of these noble insects hovering over it, but it was too quick for me, and flew away. The next day I went again to the same shrub and succeeded in catching

Photo by J. Edwards] [*Colesborne.*

BATH WHITE BUTTERFLY.

Always rare in England, though common on the Continent.

Photo by B. H. Bentley] [*Sheffield.*

GREEN-VEINED WHITE BUTTERFLY.

The cabbage-butterfly referred to on page 715.

a female, and the day after a fine male. I found it to be as I had expected, a perfectly new and most magnificent species, and one of the most gorgeously coloured butterflies in the world. Fine specimens of the male are more than seven inches across the wings, which are velvety black and fiery orange, the latter colour replacing the green of the allied species. The beauty and brilliancy of this insect are indescribable, and none but a naturalist can understand the intense excitement I experienced when I at length captured it. On taking it out of my net and opening the glorious wings, my heart began to beat violently, the blood rushed to my head, and I felt much more like fainting than I have done when in apprehension of immediate death. I had a headache the rest of the day, so great was the excitement produced by what will appear to most people a very inadequate cause."

The SKIPPERS, the last family of butterflies, are comparatively stout-bodied insects, with the antennæ widely apart at the base, and sometimes forked at the tip. They are not numerous in Europe; the prettiest of the British species is perhaps the PEARL-SKIPPER, which measures rather more than an inch across its brown and tawny wings; the under surface of the hind wings is green, and marked with several clear white spots.

Photo by J. Edwards] [*Colesborne.*

BLACK-VEINED WHITE BUTTERFLY.

A much rarer species in England now than formerly.

MOTHS.

Moths are much more numerous than butterflies, and there are about 2,000 different kinds found in the British Islands alone. Consequently we are able to notice only a few.

The HAWK-MOTHS have long, pointed

wings, thick, tapering bodies, and the antennæ thickest in the middle. The pink, greenish-striped ELEPHANT HAWK-MOTH (see page 718) is a comparatively small species. The specimens measure about $2\frac{1}{2}$ inches across the wings. Some species are much larger. The DEATH'S-HEAD HAWK-MOTH, whose caterpillar feeds on potato-leaves, is 5 or 6 inches in expanse; and some of the South American species measure as much as 9 inches. The caterpillars of the hawk-moths are generally green, often with oblique lines of a different colour on the sides. They are not hairy, though the skin is sometimes rough, and there is a fleshy appendage, called a "horn," on the back, just before the extremity of the body. The brown pupæ are found in cells in the ground.

Photo by E. C. Atkinson.

ORANGE-TIP.

Showing three different positions when wings are folded, and partly or entirely concealing upper wing.

The CHINESE MULBERRY-SILKWORM, which produces most of the silk of commerce, is a smooth, whitish caterpillar, about 2 inches long, with a horn. It is often reared in England on lettuce. The moth is a sluggish, stout-bodied insect. It is whitish, with two dusky stripes on the fore wings. The pupa is enclosed in an oval whitish or yellow cocoon of pure silk.

Photo by J. Edwards, Colesborne.

LARGE GRIZZLED SKIPPER BUTTERFLY.

Upper- and under-sides.

The EMPEROR-MOTHS, of which there is only one species in England, likewise spin large cocoons, sometimes used for commercial purposes. The caterpillars are generally more or less spiny or tufted. Some of the moths have long tails on the hind wings, like swallow-tailed butterflies, and there are several species in South Europe, South Africa, the East Indies, and North America of a beautiful sea-green colour. It will be noticed that the specimens represented on page 718 have the tails a little broken, which is a very common accident with swallow-tailed butterflies and moths. We may also notice the round

Photo by W. P. Dando, F.Z.S.] [Regent's Park.

SWALLOW-TAILED BUTTERFLY

The only British species of this butterfly is almost confined to the fen districts of Norfolk.

Photo by Highley.

ELEPHANT HAWK MOTHS.

Showing position when at rest.

Photo by Highley.

LUNA MOTHS.

A green North American moth with tail, allied to the English Emperor-moth.

or crescent-shaped spots in the middle of the wings of some of the moths represented on this page and the next. These are very characteristic of the emperor-moths, and there is often a transparent spot in the centre of the concentric markings. Two other North American species of this family are shown in the photographs on page 719, rather under natural size. The second of these, the CECROPIA MOTH, is represented with its cocoon. This moth has occasionally been captured in England, having been introduced either accidentally or by design. A year or two ago a specimen was brought to the Natural History Museum at South Kensington which had been caught in the street close by. During the summer many foreign butterflies and moths may be seen alive in the Insect-house at the Zoological Gardens, Regent's Park, and several of the photographs given in these pages were taken from specimens living there in the summer of 1901. The largest of the emperor-moths is the great ATLAS MOTH of North India, the largest of all known butterflies or moths, which occasionally measures almost a foot across its reddish-tawny wings.

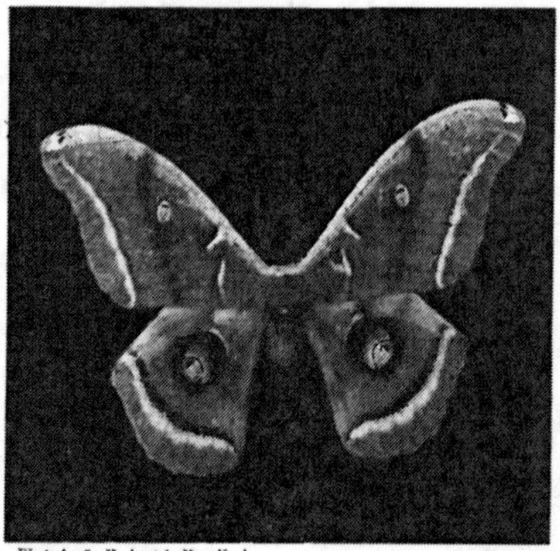

Photo by L. H. Joutel, New York.

POLYPHEMUS MOTH.

A handsome North American Emperor-moth.

The IMPERIAL MOTH, a handsome North American moth belonging to a family allied to the emperor-moths, is represented below.

The EGGARS form another allied family, also with tufted caterpillars, but with the central eye of the wings absent, or reduced to a small black spot. A set of remarkable photographs, representing the eggs, caterpillars, cocoons and sections of cocoons, and the moths of a large and handsome species—the CYPRESS-MOTH of Smyrna—appears on pages 720 and 721. We have received the following account of their habits from Mr. Mavroyeni, to whom we are indebted for the photographs: "In the month of July they start weaving their cocoons, in which they remain for seventeen days. A couple of weeks after the moths have emerged from their cocoons and laid their eggs, the eggs hatch, and the young caterpillars run up the tree, and feed from the end of August, during autumn, winter, and spring." We believe that the cocoons of this species are prepared for use as silk in Greece.

Photo by Highley.

CECROPIA MOTH.

The largest of the North American Emperor-moths.

Among other kinds, we may notice the bright-coloured TIGER-MOTHS, with their black and cream-coloured fore wings and red-and-black hind wings, which frequent gardens, and are reared from reddish-brown caterpillars with long hair. These are stout-bodied moths; and there are other moths, with brown fore wings and whitish hind wings, which fly to candles, or buzz over flowers in the evening. These are called OWL-MOTHS; but there are larger and handsomer members

Photo by L. H. Joutel] [New York.

IMPERIAL MOTH.

Yellow with purplish-brown dots and blotches. Native of North America

Photo by C. N. Mavroyeni] [*Smyrna.*

COCOONS OF CYPRESS-MOTH.

These yield silk.

Photo by C. N. Mavroyeni] [*Smyrna.*

CYPRESS-MOTHS AT REST.

In the month of July they start weaving their cocoons, in which they remain for seventeen days. A couple of weeks after their eggs are hatched, and the young caterpillars run up the tree, and feed from the end of August, during autumn, winter, and spring.

of the same family, called YELLOW UNDERWINGS, measuring nearly 2 inches across the wings, and likely to be flushed in strawberry-beds or hay-fields. They have brown fore wings, and bright yellow hind wings, with a black border. The RED-UNDERWING MOTH is about 3 inches in expanse, and has greyish-brown fore wings, and red hind wings, with a black central band; it is often seen flying about willow-trees in the afternoon, or resting on tree-trunks, when the bright-coloured hind wings are quite concealed.

The LOOPER-MOTHS are those produced from caterpillars which have only ten legs instead of sixteen, as already explained. Most have slender bodies of moderate length, and broad and rather brightly coloured wings, green, russet-brown, yellow, etc. Some, measuring about an inch in expanse, are called CARPET-MOTHS, from the zigzag patterns on the fore wings, which are generally black and white, or brown and white, and sometimes green. The YELLOW-SHELL, a yellow moth, with some zigzag brown and whitish lines across the wings, which expand about an inch, is common in hedges and bushes. The white, black-and-yellow-spotted GOOSEBERRY-MOTH, or MAGPIE-MOTH, so common in gardens, is also one of the Loopers.

Among the smaller moths are the PEARL-MOTHS, with long slender bodies, wings longer than broad, and often with a pearly lustre, one or two species of which are common among nettles. We may also mention the SNOUT-MOTH, a brown slender-bodied moth, with a pointed beak projecting in front of the head, likewise a common insect among nettles. The GRASS-MOTHS are small moths, with narrow whitish fore wings, and broad brownish hind wings, which they wrap round their bodies when at rest. They are common in every field and meadow. The BELL-MOTHS have broad truncated fore wings, and rounded hind wings. A species belonging to this family, with green fore wings and brown hind wings, may be shaken from every oak-tree in summer, and at the same time numbers of its little green caterpillars will drop themselves down, and remain swinging at the end of a thread, till they think that the danger is past, when they climb up again.

The CLOTHES-MOTHS, familiar to everybody, are representatives of an enormous family of small moths, comprising nearly two-thirds of the British species, but only a few live in houses. Most have narrow wings with long fringes, and many feed in tortuous galleries which they eat in the substance of leaves. Some are among the smallest moths known.

Photo by C. N. Mavroyeni] [*Smyrna.*

CYPRESS-MOTHS.

The inside of the cocoons, showing the pupæ.

The WHITE PLUME-MOTH, which may be noticed floating about in weedy places like a piece of thistle-down, is a representative of a small family in which the fore wings are divided into three separate feathers, and the hind wings into two. The other species are brown, and smaller. When at rest, they look like small daddy-long-legs.

The TWENTY-PLUME MOTH is a yellowish-grey species, less than an inch in expanse, often to be seen at rest on windows or palings. It might easily be taken for a small looper-moth, but that each wing is split into six feathers.

SILKWORMS.

We have now completed a rapid survey of the principal groups of Butterflies and Moths, and may fittingly conclude this part of our subject by giving a short account of the history of SILKWORMS—insects which far surpass all other butterflies and moths in their importance to mankind, on account of the valuable product which is obtained from their cocoons. The industry has been carried on from time immemorial in China; and many old Chinese works contain interesting particulars, especially relating to the rearing of silkworms by the queens and their ladies, for silk was probably a royal monopoly in old times. These Chinese records date back to about 2200 B.C., when the silk industry was already flourishing; but, according to the usually received tradition, silkworms were first reared during the reign of the Emperor Hwang-té (2640 B.C.) by his queen. The following extracts from the "Le-he Book of Ceremonies," written between 204 B.C. and 135 B.C., and quoted by Horsfield and Moore in their "Catalogue of the Lepidoptera of the East India

Photo by C. N. Mavroyeni] [*Smyrna.*

CYPRESS-CATERPILLARS.

When they leave their cocoons, the young caterpillars run up the tree to feed.

Photo by J. Peat Millar] *[Beith.*

DEATH'S-HEAD MOTH.

Remarkable for the skull-like pattern on the back.

Museum," may not be uninteresting to our readers:—

"In the first month of spring orders were issued to the forester not to cut down the mulberry-trees; and when the cooing doves were observed fluttering with their wings, and the crested jays alighting upon the mulberry-trees, people were to prepare the trays and frames for the purpose of rearing the silkworms.

"In the spring season, when the empress and her ladies had fasted, they proceeded to the east, and personally engaged in picking the mulberry-leaves. On this occasion the married and single ladies were forbidden to wear their ornaments, and the usual employments of females were lessened, in order to encourage attention to the silkworms. When the rearing of the silkworms was completed, the cocoons were divided (for reeling) and the silk weighed (for weaving), each person being rewarded according to her labour, in order to provide dresses for the celestial and ancestorial sacrifices. In all this none dared indulge in indolence.

"In the last month of summer the order was given to the female officers to dye the silk of various

Photo by W. Saville-Kent, F.Z.S., Milford-on-Sea.

DAY-FLYING MOTH OF MADAGASCAR.

Remarkable for the brilliancy of its colours—green and black, with the hind wings brilliant coppery red towards the extremity.

Photo by J. Peat Millar] *[Beith.*

CONVOLVULUS HAWK-MOTH.

A grey moth, with pink bands on the body.

Photo by C. N. Mavrogeni] [Smyrna.

GREAT PEACOCK-MOTH.

Brown with pale borders. The largest moth found in Europe.

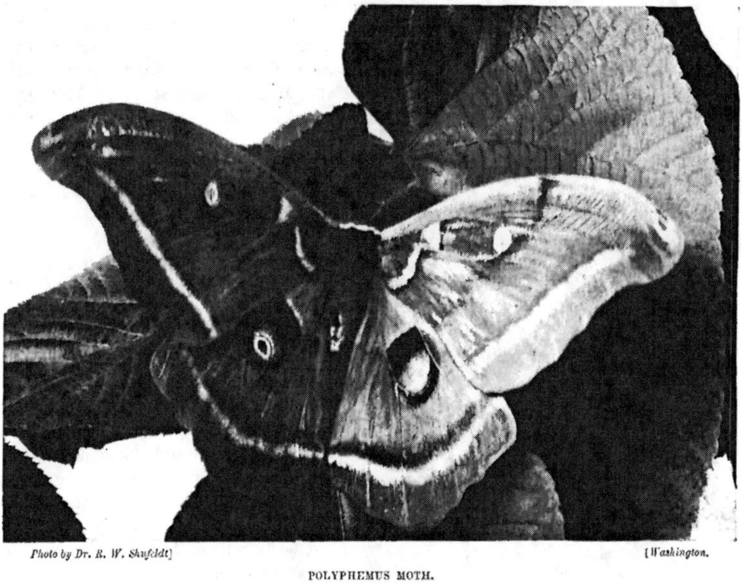

Photo by Dr. R. W. Shufeldt] [Washington.

POLYPHEMUS MOTH.

On leaves of linden-tree, just out of cocoon. A native of North America.

colours, in order to weave chequered sarcenets, comprising black and white, black and green, green and red, with red-and-white checks—all of which was to be done according to the ancient rule, without the least variation; the black, yellow, azure, and red tints were all to be correct and good, without the least fault, in order to provide dresses for the celestial and ancestorial sacrifices, and standards for distinguishing the high and low degrees.

Photo by W. Saville-Kent, F.Z.S.] [Milford-on-Sea.

WHITE PLUME-MOTH.

A very delicate insect. The wings are cleft almost to the base into separate feathers, two on the fore wings and three on the hind wings.

"In ancient times the emperor and his princes had a public mulberry garden and a silkworm establishment erected near some river. On the morning of the first day of the third month of spring, the sovereign, wearing a leather cap and a plain garment, ascertained by lot the chief of his three queens, with the most honourable amongst his concubines, and caused them to attend to the rearing of the silkworms in the above-named establishment. They then brought the eggs of the worms, and washed them in the river above alluded to, after which they picked the mulberry-leaves in the public garden, and aired and dried them, in order to feed the worms.

Photo by W. Saville-Kent, F.Z.S.] [Milford-on-Sea.

INDIAN SWALLOW-TAILED MOTH.

Resembles the American Luna Moth figured on page 718, and of an equally delicate green.

"When the season was over, the royal concubines, having completed the business of rearing the silkworms, brought the cocoons to show them to the prince, when he presented the cocoons again to his consort, whereupon his consort said, 'This is the material of which your highness's robes are to be formed.' Having said which, she covered herself with her robe, and received the cocoons. On this occasion the ladies of the court were honoured with the present of a sheep. This was the mode in which the presentation of the cocoons was anciently conducted."

In the reign of Justinian eggs of the Chinese mulberry-silkworm were smuggled into Europe by two monks, and the culture of silk rapidly spread through Southern Europe, where it has continued to form a staple industry ever since. In the Peloponnesus especially such large plantations of mulberry-trees were grown for the purpose of rearing silkworms as to give the peninsula its modern name of Morea. Silk is obtained in different parts of the world from the cocoons of various other moths, chiefly belonging to the group of Emperor-moths; but these products are only of local importance, and are not likely to compete with the mulberry-silkworm.

HALF-WINGED INSECTS, OR BUGS AND FROG-HOPPERS.

BY W. F. KIRBY, F.L.S.

THE order including the Bugs and Frog-hoppers is divided into two sub-orders. There are also one or two small groups, sometimes treated as separate orders, and sometimes regarded as aberrant sections of the order, to which we shall allude later.

The TRUE BUGS have their fore wings of a horny texture, but generally overlapping, and the extremities form a transparent membrane, resembling that of the hind wings. They have a long sucking-proboscis curved down beneath their bodies, and their antennæ usually consist of only four or five long joints. Most are vegetable-feeders, but some species feed on the juices of other insects, while a few attack warm-blooded animals, either casually or habitually.

The first family includes the SHIELD-BUGS. These derive their name from the unusual development of a part of the thorax called the "scutellum." In most insects it is only a small plate of no great importance, attached to the end of the thorax; but in the Shield-bugs it forms a great solid arch, covering the whole of the wings, and protecting them as the wing-cases protect the wings of beetles. There are only a few small species in England, but a great number of beautiful species inhabit warm countries, some of a brilliant blue or green or yellow, or spotted. Many of them are comparatively large insects, nearly an inch long, and resemble brilliantly coloured beetles, from which, however, they can easily be distinguished by the antennæ, the proboscis, and the shield, the latter of which is not divided down the middle like the wing-cases of beetles.

Photos by W. P. Dando, F.Z.S.] *[Regent's Park.*

SHIELD-BUG.

In tropical countries these bugs are often as large as cockchafers.

JUNIPER-BUG.

Some species of this family are carnivorous as well as herbivorous.

Next to the Shield-bugs, and considered by many entomologists as belonging to the same group, are the PENTAGONAL SHIELD-BUGS, so called because the scutellum, though much smaller than in the Shield-bugs, is often half as long as the abdomen, and forms a broad triangle, sometimes broken at the sides, so as to make a five-sided plate, lying above the bases of the wings. Several green or brown species of this family, about half an inch long, are common in England among bushes. Many have a very disagreeable smell, and hence they are called STINK-BUGS in America. They feed on vegetable juices, and also frequently on soft-bodied insects.

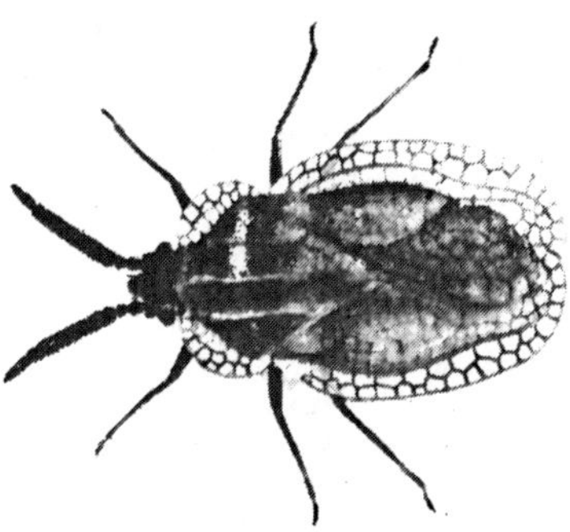

Photo by J. Edwards] *[Colesborne.*

LACE-WING BUG.

An elegant little insect, injurious to pear-trees.

Several species (chiefly foreign) among the Shield-bugs and the present group have a strong spine, or else a blunt protuberance, projecting from each shoulder.

The remaining plant-bugs are much more numerous—at least in England—than those already mentioned, and form several families, which cannot be noticed in detail. Many species are rather small and delicate creatures, narrower and softer than the Shield-bugs and Pentagonal Shield-bugs, and are adorned with various colours, black and red predominating. Some have more transparent wings than the others, such as the beautiful little LACE-WINGED BUGS, one species of which is often very destructive to pear-trees.

The BED-BUG is a reddish-brown, somewhat oval insect, common in many old houses, hiding in cracks and crevices in walls and woodwork, and coming out at night to suck the blood of sleepers with its sharp proboscis. There are allied species, sometimes found in hen-houses, pigeon-houses, and places where bats congregate. The bed-bug has only been known in England for a few centuries, and though now a great pest in all parts of the world, was probably a native of Africa originally.

The bed-bug, notwithstanding its offensive odour, is preyed upon by several other insects, among which are the common cockroach and the MASKED BUG. The latter is a black-winged bug about three-quarters of an inch long, and remarkable for the habits of its larva, which conceals itself with dust or fluff, so that it may steal upon its prey unobserved. The masked bug and its larva feed on soft-bodied insects of various kinds, and are more frequently found in outhouses than in dwelling-rooms. This bug occasionally attacks warm-blooded animals; and a short time ago a great deal of nonsense was published in the newspapers about a mysterious insect-pest in North America, called the KISSING-BUG, which seems to have been nothing more unusual than this insect. There are, however, some much larger species belonging to the same family, which are formidable pests in the Southern States of North America, Chili, and various other countries.

Photo by W. P. Dando, F.Z.S., Regent's Park.

MASKED BUG.

The larvæ of these insects cover themselves with dust, in order to creep upon their prey unnoticed.

After these insects come the WATER-BUGS, of which there are several families, though the number of species is comparatively small. Some are very slender insects, with long, slender legs, and may be seen running on the surface of ponds in England; while others, which are tropical species, are marine, and are met with running on the surface of the water in the open sea.

The largest members of the group are some of the great water-bugs found in Africa, India, and America. Their fore wings are of a light brown, and measure from 3 to 5 inches in expanse. Their legs are short and strong, and the front legs are adapted for grasping their prey, which consists of insects and small fishes. There are some smaller species in which the female lays her eggs in a cluster on the back of the male, which carries them about till they are hatched. These bugs fly about in the evening, and are frequently attracted by electric light.

In England there are two allied species called WATER-SCORPIONS, from their long front legs, which somewhat resemble the nippers of a scorpion. The commonest is a brown insect, with the abdomen red beneath. It is about an inch long, including the breathing-tube, which sticks out behind the body like a tail, and is formed of two separable parts. It is an oval insect, half as broad as long, and is common in stagnant water. The other species is twice as long, and is much more slender, with longer and more slender legs. It is yellowish brown, like most of the other water-bugs, and is a sluggish and rather scarce insect, creeping about in the mud at the bottom of deeper water than that preferred by the commoner species.

The WATER-BOATMEN are yellowish-brown insects, measuring half an inch in length, with smooth bodies, and long, hairy hind legs, with which they row themselves about on the water, as if with oars, while floating on their backs. All the larger water-bugs are capable of inflicting a severe puncture with their sharp proboscis, if handled incautiously.

Photo by W. P. Dando, F.Z.S.] *[Regent's Park.*

GREAT WATER-BUG.

Very similar species are found in Africa, Asia, and America.

Photo by W. P. Dando, F.Z.S.] *[Regent's Park.*

GREAT WATER-BUG.

These insects live in water during the day, and fly about in the evening.

The FROG-HOPPERS and their allies differ from the Bugs in the fore wings being uniform in texture throughout, and not membranous, with the tips transparent. Sometimes the fore wings are of a more or less horny texture, but they are frequently as transparent as the hind wings. All the species are plant-feeding insects.

The first family, the CICADAS, includes a number of large or moderate-sized species, in which the males are provided with a large, drum-like apparatus on the abdomen, and some of which make the loud noise for which they have long been celebrated. There is only one comparatively small species in England, which is rare, and almost confined to the New Forest. It is black, with transparent wings, about 1½ inch in expanse, and has red transverse lines on the abdomen. The largest Indian species, however, sometimes expands 8 inches. Cicadas have broad heads, broad short bodies, ending rather abruptly in a point, and their larvæ live in the ground, where they are sometimes injurious to the roots of trees. The wings are

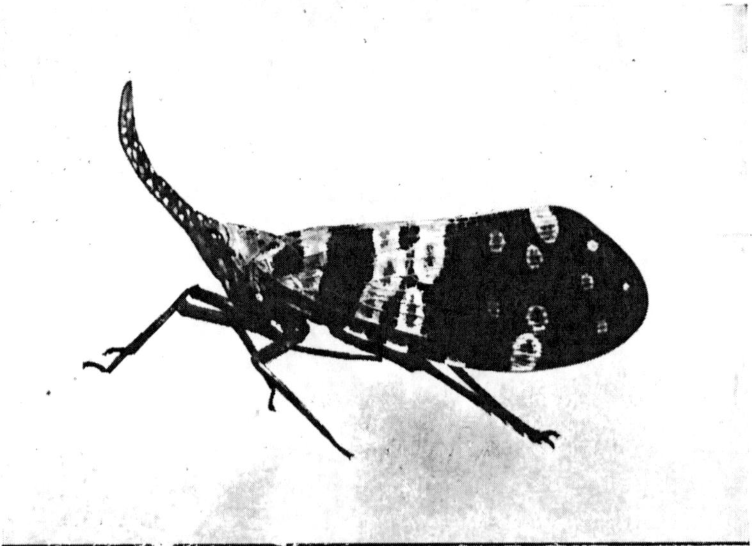

Photo by J. Edwards] [*Colesborne.*

INDIAN CANDLE-FLY.

Erroneously stated to be luminous.

usually, but not always, transparent—a very common Indian and Chinese species, about 3 inches in expanse, being black, with large yellow spots on the fore wings. In North America and Australia cicadas are often miscalled Locusts.

The LANTERN-FLIES, or CANDLE-FLIES, which form the next family, derive their name from having been stated to be luminous, a statement which is now considered very doubtful. They are insects of considerable size and bright colours, occasionally resembling butterflies and moths; the largest species, the LANTERN-FLY of South America, sometimes measures as much as 5 inches across the wings, which are of a pale yellowish or greenish tint, with a large round spot on the hind wings, formed of black rings or crescents, and enclosing one or two large white spots. On the head is an immense hollow, blunt protuberance, marked with one or two longitudinal red lines. In some species there is a curved horn in front of the head; in some the horn forms a short cross; in others it ends in a red knob; while others are destitute of such an appendage. The hind wings are often brightly coloured, red or yellow usually predominating.

The True Frog-hoppers are small insects about a quarter of an inch long, found among grass and bushes. The fore wings are of rather a stout consistency and uniform in colour (often yellowish), and the hind wings transparent. The larvæ are soft grubs, and live in the masses of froth so common in grass and bushes, which are vulgarly known as "cuckoo-spit."

Photo by W. P. Dando, F.Z.S., Regent's Park.

SCALE-INSECT.

The females die, covering their eggs with their own bodies.

Passing over several families of small species, we arrive at two which contain many very destructive insects. The Aphides, Plant-lice, or Smother-flies are the small green or brown winged or wingless insects which frequently cover the shoots of roses and other trees and plants, and exude a sweet sticky substance, called "honey-dew," very attractive to ants. One species, known as the American Blight, is extremely destructive to apple-trees, patches of a substance resembling white cotton appearing on the bark. Under these patches the bark rots from the attacks of the insects, the pest being very difficult to eradicate.

Many of the Aphides exhibit the curious phenomenon known as "alternation of generations." The first brood consists of winged males and females; but the eggs which the latter lay produce exclusively wingless females, or rather sexless creatures capable of laying eggs, and these multiply indefinitely for a time, till perfect males and females are again reproduced. In some cases the winged forms live on the leaves of trees, and the wingless forms at the roots of grass, etc. One of the most destructive of all these insects is the Vine-aphis, which was probably introduced into Europe from America, and which threatened at one time almost to destroy the vine industry in France. Wingless sexless forms live and multiply at the roots of vines; and in summer winged males and females are produced, which fly up, and lay eggs on the leaves; while some of the wingless insects also quit the ground, and form small galls on the vine-leaves. Although very abundant in America, the insect is not nearly so destructive to the plants which it attacks as in Europe.

Photo by W. P. Dando, F.Z.S., Regent's Park.

APHIS.

A sexual wingless form.

Some species of Scale-insects are almost equally destructive, especially to greenhouse plants. The male is slender and two-winged, but the female is wingless and often legless, and after depositing her eggs usually dies above them, thus forming a covering to protect them from injury. Cochineal consists of the bodies of a species of scale-insect which infests the leaves of a cactus in Mexico.

The True Lice are found on various species of mammals, and imbibe their food through a proboscis. The Bird-lice, or Biting-lice, form a well-defined group by themselves. They are sometimes regarded as forming distinct orders of insects; but some authors treat the first group as a degraded family of insects allied to the Frog-hoppers, and the second group as an equally degraded and aberrant family allied to the Lace-winged Insects.

SCALE-INSECTS.

Showing their appearance when crowded together on a branch.

TWO-WINGED INSECTS, OR FLIES.

BY W. F. KIRBY, F.L.S.

Photo by C. N. Mavroyeni] *[Smyrna.*

CICADA AND PUPÆ.

Noted for the loud drumming sound produced by the males.

THIS order of insects is probably one of the most numerous in individuals, though it may be that, when we know more of the insect population of the world, we shall find that it is outnumbered in species by the Beetles or the order to which the Bees and Ants belong. It differs from all other orders in possessing only two wings instead of four, which is the usual number in insects. The metamorphoses are complete, and the mouth is furnished with a proboscis for imbibing liquid food. Hind wings are represented in many species by a pair of organs called "poisers," resembling a knob at the end of a stick, and other species have two small additional lobes attached to the wing, called "winglets"; but there is no such thing as a really developed hind wing in any insect belonging to the group. They are always two-winged flies, except in the case of a few aberrant species, such as the Fleas, in which no wings, or only mere rudiments of wings, are to be met with. The Gnats, Daddy-long-legs, and House-flies are among the commonest representatives of this order.

The first section of the group includes the GNATS and the DADDY-LONG-LEGS, or CRANE-FLIES, the members of which may be distinguished by having moderately long antennæ, composed of more than six joints, and never terminating in a bristle. They are all vegetable-feeders, with the exception of the females of gnats and sand-flies, which are furnished with a lancet-like arrangement for sucking the blood of warm-blooded animals.

The GALL-FLIES, WHEAT-MIDGES, etc., have rather long, jointed antennæ, which are not feathered, though sometimes tufted on the sides, and their maggots produce small galls on various trees and plants, or distort and otherwise injure them. They resemble small gnats, and there are two particularly destructive species which attack corn in England and elsewhere,—the WHEAT-MIDGE, an orange-yellow fly with black eyes, which produces little yellowish or reddish maggots which injure the growing grain in the ear; and the HESSIAN FLY, which is brown, and produces semi-transparent maggots, which afterwards grow darker, and when full grown become pupæ resembling flax-seeds. The maggots attack the stalk, feeding on the sap till the stalk cracks and bends over. This is an infallible sign of their presence, and of the mischief they are doing.

Among the best-known insects of this group are the GNATS, or MOSQUITOES, of which there are many genera and species. There is no difference, however, to permit of their being classified in two separate popular categories. In England any of these troublesome insects are called Gnats; out of England they are termed Mosquitoes, if we are tormented by them, even though they may belong to the same species as the English ones—for "mosquito" is merely the Spanish word for "gnat" Anglicised.

Photo by W. P. Dando, F.Z.S., Regent's Park.

BROWN MOSQUITO.

Observe the proboscis in front of the head.

Gnats breed in standing water, fresh or otherwise, but seem to prefer rain-water, for they are very numerous about small pools and water-butts. Consequently they were formerly far more abundant in England than at present, when the fens were still undrained, and when every house had

Photo by W. P. Dando, F.Z.S., Regent's Park.

HORNET ROBBER-FLY.

Common in the south of England.

its rain-water butt. The females of some species construct small rafts of eggs, which float about on the surface of the water till hatched, and then produce small maggots with a breathing-apparatus at the end of the tail. In this condition they swim head-downwards, while the more compact pupa floats head-upwards. They may be destroyed by pouring a little kerosene into their breeding-places; and as this floats on the surface of the water, it does not interfere with the use of the water in water-butts, which is usually drawn off by a tap below. The males of gnats often have feathered antennæ and long, slender legs. The females, however, are more nocturnal in their habits, and come into houses in the evening, and keep people awake by their humming and painful "bites," or rather punctures, which frequently cause a distressing irritation for a day or two afterwards. What is worse is that they are now known to disseminate various diseases, such as elephantiasis and also malarial fever of every kind, in this manner—from the comparatively mild ague of the English fens (now nearly extinct) to the terrible malaria of Southern Europe, India, and Africa, formerly attributed to the unhealthy atmosphere of marshy countries, or to exposure to the night air in warm countries, but now known to be caused by the bites of the gnats, or mosquitoes, which breed in swampy places, and fly about in the evening. It is believed that only certain species of gnats convey the germs of these diseases; and it has been stated that, though ague-bearing species of gnats are still found in England, those which have been examined for the purpose have been free from these germs, and are therefore incapable of propagating the disease.

In many parts of the world gnats are excessively numerous and troublesome at certain seasons of the year, filling the air like clouds of dust, so that it is difficult to sleep or eat from the annoyance and irritation caused by their attacks. This will be readily credible to those who have experienced the pain which they cause even when not very numerous, and have been kept awake at night by their shrill piping as they approach. They appear to be equally numerous in cold and warm countries—Lapland, France, South Russia, Italy, various parts of America, and in fact most parts of the world being liable to the inordinate multiplication of different species.

In England they were formerly so abundant in the fenlands that mosquito-curtains were in use less than a century ago, and may be so still. But their numbers have so diminished of late years that, whenever gnats are a little more troublesome than usual, it is reported that there has been an invasion of mosquitoes. A year or

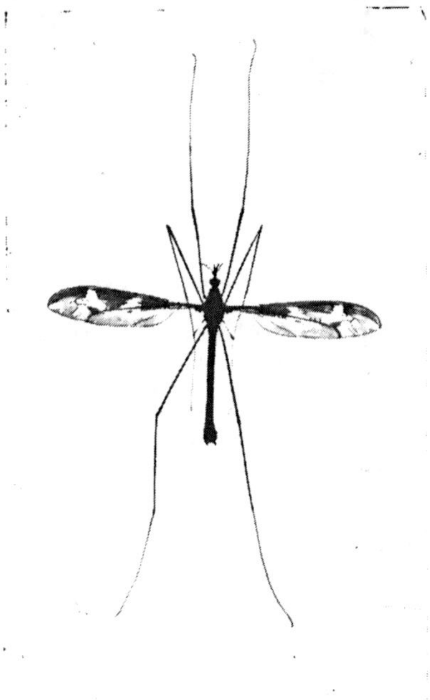

Photo by W. P. Dando, F.Z.S.] [Regent's Park.

DADDY-LONG-LEGS.

Large species, with variegated wings.

two ago there was a report that "mosquitoes" had been brought to Cromer in some fishing-vessel, and the newspapers contained paragraphs about "mosquitoes" having caused much annoyance in different parts of London. But many of the specimens submitted to the inspection of entomologists proved to be nothing more than the commonest of all the blood-sucking gnats, called the PIPING-GNAT by Linnæus, on account of its shrill note. The note is produced by the rapid vibration of the wings, which has been estimated at the rate of 3,000 per minute. Gnats do not always fly near the ground. Sometimes they have been seen ascending from cathedrals and other high buildings in such vast swarms that they resembled clouds of smoke, and gave rise to the idea that the building was actually on fire.

Equally troublesome and annoying are the SAND-FLIES, as they are called in England, or the BLACK-FLIES, as they are called in America. They are very small flies, short and broad, and with broader wings than gnats; and one of them, which actually destroys many mules and other domestic animals in the Mississippi Valley, as we learn from Professor Comstock, is called the BUFFALO-GNAT, from a fancied resemblance of the side-view of the insect to a buffalo. Other species are equally destructive to the cattle in the Banat of Hungary. It is a curious circumstance that, in the case of nearly all two-winged flies which attack men and animals, it is usually only the females which suck blood, the males frequenting flowers and being perfectly harmless.

Photos by W. P. Dando, F.Z.S.]

HOVER-FLY.

This fly has a superficial resemblance to a bee. (See page 734.)

[Regent's Park.

RAT-TAILED LARVA.

Common in filthy water.

Respecting mosquitoes in South America, Mr. H. W. Bates writes, in his work "The Naturalist on the Amazons," when passing a night in a boat about twenty-five miles from the town of Villa Nova: "At night it was quite impossible to sleep for mosquitoes; they fell upon us by myriads, and without much piping came straight at our faces as thick as rain-drops in a shower. The men crowded into the cabins, and then tried to expel the pests by the smoke from burnt rags; but it was of little avail, although we were half suffocated during the operation." But the sand-flies, encountered a little higher up the river, were much worse: "We made acquaintance on this coast with a new insect-pest, the Piúm, a minute fly, two-thirds of a line in length, which here commences its reign, and continues henceforward as a terrible scourge along the upper river, or Solimoens, to the end of the navigation on the Amazons. It comes forth only by day, relieving the mosquito at sunrise with the greatest punctuality, and occurs only near the muddy shores of the stream, not one ever being found in the shade of the forest. In places where it is abundant, it accompanies canoes in such dense swarms as to resemble thin clouds of smoke. It made its appearance in this way the first day after we crossed the river. Before I was aware of the presence of flies, I felt a slight itching on my neck, wrist, and ankles, and, on looking for the cause, saw a number of tiny objects, having a disgusting resemblance to lice, adhering to the skin. This was my first introduction to the much-talked-of Piúm. On close examination, they are seen to be small two-winged insects, with dark-coloured body and pale legs and wings, the latter closed lengthwise over the back. They alight imperceptibly, and, squatting close, fall at once to work, stretching forward their tiny front legs, which are in constant motion, and seem to act as feelers, and then applying their short, broad snouts to the skin. Their abdomens soon become distended and red with blood, and then, their thirst satisfied, they soon move off, sometimes so stupefied with their potations that they can scarcely fly. No pain is felt whilst they are at work, but they each leave a small circular raised spot on the skin, and a disagreeable irritation. The latter may be avoided in great measure by pressing out the blood which remains in the spot; but this is a troublesome task when one has several hundred punctures in the course of a day [like Prince Siror, in one of Bulwer Lytton's stories, who fell "pierced by five hundred spears"]. I took the trouble to dissect specimens, to ascertain the way in which the little pests operate. The mouth consists of a pair of thick fleshy lips, and two triangular horny lancets, answering to the upper lip and tongue of other insects. This is applied closely to the skin, a puncture is made with the lancets, and the blood then sucked through between these into the œsophagus, the circular spot which results coinciding with the shape of the lips. In the course of a few days the red spots dry up, and the skin in time becomes blackened with the endless number of discoloured punctures that are crowded together. The irritation they produce is more acutely felt by some persons than others. I once travelled with a middle-aged Portuguese who was laid up for three weeks from the attacks of Piúm, his legs being swelled to an enormous size, and the punctures aggravated into spreading sores."

Photo by W. P. Dando, F.Z.S., Regent's Park.

HOUSE-FLY (MALE AND FEMALE).

The larvæ of the house-fly live in refuse, so do not thrive where cleanliness abounds.

However, the traveller in Amazonia has one consolation: the great rivers which traverse the forests are of three different colours; and the black-water rivers—so called from the dark colour of the water, owing apparently to the amount of vegetable matter which they hold in solution—are never infested with mosquitoes. Probably the character of the water renders it unsuitable to them for breeding purposes.

The CRANE-FLIES, or DADDY-LONG-LEGS, are also very injurious insects, but in a different manner, for their subterranean maggots feed on and destroy the roots of grass in the same way as the grubs of the Cockchafers. They are insects of considerable size, with slender bodies, terminating in a short, horny point (the ovipositor) in the female, and with long, slender legs, which are liable to break off at the least touch. The commonest species has a grey body and transparent wings; but there is a larger one with the wings prettily variegated with brown, and a smaller one in which there are yellow markings towards the end of the body.

The more typical FLIES have usually shorter and broader wings, and thicker, shorter, and more hairy legs, than those just mentioned; and the antennæ have usually only three or four joints, and are often furnished with a long, slender bristle at or before the end of the last joint.

As in the case of the Gnats and Crane-flies, so as regards the more typical Flies, we have only space to notice a few of the more important families.

Some of the GAD-FLIES are no larger than house-flies, but others are as large as wasps or larger, with broader wings, and of a black, grey, or yellowish colour; they frequent fields, and settle on cattle, or on our clothes or hands. Some have transparent and others dark-coloured wings, but they are all capable of inflicting a severe puncture, often sufficient to draw blood, even in the case of the smaller species.

Photo by W. P. Dando, F.Z.S., Regent's Park.

BLUE-BOTTLE FLY, OR BLOW-FLY.

These flies deposit their eggs on meat, when it becomes "fly-blown."

The prettiest of the gad-flies are the GOLDEN-EYED FLIES. They are black, with the abdomen more or less marked with yellow; and black, or black and transparent, wings. The eyes are of a beautiful golden green, dotted and lined with purple. They are moderately stout insects, about the third of an inch long, and are not uncommon. Another insect, known as the BLOOD-SUCKING RAIN-FLY, has a rather long and slender body for a gad-fly, and is nearly half an inch long. It is of a lighter or darker grey, with reddish markings on the sides of the abdomen in the male. The wings are greyish brown with whitish dots, and a white mark towards the tip. Both these flies are very troublesome, the latter chiefly on the edges of woods or near water, especially in rainy weather.

The ROBBER-FLIES are large flies, with long, tapering bodies, of a black or partly yellow colour, and feed on smaller flies and other insects of different kinds. They have very thick, hairy legs, and a strong proboscis. A handsome Australian species, allied to these, but with a broader body, is represented in the Coloured Plate.

The HORNET ROBBER-FLY, represented on page 731, is one of the most conspicuous of the British species. Among other places, it may be seen flying over the short grass at the top of the cliffs between Brighton and Rottingdean. They are very predaceous, and are probably rather beneficial than otherwise, by contributing to keep down injurious insects. But in North America there is a species called the BEE-KILLER, which is an extremely destructive insect, taking up its station in front of a hive, and killing large numbers of bees as they fly backwards and forwards from the hive.

The HOVER-FLIES are brightly coloured, rather smooth flies, and are familiar objects in gardens, and in open places in woods. They have the habit of hovering motionless in the air, and then darting off suddenly. Some of the larger species proceed from curious maggots, with long tails, which have been compared to the tail of a rat. These live in putrid water; and as the flies have a slight resemblance to bees, the fact is believed to have given rise to the old fable that bees are generated from the rotting carcases of oxen or other large animals.

The BOT-FLIES are remarkable for being parasitic on warm-blooded animals, their maggots living in tumours on the skin of oxen, known as "warbles," or in the stomach and intestines of horses, or in the nostrils and other cavities in the heads of sheep or deer.

Photo by W. P. Dando, F.Z.S., Regent's Park.

BLUE-BOTTLE FLY, OR BLOW-FLY.

This photograph shows the wings expanded.

The HOUSE-FLIES and their allies form a very large group, divided into many families. The true house-fly is an autumn insect; but there are other flies which resemble it which live in houses at different times of the year. Most of them are harmless, although there is one species, very like a house-fly, which comes into houses in rainy weather, and inflicts a puncture like a gad-fly. This is the meaning of the popular saying that "the flies bite in rainy weather."

Although house-flies do not bite, yet they are sometimes exceedingly troublesome when they are in unusual numbers; and as they settle everywhere, they may convey infection mechanically, though not as the principal agents in the dissemination of definite diseases, like the mosquitoes. Thus, in Egypt, they are said frequently to convey ophthalmia, a very prevalent disease in that country.

The very first paper published in the "Transactions of the present Entomological Society of London" (for the existing Society had several short-lived predecessors) was a paper read by William Spence at the meeting on April 7, 1834, about a year after the Society had been definitely founded, entitled "Observations on a Mode practised in Italy of excluding the Common House-fly from Apartments." This desirable result is attained simply by stretching a net of white or coloured thread, with meshes of an inch or more in diameter, across an open window, which the flies will not venture to pass, if the room is lighted from one side only—"for if there be a *thorough* light either from an opposite or side window, the flies pass through the net without scruple." Mr. Spence's son also referred to a passage in Herodotus where he says that Egyptian fishermen in his time defended themselves from the gnats by covering their beds with the nets which they had used in the day for fishing, and through which these insects, though they bit through linen or woollen, did not even attempt to bite. The matter seems to have been overlooked in recent years, though it is evidently well worthy of consideration when flies or gnats are troublesome.

There is a conspicuous insect allied to the house-flies, but a little larger, measuring about half an inch in length. It is called the NOON-DAY FLY, and is often seen in considerable numbers, in the hottest part of the day, flying round and settling on the trunks and leaves of trees; it also settles on cow-dung. It is a shining black fly, with the sides and under surface of the head golden yellow in the male; the wings are transparent, slightly tinged with pale brown, and bright rusty yellow towards the base.

The African TSETSE-FLY is not very unlike a house-fly, and is one of the worst pests to cattle in those parts of Africa which it infests; for any horse, ox, or dog attacked by it will infallibly die after a longer or shorter period of suffering, though wild animals and sucking calves are not affected by it. It used to be supposed that the fly itself infused some deadly venom with its puncture; but later experiments have led naturalists to the conclusion that the fly is not itself poisonous, but that it forms the channel of communication of some fatal disease, just as some species of mosquitoes convey the infection of malaria.

The BLOW-FLIES, or BLUE-BOTTLES, of which there are several species closely allied to each other, are common in houses; and a smaller brilliant green fly, called the GREEN-BOTTLE FLY, is common on hedges. These are all flies which lay their eggs on fresh or putrid meat, when it is said to be "fly-blown." They will also lay their eggs in open sores; and in former days the sufferings of the wounded after a battle were often frightfully aggravated by this cause; and at the present day farmers would frequently lose sheep through their attacks, if they were not carefully tended in hot weather.

Photo by W. P. Dando, F.Z.S., Regent's Park.

TSETSE-FLY.

Destructive to horses and cattle in Africa.

Various species of flies in Eastern Europe, the Southern States of America, Jamaica, etc., habitually lay their eggs in the mouths or nostrils of men and animals, and the resulting maggots cause dreadful suffering and often death. In India, and especially in the Eastern Archipelago, there are some brilliantly coloured, smooth, metallic blue and green flies as big as humble-bees. There is also a family of flies allied to the house-fly, which have very bristly bodies, and are parasitic on caterpillars, like ichneumon-flies.

There are other flies which easily attract attention, such as the yellow hairy fly found about cow-dung, and some rather small species with prettily variegated wings, which feed on flowers or fruit. The cheese-hoppers are also the maggots of a small black fly.

Photo by W. P. Dando, F.Z.S.] [Regent's Park.

TSETSE-FLY (ENLARGED).

Showing the proboscis and veining of the wings more distinctly.

Besides these, there are some aberrant parasitic families of flies with long, hairy legs, and only one or two joints to the antennæ. These are the FOREST-FLIES and BIRD-FLIES, which attack horses and birds; and also some wingless insects, such as the so-called SHEEP-TICK (easily distinguished from a true tick by possessing only six legs), the BEE-PARASITES, and the spider-like BAT-PARASITES. This parasitic group is also remarkable for depositing full-grown larvæ or pupæ instead of eggs.

The FLEAS are a small group of small wingless insects, with such powers of leaping that it has been said that if a man was as agile as a flea he could jump over the dome of St. Paul's. The larvæ of fleas are small, worm-like creatures, with bristles, but without legs; they probably live on any sort of animal or vegetable refuse. They subsequently change to pupæ in small cocoons, and emerge as perfect fleas, which live by sucking the blood of warm-blooded

Photo by W. P. Dando, F.Z.S.] *[Regent's P.*

BEE-FLY.

Similar to the fly which destroys the locust eggs in Cyprus.

animals; or, when that fails them, they may attack caterpillars, or other small soft-bodied creatures. Though not very particular about their food, different species are more or less attached to different animals; and while in Europe the most troublesome species is the one considered to be most particularly attached to man, the species most troublesome in North America is known in Europe as the DOG-FLEA. They are all very similar in habits and appearance. Fleas are not only annoying, but, in conjunction with rats, are believed to be among the principal agents in the spread of the plague. There is another insect called the JIGGER, or SAND-FLEA, common in most of the warmer parts of America, and which has more recently been introduced into Africa. The female burrows into the feet of men or animals, where her body swells up with eggs to the size of a pea; and serious and sometimes fatal ulcers are the ordinary result, unless the insect is carefully extracted at an early stage of the attack.

USES OF FLIES.

It must not be supposed from the foregoing observations that flies are simply and solely pests to man and beast, without any redeeming qualities. Their services are less required in cold and settled countries, but in warm climates their value as scavengers can hardly be over-estimated. As regards the removal of carrion alone, Linnæus declared that the progeny of only three blow-flies would devour the carcase of a dead horse as quickly as a lion—a statement which, even if slightly exaggerated, conveys a vivid idea of their voracity and the rate at which they increase.

Flies are also useful in keeping down the multitudes of destructive insects. Numbers of caterpillars fall victims to the bristly flies alluded to on the last page; and the Bee-flies, which form a family placed next to the Gad-flies, render far greater service in destroying locusts. They much resemble small humble-bees, being very much the same shape, and they are clothed with yellow down in the British species, and the transparent wings are conspicuously marked with black bands (as in the photograph above), or with brown shading and spots. The insects have a very rapid flight, and use their long proboscis to suck the honey of flowers; but their grubs are parasitic—at least in some instances—on wild bees; and it is probable that their resemblance to bees has some reference to this mode of life. But in Cyprus, Algeria, North America, etc., the larvæ of allied species feed inside the egg-cases of locusts, sometimes destroying as large a proportion as four-fifths of the whole brood. Locusts have many enemies, but it will easily be seen that the attacks of foes like these must reduce their numbers considerably, notwithstanding the swarms which frequently survive, and which are liable to the attacks of other enemies, such as robber-flies, locust-birds, etc., after they have actually arrived at maturity.

Nor must we omit to notice the use of flies as articles of food for man or useful animals. Many persons are very fond of cheese-hoppers, which are really the maggots of a small fly; and we read in Kirby's "Textbook of Entomology," page 92: "The Rev. A. E. Eaton informs me that he believes that two species of *Ephemeridæ* (May-flies) form a portion of the so-called 'Kungu Cake,' manufactured by the natives of South Africa of gnats, and probably any other insects which can be obtained in sufficient abundance." "Gentles," which are the maggots of flies, are used by anglers for ground-bait.

Photo by W. Saville-Kent, F.Z.S., Milford-on-Sea.

PORTION OF INSHORE CORAL REEF AT THURSDAY ISLAND, TORRES STRAITS.

In the foreground are hemispherical masses of so-called Brain-Stone and Star-Corals. In the background the rocks are encrusted with various species of soft-fleshed corals, allied to the familiar "Dead Men's Fingers" of the British Seas.

BOOK VI. SHELL-FISH, LAMP-SHELLS, SEA-URCHINS, STAR-FISHES, MOSS-ANIMALS, WORMS, CORALS, JELLY-FISHES, AND SPONGES.

BY W. SAVILLE-KENT, F.L.S., F.Z.S.

CHAPTER I.

SHELL-FISH, OR MOLLUSCS.

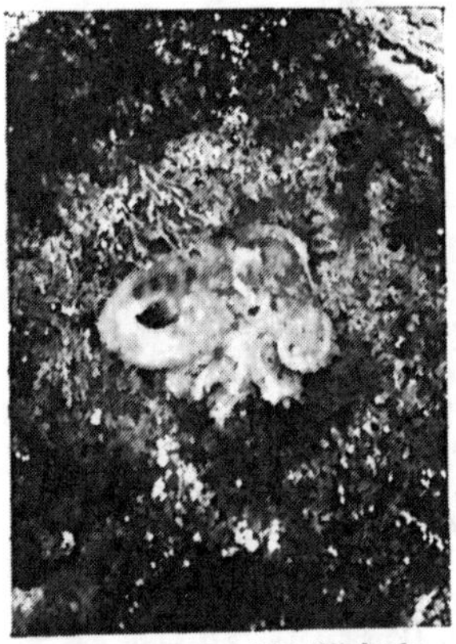

Photo by W. Saville-Kent, F.Z.S., Milford-on-Sea.

AN OCTOPUS CROUCHING IN A ROCK-POOL.

Green shore-crabs constitute the chief food of the octopus.

Photo by W. Saville-Kent, F.Z.S., Milford-on-Sea.

AN OCTOPUS ON ITS BACK AT BAY, LEFT HIGH AND DRY BY THE RETREATING TIDE.

In this attitude the octopus can use its many-suckered tentacles and its formidable parrot-like beak as defensive weapons.

THE Molluscan Group or Sub-kingdom represents one, if not the most important, of the invertebrate sections of living animals with relation both to its numbers and variety and in its commercial and economic utility to mankind. In its ranks are included all those animals generally known as Shell-fish, and familiar to the non-scientific in the shape of Oysters, Mussels, Whelks, Periwinkles, and the innumerable varieties of gorgeous or delicately tinted shells of tropical seas.

Collectively, Molluscs differ from all such invertebrate groups as Insects, Crustaceans, and Worms in that they possess neither jointed limbs nor jointed bodies, their body-substance being enclosed by a more or less distinct muscular sac, or integument, technically known as the "mantle." Molluscs possess no internal skeleton; but for the protection of their soft and otherwise defenceless bodies the mantle is among the great majority of species endowed with the property of secreting a more or less indurated calcareous shell, within which, when danger threatens, the creature can entirely withdraw. In some species the shell secreted is relatively small, and serves only as a protective shield to especially vital areas; while in a third very considerable assemblage a shell is altogether absent. The minute yet technically recognisable structural differences between the shells of even the most closely allied specific forms, and the wider and distinctly evident divergences that separate the more remotely connected varieties, furnish the basis for their classification and nomenclature by the systematic conchologist. Molluscan shells, being so extensively preserved in the fossil state, furnish the geologist with invaluable data for his determination of the age and respective relationship of the fossil-bearing strata of the earth's crust.

Having no jointed limbs, molluscs are dependent upon some other mechanical adaptation for their powers of locomotion. This, in the majority of species, is represented by a modification of the lower surface of the animal's body, which is so richly supplied with muscular tissues as to constitute an effective creeping-base. As a locomotive organ this muscular area is usually known as the "foot."

Of living molluscs some 50,000 distinct species have been recorded. The great majority of these organisms are, as is well known, marine. A very considerable number, however, are inhabitants of fresh-water; while a yet smaller proportion, like the Slugs and Snails and their allies, are especially adapted for a terrestrial existence. Excepting two relatively small and inconspicuous groups, the great natural division or sub-kingdom of Molluscs is separated by systematic zoologists into three main sections or classes. The

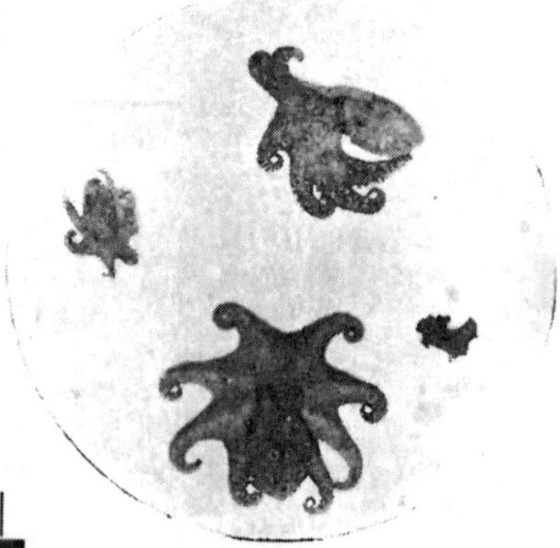

Photo by W. Saville-Kent, F.Z.S.] *[Milford-on-Sea.*

OCTOPODS.

A blue-spotted West Australian species.

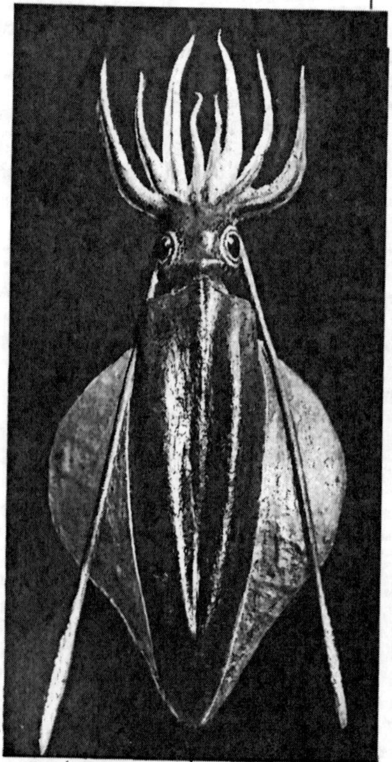

Photo by W. Saville-Kent, F.Z.S.] *[Milford-on-Sea.*

A TASMANIAN SQUID, OR CUTTLE-FISH.

Giant species of squids have been recorded in which the shorter tentacles measured 12 feet, and the two longer ones as much as 30 or 40 feet in length.

particular modification of the locomotive organ, or foot, serves, on the one hand, to readily distinguish the first or most highly organised group from the second or central class; while the third or lowest one is as clearly separated from the second and first by the character of the shell. The first and most highly developed section includes such species as the Octopus, the Cuttle-fish, the Squid, and the several varieties of Nautiluses; to the second or central group are referred all the marine and terrestrial Slugs and Snails with their innumerable modifications; while the third and lowest group comprises all the double-shelled or bivalve forms, such as Oysters and Mussels.

In the OCTOPUS and its allies the creeping-base, or foot, is prolonged round its margin into eight or more arm-like extensions. The anterior of these in the earlier phases of their development grow round and enclose the mouth, which consequently opens upon the centre of the locomotive surface. The arms of the octopus and other forms are in most instances provided throughout their length with complex sucking-disks, wherewith their owners can seize and retain their prey or walk with ease and celerity over the smoothest perpendicular or overhanging rock-surfaces. The octopus, as the type of its class, possesses yet another most effective locomotive organ. This is the so-called funnel, or siphuncle, a membranous tube connected with the capacious gill-cavity which is formed by a folding of the mantle on the under-surface. When at rest or moving leisurely, the water taken in through the pocket-like entrance to this cavity is discharged through the funnel without any particular effort. The animal can, however, at will leave go its attachment to the rocks, and propel itself swiftly through water by successive forcible expulsions of the water through the funnel. By directing the aperture of the funnel to the right or left, the creature can also direct its course in whatever direction it desires. When thus swimming, its translation is necessarily backwards. Another notable feature of the octopus is the "ink-bag," a huge gland secreting an inky-black fluid, which, as produced by the common cuttle-fish, constitutes the sepia of commerce. The contents of the ink-bag are discharged through the funnel at the will of the animal; as soon as the ink is brought into contact with the water, it becomes distributed through it in the form of a thick cloud, under cover of which the mollusc makes good its escape from any attacking enemy.

The octopus in British seas by no means attains to its maximum growth. Examples with arms from 2 to 2½ feet in length are accounted large specimens. In Mediterranean waters, however, these dimensions are much exceeded, individuals with arms 5 feet long, which are capable of covering a circular area no less than 10 feet in diameter with their fully extended appendages, being frequently recorded. In the West Indies, on the North-west American coast, and also in Chinese seas, similar, if not larger dimensions are attained by these creatures. That these monster octopods, or "devil-fish," as they are sometimes designated, prove a source of danger to human life has been abundantly demonstrated. Lurking, as is their custom, among rock-crevices, they seize hold of any moving object which approaches within reach of their extended arms. Bathers in this manner have been seized and drowned, it being impossible for even the strongest swimmer to free himself from the clutches of one of these animals, which, while retaining a firm hold on the rocks with a portion of its hundred-suckered arms, has entwined the others around its victim.

The natural food of the octopus are crabs, lobsters, and their like; and in places like the Channel Islands, where the tide retires very low, leaving the rock-fissures inhabited by the molluscs more or less exposed, their presence may be often foretold by the accumulation of empty, broken-up crab-shells around the entrances to their retreats. In common with other members of its tribe, the octopus is furnished with a strong, horny, parrot-like beak, wherewith it can with ease break through the shells of its accustomed food. The year 1900 was remarkable for the extraordinary abundance of the octopus on the English south coast, the result of their collective depredations very seriously affecting the local crab and lobster fisheries. The pots laid down over-night, in place of yielding the following morning their customary quota of marketable crustaceans, were more often than otherwise found to contain nothing but broken-up shells and a loathsome "devil-fish."

Photo by W. Saville-Kent, F.Z.S.] [Milford-on-Sea.

SHELL OF THE PEARLY NAUTILUS.

The inner lining of this shell is brilliantly iridescent.

The SQUIDS and CUTTLE-FISHES, with their large lustrous eyes, are especially adapted for an open sea life, and for this purpose are furnished with lateral fin-like membranous expansions. A more important structural distinction is their possession of two supplementary appendages, which.

Photo by W. Saville-Kent, F.Z.S.] *[Milford-on-Sea.*

SHELL OF THE ARGONAUT, OR PAPER-NAUTILUS.

The female animal only possesses a shell, and uses it as a cradle for her eggs and young.

usually retracted within special pouches when not in use, can be shot out to a length at least twice that of the eight ordinary arms. Both the cuttle-fish and the squid, or calamary, are also the possessors of an internal calcareous or horny shell which underlies and strengthens the upper-surface. The cuttle-bone used as a dentifrice and ink-eraser is the product of the first-named mollusc. The Ten-armed group, as it is named, with reference to the two supplementary arms, ten in all, possessed by its members, is notable for including species whose dimensions not only exceed those of any other invertebrate type, but whose fully extended length rivals that of the largest vertebrates. Giant squids, or calamaries, have been taken off the coast of Newfoundland, yielding, with their tentacular arms extended, a linear measurement of over 50 feet, associated with an estimated weight of as much as 1,000 lbs. There can be no doubt that these giant squids have in many instances furnished the basis of the oft-recurrent sea-serpent stories, more especially on those occasions where the supposed marine reptile and a whale have been reported as seen engaged in combat. As a matter of fact the sperm-whales habitually feed on deep-sea squids, and have been known, when mortally wounded, to vomit forth detached portions of these gigantic molluscs. The long tentacular arms of one of these monsters, thrown around the whale with which it had entered upon a death-struggle, might at a little distance be easily mistaken for some huge snake-like organism.

The various species of NAUTILUS, including the so-called "Paper" and "Pearly" species, belong likewise to this group of Molluscs. In the former case, however, it is only the female animal which secretes a shell, and this is used as a cradle wherein she deposits her eggs and rears her young. The pretty romance of the PAPER-NAUTILUS, or ARGONAUT, as it is technically termed, floating on the sun-lit waves with spreading sails and an even keel, has unfortunately been entirely dissipated by the penetrating search-light of modern science. The animal only floats on the surface when ill, or when torn from its customary pasture-fields by abnormal storms, otherwise it creeps about the sea-bottom, or disports itself in the sub-marine grottoes like an ordinary octopus, with which, in point of fact, the shell-less male agrees in all essential details. The shell-cradle of the paper-nautilus is not vitally connected with the body of the animal, as is that of the pearly species and all ordinary shell-fish. It is freely detachable from the body, and during life is grasped and held closely to it by the expanded extremities of the two lateral tentacles by which the delicate shell is mainly secreted.

The next group comprises the great bulk of Simple-shelled Molluscs, of which it is impossible in these pages to give more than a brief enumeration of some of the most prominent. The Lung-breathing section, which is usually awarded the first place on the list, includes the familiar GARDEN-SNAILS, the SHELL-LESS SLUGS, the FRESH-WATER SNAILS which come to the surface to breathe, and many distinct terrestrial species. The largest living representative of this group is the huge LAND-SNAIL of tropical West Africa, sometimes known as the AGATE-SNAIL, the shell of which is not infrequently as much as 7½ inches long.

The NAKED-GILLED SEA-SLUGS constitute a second clearly defined group. All the species are essentially marine, and most abundant among seaweeds and coral-growths, over twenty

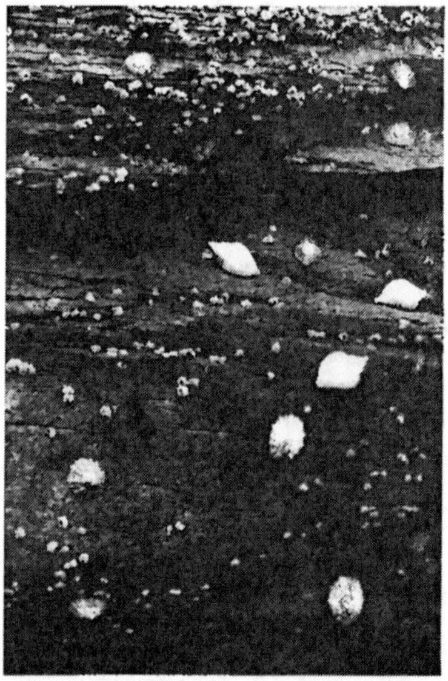

Photos by W. Saville-Kent, F.Z.S.]

LIMPETS, WHELKS, AND BARNACLES.

On the rocks at Ilfracombe when the tide was low.

[Milford-on-Sea.

SHELL BEACH, ABROLHOS ISLANDS.

Composed of iridescent top-shells.

Photos by W. Saville-Kent, F.Z.S.]

GREAT CLAM-SHELL ON CORAL-REEF.

The soft parts have been removed to show the size of the shell and the pure whiteness of the interior.

[Milford-on-Sea.

GIANT CLAM-SHELLS ON THE GREAT BARRIER REEF AS EXPOSED AT EXTREME LOW TIDE.

The shell in the foreground is 4 feet in diameter.

species occurring in British seas. They are notable for the slug-like form of their body, which is usually supplemented by the outgrowth from it of complex, variously modified gill-filaments. In some species these external gills take the form of symmetrical flower-like tufts at the posterior end of the back, while in others simple or variously branched gills may be developed on the upper-surface. The colours of many of these sea-slugs are more brilliant than those of any other molluscs, this being especially the case with the tropical coral-reef-frequenting species. Bright scarlet, yellows, and blues, separately or variously combined, are among the dominant tints. Many of these tropical species are also of considerable size. One particular kind, having a flower-like dorsal gill-tuft, observed by the writer on the West Australian reefs, was over 10 inches long and 8 inches broad. Its general ground-colour was intense vermilion, relieved, however, by a frilled border nearly an inch in width of the purest white, with radiating streaks of scarlet. It is an interesting circumstance that these naked-gilled molluscs, shell-less so far as their adult phases are concerned, emerge from the egg with a perfectly formed, but necessarily very minute, transparent shell, resembling that of a garden-snail. It is consequently inferred that the group has been derived from some permanently shell-bearing form.

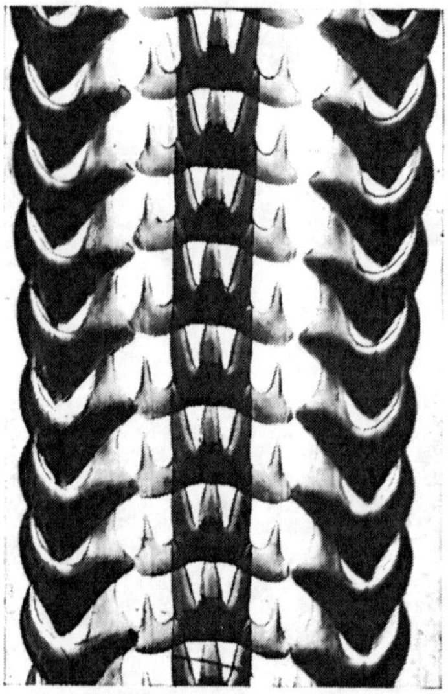

Photo by W. Saville-Kent, F.Z.S.] [Milford-on-Sea.

HIGHLY MAGNIFIED TONGUE OF A SEA-SNAIL.

With this structure its owner bores or files a hole through the shells of other molluscs upon which it preys.

The Comb-gilled section embraces the great majority of the marine molluscs having a single more or less convoluted or spirally twisted shell. They take their name from the circumstance that the gills have a compactly disposed comb-like contour. This gill-tuft is situated in an excavated chamber inside the shell, immediately over the neck. The COMMON WHELK, the PELICAN'S-FOOT SHELL, and the WINKLE are a few typical British marine representatives of this group, which, however, attains to the zenith of its development in the size, variety of form, and ornate coloration of its shells in tropical seas. The inter-tropical coral-reefs in particular yield a most abundant harvest in this direction. The shells in common use obtained from such a source include the ponderous HELMET-SHELLS, or CONCHS, employed for the manufacture of cameos; the GIANT WHELKS and TRUMPET-SHELLS, often over 18 inches long, used as signal-horns throughout Polynesia and on the tropical Australian coast; and the capacious MELON-SHELLS, made to do duty for boat-baling and as water-vessels and general domestic receptacles throughout the same tropical area. To this list may be added the HARP-SHELLS, VOLUTES, CONES, MITRES, OLIVES, THORNY WOODCOCKS, and a host of others prized by the conchologist. To this section must also be referred the innumerable species of COWRIES, of which the large, boldly mottled "TIGER" and "PANTHER" species are well known. The comparatively small, yellowish, thickly built, porcelain-like shell of the "MONEY-COWRIE" constitutes, as is well known, the current coin throughout extensive areas of Africa and India. It is recorded that as large a quantity as sixty tons of these small shells, originally collected from tropical seas, have been shipped from one British port alone to the African coast for commercial use within a single year. One very diminutive cowrie, pale pink in colour, with a delicately streaked surface, is indigenous to British waters.

The third large group of Molluscs which demands attention is that of the Bivalves, or

Leaf-gilled group. Though not so numerous in species as the last, it outrivals it in the enormous abundance in which the individuals of many varieties are produced. OYSTERS, MUSSELS, COCKLES, SCALLOPS, and other allied forms occur in closely associated colonies, constituting natural "beds" or "banks," which may be of vast extent and, in at any rate the case of oysters, several feet in thickness. From a commercial and economic standpoint this group is undoubtedly of the highest importance to the human race. Not only do its members, as instanced by the foregoing forms, contribute largely to the world's commissariat, they also yield the much-prized material known as "mother-of-pearl" and the purest and most æsthetically beautiful gems—orient pearls. Pearls and mother-of-pearl are the products of two groups of shell-fish, respectively known as PEARL-OYSTERS and PEARL-MUSSELS. There are a considerable number of species, mainly denizens of tropical seas, which, like ordinary oysters and mussels, occur naturally in banks and beds of vast extent. In some species, such as the CEYLON PEARL-OYSTER, the shell is small, and the mother-of-pearl substance, or "nacre," as it is technically termed, so thin as to be of relatively little value. Hence the fishery for this species is conducted almost exclusively for the sake of the pearls, which are fairly numerous and frequently of the finest quality. From the tropical Australian seas pearl-shells of the largest size, which produce the thickest and most valuable mother-of-pearl, are obtained. Pearls of the best quality are more rarely found in this description of shell, and its fishery is prosecuted primarily on account of the substantial substance and magnificent quality of its nacre. A single pair of shells of this species will attain in its adult state to a weight of from 12 to 18 lbs. The fishery for this pearl-shell has, however, been prosecuted so relentlessly that bivalves of such matured age and weight are now of rare occurrence, and obtained only from almost inaccessibly deep waters. Unless, in point of fact, systematic methods of conservation and cultivation are resorted to on an extensive scale and on lines corresponding fundamentally with those successfully followed in the culture of ordinary commercial oysters, there would seem to be an imminent risk of the valuable Australian pearl-shell fisheries becoming depleted to more or less complete exhaustion.

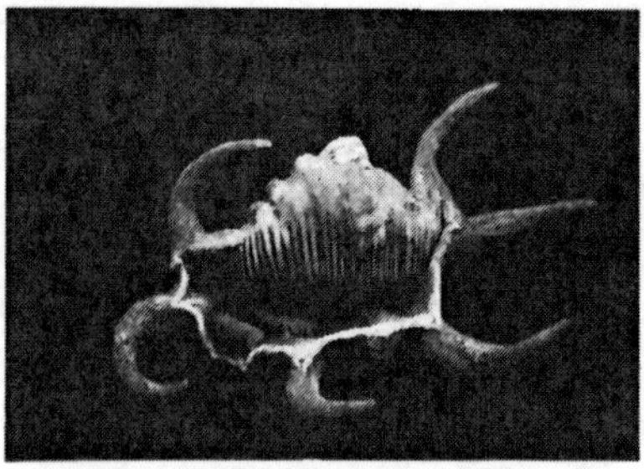

Photo by W. Saville-Kent, F.Z.S.] *[Milford-on-Sea.*

A SCORPION-SHELL.

Closely allied to the "Pelican's Foot," found on the British coast.

The tropical Australian seas, and notably those which wash the Great Barrier Reef, are famous for the production of the largest of living bivalve molluscs. These are represented by the GIANT CLAMS, which, dwelling among the coral-growths, are left exposed to view for brief periods during abnormally low spring tides. A photograph of a colony of these monster bivalves, taken by the writer amidst this mollusc's characteristic surroundings, is reproduced on page 741. The example in the foreground measured no less than 4 feet in diameter and weighed several hundred-weights. In many clams the living tissues, or mantle-borders, that are exposed to view when the shell-valves are partly open, are brilliantly tinted.

Photo by W. Saville-Kent, F.Z.S.] *[Milford-on-Sea.*

ROCK-OYSTERS.

This is the ordinary commercial oyster of the Australian shores.

Photo by W. Saville-Kent, F.Z.S.] [*Milford-on-Sea.*

A QUEENSLAND OYSTER-BANK.

Illustrating another characteristic growth-phase of the Australian rock-oyster.

Of the SCALLOPS many of the larger species are highly esteemed for the table. It is notable of them that they can progress through the water in a jerky, flight-like manner by the repeated flapping of their opposing shells. In many scallops the jewel-like eyes are developed in a row round the margin of the mantle.

The Bivalve Class includes certain representatives which are held in evil repute, on account of their destructive habits. PHOLAS and its allies bore their way into solid rock, bringing about its complete disintegration. From the dreaded SHIP-WORM, or TEREDO, on the other hand, there would appear to be no description of wood that can withstand its ravages.

The Bivalve Molluscs are not without fresh-water representatives. The well-known POND- and RIVER-MUSSELS, which form the most conspicuous examples of this group, number several hundred species. While insipid and of no account for the human commissariat, many of its members produce pearls of value. One such, obtained from the river Conway, in North Wales, is said to occupy a place in the crown of England.

The CHITONS, or MULTIVALVE MOLLUSCS, invite brief notice. As the last-named title implies, the shell-elements in this group are relatively numerous, consisting of eight pieces, or plates, which may form contiguous transverse shelly shields that entirely cover in and protect the dorsal surface of the elongate, boat-shaped body, or may be more or less isolated from one another. In the former instance the animal bears some considerable resemblance to a gigantic limbless wood-louse, and, like that familiar terrestrial crustacean, it is capable of rolling itself into a spheroidal shape as a means of protection. None of the chitons are provided with eyes in the adult state in that region of their body—namely, the head—where they might be most naturally expected to exist. Recent scientific investigation has, however, elicited the fact that in various species the respective shell-plates are studded with minute eye-specks, the aggregate number of visual organs thus possessed by certain forms reaching to the astonishing figures of 11,000 or 12,000. The majority of the chitons are shallow-water, rock-frequenting molluscs, which may be successfully sought by turning over stones at low water. Several species are inhabitants of British seas.

CHAPTER II.

LAMP-SHELLS.

A LITTLE group of double-shelled creatures, formerly regarded as near allies of the Oysters and Mussels, are the LAMP-SHELLS. Their scientific appellation, signifying "arm-footed," relates to the two spirally convoluted arm-like structures which constitute the salient features in these animals. That of lamp-shells bears reference to the small circular perforation near the extremity, or "beak," of the united shells, which imparts to the entire structure a not altogether remote resemblance to an ancient Greek or Roman lamp with its sub-terminal wick-hole. In all essential points of their organisation the lamp-shells differ so essentially from ordinary bivalves that they are now generally recognised as representing an independent animal class, having, as a matter of fact, a closer relationship with Worms than with Molluscs. In their earlier condition certain lamp-shells are indistinguishable from larval worms; while the convoluted arms of the adult animals, thickly beset with bristles and hairs, closely resemble

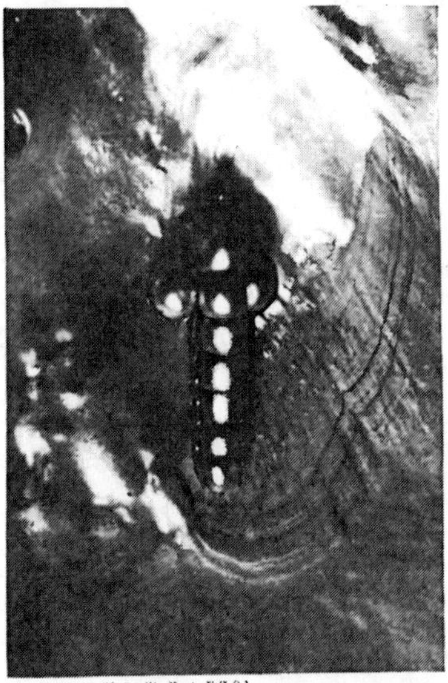

Photos by W. Saville-Kent, F.Z.S.]

SOUTHERN CROSS PEARL, VALUED AT £10,000.

Consists of nine laterally united pearls corresponding in shape and size.

[Milford-on-Sea.

PEARL-SHELL WITH GROUP OF GOLDEN PEARLS.

Many thousand shells may be opened without finding a single pearl.

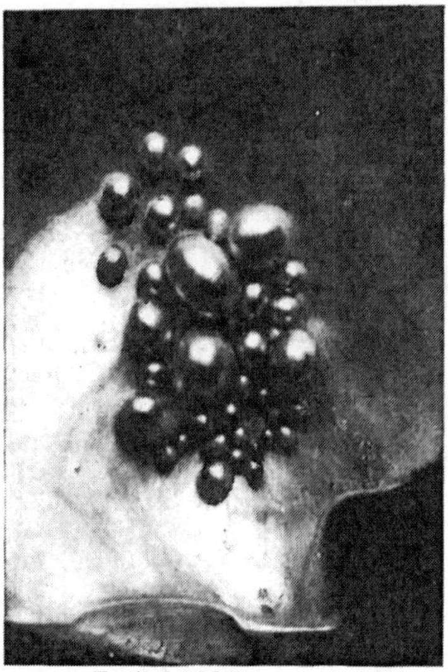

Photos by W. Saville-Kent, F.Z.S.]

QUEENSLAND PEARLS ON BLACK-LIPPED PEARL-SHELL.

The black-lipped shell produces pearls of great value.

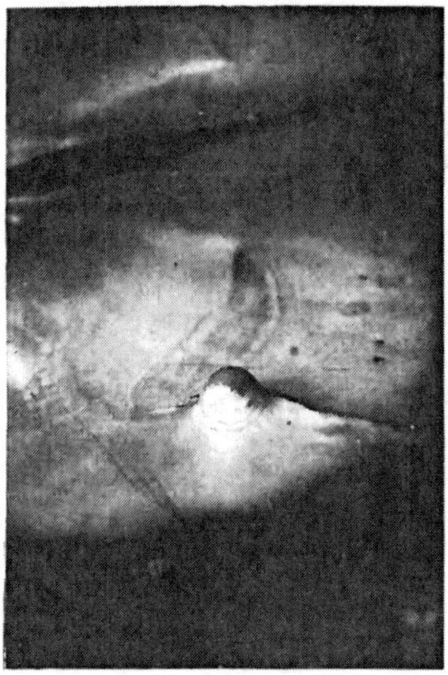

[Milford-on-Sea.

PEARL PRODUCED BY OPERATION ON THE ANIMAL.

The pearl produced is a solid hemispherical or "button" pearl.

the arms, or "cirrhi," of many sea-worms. The superadded valves of the lamp-shells differ fundamentally from those of the bivalve molluscs in the circumstance that they are developed upon the upper and lower surfaces respectively of the enclosed animal, and not on the sides. The union between the two valves is also accomplished through the medium of interlocking calcareous teeth, in place of a horny or ligamentous hinge-joint, as obtains in an oyster or a mussel. A supplementary calcareous support, having a corresponding spiral shape, is also developed in connection with the convoluted arms. This structure varies in the contour of its minuter details in every specific form, which thus furnishes zoologists with a basis for systematic classification. The lamp-shells collectively form two natural groups or orders. In one of these the shells are hinged together, and are of conspicuously unequal dimensions. The larger shell of the two is more distinctly concave and produced into a perforated beak. It is this structure that in some species resembles the wick-hole of an antique lamp, and has given rise to the popular title by which these shells are distinguished. The second or hingeless group is further distinguished by the shells being of almost uniform shape and size. In the most interesting example of this group, known as LINGULA, the two shells are thin, horny, of a green tint, and mounted on a long, flexible, worm-like stalk. Like a worm, this creature moves about in the mud, and constructs a sand-lined dwelling-tube.

Although lamp-shells are represented by comparatively few species at the present day, in the older epochs they existed in enormous abundance. It is further remarkable of this group that many species are scarcely distinguishable from their fossil ancestors. Lingula, the type last referred to, is especially notable in this respect.

CHAPTER III.

STAR-FISHES, SEA-URCHINS, ETC.

THE somewhat varied assemblage of marine animals familiarly known as STAR-FISHES, FEATHER-STARS, BRITTLE-STARS, SEA-URCHINS, and SEA-CUCUMBERS all agree structurally with one another and differ from all other living organisms in several conspicuous features. Prominent among these is the circumstance that their protecting skin is more or less extensively impregnated externally and strengthened internally with calcareous elements which take the form of plates and spines and spicules.

Photo by W. Saville-Kent, F.Z.S.] *[Milford on-Sea.*

COMMON OR SHORT-SPINED SEA-URCHIN.

This species is used for food in Italy and other Continental countries.

The COMMON SEA-URCHIN may be cited as an example in which these calcareous elements attain their maximum development. The sub-spherical box-like case or shell, wherein all the vital organs are enclosed and safely protected, is a common object of the seashore, and, empty and denuded of its external coating of prickly spines, familiarly known as a "sea-egg." Examined closely, this shell is found to consist of a series of calcareous plates, which dovetail or fit together in juxtaposition with the utmost nicety. The surface of the shell is studded throughout with rounded hemispherical knobs, those of a larger size having a very distinctly symmetrical plan of distribution. These rounded knobs are the bases of attachment of the spines, which radiate at all points from the surface of the shell when the animal is alive. It will be further recognised on a nearer examination that the walls of the shell are pierced on a definitely symmetrical pattern with minute perforations, such perforations being most distinctly visible on the inner surface of the shell. These minute punctures are the apertures through which in life the delicate tubular locomotive organs, or so-called "feet," are thrust out and retracted. The majority of these tubular organs terminate in a circular sucking-disk, wherewith, collectively, the urchin is able to adhere to and travel over the surface of the smoothest rock, or even up the glass walls of an aquarium. In the empty beach-gathered urchin-shell a circular hole may be observed at the two opposite poles, the one in the centre of the lower and flatter surface being the larger of the two. It is within this lower and larger one that the mouth, with its complex apparatus of teeth, is suspended.

Photo by W. Saville-Kent, F.Z.S.] *[Milford-on-Sea.*

LONG-SPINED SEA-URCHINS.

The needle-like spines of these sea-urchins are over a foot in length. Acres of these creatures may be sometimes seen on tidally exposed areas of the Queensland Great Barrier Reef, where this photograph was taken.

The membranous disk which covers the upper and smaller circular aperture in the living animal is perforated centrally by the vent, and around it are grouped the eye-spots and sundry excretory apertures.

A noteworthy feature associated with the greater portion of the structural details of the sea-urchin which have been enumerated is the dominance of the number five in the constituent elements. It is found, for instance, that the perforated areas through which the tube-feet are protruded form, as with the petals and other elements of many flowers, five symmetrically corresponding segments. The dental apparatus comprises five equivalent tooth-like structures, and there are five eye-spots and five excretory apertures at the upper pole. This particular number, with multiples of the same, is furthermore characteristic of all the typical members

Photo by W. Saville-Kent, F.Z.S.] *[Milford-on-Sea.*

THICK-SPINED SEA-URCHIN.

In large specimens the spines are as thick as a slate-pencil, and may be used for the same purpose.

of the class. Thus, in the COMMON STAR-FISH, there are five so-called arms, five eye-spots, one at the tip of each arm, and five equivalent elemental components of all the more important viscera. In the SEA-CUCUMBERS, which have elongate worm-like bodies, there is a similar apportionment of the nerves and muscles of the body generally into fives, and also of the branching tentacles which surround the mouth. Tubular locomotive organs, the so-called "tube-feet," are common to all the three types enumerated. The calcareous plates and spinules, while attaining to a maximum development in the urchins, are also abundantly represented in the other groups. In the common star-fish these calcareous elements form within the skin an openly reticulated trellis-like framework, while in the ordinary sea-cucumbers they more usually take the form of innumerable microscopically minute spicules. The two less familiarly known groups of the FEATHER-STARS and BRITTLE-STARS fully agree with the previously-enumerated types in their five-fold structural composition. The brittle-stars have almost invariably five arms only, but they are independent outgrowths from the body proper, instead of being prolongations of it, as in the common star-fish.

The FEATHER-STARS, which include some of the rarest and most beautiful representatives of the group, are mostly inhabitants of deep water, and remarkable for the circumstance that either throughout life or in their early phases they are affixed to submarine objects by slender stalks. This peculiarity imparts to the animals such a flower-like aspect that, in conjunction with the indurated calcareous nature of their skeletons, they have received the title of "Stone-lilies." This appellation, however, was originally more particularly applied to their fossilised remains, which occur in remarkable abundance in the older geological strata.

The most familiar British representative of the group is the ROSY FEATHER-STAR, occasionally obtained among seaweed in rock-pools on the southern coast, but more often brought up with the dredge from deeper water. In this form the elongate feather-like arms radiate from the central, relatively small, five-rayed body. There is no supporting foot-stalk in this adult stage, the animal being freely movable, and clinging to seaweeds and other objects by means of a cluster of claw-like filaments developed upon its under-surface. Releasing its hold upon its temporarily selected position, it can crawl about with the aid of the hooked extremities of its arms and their radiating joints. It can also propel itself through the water in a somewhat clumsy fashion by the consecutive flexion and extension of these appendages. This freedom of locomotion was not, however, always possessed by the feather-star. In its early days, and when of very small size, it was affixed to a slender foot-stalk, and dependent for its food on the animalcules and other minute organisms which drifted or swam within reach of its extended arms. The rosy feather-star takes its name from the bright rose-red tints by which it is usually characterised. Individuals of the species are, however, subject to considerable colour-variation. On the Australian coast, where many forms are abundantly represented, examples tinted deep crimson, black, bright golden yellow, or sundry admixtures of these several hues are not uncommonly found associated among a dredge-haul of these elegant sea-stars.

The PERMANENTLY STALKED STONE-LILIES are at the present day of rare occurrence. Up

Photo by N. Lazarnick] [*New York.*

STAR-FISH IN WATER.

If pulled to pieces, each of the five arms, or fingers, will grow into a perfect star-fish.

to within comparatively recent years the so-called MEDUSA'S-HEAD LILY was, indeed, regarded as the only living representative of the group. This species has a pentagonal jointed foot-stalk that may be 3 feet long, with five slender appendages developed in whorls at short sub-equal distances throughout its length. From the shallow cup-shaped body at the apex of the stalk a tassel-like bundle of arms is developed, all of these being produced by repeated bifurcation from one of the five equivalent basal stem-joints. Dredging expeditions have within the last quarter of a century revealed the existence of a considerable number of previously unknown species of stone-lilies in the abysses of the ocean, a depth of no less than 3,200 fathoms representing the habitat of one such type.

The Star-fish group is represented by the COMMON FIVE-FINGERS, or CROSS-FISH, as it is sometimes called, and includes a very numerous assemblage of species of varying size and shape and colour. The British seas alone yield some twenty forms. Among the more notable of these is the SUN STAR-FISH, which, departing from the rule of possessing five arms only, has twelve or more, its contour, from which it derives its name, somewhat resembling that of a symbolic sun. The colours of this species are particularly brilliant, consisting usually of a variably patterned admixture of crimson, pink, and white. An extreme contrast in contour to the sun-star is presented by the so-called BIRD'S-FOOT species, in which the body is pentagonal and so flattened out as to somewhat resemble the foot of a duck. In the CUSHION-STARS the body, while pentagonal, is comparatively thick.

The so-called SNAKE-ARMED SAND-STARS and BRITTLE-STARS constitute a section distinguished from the preceding by the character of the arms, which branch separately from the central body, and are composed of an innumerable series of calcareous joints, which snap asunder under the slightest provocation. The great majority of the species are provided with five simple arms only. In an exceptional form, however, known as the SHETLAND ARGUS, and its allies, these five arms, while simple at their base, bifurcate repeatedly and in geometrical progression to such an extent as to form in life a complex network of writhing, snake-like tendrils, that has been appropriately likened to a Medusa's head. It has been calculated that there are no less than 80,000 terminal arm-subdivisions in adult examples of this species.

Photo by E. Connold.] [*St. Leonards.*

STAR-FISH, OUT OF WATER, TURNING OVER.

The sucker-tipped tubes with which the star-fish effects locomotion are well shown in this photograph.

Among the Sea-urchin Tribe there are many notable departures from the typical form previously referred to. In some, while the sub-spheroidal form of the case, or test, is still retained, the external spiny armature is greatly varied. In one series these spines are exceedingly long, slender, and of needle-like contour and sharpness. In others, while long, they are abnormally thick and cylindrical, somewhat resembling slate-pencils, for which they are sometimes used as a substitute; or they may be club-shaped, branched, or reduced to flattened plates. In other forms the shell itself is conspicuously modified. With some known as BISCUIT- or CAKE-URCHINS it is flattened out to the resemblance of a cake or biscuit, the spines being minute and inconspicuous. In another group, distinguished as HEART-URCHINS, the shell is oval and bilaterally symmetrical, though the dominant number of five still holds good with regard to the building up of its structural details. One of the most interesting is the LEATHER-URCHIN, so called on account of the flexible and loosely jointed character of its shell, the way being paved by such a form to the normally soft- and flexible-skinned sea-cucumbers. Sea-urchins are to a great extent vegetable-feeders, and the larger species are appreciated as an article of food in many countries, the ovaries, or roe, with which at certain periods the shell is mostly filled, forming the edible portion.

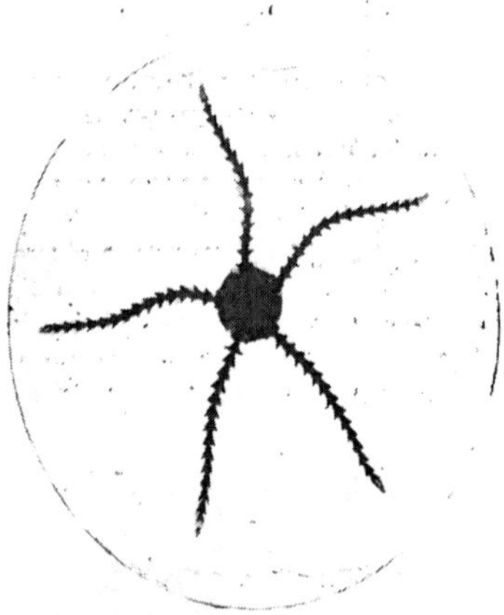

Photo by W. Saville-Kent, F.Z.S.] [Milford on-Sea.

A YOUNG BRITTLE STAR-FISH (MUCH MAGNIFIED).

The arms of the brittle-stars are composed of loosely fitting, readily fractured joints.

The SEA-CUCUMBERS—better known in the commercial world as Bêche-de-mer, or Trepang—represent the only group which possesses a substantial market-value. Its typical members present an elongate worm-like contour, but progress by means of extensile tube-feet, after the manner of the Urchins and Star-fishes, and have their dental, nervous, and muscular systems fashioned on the same five-sectioned basis. The mouth, which is situated at one extremity of the body, is surrounded by a series of ten or twenty delicately branched or mop-like tentacles, which can be protruded or retracted at the animal's will, and are used for seizing food. The skin of the typical sea-cucumber is more or less soft and flexible, and has embedded within its substance innumerable minute calcareous spinules.

The commercially valuable sea-cucumbers, or bêche-de-mer, are all inhabitants of tropical waters, the North-eastern Australian coast and the Malay seas yielding the most highly prized forms. The Queensland Great Barrier Reef, consisting of a series of coral-reefs extending for upwards of 1,000 miles at a little distance from the Australian mainland, represents one of the most productive areas for this marine delicacy, the bulk of which goes to the Chinese market. The fishery is prosecuted with the assistance mainly of the Queensland natives, who, either by diving or wading on the reefs at low tide, collect the creatures in vast quantities. On being brought to the curing-stations, the animals are emptied from the collecting-sacks into large caldrons, where they are allowed to stew in their own juice for about twenty minutes. Taken out of the caldrons, they are split open and eviscerated, dried for a short interval in the sun, and then placed in tiers on wire gratings in a smoke-house, where they remain for twenty-four hours. They should at this stage have shrunk up to about one quarter of their normally extended size, much resemble charred sausages in aspect, and should rattle like dry walnuts when bagged up for exportation. From £50 to £150 per ton are the prices that the better qualities of bêche-de-mer realise when well cured and delivered at Chinese ports. The chief culinary use to which the cured sea-cucumbers are applied is that of the concoction of soup, the best quality prepared taking rank with that made from swallows' nests. At the hotels and clubs in the leading Australian cities bêche-de-mer soup is held in high favour, and its more extensive introduction on the menu-cards of Western civilisation may be only a question of time.

Many species of sea-cucumbers inhabit British seas, but none possess that density of tissue which is essential for their economic conservation; the majority, moreover, are of comparatively small size, some few inches long only when fully extended, whereas the commercially valuable tropical ones may measure as much as from 2 to 3 feet. The mode of feeding of sea-cucumbers is somewhat interesting; the smaller species, with much-branching tentacles, generally affix themselves by their tube-feet to some object, and, extending their tentacles in all directions, utilise them, like those of a sea-anemone, for seizing any minute and suitable prey which may strike against them. The microscopic organisms on which they chiefly feed abound in the waters they inhabit, and one after the other, the branched tentacles having effected a capture, are gathered together and tucked bodily into the creature's central mouth and apparently half-way down its throat. The larger coral-frequenting species are provided mostly with mop-shaped tentacles. They crawl about leisurely in search of their food, mopping over the ground, and gathering up in their tentacles the minute shells and other organisms on which they subsist, which are collectively thrust with an indrawn tentacle into the throat. In some of the lower forms the tube-feet have disappeared, the integument is thin and semi-transparent, and the worm-like animal crawls about by means of its skin-spinules, which take the form of anchors or grappling-hooks. In an opposite direction they may develop a supplementary covering of dermal plates and a more rigid integument, which indicate their nearer relationship with sea-urchins.

Photo by W. Saville-Kent, F.Z.S.] *[Milford-on-Sea.*

A BRANCHING-ARMED BRITTLE-STAR.

The specimen is attached to a brilliant scarlet sponge.

Photo by W. Saville-Kent, F.Z.S.] *[Milford-on-Sea.*

SEA-CUCUMBERS, SOME WITH EXTENDED TENTACLES.

A West Australian species whose colours are bright pink and yellow.

The majority of sea-urchins and star-fishes pass through a series of interesting metamorphoses before arriving at the adult state. The larval phases in these instances are free-swimming organisms, having arm-like processes, strengthened by calcareous rods that have been likened in contour to a clock-stand. A small spherical central area, like a clock in its case, representing the stomach of the larva, develops spicules around it, and becomes the body of the urchin, the other

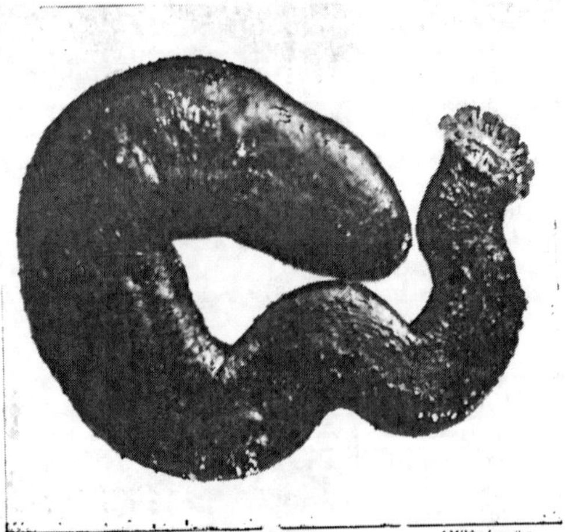

Photo by W. Saville-Kent, F.Z.S.] [Milford-on-Sea.

SEA-CUCUMBER, OR BÊCHE-DE-MER.

These animals are collected in vast quantities on the Australian Great Barrier Reef, smoked, and sent to the Chinese market.

outlying portions becoming gradually absorbed. Some of the brittle-stars and sea-cucumbers bring forth their young in the adult form, nursing them from the egg in special breeding-chambers.

The capacity of a star-fish to renew its lost arms is commonly manifested. A single detached arm, moreover, in such a type as the common five-fingered species, can reproduce its body and the remaining four arms. Fishermen, who are in the habit of tearing up star-fishes and throwing them back into the water, under the impression that they are thus effectually incapacitating them from further injury to their oyster-beds, commit an error, such mutilation tending to the multiplication of their numbers.

In the matter of colour-ornamentation the Star-fish group is richly endowed. Allusion to the brilliant crimson and pink-and-white tints of the British sun star-fish has been already made. As with most animal groups, however, it is amid their tropical representatives that the most striking colour-variations obtain. One form which is common among the coral-reefs on the Queensland coast-line, and much resembles the common British "five-fingers" in size and shape, is brilliant ultramarine-blue. Another large pentagonal species, belonging to the group known as Cushion-stars, has a golden-brown ground, upon which are thickly scattered small bead-like tubercles of turquoise. A third form, not uncommon on the Tasmanian coast-line, which is nearly related to the Bird's-foot species, previously mentioned, is distinguished by tints which range through several shades of crimson to brilliant violet.

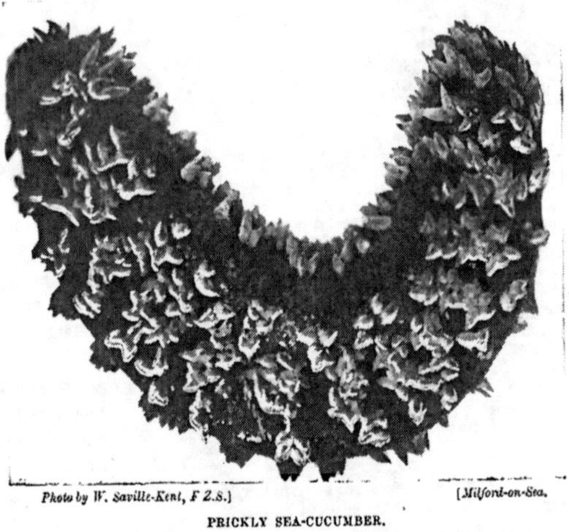

Photo by W. Saville-Kent, F.Z.S.] [Milford-on-Sea.

PRICKLY SEA-CUCUMBER.

This species of bêche-de-mer commands a high price in China, and makes delicious soup.

Not a few of the star-fishes are notable for their eminent phosphorescent properties. The group of the Snake-armed and Brittle-stars are more especially distinguished in this respect. Many of these species occur in such numbers in

Photo by W. Saville-Kent, F.Z.S.] *[Milford-on-Sea.*

BLACK SEA-CUCUMBER.

This photograph was taken through the water in a coral-pool. A large clam-shell, with its expanded fringe of tentacles, is close beside the sea-cucumber.

comparatively deep water that the dredge may be filled with a tangled mass of their writhing snake-armed bodies. Should it be night when the dredge is brought aboard, and its contents are emptied upon the deck, the spectacle presented as the star-fishes scramble in all directions, their bodies and arms aglow with pale green or blue phosphoric coruscations, is highly remarkable.

CHAPTER IV.

MOSS-ANIMALS.

A LITTLE group of animals whose relationship with the sub-divisions previously and hereafter described cannot be very definitely determined is that of the MOSS-ANIMALS, sometimes designated CORALLINES, or LACE-CORALS. All its members are of exceedingly minute size, and if living separately would be scarcely discernible to the unaided vision. They are, however, in the habit of forming stocks, or colonies, after the manner of corals, by a process of continual budding, and in this way build up social aggregations which may be of considerable dimensions. The majority are marine, and largely in evidence on almost every seashore in the form of the so-called SEA-MATS, consisting of masses of minute, light brown, horny cells, which take the form of seaweeds, or are spread in thin, lace-like encrustations upon the surfaces of shells, stones, and the larger seaweeds. The living inhabitants of these cells are as transparent as glass, their most characteristic feature being the elegant shuttle-cock-shaped crown of tentacles which is thrust out or withdrawn at will from the aperture of each tiny tenement. The assistance of the microscope is requisite for the apprehension of these details, as also of the somewhat complex alimentary and other organs enclosed within the component cells.

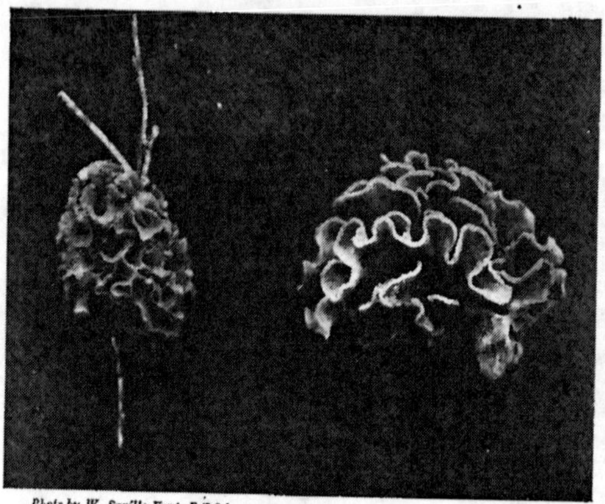

Photo by W. Saville-Kent, F.Z.S.] *[Milford-on-Sea.*

MOSS-ANIMALS.

These coral-like masses are composed of many thousand closely united dwelling-cells of microscopic dimensions.

A comparatively small number of these moss-animals are inhabitants of fresh-water, forming brown tubular aggregations on the under side of the leaves of water-lilies or other submerged objects. It is interesting to observe that the tentacular crown in almost all these fresh-water species is horseshoe-shaped, instead of like a shuttle-cock, as in the marine forms. One very notable fresh-water species is remarkable for the circumstance that in place of horny tubes the component individuals secret a common transparent gelatinous matrix, which is provided with a creeping-base, wherewith the colony-stock is enabled to travel over the surfaces of the water-plants among which it lives, or up the glass sides of an aquarium. In some respects, and more especially their earlier developmental phases, the Moss-animals show affinities with the Lamp-shells, while the tentacular crown of the adult individual is closely imitated in certain worms.

CHAPTER V.

WORMS.

THE Worms and their allies embrace a numerous assemblage of animals which exhibit a remarkable amount of variation both in structure and habits. A fundamental distinction which serves to separate readily even the most highly organised members of the group from the other articulate or jointed-bodied animals, such as Crabs, Insects, or Centipedes, is furnished by the character of the locomotive appendages. These in the Worm Tribe never assume a jointed character, but take the form of unjointed membranous processes which may or may not be supplemented by bristles. Frequently bristles alone constitute the essential locomotive organs. In certain groups, such as the Leeches, Flat-worms, Thread-worms, and others, even these are unrepresented.

The appropriate title of Bristle-worms has been conferred upon the section in which the locomotive organs take the form of bristles. Among these the Common Earth-worm is included. At first sight the worm's body appears to be perfectly smooth and naked; it is found, however, on closer investigation to be furnished, according to the species, with either two or four longitudinal rows of fine, hook-like bristles. Although these bristles project but slightly above the surface of the skin, they constitute very effective aids to locomotion, enabling the animal to obtain a secure grip upon the surface of the ground over which it may be travelling. Progression under such conditions is effected, in fact, on the same principle as that of the snake, the ends of the stiff bristles with which the segments are armed fulfilling the same rôle as the projecting edges of the reptile's scales. Earthworms are chiefly vegetable-feeders, dragging into their holes fallen leaves, straws, and every other description of vegetable débris. They also swallow and pass through their systems large quantities of earth, absorbing from it its organic constituents, and depositing the indigestible residuum therefrom in the form of "earth-casts." The useful function thus performed by worms in bringing up earth from considerable depths and redepositing it upon the surface of the ground has been fully demonstrated in one of Mr. Darwin's works. There are some twenty species of British earth-worms, none of which, however, attain to the proportions of certain kinds indigenous to Australia and South Africa. Some of these giant species are as much as 3 or 4 feet long when unextended, and will on the stretch measure twice such lengths. Their thickness, which is proportionate, may vary from that of a man's finger to that of an ordinary sausage.

The most numerically abundant and structurally varied representatives of the bristle-bearing worms are inhabitants of the sea, and are divisible into two easily recognised natural groups. In one of these the animals resemble earth-worms in their ability to move about freely from place to place. In the other group they secrete and permanently reside within a tubular edifice, which may be calcareous and of shell-like hardness, or composed of particles of sand, mud, or other substances. The free-roving group, which embraces by far the larger number, includes such forms as the LUG-WORM, or LOB-WORM (held in high repute for fishing-baits), and a host of other allied species. In all of these the development of bristles and other appendages is more pronounced than in the Earth-worms. In another group, known as the NEREIDS, the elongate worm-like body is more or less flattened in shape; unjointed leg-like appendages, supplemented by bristles, are developed from the majority of the segments, and the animal presents a somewhat centipede-like aspect. This likeness is further enhanced by the presence of antennæ-like organs at the anterior extremity, while the mouth is armed internally with a pair of sharp-pointed, horny jaws. In many of the nereids the lateral organs are flattened out and paddle-like, constituting effective swimming-structures. Some of the larger species attain a length of several feet, and are especially noteworthy for the brilliantly iridescent tinting of their skins. The palm of beauty with respect to its brilliant colouring must undoubtedly, however, be awarded to the so-called SEA-MOUSE, frequently cast up by storms on the British coast. In this creature the body is comparatively short and thick, 3 or 4 inches long by $1\frac{1}{2}$ to 2 inches wide. The centre of the back is covered in by a felt-like mass of fine interlacing hairs of a brownish hue, underneath which are broad, flat scales which protect the breathing-apparatus. The sides are, however, thickly clothed with long, slender hairs and bristles, each of which reflects the

Photo by W. Saville-Kent, F.Z.S.] *[Milford-on-Sea.*

TUBE-WORMS.

Some with their flower-like gill-tufts expanded.

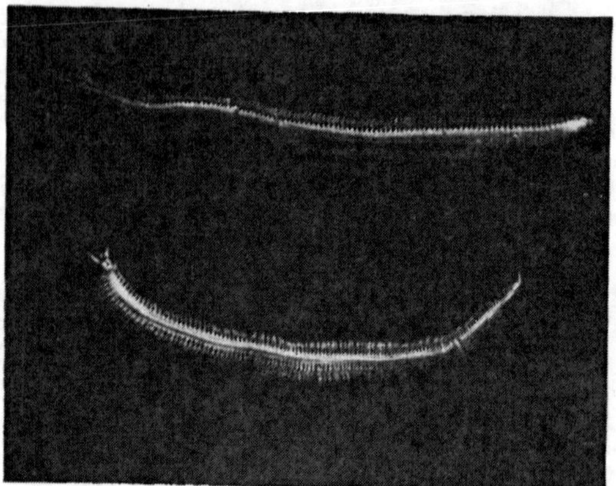

Photo by W. Saville-Kent, F.Z.S.] *[Milford-on-Sea.*

SEA-WORMS, OR NEREIDS.

Their innumerable "false feet" impart to them a centipede-like aspect.

most brilliant prismatic tints.

The TUBE-DWELLING WORMS are noteworthy for the elegant and often beautifully coloured flower-like gill-tuft with which the head is crowned. Its separate filaments are clothed with vibrating hairs, which create currents bringing food-particles to the mouth. In those forms which build up a hard calcareous dwelling-tube, one of the gill-filaments is usually so modified as to constitute a stopper-like organ, wherewith the animal, on retreating into its domicile, can effectually bar out the ingress of intruders. In some members of the group the gill-tufts are elegantly branched and supplemented by long, simple, thread-like filaments, that are thrust out to long distances in every direction both for food and the materials required for the further lengthening and enlargement of the tube.

The LEECHES differ essentially from the Bristle-worms in the absence of bristles or supplementary appendages, in the presence of an adhesive sucking-disk at the posterior and sometimes also the anterior extremity, and on their well-known blood-sucking propensities. While the MEDICINAL and so-called HORSE-LEECHES inhabit fresh-water, some, more especially in tropical countries, infest the moist jungles and scrubs in vast numbers, and are among the most actively aggressive pests with which the traveller has to contend. A few leeches also inhabit the sea, preying upon the skate and other fishes. The bodies of these marine species are cylindrical, with a sucker at each extremity, and roughly corrugated or warted.

The FLAT-WORMS embrace a large number of intestinal and other parasitic species, including TAPE-WORMS, THREAD-WORMS, LIVER-FLUKES, and others. Among the free-living non-parasitic members of this group, the so-called INDIA-RUBBER-WORM is remarkable for the extraordinary elasticity of its tissues. Black in hue, it lives among rocks and sea-weeds, and preys upon small fishes and other organisms. These, being seized by the suctorial mouth, are unable to effect their escape, the worm's body being capable of stretching out to a length of 20 feet or more, and "playing" the captured victim like a living elastic fishing-line until its struggles are exhausted.

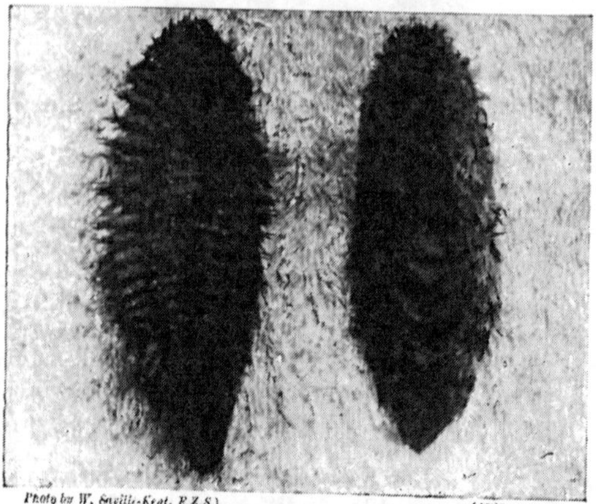

Photo by W. Saville-Kent, F.Z.S.] *[Milford-on-Sea.*

SEA-MICE.

Worms, with remarkably iridescent hairs, which burrow in the sand.

Photo by W. Saville-Kent, F.Z.S.] [*Milford-on-Sea.*

PORTION OF THE GREAT BARRIER REEF OF AUSTRALIA.

Showing soft or leathery and other corals.

Photo by W. Saville-Kent, F.Z.S.] [*Milford-on-Sea.*

ANOTHER PORTION OF THE GREAT BARRIER REEF.

Composed chiefly of stag's-horn corals. This coral varies in colour, being sometimes brown with white tips, in other instances grass-green or even brilliant violet.

Photo by W. Saville-Kent, F.Z.S.] [*Milford-on-Sea.*

A MUSHROOM-CORAL FULLY EXPANDED.

In this condition the coral, or skeleton of the animal, is entirely concealed.

CHAPTER VI.

CORALS, SEA-ANEMONES, AND JELLY-FISHES.

WITH the Sea-anemones and Jelly-fishes almost the lowest organised group of living animals is reached. As typified by an ordinary sea-anemone, the body may be described as a simple sac, the orifice of which is inverted for some little distance, and held in position with relation to the outer wall by a series of radiating partitions. One or more rows of tentacles, varying in number and character according to the species, surround the mouth of this partially inverted sac. There is no distinct intestinal track, the whole space enclosed within the outer wall and ramifying among the radiating partitions containing the digestive juices. The radiating membranous partitions develop upon their surfaces the reproductive elements, and in the case of Corals, which are merely skeleton-producing sea-anemones, partly secrete within them the symmetrical radiating calcareous plates so characteristic of the group.

Some thirty odd species of sea-anemones are indigenous to British waters, and one or more of these will be familiar to most readers. The STRAWBERRY-ANEMONE, clinging to the rocks as a hemispherical lump of crimson, green, brown, or red and yellow speckled jelly when the tide is down, and expanding like a beautiful flower when the waters flow back upon it, is the commonest and in many respects the most beautiful of all, the circlet of turquoise beads, regarded as rudimentary eyes, developed around the outer margin of the tentacles, adding a charm possessed by few other species. The DAHLIA-ANEMONE, whose expanded disk and innumerable petal-like tentacles may measure as much as 6 or 8 inches in diameter, is the largest British species. These dimensions are, however, vastly exceeded by

Photo by W. Saville-Kent, F.Z.S.] [*Milford-on-Sea.*

MUSHROOM-CORALS, WITH THE ANEMONE-LIKE POLYP EXPANDED.

Taken through the water on a coral-reef.

Photo by W. Saville-Kent, F.Z.S.] [*Milford-on-Sea.*

PART OF THE GREAT BARRIER REEF OF AUSTRALIA.

Chiefly composed of star-corals, many of them resembling human skulls. The Great Barrier Reef of Australia, consisting of innumerable detached reefs and coral-islets, is over 1,200 miles in length.

Photo by W. Saville-Kent, F.Z.S., Milford-on-Sea.

PORTION OF A STAG'S-HORN CORAL.

Each minute circular cell represents the situation in life of a small sea-anemone-like animal, or coral-polyp.

its tropical allies. The Australian coast produces giant species which may measure no less than from 18 inches to 2 feet across their expanded disks. These giant anemones are further interesting on account of the circumstance that they are self-constituted "harbours of refuge" to sundry species of fishes and crabs, which nestle among their tentacles like birds in a leafy bower. The anemones are themselves bright in colour, but the associated fishes are even more so. In an example which was photographed by the writer on the Western Australian coast, the anemone was olive-green, with the tips of the tentacles bright mauve. The fishes, of which three examples were present, were brilliant orange-scarlet with white bands. In addition to the fishes a small flat-clawed crab shared the sheltering hospitality of the anemone. Some of the tropical coral-reef-frequenting anemones, which have their tentacles beautifully branched, must be cautiously handled, in consequence of their notable stinging properties. All sea-anemones and corals are, in fact, provided with peculiar stinging-cells, with which they benumb and thus make an easy capture of the living organisms on which they prey. While the majority of the sea-anemones live single or individually separate lives, there are some which form aggregations or colony-stocks of numerous units. These compound growths are brought about by repeated budding, or the sub-division or fission, without complete separation, of an originally single individual. It is by a similar process of recurrent sub-division that the wonderful fabrications of the coral-polyps are built up.

An ordinary coral-animal or polyp, as previously stated, differs in no respect from a sea-anemone, excepting for the possession of a calcareous skeleton secreted within its basal tissues, including portions of the membranous radiating partitions. Some coral-animals, like the majority of the Anemones, are solitary, and form single attached or loosely lying corals. The well-known MUSHROOM-CORAL is one of the latter. One species observed, which was photographed through the water by the writer as it lay expanded in a tide-pool on the Australian Great Barrier Reef, might easily be

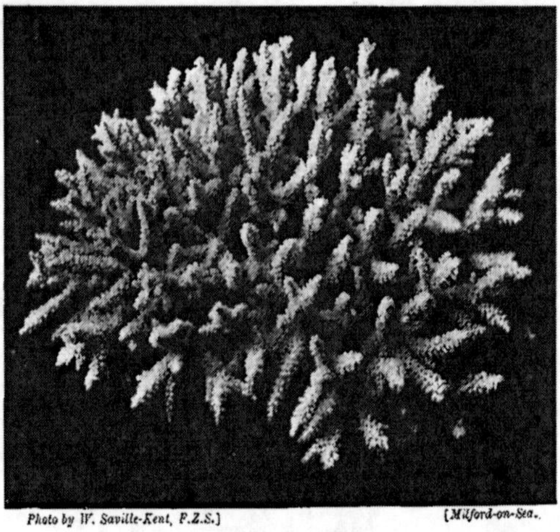

Photo by W. Saville-Kent, F.Z.S.] *[Milford-on-Sea.*

A CLUMP OF STAG'S-HORN CORAL.

The life-colours of this coral are a delicate cream with brilliant magenta tips.

mistaken for a big sea-anemone allied to the dahlia-anemone. On being disturbed, however, it immediately shrinks back upon its base, ejecting all the water with which its expanded tissues were filled, and revealing the presence of the hard radiating coral beneath. Each of the calcareous radii, which are now clearly defined through the thin semi-transparent skin, corresponds in position with one of the internal membranous partitions, and also with the origin of one of the tentacles. New mushroom-corals are produced as buds thrown off from the parent, which attach themselves and secrete a foot-stalk, to which they remain affixed, like the young of the feather star-fish, for the earlier epoch of their existence. Ultimately, however, they become detached, and, falling from their stalks, lie loosely on the sea-bottom, after the manner of their parents. The huge

Photo by W. Saville-Kent, F.Z.S.] [*Milford-on-Sea.*

BLEACHED CORALS FROM THE GREAT BARRIER REEF.

Branching stag's-horn corals are chiefly represented in this group. Several of the large solitary mushroom-corals may, however, be observed in the foreground.

coral-masses commonly known as MADREPORES, out of which coral-islands and reefs are constructed, all commence as a single coral-animal, with its contained skeleton analogous to the mushroom-coral, though in all instances much smaller. The buds developed by the coral-polyp in these instances remain attached to the parent. If they spread out laterally, they build up by accumulation the large flattened or sub-spherical masses known as BRAIN-CORALS and STAR-CORALS, which are most abundant on coast-line reefs, or form the bases of the outer barrier-reefs. Where, on the other hand, the budding is terminal or oblique, branching tree-like growths such as the STAG'S-HORN CORALS, with their innumerable allies and variations, are produced. The colours of the coral-polyps are as brilliant and diverse as those of ordinary sea-anemones, living reefs, whereon a number of different species are in a condition of healthy growth, yielding a spectacular effect that vies with that of any floral parterre. Sometimes large areas, acres upon acres in extent, may be covered with one almost uniform purple, green, brown, or other coloured growth of the branching stag's-horn species. The aspect presented is not unlike that of a heath-covered common.

In addition to the solid, calcareous-skeletoned Madrepores, or "Stony Corals," as they are often termed, there are a number of species in which a skeleton composed only of loosely aggregated calcareous spicules is produced. The so-called FLEXIBLE CORALS, or SEA-FANS, belong to this category, as also the precious CORAL OF COMMERCE. In the last-named species the solid, brilliantly coloured skeleton so much prized as an article of jewellery is deposited as a supplementary basis outside the tissues by which the star-patterned skeletons of the stony corals are secreted.

Photo by W. Saville-Kent, F.Z.S.] *[Milford-on-Sea.*

A QUEENSLAND STAR-CORAL.

This species in life is of a pale lemon-yellow tint.

A group which demands brief notice is that of the HYDROID POLYPS. These include the majority of the JELLY-FISHES, a few coral-secreting species, and the organisms whose seaweed-like horny skeletons, known as SEA-FIRS, are, in common with those of Sea-mats, included among the flotsam and jetsam on every sea-beach. In the COMMON HYDRA, or FRESH-WATER POLYP, an exceptional fresh-water representative of this group is presented. It may be likened to a tiny sea-anemone, having, when extended, a slender foot-stalk and long thread-like tentacles. Like a sea-anemone, it will shrink up when disturbed into a mere button of jelly. Its organisation is more simple than that of the anemone, its body-cavity being a simple sac, without any intucking of the orifice, or strengthening by supplementary membranous partitions. A similar simple structural plan is characteristic of all the organisms belonging to the series. An interesting phenomenon connected with the fresh-water hydra is the circumstance, demonstrated now over a century ago, that, if one of these animals be cut up into little pieces, each separate fragment is capable of repairing itself and growing into a new polyp.

The JELLY-FISHES, or MEDUSAS, and their allies would appear at first sight to possess but little structurally in common with the Coral-polyps and Sea-anemones. In their most familiar form they are represented by a more or less translucent bell-shaped body, which drifts with the current or propels itself through the water by its alternate expansions and contractions. In the centre of the lower surface, occupying the position of the bell's clapper, a polyp-like, tubular mouth is usually discernible, and this is frequently surrounded by a circle of tentacles, sometimes simple and sometimes elaborately ramified. Long, thread-like tentacles are also commonly developed around the margin of the swimming-bell.

Photo by W. Saville-Kent, F.Z.S.] *[Milford-on-Sea.*

A GIANT ANEMONE FROM THE GREAT BARRIER REEF.

From 18 inches to 2 feet in diameter when expanded. Bright apple-green in colour, and with almost spherical bead-like tentacles.

The larger number of the jelly-fishes are, as a matter of fact, transitional phases only of the fixed hydroid polyps previously referred to. In certain instances the body of the fixed polyp becomes elongated, and splits up horizontally into a series of jelly-fishes, or medusas, resembling a pile of saucers, which consecutively break away and lead a free-roving existence. In other forms a compound tree-like growth gives birth to medusa-like buds, like the flowers on a plant, which ultimately become detached and swim away. What are known as the COMB-BEARING JELLY-FISHES—their locomotive organs consisting of comb-like bands of vibratile hairs—are especially noteworthy. In some of these the body is nearly spherical or ovate, one of the species, in reference to its shape, being popularly known as the SEA-LEMON. A notable feature of these medusas is their remarkable glass-like transparency, their presence in the water in many instances being recognisable only by the prismatic glimmerings of their rows of vibratile hairs when the light falls upon them at a favourable angle. The most remarkable member of this particular group is undoubtedly the form known as VENUS'S GIRDLE. This species takes the form of a long, ribbon-like band of transparent jelly. The edges of the ribbon are clothed with vibratile hairs, and the mouth is situated in the centre of one of the edges. The animal progresses by the action of its hairs alone, or may be assisted by the twistings and undulations of its ribbon-like body.

Many jelly-fishes possess an unenviable reputation with reference to their stinging properties. The so-called PORTUGUESE MAN-OF-WAR is one of the more noteworthy of these. The organism consists of an ovately pointed air-bladder, which floats on the water, and from which depend numerous nutritive polyps and a mass of capturing-filaments, or tentacles.

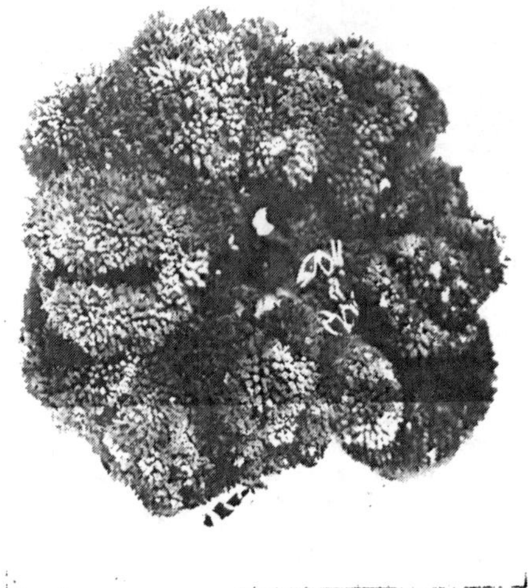

Photo by W. Saville-Kent, F.Z.S.] *[Milford-on-Sea.*

A GIANT SEA-ANEMONE.

Measures, when opened, 18 inches in diameter. Is almost always associated with companion or "commensal" fish and crabs of brilliant colour. The fish cruise round in search of food, but always return to shelter among the anemone's tentacles. Photograph taken through the water.

Photo by W. Saville-Kent, F.Z.S., Milford-on-Sea.

FRILLED SPONGE.

A species not infrequently dredged up by the pearl-shell fishers in Sharks Bay, Western Australia.

CHAPTER VII.

SPONGES AND ANIMALCULES.

THE SPONGES are regarded as a group standing on the borderland between the Polyps and the lowly organisms which follow.

The familiar BATH- and TOILET-SPONGES of commerce represent but an insignificant fraction in comparison with the many hundred species which find no place in the world's market. Toilet-sponges owe their intrinsic value to the relative fineness and elasticity of their component fibrous skeletons. In these particular species the skeleton is composed of a substance akin to horn. In other sponges the skeleton may consist of horny fibres mixed with flinty spicules, or it may be of flint only, or of spicules of carbonate of lime. Finally, there are sponges which possess no internally supporting skeleton, fibrous or spicular, and whose substance is consequently little more than gelatinous. All these numerous forms, however, agree with one another in the identity of their most essential vital elements. In the living sponge the skeleton, fibrous or otherwise, is embedded within a gelatinous matrix by whose component cells it is excreted. Externally the sponge-body is perforated over the greater portion of its extent by minute holes or pores, while one or more holes of relatively large size occupy the summit of the sponge, or are scattered here and there among the numerous smaller pores. The smaller pores represent incurrent apertures, and lead to chambers within the sponge's substance lined by cells. Each of these is provided with a long whip-like appendage, with a transparent wineglass-shaped cup or collar, which is a beautifully constructed food-trap. The lashings of the whips of the collar-cells cause currents of water bearing nutrient particles to flow in at all the smaller pores. Arriving at the chambers, these particles are caught by the outstretched collar-traps and absorbed into the cell's substance. The water, together with rejected and waste materials given off by the sponge-body, is carried forward, and passes out at the larger orifices or vents.

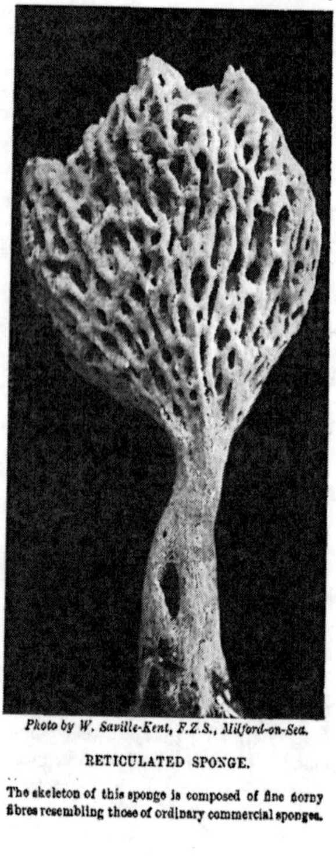

Photo by W. Saville-Kent, F.Z.S., Milford-on-Sea.

RETICULATED SPONGE.

The skeleton of this sponge is composed of fine horny fibres resembling those of ordinary commercial sponges.

Among the more remarkable sponges may be mentioned the NEPTUNE'S-CUP SPONGE, like a huge chalice 3 or 4 feet high, indigenous to the South Seas; the wonderful cornucopia-shaped LACE-SPONGE, consisting of a lace-like reticulation of flinty fibres; and its near ally the GLASS-ROPE SPONGE, forming a cup- or bird's-nest-shaped body, supported on a long cylindrical stalk

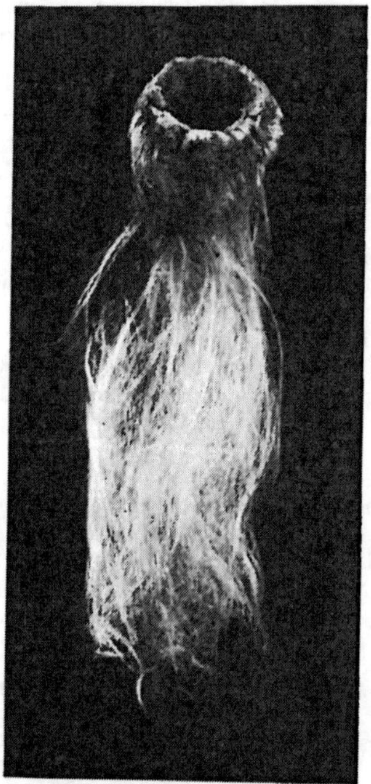

Photo by W. Saville-Kent, F.Z.S., Milford-on-Sea.

PORTUGUESE BIRD'S-NEST SPONGE.

Dredged from a depth of 600 fathoms off the coast of Portugal. In life the body, or "cup," of this sponge was deep orange colour, from which the grey beard-like mass of anchoring fibres depended.

of flinty fibres that may be over a foot in height. One of the compound or social sea-anemones is in the habit of forming bark-like encrustations on this glassy stem, and it was for a long time doubtful whether the sea-anemone or the sponge produced the supporting-stalk.

The ANIMALCULES, which represent the simplest and lowest forms of living animals, consist chiefly of organisms which are the equivalents of one of the single cells, or, as they might be termed, the "life-bricks," out of which all the higher animals, and also plants, are built up. They are of minute dimensions, and require the aid of the microscope for their proper investigation. Among the most highly organised members of this sub-kingdom mention must be made of the CILIATED ANIMALCULES, or INFUSORIA, so called because they were first discovered inhabiting decaying vegetable and animal infusions. The so-called SLIPPER-ANIMALCULE is one of the commonest forms which makes its appearance amidst such environments. The length of this single-celled animal scarcely averages the one-hundredth part of an inch, but within this restricted space an amazing degree of structural and functional differentiation is included. Its outer surface is, in the first place, densely clothed with hairs, which represent its organs of locomotion. This outer cell-wall has a subjacent somewhat softer layer, in which are developed as crowded a series (as compared with the hairs) of minute rod-like bodies, which, under various stimuli, can be shot out like darts through the skin, and are adjudged to be offensive and defensive weapons, partaking much of the same nature as the thread- or stinging-cells of sea-anemones. Among other noteworthy structures, the slipper-animalcule

Photo by E. Connold] [*St. Leonards.*

CHALINA SPONGE.

A British species, composed partly of horny and partly of flinty elements.

has a distinct throat-opening, two rhythmically contracting cavities fulfilling a respiratory function and a complex reproductive nodule, or nucleus. Compared with a host of its kindred, this animalcule is a giant, the longest diameter of many of the smaller varieties measuring no more than the $\frac{1}{1000}$th part of inch, or even less.

The elegant little BELL-ANIMALCULE, with its crystal wineglass-shaped body, crown of vibrating hairs, and long spirally contractile foot-stalk, is a familiar object to the possessor of a microscope. Most commonly these single-celled organisms, like the single-celled elements of organic tissues, multiply by repeated sub-division, the number that can be reproduced in a short space of time by this simple process being almost incredible. As many as a million, it has been calculated, of some species may be thus derived from an original single individual within twenty hours. In this connection these lowly organisms can among living animals most logically lay claim to immortality. The individual, in point of fact, never dies. Finding itself growing old and obese at the ripe age of, say, sixty minutes, it has simply to split itself up into two offsets, which swim away and repeat the process. Occasionally, for the rejuvenescence of the race, two individuals coalesce completely with one another, and multiplication by splitting takes place.

Some near relations of the little bell-animalcule, while sub-dividing so far as their bodies are concerned, remain united by their foot-stalks, and thus in time build up beautiful tree-like structures, laden as it were with crystal bells or fruit. In some of these the common branching foot-stalk is erect and rigid, while in others it is flexible, and contains, as in the ordinary species, a central elastic ligament. Under these circumstances the whole tree-like structure, with its crystal bells, collapses and expands again under the slightest stimulus, and constitutes one of the most beautiful objects that can be viewed through the microscope.

In lower forms of the infusorial animalcules one or more long, lash-like organs take the place of locomotive hairs. In this category are included the COLLAR-BEARING ANIMALCULES. Some of these build up tree-like growths by repeated sub-divisions and imperfect separation, after the manner of the bell-animalcules, while others excrete tubular dwelling-cases, inhabited by the resultants of the splitting process. Such forms can with difficulty be distinguished from skeletonless sponges.

The animalcule NOCTILUCA, which by its countless myriads is the chief constituent of ocean phosphorescence, is a member of the Lash-bearing group. This noteworthy form invites a somewhat more extended notice. It is to the presence of the Noctiluca in

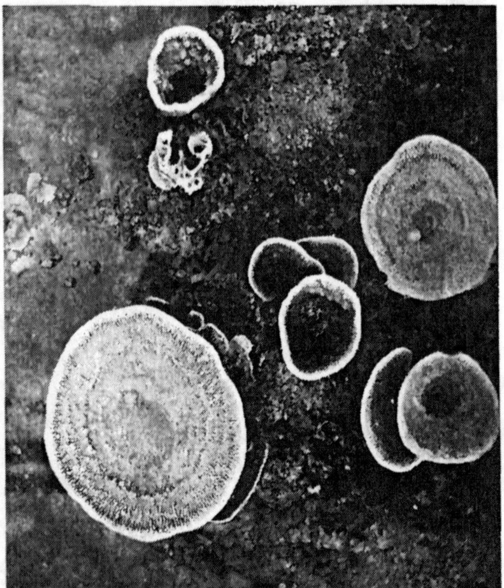

Photo by W. Saville-Kent, F.Z.S.] *[Milford-on-Sea.*

CUP-SPONGES, PHOTOGRAPHED AS GROWING IN A CORAL-POOL.

The Neptune's-cup Sponge, allied to this species, is sometimes 2 or 3 feet in height and diameter.

countless myriads upon the upper stratum of the water on calm summer nights that is especially due the diffused form of phosphorescence which is more essentially characteristic of temperate latitudes. Under the most favourable of these conditions, the waves falling upon the strand leave as they retreat a glittering carpet of scintillating points; the oars of the passing boat seem as it were to dip into molten silver; while on the high seas the revolving screw or paddle of the steam-vessel leaves in its wake a broad, luminous track as far as the eye can reach. A glassful of water taken from the sea at such times immediately reveals the origin of these wonderful phenomena. Here and there will be seen floating minute bladder-like transparent spheres, resembling as nearly as possible small granules of boiled sago. Investigated more closely with the microscope, each individual speck will be found to exhibit a pouch-like contour, having a central furrow, from the which lash projects, and upon which the minute mouth-aperture opens. Irritated by agitation in any shape or form, the Noctilucas at once respond by, as it were, angry flashes of silvery-greenish light, and it is to the coruscations in their aggregate condition of many millions of these minute organisms that the several phenomena above recounted are produced.

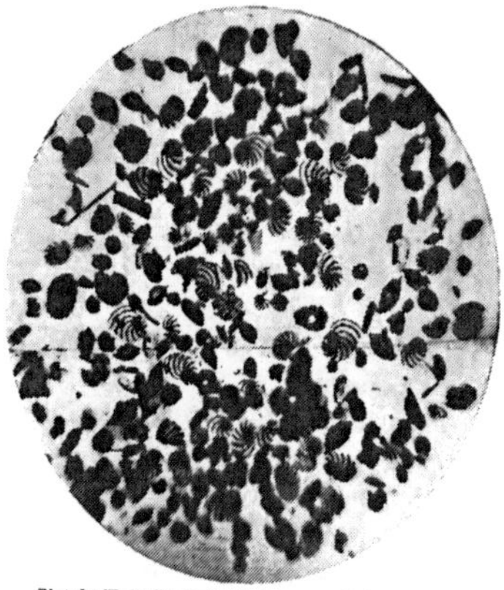

Photo by W. Saville-Kent, F.Z.S.] *[Milford-on-Sea.*

SHELLS OF FORAMS HIGHLY MAGNIFIED.

The chalk cliffs of Dover and many other strata are mainly composed of similar microscopically minute shells.

One other characteristic manifestation of ocean phosphorescence dependent upon the presence in countless numbers of these minute animalcules may be recorded. To those accustomed to a seafaring life the spectacle is a common one, on nights when the luminosity is most in evidence, of fishes following or darting away from the sides of the vessel apparently aglow themselves with phosphoric light, and leaving behind them, in accordance with their size, a more or less conspicuous luminous path in the murky waters. It is commonly supposed that such form of luminosity is emitted by the fishes themselves; but on closer investigation it will be found that this also is due to the presence of the animalcules under notice in countless numbers, which are disturbed into a sudden display of their phosphoric properties by the passage of the fishes through their midst. This light is reflected, as from a mirror, by the fishes' glittering scales, while the Noctilucas continue scintillating for several seconds in the path or wake through which the fishes have passed.

There are other animalcules nearly allied to Noctilucas which sometimes occur in such vast abundance in both salt and fresh water as to visibly affect its character. In addition to a very long lash they have a girdle of vibratile hairs. The fresh-water representatives of this group are sometimes brilliant green, at others bright scarlet. That instance among the Biblical Egyptian plagues

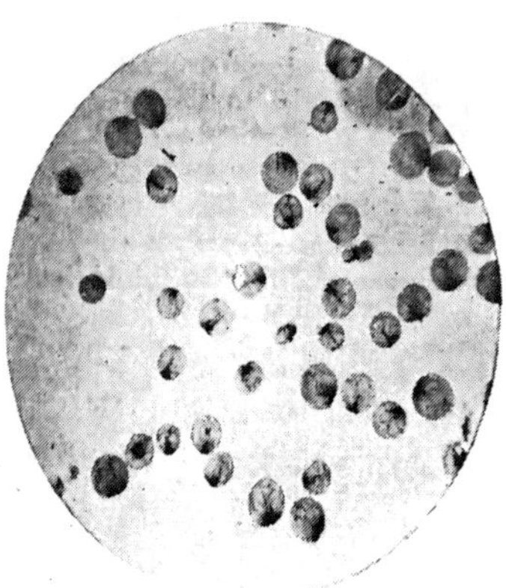

Photo by W. Saville-Kent, F.Z.S.] *[Milford-on-Sea.*

NOCTILUCAS.

These are the animalcules which chiefly produce marine phosphorescence.

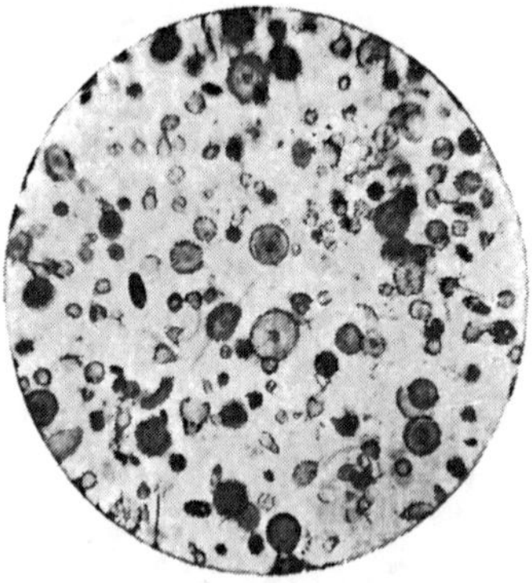

Photo by W. Saville-Kent, F.Z.S.] [*Milford-on-Sea.*

POLYCYSTS.

Flinty-shelled organisms of microscopic dimensions. The living animals consist of tiny specks of transparent jelly, from which radiate innumerable false feet of hair-like fineness.

in which the water of the Nile was as it were "turned to blood, and all the fish died," has been attributed to a phenomenal development of these animalcules, which, on dying, polluted and putrefied the water. Instances of fishes being destroyed in vast quantities through a like agency throughout even extensive sea-areas have been occasionally recorded. While these pages are going to press an account has appeared in an American journal of red water caused by these flagellate animalcules, which occurred last July for an extent of at least 200 miles along the coast of California, producing with their decomposition a most sickening odour, and the death of shoals of fishes, octopods, sea-cucumbers, and other organisms.

Next to the Flagellates come the ROOT-FOOTED ANIMALCULES, which possess no mouth and no hairs or lashes, but progress by pushing out lobes of their jelly-like substance in any desired direction, into which the rest of the body flows. Food is picked up at any point with which an acceptable morsel may be brought in contact. The little gelatinous animal known as an AMŒBA is one of these. Related forms of this jelly animalcule secrete shells of varying form and structure. Some of these, known as FORAMS, are of carbonate of lime, and wonderfully like nautiluses and other of the higher molluscan shells in aspect. Though so minute, scarcely visible to the unassisted eye, they occur in the sea in such numbers as to form by their aggregations the more considerable ingredients of vast areas of the earth's strata, both past and present. The chalk cliffs of Albion and the white tenacious ooze of the broad Atlantic are thus to a large extent composed of the shells of minute organisms, which formerly flourished near the surface of the ocean, but sank on their death to its abysmal depths.

The simplest of the forams fabricate shells with a single chamber, which are often elegantly vase- or flask-shaped. More usually, however, the shell represents the product of repeated buddings or outgrowths, and may attain considerable dimensions. Flattened circular forms of this type much resemble time-worn coins, and are hence called NUMMULITES. Their fossil-shells enter mainly into the composition of rocks which extend through North Africa and Asia to the Himalaya, and supplied the stone of which the Pyramids are built.

Allied to the Forams, but distinguished by the radiating, needle-like contour of their false feet and the flinty texture of their shells, are an equally numerous assemblage of organisms known as RADIOLARIANS. Like the Forams, they are inhabitants of the sea, and their discarded shells enter extensively into the constitution of strata. A little globular fresh-water form, devoid of a shell, and with slender bristle-like feet radiating in every direction, is known as the SUN-ANIMALCULE, and forms a connecting-link between the last two groups.

From Man to Egg-laying Mammals, Molluscs to Animalcules, the vast scheme of the Animal Creation has now been successively portrayed. With such simple gelatinous life-specks as the Amœba and its allies THE LIVING ANIMALS OF THE WORLD make their exit: unorganised organisms, groping blindly in the darkness—"Sans teeth, sans eyes, sans taste, sans everything."

END OF VOL. II.

INDEX.

97